SHEMARYAHU TALMON

THE WORLD OF QUMRAN FROM WITHIN

For Penina

THE WORLD OF QUMRAN FROM WITHIN

Collected Studies

SHEMARYAHU TALMON

JERUSALEM – LEIDEN
THE MAGNES PRESS, THE HEBREW UNIVERSITY
E. J. BRILL

© The Magnes Press, The Hebrew University, Jerusalem 1989
All rights reserved
Printed in Israel
Typesetting: Beverly Butrin Fields, Jerusalem

Distributed in Israel by the Magnes Press, the Hebrew University,
Jerusalem
Distributed in the other territories of the world by E. J. Brill, Leiden

Library of Congress Cataloging-in-Publication Data

Talmon, Shemaryahu, 1920-
  The World of Qumran from Within

  Includes bibliographical references.
  1. Qumran community. 2. Dead Sea scrolls—
Criticism, interpretation, etc. I. Title.
BM175.Q6T35 1989   296.8'15   89-17265
ISBN 90-04-08449 5 (Brill)

CONTENTS

PREFACE

As the title indicates, the studies collected in this volume evince my endeavor to view the conceptual universe of the Qumran Covenanters *from within*. I purport to extract from their writings pertinent information on their theology, their world of ideas, and their comprehension of Israelite history; on the structure of their community, or *commune*, in its historical setting; and on their vision of an ideal future age in which their *Yaḥad* would become the reconstituted biblical people of Israel. I aim at clarifying the seminal beliefs which inspired these millenarian messianists, who established a closely-knit community in the first half of the second century B.C.E. which ensuingly existed for close to 300 years.

The Covenanters are viewed here as a socioreligious phenomenon *sui generis,* whose unique interpretation of the biblical heritage which they shared with all other groups in the Judaism of the outgoing Second Temple Period calls for elucidation. The emphasis laid on an analysis *from within* causes the discussion to focus first and foremost on the Qumranites themselves and on their characteristic writings, and steers clear of a premature comparison or identification of this peculiar community with other nonconformist groups in late Second Temple Judaism (above all the Essenes) on which ancient reports enlighten us. Such an identification should be attempted only after the ideational and organizational profile of the Covenanters' community has been sufficiently delineated, to the degree that such a delineation can be distilled from their literature.

Our knowledge of mainstream Judaism in the last centuries B.C.E. has previously been based on inference from information extracted from sources which actually document *normative Judaism* of the tannaitic period, the first and second centuries C.E. The non-existence of contemporary documentation concerning the roots and the founders of what later was to become *normative Judaism* resulted in a lack of criteria available for us to determine the prominence and weight of *mainstream Judaism* in late pre-Christian times relative to that of *dissenting* groups. It is in this context that the paramount importance of the Qumran literature comes to light. These writings provide

7

firsthand information on a structured socioreligious entity in Judaism of the Greco-Roman times such as scholars never before have had at their disposal.

Because of the only vaguely ascertainable appraisement of the constitution and the characteristics of mainstream Judaism in the last two centuries B.C.E., I prefer to designate the Covenanters of Qumran as *dissenters* or *nonconformists* rather than defining them by the technical terms *sect* or *sectarian,* as I did in the past. These latter terms presuppose the existence of a sociologically and credally clearly delineated mother community (*Church* or *Synagogue*) from which differently constituted groups deviated and ultimately seceded.

The studies included in this volume were published over a period of almost four decades. The first, "Yom Hakippurim in the Habakkuk Scroll," appeared not long after the scrolls from Cave 1 were made available to scholars. The most recent one, "Between the Bible and the Mishna," was written for the occasion of the 40th anniversary of the Qumran discoveries. Thus they bear the imprint of Qumran research in its development. At the same time they reflect my own thoughts on Qumranic matters as they evolved in these close to 40 years. I did not attempt to update the studies to the present state of the art. But no effort was spared to emend mistakes and typographical errors and to achieve uniformity of quotation techniques, sigla, *et sim.* While some duplication cannot altogether be avoided in a collection of essays pertaining to one overall topic, which were written over an extended span of time, I did my best to reduce them to a minimum. Thus the present text of "The Emergence of Institutionalized Prayer" is in fact a reworked version of two separate studies which were amalgamated here.

Work on the preparation of the essays for republication in this collection was carried out to a large extent while I was a Fellow at the National Humanities Center in North Carolina, U.S.A., a research institute which provided excellent study facilities in a congenial scholarly atmosphere. I am indebted to the staff of the Center for unfailing assistance willingly given.

My thanks are due to Dr. Weston Fields and Ms Dorit Josef, who furthered in various ways the production of this volume, Ms Josef also taking care of the indexes. Special thanks go to Mrs. Beverly Fields, who edited, typeset, and proofread the entire manuscript with the utmost care.

I wish to thank the Academic Committee and the director of the Magnes Press for resolving to publish this collection of my studies, like the previous one entitled *King, Cult and Calendar* (1986), and two more which are being prepared for publication.

Preface

My thanks are due to the editors and publishers of the various periodicals and coauthored volumes in which these essays originally appeared, who granted permission to have them republished in this collection.

I dedicate this volume to my wife, Dr. Penina Talmon-Morag, companion and partner, in times of hardship and happiness.

BETWEEN THE BIBLE AND THE MISHNA

I

Some forty years have passed since the accidental discovery of a cluster of ancient scrolls in a cave near a site in the Judean Desert known by the Arabic name Qumran.[1] In the ensuing systematic exploration of that wilderness area, scholars produced a hoard of partial scrolls and fragments from eleven of the many more caves which were methodically investigated. The finds opened an entirely new field of intensive research. Notwithstanding the energy and expertise brought to bear on the elucidation of the intricate problems which these documents pose for us, all the acumen and wisdom mustered by a legion of scholars cannot dispel the doubts which beset the solutions that have been offered in the search for answers to the questions which abound in the Qumran documents. Unlike the Covenanters of Qumran who gave twenty years as the length of the period of their own initial bewilderment (CD i 9-10), we have in fact been "like the blind groping their way," in respect to most of the issues which have come under review, for the stereotypical span of forty years which biblical tradition accords to the aberrant wilderness generation and henceforth to every generation.[2]

1. An account of the circumstances surrounding the discovery of the scrolls is offered in several comprehensive surveys. See int. al.: F. M. Cross (*The Ancient Library of Qumran and Biblical Studies* [New York: Doubleday, 1980]); J. T. Milik (*Ten Years of Discovery in the Wilderness of Judea* [Naperville, IL: Allenson, 1959]); G. Vermes (*The Dead Sea Scrolls: Qumran in Perspective* [London: SCM, 1982]). While these surveys are 20 years apart, they address themselves in essence to the same basic issues and problems. See further: J. A. Sanders ("The Dead Sea Scrolls—A Quarter Century of Study," *BA* 36 [1973] 110-48); M. A. Knibb (*The Qumran Community* in *Cambridge Commentaries on Writings of the Jewish and Christian World 200 B.C. to A.D. 200* [Cambridge: Cambridge University Press, 1987], vol. 2).
2. For this motif, see S. Talmon ("מדבר, miḏbār; ערבה, arābāh," *TWAT* 4 [1983] 660-95; idem, "The 'Desert Motif' in the Bible and in Qumran Literature," *Biblical Motifs, Origins and Transformations* [Studies and Texts of the Philip L. Lown

Judging by the past achievements, which have resulted in only partial success, one wonders whether at the end of the next decade (which will mark the jubilee of Qumran research) we shall be better informed on these perplexing issues. It remains to be seen whether we shall then have reached the *terra firma* of an adequate and full understanding of what these scrolls were meant to tell their ancient readers, exactly who these readers were, and why and by whom the manuscripts were deposited in the caves and were thus preserved for posterity. We seem to stand in need of another מורה הצדק or another דורש התורה "to make known to the last [i.e., "our"] generation" (CD i 11-12) ways and means for solving the many puzzles which confront us.

In view of the unsolved problems, current Qumran research patently stands in need of a periodic assessment of the state of the art,[3] even though a considerable part of the documents salvaged from the caves still has not been made available for study. The publication of additional materials is bound to enlarge the compass of the evidence on which theories can be founded. Some of the extensive manuscripts and fragments which still remain unpublished may eventually shed new light on some unresolved pivotal questions, and others may even hold surprises. But the experience of recent decades prompts the assumption that we should not expect a fundamental reformulation of any of the mainline theories propagated in the past. The considerable volume of materials, published over the last two or three decades, albeit fragmentary, has not appreciably corroborated or countervailed proposals put forward in the first ten or fifteen years on the basis of the documents available then. It suffices to make reference only to the most important of these more recently published manuscripts and fragments: the several volumes in the DJD series,[4] extra-series publications such

Institute of Advanced Judaic Studies, ed. A. Altman; Cambridge, MA: Harvard, 1966], 3. 31-63).

3. Such an assessment was indeed proffered in several conferences which were convened to celebrate four decades of Qumran discoveries. The proceedings of these meetings, once they are published, should provide a detailed picture of the state of the art. For the present, see the partial overview given by M. Wise ("The Dead Sea Scrolls, Part 1: Archaeology and Biblical Manuscripts," *BA* 49 [1986] 140-56; "Part 2: Non-Biblical Manuscripts," *BA* 49 [1986] 228-43). Some of the papers presented at a conference held at the Warburg Institute in London were published in *JJS* 39 [1988] 5-79). See also G. Vermes (*The Dead Sea Scrolls Forty Years On. The Fourteenth Sacks Lecture* [Oxford: Centre for Postgraduate Hebrew Studies, 1987]).

4. J. A. Sanders, *The Psalms Scroll of Qumran Cave 11 (11QPs^a)*, (DJD; Oxford: Clarendon, 1965), vol. 4; J. M. Allegro, *Qumran Cave 4:1 (4Q 158—4Q 186)*

as the *Targum of Job*,[5] the Paleo-Hebrew Exodus[6] and Leviticus Scrolls,[7] and the *Temple Scroll*.[8] They did not provide any pertinent new information which would lead to a fully satisfactory solution of old questions, but rather added new queries to the extant roster.

Some off-beat hypotheses which were formulated in the early stage of Qumran studies have indeed been abandoned. They are now passed over in silence or are cursorily referred to in retrospective surveys of Qumran research. We need but to mention the most conspicuous of these phased-out theories: the attempted invalidation of the scrolls by debunking them as spurious modern fabrications;[9] their presentation as medieval documents of Karaite origin;[10] the various proposals to affiliate their authors with sundry factions that flourished in the early Christian Era—the Ebionites;[11] or in the outgoing Second Temple

(DJD, 1968), vol. 5; R. de Vaux and J. T. Milik, *Qumrân Grotte 4: II. Archéologie; Tefillin, Mezuzot et Targums (4Q 128—4Q 157)* (DJD, 1977), vol. 6; M. Baillet, *Qumran Grotte 4: III (4Q 482—4Q 520)* (DJD, 1982), vol. 7.

5. A. S. van der Woude and J. P. M. van der Ploeg, *Le Targum de Job de la Grotte XI de Qumrân* (Leiden: Brill, 1971); R. Weiss, *The Aramaic Targum of Job* (Tel Aviv: University, 1979) Heb.

6. J. E. Sanderson, *An Exodus Scroll from Qumran. 4QpaleoExod[n] and the Samaritan Tradition* (Harvard Semitic Studies; Atlanta, GA: Scholars Press, 1983), vol. 30.

7. D. N. Freedman and K. A. Mathews, *The Paleo-Hebrew Leviticus Scroll (11QpaleoLev)* (Winona Lake, IN: ASOR, 1985).

8. Y. Yadin, *Megillath ham-Migdash. The Temple Scroll* (Jerusalem: IES and Hebrew Univ., 1977) Heb.; (Jerusalem: IES, 1983) Eng. Ed.

9. S. Zeitlin voiced this opinion in a series of essays published in *JQR*. See especially *The Dead Sea Scrolls and Modern Scholarship* ([JQRMS; Philadelphia: JQR, 1956], vol. 3).

10. Foremost, S. Zeitlin, *The Dead Sea Scrolls* (above, n. 9); N. Wieder, *The Judaean Scrolls and Karaism* (Oxford: Clarendon, 1962); N. Golb, "Literary and Doctrinal Aspects of the Damascus Covenant in Relation to Those of the Karaites," *JQR* 47 (1957) 354-74.

11. This identification had already been proposed by Kaufmann-Kohler on the basis of the Zadokite Fragments from the Cairo Genizah but was developed by J. Teicher on the strength of the Qumran discoveries in a series of essays published in *JJS* (2-5 [1950-54]). See especially "The Dead Sea Scrolls— Documents of the Jewish-Christian Sect of Ebionites" (*JJS* 2 [1951] 67-99); "The Damascus Fragments and the Origin of the Jewish-Christian Sect" (*JJS* 2 [1951] 115-43); "Jesus in the Habakkuk Scroll" (*JJS* 3 [1952] 53-56); "The Teachings of the Pre-Pauline Church in the Dead Sea Scrolls" (Part I, *JJS* 3 [1952] 111-18; Part II, *JJS* 3 [1952] 139-50; Part III, *JJS* 4 [1953] 1-13; Part IV, *JJS* 4 [1953] 49-58; Part V, *JJS* 4 [1953] 93-103; Part VI *JJS* 4 [1953] 139-53); "Jesus' Sayings in the Dead Sea Scrolls" (*JJS* 5 [1954] 38).

Period—the Samaritans[12] or the Zealots.[13] These and similar theories have altogether lost credibility. The ever-increasing cumulative evidence brought to light by scholarly investigation in a variety of disciplines, history, archeology and numismatics,[14] paleography,[15] and science,[16] has proven them to be unfounded.[17] But on the whole, scholars remain entrenched in positions which they had originally taken up, steadfastly defending hypotheses worked out on the strength of the evidence available then, and passing them on to new generations of their disciples. We seem to have reached an impasse.

12. J. Bowman, *The Samaritan Problem: Studies in the Relationships of Samaritanism, Judaism and Early Christianity* (Pittsburgh: Pickwick Press, 1975).

13. C. Roth, *The Historical Background of the Dead Sea Scrolls* (Oxford: Blackwell, 1958).

14. See R. de Vaux, *Archaeology and the Dead Sea Scrolls. The Schweich Lectures of the British Academy. 1959* (Oxford: Oxford University Press, 1973); idem, "Archéologie," *Qumrân Grotte 4 II*, ed. R. de Vaux and J. T. Milik (DJD; Oxford: Clarendon, 1977), 6. 3-28.

15. See int. al.: S. A. Birnbaum, *The Hebrew Script. Part One: The Texts* (Leiden: Brill, 1971); *Part Two: The Plates* (London: Paleographia, 1957); N. Avigad, "The Paleography of the Dead Sea Scrolls and Related Documents," *ScrHier*, ed. C. Rabin and Y. Yadin (Jerusalem: Magnes, 1958), 4. 56-87; M. Martin, *The Scribal Character of the Dead Sea Scrolls* (Louvain: Publications Universitaires, 1958); F. M. Cross, "The Development of the Jewish Scripts," *The Bible and the Ancient Near East: Essays in Honor of W. F. Albright* (ed. G. E. Wright; New York: Doubleday, 1961) 133-202; J. P. Siegel, "The Scribes of Qumran. Studies in the Early History of Jewish Scribal Customs, with Special Reference to the Qumran Biblical Scrolls and to the Tannaitic Traditions of Massekhet Soferim" (Ph. D. Diss., Brandeis Univ., 1972).

16. See, e.g., O. R. Sellers, "Radiocarbon Dating of Cloth from the 'Ain Feshkha Cave,'" *BASOR* 123 (1951) 24-26.

17. The discovery on Masada of fragments of the *Širat ʿOlat Haššabat*, the *Ben Sira Scroll* (see below, n. 63) and some additional fragments which are Qumran-related provide the definite ante quem date 73 C.E. for the Covenanters' community and their literature. See Y. Yadin ("Qumran and Masada," *BIES* 30 [1966] 117-27, esp. 123-27 [Heb.]). Further, C. Newsom and Y. Yadin ("The Masada Fragment of the Qumran Songs of the Sabbath Sacrifice," *IEJ* 34 [1984] 77-88); C Newsom (*Songs of the Sabbath Sacrifice: A Critical Edition* [Harvard Semitic Studies; Atlanta, GA: Scholars Press, 1985], vol. 27); J. Strugnell ("The Angelic Liturgy at Qumran—4Q Serek Širōt ʿOlat Haššabat," *Oxford Congress Volume* [VTSup; Leiden: Brill, 1960], 7. 318-45).

II

It is appropriate that at this juncture we be reminded of the enthusiastic reactions when the news of the initial discovery of the Qumran Scrolls came to the attention of scholars. Expectations soared high. The manuscripts appeared to hold out great promise for opening up new possibilities of scholarly inquiry into the late Second Temple Period before the emergence of Christianity. In the early 1950s H. H. Rowley assured students of the Hebrew Bible troubled by a nagging doubt whether significant contributions could yet be made in that intensively ploughed-over field of research, that the new documents would provide at least two generations of scholars with interesting, problematic, and yet revealing materials into which to put their teeth.[18]

The veritable "megillo(th)mania" which spread in the 1950s and 1960s seemed to prove that prognosis correct. The new art of "scrolling" attracted many a scholar who had previously been engaged in another area of Ancient Near Eastern studies. [19] The new pursuits caused an avalanche of Scroll publications in the one and a half decades after the discovery of the Qumran Caves. In the first volume of the comprehensive Qumran bibliography published in 1957, Christoph Burchard could already list approximately 1500 entries.[20] In the second volume, which brought the survey up to 1962, the number of entries grew to some 4500.[21] No comprehensive inventory is available for the quarter of a

---

18. This may be an "oral tradition." I cannot trace this remark to a written source. A similar appreciation was expressed by A. Dupont-Sommer: "It is clear that Qumran studies, affecting as they do all sorts of spheres—paleographic, linguistic, literary, historical, theological—will continue to develop, and will require the co-operation of very many scholars for a long time to come, whether with regard to the biblical manuscripts or the non-biblical writings" (*The Essene Writings from Qumran* [trans. G. Vermes; Oxford: Blackwell, 1961] 8).

19. In 1959 Mitchell Dahood voiced the complaint that the Qumran finds turned students away from the pursuit of Ugaritic studies, due to widespread feeling that "the Ras Shamra tablets have contributed as much to biblical studies as they ever will." (M. Dahood, "The Value of Ugaritic for Textual Criticism," *Bib* 40 [1959] 160ff.)

20. C. Burchard, *Bibliographie zu den Handschriften vom Toten Meer* (Berlin: Töpelmann, 1957).

21. Idem, *Bibliographie zu den Handschriften vom Toten Meer* (Berlin: Töpelmann, 1965).

15

century after 1962.[22] While it cannot be established for certain whether the pace of publications continued at the same speed, we may presume that it did not slow down perceptibly.

A possible explanation of this rapid development lies in the fact that since the inception of critical Judaic research, scholars have never before had access to pristine copies of Hebrew writings which date from the otherwise undocumented latter half of the Second Temple Period. All previously available information relative to those times gleaned from Hellenistic, Jewish, or Christian sources is retrospective. It derives from reports in which that period is viewed from the vantage point of later generations that were removed from it by several centuries. In contradistinction, the writings which emanate from the Qumran Caves were evidently produced by Jewish authors who lived in the last centuries before and the first century after the turn of the era. These documents thus contain contemporaneous, firsthand evidence which relates directly to this crucial period. One could expect with much justification that they would enlighten us on that "dark age" in the history of Judaism.

These great hopes did not materialize. The most painstaking analysis of the Qumran documents has not shed new light on historical events which affected Judaism as a whole in those times, nor on significant developments which then occurred in Jewish concepts and beliefs. Moreover there remains, as said, much uncertainty even in regard to matters which pertain specifically, in fact exclusively, to the Qumran Covenanters themselves: int. al., the genesis, history, and societal structure of their community, their particular theology and ritual code.

In the present framework a full review of all the relevant issues cannot be offered. It must suffice to list only some important questions which remain

---

22. See, int. al.: W. Lasor, *Bibliography of the Dead Sea Scrolls 1948-1957* (Pasadena, CA: Fuller Theol. Sem., 1958); M. Yizhar, *Bibliography of Hebrew Publications on the Dead Sea Scrolls. 1948-1964* (Cambridge, MA: Harvard, 1967); B. Jongeling, *A Classified Bibliography of the Finds in the Desert of Judah. 1958-1969* (Leiden: Brill, 1971); J. Fitzmyer, *The Dead Sea Scrolls: Major Publications and Tools for Study* (Missoula, MT: Scholars Press, 1977); C. Koester, "A Qumran Bibliography: 1974-1984," *Biblical Theology Bulletin* 15 (1985) 110-20; E. Schürer, *The History of the Jewish People in the Age of Jesus Christ,* ed. G. Vermes, F. Millar, M. Goodman (Edinburgh: Scribner, 1986), 3,1. 380-469; further: the current bibliographical information given in *RQ* and *Bib*.

under scrutiny and are debated with the same or similar pro and con arguments that were adduced when Qumran research was in its infancy.

We have as yet no universally accepted identification of the Covenanters' community. We cannot establish for certain the identity of the authors who presumably produced the substantial number of documents which exhibit a specifically Qumranite stance. Nor do we know any better the provenance of writings in the collection which were probably not produced locally by members of the New Covenant but had been brought to Qumran by new recruits who joined the יחד.[23]

The proposed identification of the Covenanters with the Essenes is certainly more persuasive than all other suggestions and has accordingly attracted wide scholarly acclaim. But at the same time, it met from the outset with some opposition which may now draw strength from new sources.[24] The first halakhic document which issued from the fourth Qumran Cave, מקצת מעשי/דברי התורה (4QMMT), so far only known in general outline, presumably reflects legal and

23. There are as yet no generally agreed-upon criteria for differentiating imported from locally produced manuscripts. There is much to be said for E. Tov's proposal to use objective linguistic and scribal criteria, such as defective vs. (excessive) plene spelling as means for telling one group from the other. See E. Tov ("The Orthography and Language of the Hebrew Scrolls Found at Qumran and the Origin of These Scrolls," *Textus* 13 [1986] 31-57; idem, "Hebrew Biblical Manuscripts from the Judaean Desert: Their Contribution to Textual Criticism," *JJS* 38 [1988] 5-37). The hypothesis that all scrolls were brought to Qumran from (the Temple archives in) Jerusalem is not convincing, since it disregards the obvious connection of the manuscripts with the Qumran caves and the nearby settlement. See K. H. Rengstorf (*Hirbet Qumran und die Bibliothek vom Toten Meer. Studia Delitzschiana* 5 [Stuttgart: Kohlhammer, 1960]); E. Y. Kutscher (*The Language and Linguistic Background of the Isaiah Scroll [1QIsa^a]* [Leiden: Brill, 1974] 89-95); N. Golb ("The Problem of Origin and Identification of the Dead Sea Scrolls," *PAPS* 124 [1980] 1-24).
24. There is no need to give a list of the proponents of the Essene theory. The reader is referred to the surveys and bibliographies and especially Jongeling's classified bibliography mentioned above (nn. 1, 18, 20-22). The identification of the Covenanters with the Essenes was rejected by several scholars. See, e. g., C. Roth ("Why the Qumran Sect Cannot Have Been Essenes," *RevQ* 1 [1958-59] 417-22; idem, "Were the Qumran Sectaries Essenes? A Re-examination of Some Evidences," *JTS* 10 [1959] 87-93). I have recurrently questioned the proposed identification. See "The New Covenanters of Qumran" (*Scientific American* 225:5 [1971] 72-81); "Qumran und das Alte Testament" (*Frankfurter Universitätsreden* 42 [1971] 71-83); "The Calendar of the Covenanters of the Judean Desert" (in this vol., 147-85); "Waiting for the Messiah—The Conceptual Universe of the Qumran Covenanters" (in this vol., 274-301).

ritual peculiarities which rabbinic tradition associates with the Sadducees.[25] For this reason and because of some other particular traits which mark Qumran theology and religious practice (which had indeed been known for a long time but were not given the attention they deserve), the prevalent identification of the Qumran community with the Essenes must again be brought under review.

No manifest progress can be registered in the endeavor to establish conclusively the identity of the central *agonistes* in the contention between the Covenanters and their adversaries. The designations מורה הצדק and הכוהן הרשע, by which they are known in the Qumran literature, have an enigmatic ring to them in the ears of the modern reader and cannot be related unequivocally to historical figures of whom the classical sources speak. The epithets דורש התורה and מטיף הכזב may equally pertain to these opposing leaders. Alternatively they may designate some other *dramatis personae* who at a later stage played an important role in the controversy between the יחד and the main community.[26]

The arguments adduced in favor of the thesis that the Covenanters entertained a vision of "Twin Messiahs," who were expected to arise in an undetermined future, have not materially changed since this issue came to the attention of scholars in the wake of the discovery of the Zadokite Fragments in the Cairo Genizah (CD). The very same holds true for the counterarguments which the defenders of the "One Messiah" thesis brought to bear upon the matter.[27]

Similarly, novel theories concerning the history of the text of the Hebrew Bible and its historical development, promulgated on the strength of the two Isaiah scrolls (1QIsa[a] and 1QIsa[b]) which issued from Cave I and some additional biblical manuscripts published in the first decade of Qumran research, are in the

25. See the preliminary report by E. Qimron and J. Strugnell ("An Unpublished Halakhic Letter from Qumran," *Biblical Archaeology Today* [Jerusalem: IES, Israel Academy of Arts and Sciences and ASOR, 1985] 400-407).

26. The question whether the titles מורה הצדק and דורש התורה designate the same or different personalities does not need to occupy us here. The same pertains to the titles כוהן הרשע and מטיף הכזב. The reader is referred to the publications listed by Jongeling (above, n. 22), to which should be added, int. al., R. Thiering (*Redating the Teacher of Righteousness* [Sydney: Theological Explorations, 1979]); J. Carmignac ("Qui était le Docteur de Justice?" *RQ* 38 [1980] 235-46); H. Burmann ("Wer war der 'Lehrer der Gerechtigkeit,' " *RQ* 40 [1981] 553-78); B. Z. Wacholder (*The Dawn of Qumran. The Sectarian Torah and the Teacher of Righteousness* [Cincinnati: HUC, 1983]).

27. See Wacholder, *The Dawn* (above n. 26); Talmon, "Waiting for the Messiah" (in this vol., pp. 273-300).

main still discussed on the same premises that initially formed the basis of the debate.[28]

Again, no discernible progress was made in gauging the process of the gradual emergence of the "Hebrew Bible Canon" and its final closure. The questions pertaining to this matter remain unanswered. They result, inter alia, from the absence in the Qumran manuscript finds of even one fragment of the book of Esther or of one evident quotation from that book in the Covenanters' particular literature. The publication over the last quarter of a century of a large number of additional, partial copies and fragments of biblical books and of typical Qumranite works did not contribute new data which would induce scholars to change their earlier pronouncements on the issue of canon-formation.[29]

There is no need to proliferate examples which buttress the conclusion that the materials published since the mid-sixties have not introduced new arguments into the debates over questions which had been raised in the past, nor did they perceptibly affect the insights gained in the preceding period.[30]

III

Before proceeding it should again be emphasized that the Qumran documents must be judged an unprecedented phenomenon in the study of ancient Jewish history and civilization. Viewed comprehensively, they provide the means for reconstituting to an impressive extent an exceedingly detailed and intricate self-portrait of a closely knit socioreligious entity in Second Temple Judaism such as

28. See the collection of pertinent studies in F. M. Cross and S. Talmon, eds. (*Qumran and the History of the Biblical Text*, hereinafter QHBT [Cambridge, MA: Harvard, 1975]); Vermes (*The Dead Sea Scrolls*, above n. 1); Tov (*JJS* 38 [1988] 5-37 [above, n. 23]; idem, "A Modern Textual Outlook Based on the Qumran Scrolls," *HUCA* 53 [1982] 11-27); E. Ulrich ("Horizons of Old Testament Textual Research at the Thirtieth Anniversary of Qumran Cave 4," *CBQ* 46 [1984] 613-36); et al.

29. See S. Talmon, "Heiliges Schrifttum und Kanonische Bücher aus jüdischer Sicht—Überlegungen zur Ausbildung der Grösse 'Die Schrift' im Judentum," *Mitte der Schrift? Ein jüdisch-christliches Gespräch. Texte des Berner Symposions vom 6.-12. Januar 1985* (Judaica et Christiana, ed. M. Klopfenstein, U. Luz, S. Talmon, E. Tov; Bern: Lang, 1987), 11. 45-79.

30. See the surveys provided by Vermes, Sanders, Knibb (above, n. 1) and Wise (*BA* 49 [1986], above, n. 3).

cannot be gained from any other ancient sources. The emerging picture has, moreover, the quite special distinction of being contemporaneous with the events which it depicts. This literature provides information on a nonconformist movement that flourished in the Judaism of that period, which must be accorded more, and certainly not less, credibility than the retrospective reports found in Hellenistic, Rabbinic, and Christian sources on other groups of dissenters. True, the Qumran evidence needs to be viewed with circumspection. It is most probably marred by distortions which can be expected to occur in such a literary self-portrait. But we should bear in mind that the classical sources are also tainted by their authors' prepossessed notions and are to a large measure founded on hearsay. Therefore they too must be taken *cum grano salis*.

Because of the characteristics of the Qumran literature, it is appropriate to study the scrolls first and foremost with the aim of extracting from them substantive and intimate information on the Covenanters' community and their *Eigenbegrifflichkeit*.[31] It is to be expected, however, that when all is said and done there will still remain unsolved and possibly unsolvable problems which result from the many veiled references and an often baffling terminology which abound in the Covenanters' writings. However, these enigmatic allusions should not be construed as evidencing the writers' calculated attempts at mystification. It stands to reason that in antiquity the seemingly elusive references were fully understood by the initiated. The Qumran authors did not compose their opuscules as missionary tracts intended for outsiders whom they wished to attract into their fold, as some scholars opine.[32] Their compositions addressed an informed audience and were expressly designed for transmitting to discerning readers instructive and normative teachings which were to regulate the life of the individual member and the communal life of the יחד.

These considerations prescribe the methodology which will govern the ensuing discussion: the יחד literature will primarily be viewed and analyzed as firsthand documents which give witness to the particular world of ideas and the history of an ancient, self-contained, socioreligious entity *sui generis*. Once a comprehensive understanding of the Qumran commune has been achieved, as far as this is possible, the comparative approach can be attempted. A premature

---

31. For this term and the underlying concept, see B. Landsberger ("Die Eigenbegrifflichkeit der babylonischen Welt," *Islamica* 2 [1926] 355-72).

32. See especially J. Murphy-O'Connor, "An Essene Missionary Document? CD II,14—VI,1," *RB* 77 (1970) 201-29; P. Davies, *The Damascus Covenant* (Sheffield: JSOT, 1983).

comparison and the hypothetical identification of the novel phenomenon with one or another schismatic group known from the classical sources on the strength of discrete features which they appear to have in common, is bound to obfuscate the Covenanters' idiosyncratic religious and societal profile. In the comparison attention should be given not solely to similarities which the יחד shares with one or the other *Strömung* in Second Temple Judaism, but also to dissimilarities which set it apart from all other known contemporaneous socioreligious manifestations. Moreover, the emerging analogous and disparate features should not be assessed in isolation but rather should be accorded their specific weight in the holistic makeup of each of the groups under consideration. Only thus can we hope to gauge the specific historical, social, and credal characteristics of the יחד and define its place in late Second Temple Judaism. The Qumran commune will probably emerge from this analysis as a unique socioreligious configuration of Judaism in the transition period from the biblical to the rabbinic era.

In the ensuing deliberations I aim at highlighting the distinctive posture of the יחד. I purport to show that the Qumran Covenanters were poised between an ideational attachment to the world of the Hebrew Bible and the emerging world of the Mishna. They hovered between the historical reality of the Hellenistic-Roman era and a utopian identification with the historical past of biblical Israel. This setting of the יחד in an existential twilight zone appears to cause a good many of the immense difficulties which confront the modern interpreter of the Covenanters' literature and their spiritual universe.

IV

This above depiction of the historical setting and the ideational character of the יחד connects the issue under review with a well-known problem to which some thought must now be given. There is no universally or even widely accepted criterion by which one can securely define the termination of the biblical age. The total lack of reliable historical data defies any attempt to delimit the ending of that period in precise chronological terms. Therefore in endeavoring to draw the demarcation line between the biblical and the postbiblical era, scholars tend to have recourse to a variety of somewhat intangible indicators.

There is a prevalent disposition to distinguish between a "Biblical Israel" and an "Early Judaism" and to conceive of the one as being entirely different from the other. This radical disjunction is determined by subjective predilections rather than by conclusions which result from an objective scholarly analysis. It is predominantly based on theological notions or credal preconceptions and not on chronological facts and historical considerations.[33]

One registers attempts to define the ending of the biblical era by equating that critical caesura in the history of ancient Israel with the effective closing of the Hebrew Canon of Scripture.[34] However that literary-cultural phenomenon also cannot be dated unequivocally.[35] Scholarly opinion remains divided in respect to the chronological determination of almost every phase in the progressive accumulation of the collection of books contained in the Hebrew Canon.[36] No reliable criteria are at hand for convincingly and accurately dating the inclusion of the book of Esther, assumedly the last book that was accepted into the corpus of Holy Scriptures.[37] Likewise there is no *communis opinio* relative to the date and the circumstances pertaining to the closure of the third major constituent part of the Hebrew Bible (the כתובים or "Writings"), which would have been coterminous with the culmination of the cumulative process and the fixation of the comprehensive canon.

It appears that already in antiquity concrete and precise data pertinent to the issue were no longer available. A rabbinic dictum which connects the closure of the corpus of biblical writings with the demise of the last prophets (Haggai, Zechariah, and Malachi), when "divine inspiration departed from Israel" (*t. Soṭa,*

---

33. An illustration of this approach may be found, int. al., in M. Noth, *The History of Israel* ([New York: Harper, 1960] 454). See R. Rendtorff's criticism of this modus operandi: "Das Ende der Geschichte Israels" (*Gesammelte Studien zum Alten Testament* [München: Kaiser, 1975] 267-76); further, S. Herrmann, *A History of Israel in Old Testament Times* (Philadelphia: Fortress, 1975).
34. See Talmon, "Heiliges Schrifttum," above, n. 29.
35. The discussion of this matter is surveyed, int. al., in S. A. Leiman (*The Canonization of Hebrew Scripture—The Talmudic and Midrashic Evidence. Transactions of the Connecticut Academy of Arts and Sciences* [Hamden, CT: Archon Books, 1976]); B. S. Childs (*Introduction to the Old Testament as Scripture* [Philadelphia: Fortress, 1979] 27-67); J. A. Sanders (*From Sacred Story to Sacred Text. Canon as Paradigm* [Philadelphia: Fortress, 1987]).
36. See the publications cited in nn. 29 and 35.
37. See S. Zeitlin, "An Historical Study of the Canonization of the Hebrew Scriptures," *PAAJR* 3 (1931/2); repr. in S. Z. Leiman, ed., *The Canon and Masorah of the Hebrew Bible* (New York: Ktav, 1974) 164-99.

ed. Zuckermandel 318.21-23; *b. Soṭa* 48b; *Sanh.* 11a; *Yoma* 9b), is altogether indeterminate. The same pertains to a later saying which probably evolved out of the former, in which the cessation of prophetic inspiration is dated in the time of Alexander the Macedonian (SOR 6, ed. Ratner 140; cp. Josephus, *Ag. Ap.* 1.40-41). It is more than doubtful that these pronouncements reflect reliable information of which the sages could yet avail themselves but which escapes our knowledge. They seem, rather, to reveal the ancient tradents' ignorance of the precise circumstances which surrounded the definitive delimitation of the canon of Holy Scriptures. Concomitantly they point up the ancients' ignorance of the exact conditions under which the new and distinct literary genres which mark the commencement of the rabbinic age concurrently emerged.[38]

We should give attention to a prominent and telling characteristic which the ancient rabbinic sayings (concerning the closure of the Hebrew Canon and the termination of the biblical era) seem to share with modern scholars' opinions in these matters. The dichotomy between the world of "Biblical Israel" and the world of "Early Judaism" is thrown into sharp relief as a result of focusing solely on the one central configuration of Second Temple Judaism that came into full view in the tannaitic period, the first and second centuries C.E. From then on it constitutes the mainstream community, which George Foot Moore designated "normative Judaism."[39] Persuasive validity attaches to the claim that the roots of that core community of the tannaitic age can be traced to the preceding centuries, back to the return from the exile in the sixth and fifth centuries B.C.E.[40] But this very plausible assumption cannot be substantiated by tangible contemporaneous evidence.

In this context the significance of the Qumran Scrolls becomes apparent: they reflect a socioreligious entity in Second Temple Judaism which did not link up with either the "normative" community that crystallized in the tannaitic era or with nascent Christianity. The cluster of dissidents who established "The New Covenant" and consolidated the יחד in the Judean Desert remained outside the compass of Rabbinic Judaism and Christianity, each of which perceived (through

---

38. See below.
39. G. F. Moore, *Judaism in the First Century of the Christian Era: The Age of the Tannaim* (Oxford: Clarendon, 1927), 1. 3.
40. See S. Talmon, "The Emergence of Jewish Sectarianism in the Early Second Temple Period," *King, Cult and Calendar,* hereinafter KCC (Jerusalem: Magnes, 1986) 176-201.

its own interpretation) biblical Israel as the source from which its particular societal-credal universe sprang.[41]

This conceptual implantation in the biblical world was also shared by the יחד. However, as will yet be specified, the Covenanters' ideational integration into the framework of biblical Israel rests upon a rather singular interpretative notion that differs fundamentally from the perception of the biblical legacy by both Judaism and Christianity. A close reading of the Qumran documents reveals some hitherto unknown aspects of the spiritual makeup of Jewry before the turn of the era. These particular facets evince a possibly unique existential understanding of the meaning and import of the biblical heritage which that group fostered and which has left no lasting imprint on the later Jewish and Christian evaluation and formative exegesis of the Hebrew Bible. Notwithstanding the ephemeral nature of their community, the Covenanters' idiosyncratic attachment to the biblical world throws further light on the internal multiformity within Jewry at the height of the Second Temple Period.[42]

At this juncture we need to remember that a substantial number of the Covenanters' writings stem from the second or possibly even from the third century, B.C.E. This means that they were written when biblical literary creativity was still ongoing. Now it is a *communis opinio* that the book of Daniel, or at least its second part, was probably composed somewhat later in the Hellenistic Period.[43] Many scholars concur that the book of Esther was also written at that time.[44] Some maintain that it was integrated into the Hebrew

41. Ibid., 186-201.
42. Ibid., 176-97.
43. See R. D. Wilson ("The Book of Daniel and the Canon," *Princeton Theological Review* 13 [1915] 352-408). A concise presentation of the arguments is given by Childs (*Introduction,* [above, n. 35], 608-23); further, S. Talmon ("Daniel," *The Literary Guide to the Bible* [ed. R. Alter and F. Kermode; Cambridge, MA: Harvard, 1987] 343-56). The discovery at Qumran of fragments of several Daniel manuscripts has added a new dimension to the discussion. See E. Ulrich, "Daniel Manuscripts from Qumran, Part I: A Preliminary Edition of 4QDan^a," *BASOR* 268 (1987) 17: "It (4QDan^a) is closer to the time of the original composition than any other extant manuscript of a book of the Hebrew Bible. The early semicursive script of 4QDan^a is to be dated in the 'late second century' B.C. 'no more than about half a century younger than the autograph,' ca. 168-165, 'of that book'" (quoted from Cross, *The Library* [above, n. 1] 43).
44. A summary of the arguments may be found, int. al., in S. Talmon, "Wisdom in the Book of Esther" (*VT* 13 [1963] 419ff.); Childs, *Introduction* (above, n. 35); R. Bardtke, "Neuere Arbeiten zum Estherbuch. Eine kritische Würdigung" (*Ex Oriente Lux* 19 [1965-66] 519-49).

Canon only in the second century C.E.[45] (While various aspects of these conjectures remain under debate, the comparative lateness of those books is a matter of scholarly consensus.) Accordingly it may be considered certain that various Qumran works originated concurrently with the latest books contained in the Hebrew Canon, and that the historical reality of the יחד coincided with the last stage of the waning biblical age.

This partial chronological overlap with the end phase of the biblical era also applies to the mainstream Jewish community of the last two centuries B.C.E., the days of the *Zugoth,* the pairs of contending sages, the founding fathers of Rabbinic Judaism. However the partial concurrence of their existential situation with the biblical world generated in the Qumran יחד and in the community of sages intrinsically different responses. (Proto)Rabbinic Jewry viewed the biblical era as a closed chapter and their own times as being profoundly different from that preceding age. In contradistincition, the Covenanters perceived themselves as standing within the orbit of the biblical era and their community as the rejuvenated embodiment of biblical Israel: they were the "righteous remnant" whom God had spared when he delivered Judah and Jerusalem to the sword of the Babylonians; they were divinely appointed to reconstitute Israel of old in the present (CD i 1ff.) and to write the next chapter in the yet ongoing history of the biblical people.

V

The fundamental divergence of the stance of the יחד from that of Rabbinic Judaism surfaces in various facts of the two communities' public life and spiritual universe. Some of these will now be brought under consideration.

תורה שבעל פה and *תורה שבכתב*

From the early days of the mishnaic, or protomishnaic period, the sages accorded a special status of sanctity to the biblical books. They were *in toto* designated תורה שבכתב and were considered to have been authored under divine inspiration. The corpus of "Holy Writings" was distinguished from all other compositions then known. These also included the teachings of the sages, which were subsumed under the comprehensive appellation תורה שבעל פה. The Hebrew

---

45. See Zeitlin, *PAAJR* 3 (1931-32) 12-14 (above, n. 37).

expressions and their prevalent English translations, "Written Law" and "Oral Law," convey the notion that the distinction between the two corpora of traditions is rooted in a purely technical circumstance: one could and should be handed down in writing; the other should exclusively be transmitted orally (*y. Meg.* 4.1 74d; cp. *b. Giṭ.* 66b; *b. Tem.* 14b).[46]

This understanding of the collocations is based on fully justified etymological considerations. The implied technical particularity of transmission may indeed initially have set apart one category of literary works from the other. But in a subsequent stage of development, the תורה שבעל פה was also committed to writing. Therefore its presumed differentiation from the תורה שבכתב by the merely technical criterion of "oral" versus "written" fails to do justice to the intrinsic significance of these collocations. They should be understood, rather, as ciphers for "biblical," viz., "holy" books conceived under divine inspiration, and "extra-biblical" books which are not thus distinguished, irrespective of their being transmitted orally or in manuscript form.

Rabbinic tradition considered the category of biblical books to be totally different in tenor from the works of the sages. They were distinguished from each other by the distinct "language" in which they are severally clothed: "the language of Torah [i.e., the books of the Bible] is one matter; the language of the [teachings of the] sages is another matter," לשון תורה לעצמה לשון חכמים לעצמו (*b. ʿAbod. Zar.* 58b; *b. Menaḥ.* 65a). In this context the term לשון should not be taken to connote only the linguistic medium in which one or the other complex of writings was cast. Its meaning also extends to the terminology in which they were couched, to style and conceptual content.[47] In short, the above pronouncement declares the biblical literature in its totality to be essentially different from the rabbinic.[48]

The traditions which evince this distinction are mostly attributed to talmudic teachers of later generations, viz., to *Amoraʾim*. It follows that in their present

---

46. See S. Lieberman, *Hellenism in Jewish Palestine* (New York: JTS, 1962) 87.

47. For the style and formulation of mishnaic legal literature see J. Neusner ("The Meaning of Oral Torah," *Early Rabbinic Judaism* [Leiden: Brill, 1975] 1-33; "Accomodating Mishnah to Scripture in Judaism: The Uneasy Union and Its Offspring," *Michigan Quarterly Review* 22 [1983] 465-79); et al.

48. See E. Rivkin, *A Hidden Revolution: The Pharisaic Search for the Kingdom Within* (Nashville: Abingdon, 1978) 223-27. This distinction may explain the striking circumstance noted by W. D. Davies "that the Oral Law of Judaism often bears little relation to the Written Torah" ("Reflections about the Use of the Old Testament in the New in Its Historical Setting," *JQR* 74 [1983] 132).

wording they stem from the third to the fifth century C.E. But it may confidently be assumed that they reflect a situation which obtained from the days of the very first *Tannaʾim* or from even earlier times.

Various categories of literary compositions were excluded from the corpus of "Holy Writings." Some were of a patently secular nature, like the ספרי המירן, possibly a mispronunciation of *homeros* (*m. Yad.* 4.6), which were current either in an original Greek version or else in Hebrew translation. Others, foremost the Proverbs of Ben Sira, admittedly contained significant teachings. But they were nevertheless relegated to the extracanonical status of חיצונים,[49] since they did not meet with the above-mentioned qualitative and temporal requirements (*m. Sanh.* 10.1), viz., they were not conceived under divine inspiration and were known to have been authored after מכאן ואילך. Standardized prayer texts and compilations of prayers[50] were similarly precluded from inclusion in the book of Psalms and from thereby becoming an integral part of the biblical canon.

The canonical books *in toto* come under the headings כתבי הקדש, מקרא, תורה, et sim.[51] They are further defined by the phrase מטמאים את הידים, which sets them apart from all other books. The exact signification of this designation too cannot be unequivocally established. Its meaning may, in fact, have already escaped the knowledge of the rabbinic tradents who offer seemingly farfetched suggestions for its explanation.[52] The prevalent English rendition, "(books which) defile the hands," is etymologically correct. But it does not convey the intrinsic technical sense of the Hebrew term. There is no reference to an actual ritual "defilement" incurred by the handling of books which are specifically said to be מטמאים את הידים. Nor is there any mention of an ensuing purification rite required after contact with "defiling" objects. These circumstances prompt the conclusion that the characterization of the biblical books as מטמאים את הידים does not show that they actually impart "impurity." Quite the contrary. The expression defines and highlights their unique sacred and authoritative status in which no extra-canonical book has a part. This term too must be understood as a

---

49. The Hebrew expression חיצונים is echoed in the Aramaic term ברייתא, which defines an extracompendium mishna.
50. On the exclusion of prayers from the "Holy Writings," see S. Talmon, "Institutionalized Prayer," in this vol., pp. 200-243.
51. For the use of these terms in rabbinic literature, see Leiman, *Canonization* (above, n. 35), 56-72.
52. The putative rabbinic explanations of this term are surveyed in Ibid., 102-20.

cipher which had a specific and restricted applicability. It pertains positively to acclaimed biblical books only. In the negative sense it applies exclusively to writings which appear to have stood a chance of infiltrating the canon and therefore needed expressly to be precluded from entering it. In neither of these connotations was the phrase ever used in reference to a work for which no one claimed a "biblical" status, nor to rabbinic compositions of the תורה שבעל פה category. While these works were held in highest esteem, they were extrabiblical by definition.

In sum, the above technical terms and others not mentioned, which in rabbinic literature pertain exclusively to canonical books and segregate them from all nonbiblical writings, reveal the sages' perception of the Hebrew Canon as a closed corpus to which nothing can be added and from which nothing can be subtracted.

The Qumran Covenanters' outlook was entirely different. There is no explicit or implicit statement in their literature which could give pause to think that they subscribed to a similarly clear-cut distinction between books which "defile" and others which "do not defile the hands." Likewise nothing indicates that they discriminated between books of the category תורה שבכתב and others which were subsumed under the category תורה שבעל פה, irrespective of whether these terms are understood as distinctive designations of canonical vis à vis extracanonical works as proposed above, or whether, in accord with the prevalent opinion, they distinguish between books which should be transmitted in writing and others which should be only orally tradited. The total absence of relevant pronouncements suggests that the Covenanters did not subscribe to such a categorization of the literary works which they preserved.

This conclusion is borne out by the large number of distinctive יחד opuscules which issued from the Qumran Caves. These finds prove beyond doubt that the prolific יחד scribes committed to writing a considerable amount of various, partly legal, materials of a type which the sages would have deemed to belong to the category of תורה שבעל פה.

We mention here only some instructive examples. From Cave 1 issued the *Serek hayyaḥad* (1QS), a compilation of legislation peculiar to Qumran. Extrapolations of biblical laws and additional injunctions are also contained in the *Zadokite Documents* (CD ix 1ff.). This work is known *in extenso* from medieval manuscripts which stem from the Cairo Geniza.[53] But its יחד origin is proven beyond doubt by manuscript fragments of the work which were found at Qumran.[54] Further statutes surface in the *War Scroll* (1QM) and in the *Temple Scroll* (11QT). Special weight must be accorded in this context to the treatise מקצת מעשי/דברי התורה (4QMMT), only partially preserved and not yet published, which lists a series of halakic rulings in which the Covenanters differed from their opponents.[55] The tractate is extant in fragments which hail from six different copies, evidence to the exceeding importance which the Covenanters attached to it.

These distinctive extrabiblical law compilations, which differ from each other in their stylistic formulations, were all handed down at Qumran in manuscript form, viz., as תורה שבכתב. They were invested with a binding force that was evidently on a par with the normative nature of the legal decrees and dispensations which in the contemporaneous rabbinic community of that time were transmitted exclusively as תורה שבעל פה. The transmission in writing of such extrabiblical legislation at Qumran sustains the conclusion that the Covenanters, unlike mainstream Judaism, did not distinguish between a "Written Law" and an "Oral Law."

The Withdrawal of Divine Inspiration

It can equally be shown that the יחד did not embrace the rabbinic distinction between the books contained in the biblical canon which were believed to have been authored under divine inspiration in the era that preceded the caesura termed מכאן ואילך and all other works known to have been composed after that indefinable date when divine inspiration (viz., the prophetic spirit) had withdrawn from Israel.

---

53. S. Schechter, *Fragments of a Zadokite Work* in *Documents of Jewish Sectaries* (Cambridge: Cambridge University Press, 1910), vol. 1.
54. M. Baillet published the fragments from Cave 6 in *Les 'Petites Grottes' de Qumrân* ([DJD; Oxford: Clarendon, 1962], 3. 128-31). J. T. Milik published a fragment from Cave 5 (ibid, 181) and another fragment from Cave 4 ("Fragment d'une source de psautier [4QPs 89] et fragments des Jubilés, du Document de Damas, d'un phylactere dans la grotte 4 de Qumrân," *RB* 73 [1966] 105).
55. See the preliminary report by Qimron and Strugnell (above, n. 25). For a discussion of the specific Qumran *halakhah* see, int. al., L. H. Schiffman (*The Halakhah at Qumran* [Leiden: Brill, 1975]) and J. Baumgarten (*Studies in Qumran Law* in *Studies in Judaism in Late Antiquity,* ed. J. Neusner [Leiden: Brill, 1977], vol. 24).

Nothing indicates that the Covenanters subscribed to the notion that prophecy was phased out after the demise of the last biblical prophets. Quite the contrary. The prophetic spirit was seen still to be implanted in some of their leaders, even though the inspiration of the מורה הצדק[56] and possibly the author of the *Hôdāyôt* (1QH) was expressed in forms which differed from the hypostatizations of prophecy in the biblical age.

The Covenanters preserved in writing commentaries on books of biblical prophets, such as the *Pesher on Habakkuk* (1QpHab) or *Nahum* (4QpNah); midrashic extrapolations of biblical books such as the *Genesis Apocryphon* (1QapGen);[57] translations of biblical books into Greek[58] or Aramaic;[59] sundry prayer collections;[60] and also several extracanonical works which in rabbinic parlance would come under the heading חיצונים,[61] such as *Jubilees*,[62] Ben Sira,[63] *Enoch*,[64] and the *Testaments of the Twelve Patriarchs*.[65]

56. See G. Jeremias, *Der Lehrer der Gerechtigkeit* (Göttingen: Vandenhoek & Ruprecht, 1963).

57. N. Avigad and Y. Yadin, *A Genesis Apocryphon* (Jerusalem: Magnes and Shrine of the Book, 1956).

58. Only a few fragments of a Greek translation of the Bible were preserved at Qumran: pap7QLXXEx; 4QLXXLev[a]; pap4QLXXLev[b]; 4QLXXNum; 4QLXXDeut. See P. W. Skehan ("The Qumran Manuscripts and Textual Criticism" [VTSup; Leiden: Brill, 1957], 4. 155-59; idem, "4QLXXNum: A PreChristian Reworking of the Septuagint" *HThR* 70 [1977] 39-50); E. Ulrich ("The Greek Manuscripts of the Pentateuch from Qumran, Including Newly Identified Manuscripts of Deuteronomy [4QLXXDeut]," *De Septuaginta. Studies in Honor of J. W. Wevers on His Sixty-Fifth Birthday* [ed. A. Pitersma and C. Cox; Missiauga, Ont.: Benben, 1984]); C. H. Roberts ("On Some Presumed Papyrus Fragments of the NT from Qumran," *JTS* 23 [1972] 321-25); A. C. Urban ("Observaciones sobre ciertos papiro de la cueva 7 de Qumran," *RB* 8 [1973] 16-19); A. R. C. Leaney ("Greek Manuscripts from the Judaean Desert," *Studies in New Testament Language and Text* [ed. J. K. Elliott; Leiden: Brill, 1976] 283-300. The authors of these essays refute J. O'Callaghan's reading of these fragments as NT texts: "Los papieros griegos de la cueva 7 de Qumran," *BAC* 353 [Madrid, 1974]); Tov (*JJS* 38 [1988] 18-19 [above, n. 28]); further, D. Barthélemy (*Les Devanciers d'Aquila* [VTSup; Leiden: Brill, 1963], vol. 10).

59. Van der Woude and van der Ploeg, *Le Targum* (above, n. 5).

60. See Talmon, "Institutionalized Prayer," in this vol. pp. 200-243.

61. Manuscript fragments of a variety of such "extraneous" books issued from the "smaller" Qumran Caves (2-10). See Baillet (*Les 'Petites Grottes,'* DJD 3 [1962], above, n. 54).

62. 2Q19 and 2Q20, Baillet, Milik, and de Vaux, *Les 'Petites Grottes' de Qumrân* (DJD; Oxford: Clarendon, 1962), 3. 77-79; further M. Kister, "Newly-Identified Fragments of the Book of Jubilees: Jub. 23:23-23, 30-31," *RQ* 48 (1987) 529-

The יחד members considered many, if not all, of these works to have been authored under divine inspiration and invested them with the sanctity which attaches to the biblical books. The book of *Jubilees* is expressly cited in the Zadokite Documents (CD xvi 3-4) as the ספר in which "the divisions of times according to jubilees and sabbath years" are authoritatively explicated. That opus is thus presented as the source which proves the exclusive legitimacy of the Covenanters' particular calendar reckoning. This issue was an important factor of contention with the main community and eventually led to their dissent from it.[66]

In addition, the Covenanters ostensibly attached inspired sanctity to some works of a legal nature which are in no way Bible-connected and were authored by their own members. They considered these books pillars of the Renewed Covenant that God had established with them and held them in highest esteem. It suffices to refer, int. al., to the *Manual of Discipline* (1QS) and the related *Serek Ha'edah* (1QS[a]), the *Temple Scroll* (11QT), the Zadokite Documents (CD), and the yet unidentified ספר ההגי/ו which is mentioned there together with the titles of several other works (CD x 6).

The continuance of inspired literary activity in the biblical mode supports the proposition that the Qumran Covenanters did not see the biblical period as a closed chapter in the history of Israel. Far from it. In their *Eigenverständnis* they viewed their community as a new link in the reconstituted generation-chain of biblical Israel (CD i 1-10).

36; J. van der Kam, *Textual and Historical Studies in the Book of Jubilees* (HSM; Missoula, MT: Scholars Press, 1977), vol. 14; A. S. van der Woude, "Fragmente des Buches Jubiläen/aus Höhle XI (11QJub)," *Tradition und Glaube. Das frühe Christentum in seiner Umwelt* (ed. G. Jeremias, H. W. Kuhn, H. Stegemann; Göttingen: Vandenhoek & Ruprecht, 1971) 140-46.

63. Y. Yadin, *The Ben Sira Scroll from Masada* (Jerusalem: IES and Shrine of the Book, 1965).

64. J. T. Milik, *The Books of Enoch. Aramaic Fragments of Qumran Cave 4* (Oxford: Clarendon, 1964).

65. J. T. Milik, "Le Testament de Lévi en araméen. Fragment de la grotte 4 de Qumrân," *RB* 62 (1958) 498-506; for the Testament of Juda (4Q484 T. Juda), see Baillet (*Qumran Grotte 4* [DJD7], above, n. 4); J. T. Milik ("Écrits préesseniens de Qumrân," *Qumrân, sa piété, sa théologie et son milieu* [ed. M. Delcor; Paris/Leuven: Duculot et U. P. Louvain, 1978]) 91-106.

66. See Talmon, "The Calendar of the Covenanters," in this vol., pp. 147-85.

VI

The Living Bible

Many יחד compositions are manifestly couched in an archaizing style and wording which reveal their authors as epigones who intentionally infused biblical linguistic coinage into their vernacular Mishnaic Hebrew. However other Qumran works, which by theme and content are more closely related to canonical writings, display linguistic, terminological, and stylistic characteristics reminiscent of distinctive features which are intrinsic to the language, style, and spirit of the biblical literature. Against the background of these compositions, we can better appreciate the ongoing literary creativity at Qumran in the diverse genres and the distinctive essence which marks the books of the Hebrew Canon.

The following examples will illustrate the persistence of biblical literary styles at Qumran:

(1) Several noncanonical songs which are interspersed among "canonical" psalms in the *Psalms Scroll* of Cave 11 (11QPs[a]) give evidence to the preservation at Qumran of extrabiblical psalmodic creations which for one reason or another were not included in the canonical book of Psalms. We find in that scroll a variant version of Sir 51:13-30 (11QPs[a] xxi 11-17; xxii 1) and three Hebrew songs (cols. xviii—xix). The latter are extant in a Syriac translation which the 11th century Nestorian patriarch Elias of Anbar had included in his homiletical opus *Kitabʾal ʾAnwaʾr* (together with two others which are not attested to at Qumran). The Covenanters invested these songs and similar, hitherto altogether unknown, psalm-like compositions preserved in 11QPs[a] and other cave manuscripts,[67] with the same aura of sanctity which they attached to the canonical psalms.

We cannot say for certain whether those supernumerary psalms originated *in toto* or in part at Qumran or whether they were brought there by recruits who joined the יחד. It is safe, however, to conclude that the art of biblical psalmody was still practiced in the Covenanters' community and in all likelihood also in other contemporary sectors of Second Temple Judaism.

(2) The self-identification of the יחד with biblical Israel shows in the liberty which Qumran men of letters took in rearranging tradited biblical

---

67. See E. M. Schuller (*Non-Canonical Psalms from Qumran—A Pseudepigraphic Collection* [Harvard Semitic Studies; Atlanta, GA: Scholars Press, 1986], vol. 28) and bibliography cited there.

psalmodic materials and changing their textual formulations. A case in point is the sequence of the "canonical" psalms in 11QPs[a] [68] which diverges from the order in the MT, and the internal restructuring of several "canonical" psalms with the obvious aim of casting them in the form of the *responsorium*. This mode of recitation is preeminently suited to their use in prayer worship. Moreover, going beyond the liberal restructuring of biblical psalms, they extracted constitutive parts from diverse songs and rearranged and combined them into new compositions which are molded after the typical patterns of biblical psalmody or else resemble them closely.

These features presumably evidence the use of the *Psalms Scroll* as a breviary[69] in the prayer service which the Covenanters instituted as replacement for the sacrificial service in the Jerusalem Temple from which they had withdrawn.[70] 11QPs[a] shares the postulated breviary character with the prayer manuals which in mainstream Judaism became current in postbiblical times. It is therefore of importance to point out a prominent difference between the two sets of liturgical traditions. The authors, redactors, and arrangers of the later normative Jewish synagogal compendia never took recourse to such a liberal revamping of canonical psalms. When incorporating passages from Psalms and other biblical books in their compilations, the sages and later rabbinic authorities took pains to preserve the borrowed materials in their transmitted forms and textual formulations. The firm adherence to the hallowed tradition clearly indicates that also in this matter rabbinic authors and authorities assumed a consciously *postbiblical* stance.

The Qumran authors' attitude is the exact opposite. They freely adapted canonical texts to the particular requirements of their community and their time. Their procedures reflect that pronounced *inner-biblical* attitude toward the texts

---

68. The editor of 11QPs[a] defined the MS as a copy of the biblical book of Psalms. (See J. A. Sanders, *The Psalms Scroll of Qumran Cave 11 [11QPs^a]* [DJD; Oxford: Clarendon, 1965], vol. 4; idem, "Cave 11 Surprises and the Question of Canon," *New Directions in Biblical Archaeology* [ed. D. N. Freedman and J. Greenfield; New York: Doubleday, 1971] 113-30; idem, "The Qumran Psalms Scroll [11QPs^a] Reviewed," *On Language, Culture, and Religion. In Honor of E. A. Nida* [ed. M. Black and B. Smalley; The Hague: Mouton, 1974] 19-99).

69. The presentation of 11QPs[a] as a biblical MS has been questioned by scholars who would rather view it as an early liturgical composition. See M. Goshen-Gottstein ("The Psalms Scroll [11QPs^a]. A Problem of Canon and Text," *Textus* 5 [1966] 22-33); S. Talmon ("Extra-Canonical Hebrew Psalms," below, 244-72).

70. See Talmon, "Institutionalized Prayer," in this vol., pp. 200-243.

which was already pointed out and which is akin to the posture maintained by the biblical psalmists.

Psalm 108 is an instructive example of this liberal, structurational technique which biblical poets were wont to use. Several originally independent elements (e.g., Pss 57:8-12 and 60:7-14) were combined in this song to form a new comprehensive unit.

Another illustration is provided by the textual and structural divergencies between two versions of one and the same psalm which are extant in different books of the Hebrew Bible or even in the book of Psalms itself. For example, there are two versions extant of David's מזמור, one found in 2 Samuel 22, the other in Psalm 18. Similarly the opening passage common to Psalms 31 and 71 is preserved there in variant formulations.

Quotations and paraphrases drawn from one or several biblical books will result in the constitution of a new song, as is the case with Psalm 86 or with Jonah's Psalm (Jonah 2:3-10). One can further compare the liberal use of excerpts from Psalm 107 (vv 40-42) in Job 5:16; 12:21, 24; 22:19.[71]

Even more persuasive is the comparison of the Covenanters' approach with the compositional methods to which the Chronicler had recourse when he inserted in his work a hymn (1 Chr 16:8-36) which is constituted of several pieces drawn from a variety of canonical psalms (105:1-15; 96:1-13; and 106:1-2, 47-48).

The author or compiler of 11QPs[a] (or possibly one of his predecessors) seems to have pursued this course when he set about the rewording and re-structuring of some canonical psalms which he adopted into his compilation. Other Qumran literati proceeded along similar lines.

(3) A Qumran biblical manuscript will at times exhibit a variant text that diverges from the MT in the same characteristic details and overall manner in which differ the MT readings of a pericope which is preserved in parallel versions in two canonical books, and occasionally in one and the same book. The phenomenon can be illustrated by making reference to just a few of these well-known textual doublets or triplets.

71. The borrowing may have been in the reverse, but this would not affect our argument.

The concise note concerning the capture of Samaria by Sennacherib's forces is recorded in 2 Kgs 17:5-6 and 18:9-12 in two significantly different readings, one possibly preserving an Ephraimite, the other a Judean tradition.[72]

Again, the much more extended report on the siege which Sennacherib's army laid on Jerusalem is extant in 2 Kgs 18:13—19:36 in a reading which diverges textually and structurally from the parallel in Isa 36:1—37:38. A third, evidently compressed, version turns up in 2 Chr 32:1-22.

Similarly the conquest of Judah and the destruction of Jerusalem by Nebuchadnezzar's troops are reported in 2 Kgs 25:1-21 in a wording and composition which differ substantially from the parallel found in Jer 52:1-27. Another version of this account in the book of Jeremiah (Jer 39:1-10) exhibits a text and literary structure that do not tally with either of the aforementioned sources.[73]

It stands to reason that a great number or possibly most of these variant formulations resulted from a variety of secondary phenomena which affected one pristine *Vorlage* in the process of transmission, whether involving scribal lapses or premeditated linguistic and theological/ideational changes.[74] But there is room for another explanation of the emergence of such variations in the biblical text tradition, both in the original Hebrew and in the ancient versions. I have suggested that some such variants persisted from a precanonical stage in which traditions could still be transmitted legitimately in somewhat differing formulations which did not affect the intrinsic content of the text. Such diverging readings should be judged "original."[75]

72. See S. Talmon, "Polemics and Apology in Biblical Historiography: 2 Kings 17:24-41," *The Creation of Sacred Literature—Composition and Redaction of the Biblical Text* (ed. R. B. Friedman; Los Angeles: UCLA, 1981) 57-68.

73. We should also mention the preservation of two divergent wordings of a pericope as pivotal as the Ten Commandments (Exodus 20 and Deuteronomy 5). Their ascription to two different "sources" is of no concern in the present context.

74. This assumption underlies, e.g., the attempt to reconstruct an original common *Vorlage* for the two extant versions of David's psalm: F. M. Cross and D. N. Freedman ("2 Sam 22 = Ps 18," *JBL* 72 [1953] 15-34).

75. See S. Talmon, "Double Readings in the Massoretic Text," *Textus* 1 (1960) 144-84; idem, "Synonymous Readings in the Textual Tradition of the Old Testament" (ScrHier, ed. C. Rabin; Jerusalem: Magnes, 1961), 8. 335-85; idem, "The Old Testament Text," in *From the Beginning to Jerome,* ed. P. R. Ackroyd and C. F. Evans, *Cambridge History of the Bible* (Cambridge: Cambridge University Press, 1970), 1. 159-99 = QHBT (above, n. 28) 321-400.

This understanding of the data differs from a prevalent appreciation of the facts. E. A. Speiser, e.g., has succinctly argued: "The canonical tradition . . . much older than the pentateuchal writers, older indeed than the time of Moses," conferred a binding sanctity upon the narratives, and no biblical writer "would have felt free to recast them in terms of his own time and environment."[76] The very opposite appears to be the case. Compilers, redactors and even copyists of the biblical age acted as the authors' minor partners in the creative literary process in varying degrees, occasionally injecting their personalities into the materials which they transmitted.[77] Whenever they deemed that textual adjustments were called for, they would not abstain from adapting formulations which they found in their *Vorlagen* to their own preferences and predilections. At times they would go beyond what appears to have been tacitly accepted as a "legitimate latitude of variation" in respect to wording, style, and structure.[78]

The Persistence of Biblical Literary Genres at Qumran

The variance in attitude toward the biblical world which, as proposed, distinguishes the יחד from rabbinic Judaism and at the same time evidences the Covenanters' "biblical stance," is not exhausted by a review of the divergent procedures in the handling of the hallowed biblical texts and traditions and the continuance of biblical linguistic and stylistic conventions which obtained at Qumran. It also shows in the persistence of biblical literary genres which evidently relapsed in the rabbinic literary tradition.

(1) *Qumran Law Literature*. The formulations of Qumran enactments bear a close resemblance to the characteristic style and structure which mark the pentateuchal legal compilations. The similarity shows both in the extrapolation and amplification of biblical laws and in the wordings of new ordinances which pertain in particular to the יחד membership. The following examples may serve as illustrations of this phenomenon.[79] The supplementary Sabbath prescriptions

76. See E. A. Speiser ("The Biblical Idea of History," *IEJ* 7 [1956] 201-16 [esp. 206-9] = *Oriental and Biblical Studies* [Philadelphia: Univ. of Penn., 1967] 187-200).

77. See S. Talmon, "The Textual Study of the Bible—A New Outlook," QHBT (above, n. 28) 321-400.

78. We cannot accurately define the extent to which such variation was considered legitimate. For some of the relevant phenomena which seem to be involved, see Talmon ("The Textual Study," QHBT).

79. The issue can only be touched upon here. The required detailed analysis must be undertaken in a separate framework.

listed in the Zadokite Documents are introduced severally by the biblical conclusive אל formula, [אל [יעש, יתהלך, ישאב, which parallels the biblical apodictic אל/לא model. Both preclude the voicing of any objections or dissenting opinions (CD x 16ff; cp. Exod 3:5; 12:9; 16:29; 19:15; Lev 10:6, 9; 25:14; etc.). At times that same formula precedes intrinsically Qumranite purity injunctions (e.g., CD x 10-14; x 21—xii 2, 12-15) and other precepts which are derived from and enlarge upon biblical legislation.

Qumran legislation is sometimes couched in wordings which resemble the biblical casuistic mode,[80] e.g., כל (איש) אשר (CD xii 2) or וכל אשר (CD xii 4), et al. (cp. Lev 20:9-21, et al.).

Practically all formulae which Qumran authors apply in the expansion and amplification of biblical laws are also applied in the distinctive יחד legislation; one may cite phrases such as כל אדם or כל איש אשר followed by a verb (CD ix 1, 2), which turn up in a roster of precepts regulating the life of the community. The violation of these statutes engendered harsh punishment (CD ix—x 10).

The roster of purity laws in the halakic compilation מקצת מעשי/דברי התורה (4QMMT) is arranged in units of itemized related phenomena, each introduced by the protasis על. The same superscription is found in the Zadokite Documents: על הטהר במים (CD x 10); על השבת (CD x 14). A similar purpose in the organization of legal materials is served by the standard phrase זה הסרך (CD x 4; xii 19, 22; xiii 7; 1QS passim) and equally by the typical biblical collocation ואלה הח(ו)קים (CD xii 21). This latter structurational model may be compared with the formula זאת התורה or זאת תורת, which in biblical law texts precedes and/or summarizes the enumeration of distinct categories of statutes (e.g. Lev 6:7; 7:1, 11, 37), especially in reference to ritual purity (Lev 11:46; 12:7; 13:59; 14:1, 32, 54; Num 5:29-30).

In contrast, rabbinic legal literature is predominantly cast in the form of שקלא וטריא: the presentation and evaluation of discordant views leads to the promulgation of normative statements based on majority decisions or on past pronouncements of acknowledged authorities. Unlike Qumran tradition, the style

---

80. These terms were introduced into the discussion by A. Alt (*Die Ursprünge des israelitischen Rechts* [Leipzig: Hirzel, 1934]) and have recently come under criticism from various quarters. See the review of the discussion *apud* Childs (*Introduction* [above, n. 35], part 2); and R. Rendtorff (*Das Alte Testament. Eine Einführung* [Neukirchen-Vluyn: Neukirchener, 1983]).

and procedures which denote these rabbinic debates[81] are fundamentally distinct from the ones which predominate in the legal corpora of the Hebrew Bible.

(2) *Qumran Historiography*. Early rabbinic Judaism evidently did not cultivate the historiographical genre. Rabbinic literature does not comprise any composition which is similar to the inclusive biblical historiographies, such as the Pentateuch and the Former Prophets or Chronicles and Ezra-Nehemiah, which offer wide-ranging surveys of past events and also encompass contemporary occurrences and situations. The comprehensive presentation of history in perspective will reemerge only in medieval times, when a compilation such as *Seder ʿOlam Zuta* (sixth-eighth centuries) presents an overview of events from the creation of the world to the days of the Babylonian exilarchs in the sixth century C.E.[82]

This late work draws heavily on the *Seder ʿOlam (Rabba)*,[83] which the third-century Palestinian Amoraʾ R. Jochanan ascribes to the second-century Tannaʾ Jose b. Halafta (*b. Šabb.* 88a; *Yebam.* 82a-b; *Nid.* 46b). In the present context, it is of significance to note that this earlier opus is dedicated in its entirety to a presentation of the biblical era. Only one part of its final chapter (chap. 30) contains a compressed summary of events from Alexander's conquest of Persia to the Bar Kochba revolt. It appears that this excerpt, a mere literary torso, stems from the pen of an editor who was evidently "uninterested in postbiblical history."[84] The chronological discontinuity between the end of the biblical period and the ensuing period invites the conclusion that the author of *Seder ʿOlam (Rabba)* deliberately refrained from directly linking the "postbiblical" rabbinic age (including his own times) with the biblical era.

The sages' distinction between the biblical and their own world (which, int. al., found a salient expression in the above-quoted saying (לשון תורה לעצמה;

---

81. See Neusner, "The Meaning" (above, n. 47) 1-33 and see idem, "Mishnah and Messiah," *Judaisms and Their Messiahs at the Turn of the Christian Era* (ed. J. Neusner, W. S. Green, E. Frerichs; Cambridge: Cambridge University Press, 1987) 267: "The framers of the [Mishna] code . . . barely refer to Scripture, rarely produce proof texts for their own propositions, never imitate the modes of speech of ancient Hebrew, as do the writers of the Dead Sea Scrolls at Qumran."

82. M. Grossberg, ed., *Seder Olam Zuta* (London: Naroditzky, 1910); M. J. Weinstock, ed., *Seder Olam Zuta ha-Shalem* (Jerusalem: Metibta' Torat Hesed, 1957); J. M. Rosenthal, "Seder Olam," *EJ* (Jerusalem: Keter, 1972), 14. 1092-93.

83. B. Ratner, ed. *Seder Olam Rabba* (Vilna: Romm, 1897), repr. with an introduction by S. K. Mirsky (Jerusalem: Kook, 1966); A. Marx, ed., *Seder Olam* (Berlin: Itzkowski, 1903).

84. Rosenthal, *EJ* (above, n. 82), 14. 1091-92.

לשון חכמים לעצמו) invites the conclusion that the nonexistence of the specifically biblical genres of historiography, prophecy, and psalmody in rabbinic literature is not accidental but rather points up a premeditated discontinuance.

An altogether different picture emerges from the Qumran finds. יחד authors purposefully added new features to the rich canvas of past events which their biblical predecessors had bequeathed to them and spun out anew the historical thread which had snapped some four centuries prior to their own times. They present the experiences of their community as another link in the narrative chain which opened with the creation tradition, related the story of biblical Israel's progress in history, and was severed when the Babylonians put an end to Judah's sovereignty in 586 B.C.E. (CD i 1ff.).

A partial account of events in the Covenanters' history is contained in the Zadokite Documents whose overall literary structure is reminiscent of the Pentateuch and especially of the book of Deuteronomy: a core of legislative material is embedded in a historical-narrative framework which consists of a series of addresses, probably delivered by the "Righteous Teacher," the Moses-like spiritual leader of the יחד. Further pieces of historical data are found in the pesharim, e.g., 1QpHab, 4QpNah, and 4QpPs, and in other Qumran documents of different literary genres.

There is also ground for assuming that יחד writers also authored comprehensive historiographies as well. Some such opuscules are mentioned by title in the Qumran literature. However, no copies of them are extant among the published manuscripts, just as there has not yet been found a copy of the already-mentioned ספר ההגו/י. These יחד works may have been somewhat similar to the lost compositions to which biblical writers, especially the authors of Chronicles (1 Chr 29:29; 2 Chr 9:29; 12:15; 20:34; 32:32; et sim.) and Kings (1 Kgs 11:41; 14:19; 15:31; et sim.) refer,[85] occasionally recording quotations from such works (Num 21:14; Josh 10:12-13; 2 Sam 17-18; and possibly 1 Kgs 8:13, LXX).

In this context we should give special attention to the מספר, viz., the ספר, mentioned in the Zadokite Documents, which was most probably a written account couched in the style of a chronicle (cp. 2 Chr 24:27). That work

---

85. Leiman (*Canonization* [above, n. 35]) counts 24 lost books, which number would correspond to the number of books included in the Hebrew Canon. See also Talmon ("Heiliges Schrifttum," 55 [above, n. 29]; idem, *Literary Guide* [above, n. 43] 368ff.).

evidently contained a record of events in the Covenanters' history, from their "Exodus" after the destruction of the Temple and their experiences in "Exile," to their "Return" to the land, together with a reference to an as yet uncharted future age[86] termed אחרית הימים:

> the returners [and/or repenters][87] of Israel, שבי ישראל, . . . who had left the land of Judah[88] . . . they are the elect of Israel, the men of renown who [will] arise באחרית הימים. Here is the roster of their names according to their families, לתולדותם and the appointed time[89] of their *constitution* [as a community], קץ מעמדם; the account, מספר, of their afflictions [during] the years of exile, שני התגוררם; here is, הנה, the [overall] exposition of their affairs (CD iv 2-6).

I presume that this compilation was in fact a Qumran parallel of the biblical reports which pertain to the returned exiles and are preserved in the books of Haggai, Zechariah, Malachi, and Ezra-Nehemiah. Those reports also include various detailed lists of returnees arranged according to their paternal houses (Ezra 2 = Nehemiah 7; Ezra 8:1-14; 10:16-43; Neh 3:1-32; 10:1-28, et sim.) and itemized accounts of the events which befell them (passim), together with an unmistakable reference to the future era of אחרית הימים in the prophecy which closes the book of Malachi:

> the day when I [God] will [again] make [them] my [special] possession and will have mercy upon them as a man has mercy on his son who serves him (Mal 3:17).

86. For this understanding of the Hebrew term, see S. Talmon, *Eschatology and History in Biblical Judaism. Occasional Papers* 2 (Jerusalem: Ecumenical Institute, Tantur, 1986).

87. שוב is employed here by way of a *double entendre,* similar to some of its uses in Biblical Hebrew.

88. Undoubtedly an allusion to the enforced deportation of Judeans in the wake of the debacle of 586 B.C.E.

89. This is the predominant connotation of קץ in the Qumran writings as, e.g., in גמר קץ (1QpHab vii 1-2). The term has the same signification in some late (postexilic) biblical books. This meaning becomes especially apparent when קץ is used coterminously or in conjunction with עת (Ezek 21:30, 34; 35:5; Dan 8:17; 11:35, 40; 12:4, 9) or מועד (Dan 8:19; 11:27). We can also compare the rabbinic collocation קץ משיח (*b. Meg.* 3a; further: *Gen. Rab.* 88 *ad* Gen 49:1, ed. Theodor-Albeck, 1251). In the sense of "end," קץ is only rarely used in the Qumran literature. See, e.g., 4QpNah 3-4 ii 4-6.

It is of interest that the formula הנה, which in the Zadokite Documents introduces the reference to that historical account (no longer extant), echoes incipits which in the Hebrew Bible precede several comparable allusions to books that are not preserved in the canon: הנה (2 Sam 1:18; 2 Chr 16:11); הנם (1 Kgs 14:19; 1 Chr 29:29; 2 Chr 20:34; 27:7; 32:32) and הלא הנם (2 Chr 25:26).[90] Especially noteworthy is the resemblance of the Qumran phrase הנה פרוש שמותיהם לתולדותם to the collocation וכל ישראל התיחשו והנם כתובים, which prefaces the postexilic inventory of returning families in 1 Chr 9:1.

It seems plausible that the מספר which bridged the gap between the ending of biblical Israel's history and the early stages of the Covenanters' community was actually a component of a comprehensive historiographical account in which the "appointed epochs," קצים, were set out in their sequential order, וכל קציהם לדורותם (1QS iv 13). The writer of that composition had recorded the divinely imparted information concerning "the years of [their] existence and the full account of their epochs, ומספר ופרוש קציהם, for all that was and is, unto what will befall them in their [future] epochs for all times" (CD ii 9-10).

That opus and similar compositions inspired other Qumran authors to employ in their own creations (which are not necessarily of the historiographical genre) the specific vocabulary and imagery used there.[91] A striking example may be found in the series of speeches which the Zadokite Documents ascribe to the Righteous Teacher.[92]

(3) *Exile-and-Return Phraseology and Imagery*. The conceptual proclivity to identify with and present themselves as biblical Israel finds a salient expression in the socioreligious vocabulary of the יחד. When recording their community's history, Qumran writers appropriate the idiomatic phraseology which the authors of the postexilic biblical books employ in the presentation of the period of the Return. This tendency can be illustrated by some pivotal examples:

90. הלא הנם may have arisen from a conflation of הנה with the parallel formula הלא היא (Josh 10:12; 1 Kgs 15:31; 2 Chr 9:29; 12:15).

91. Thus we read, e.g., in the first *Hôdāyah*: הכול חקוק בחרט זכרון לכול קצי נצח ותקופות מועדיהם מספר שני עולם בכול. The phrase הקוק בחרט זכרון is not attested in Biblical Hebrew, as J. Licht (*The Hymn Scroll* [Jerusalem: Bialik, 1965] ad loc [Heb.]) correctly points out. It may be a paraphrase of Mal 3:16, with an adjustment of the biblical text to the typical יחד vocabulary.

92. His historiographical sermons appear to be modelled upon the parenetic speeches ascribed to Moses in Deuteronomy. Cp. also the prayers of Daniel (Daniel 9), Ezra (Ezra 9), and Nehemiah (Nehemiah 9), which also carry the stamp of the historiographical genre upon them.

(a) The triad גולה—מדבר—שוב/שיבה, in which the essence of the biblical exile experience is concretized, also figures prominently in the Covenanters' literature. This is true, e.g., of a pesher in CD vii 14-17 (not expressly stated but clearly implied), where the author extrapolates from Amos' visionary threat of Israel's deportation to the north of that city a prospective allusion to the divine "Covenant in Damascus" of the יחד, והגליתי אתכם מהלאה לדמשק (Amos 5:26-27).

Similarly the reference to the Righteous Teacher's flight into the desert (of Qumran) is also couched in exile terminology. The Wicked Priest pursued him and his adherents אבית גלותו (1QpHab xi 4-6), so as to prevent them from observing the Day of Atonement at a date which accords with their special calendar.[93]

The same concept permeates the depiction of the future eon. In the *War Scroll* the Covenanters are termed בני לוי ובני יהודה ובני בנימין (1QM i 2-3; cp. Ezra 1:5; 4:1; Neh 11:4; further: Ezra 2:1, 70 = Neh 7:6, 72, et sim.). They are the מדבר העמים, viz., גולת בני אור, גולת המדבר, who "will return . . . from the מדבר העמים and encamp in the מדבר [outskirts] of Jerusalem."[94] From there they will launch their victorious attack on the city and its inhabitants, who are the Wicked Priest's followers and the implacable adversaries of the יחד.

(b) The intended existential implantation in the conceptual "Returners" matrix may shed some light on the Covenanters' pointed employment of the biblical term יחד as the most conspicuous designation of their community. In Biblical Hebrew יחד serves prevalently as an adverb, like יחד(י)ו. Only rarely does the word occur as a noun. The most important one for our purpose is found in the opening passage of Ezra chap. 4, which reports on an encounter between the repatriated Judeans and their "adversaries" who offer to join with the returnees in the rebuilding of the Temple. Zerubbabel, Jeshua the High Priest, and the leaders of the people, ראשי האבות, reject these overtures. They maintain that only they had been instructed by King Cyrus to undertake this project and that they alone are permitted to carry it out: אנחנו יחד נבנה (Ezra 4:3).

I have proposed that in this instance יחד serves as a noun which circumscribes the community of the repatriated exiles, to the obvious exclusion of the petitioners who are referred to as צרי יהודה ובנימין (Ezra 4:1).[95] It may be presumed that the letter ה was elided in the MT, possibly due to a *lapsus calami*

93. See Talmon, "Yom Hakippurim," in this vol., pp. 186-99.
94. For this meaning of the term, see Talmon, "miḏbār," *TWAT* 4 (1983), above, n. 2.
95. See Talmon, "The Qumran יחד," in this vol., pp. 53-60.

involving a quasi-haplography ו-הי, and that the text originally read אנחנו היחד
נבנה, viz., "[only] we, the יחד [of the returnees] will rebuild [the Temple]." This
conjecture restores a reading in which יחד is used as a noun. It is also the only
instance in which it serves as a socioreligious term that defines solely the
community of the erstwhile exiles. The Qumranites' appropriation of this
singular designation again reveals their intention to present themselves as the
only true successors of predestruction Israel.

(c) Nevertheless, against the background of the evident linguistic similarities,
a telling difference between the Qumran and the biblical vocabulary pertaining to
"exile and return" should not go unnoticed.

In postexilic historiography the notion of a return to the Land is
preponderantly expressed in words belonging in the semantic field of עלה, which
connotes physical movement from a remote place (in the Diaspora) towards the
Promised Land. Viewed in their totality, vocables derived from עלה constitute an
ideational motif. They serve as signifiers of the returnees and their community
(Ezra 1:3, 5, 11; 2:1, 59 = Neh 7:6, 61; Ezra 4:2; 7:7, 9, 28; Neh 7:5; 12:1; et
al.), which distinguish them from the inhabitants of the Land, the עמי/גויי
(הארץ(ות). In contradistinction, עלה vocables are predominantly used in Qumran
literature in the general sense of "rise, go up" or in the technical connotation of
"sacrifice" and are seldom found in texts which have a socioreligious import.[96]

At the same time vocables derived from the root שוב which can also denote
a "physical return," are comparatively rare in postexilic historiography.[97] As
against this, one registers a plethora of words in the יחד documents belonging in
this semantic field. It is significant, however, that Qumran authors employ שוב
terminology predominantly in the connotation of "moral repentance," with the
concomitant muffling of the notion of physical movement. The preference for
the ideational over the physical aspect of שוב, both of which are within the
twofold semantic range of the root in Biblical Hebrew, appears to be intentional.
These data suggest that for the יחד authors, שוב terminology and related language
signify moral-credal repentance rather than spatial return. The entire complex of
exile and repatriation imagery in Qumran literature pertains to a religious "turn

96. S. Iwry ("Was There a Migration to Damascus? The Problem of שבי ישראל," *EI* 9,
    W. F. Albright Volume [Jerusalem: IEJ, 1969] 80-88) remarked on this
    circumstance *en passant* (p. 87) but failed to discern its heuristic importance.
97. Only three instances of שוב are extant in Ezra-Nehemiah (Ezra 2:1 = Neh 7:6; Ezra
    6:21; Neh 8:11).

of the mind" and should not be construed as evidence for a "bodily return," which the Covenanters presumably experienced in a sociopolitical reality.

(d) The correlation of significant Qumran vocabulary and imagery with equally important postexilic biblical phraseology did not escape the attention of scholars. However, one is usually content with simply registering the fact. At best this similarity of language and wording is taken to reveal the evident temporal proximity of the composition of the latest biblical books and the earlier Qumran writings.[98] Mention should be made, however, of some attempts to probe the significance of this similarity beyond the merely linguistic aspects. The probe led some scholars to interpret this circumstance as revealing a real-historical connection, or else a parallelism between the יחד and the community of returnees of which the biblical books speak.

Assigning a much earlier date to the Qumran scrolls than is generally assumed, J. Brand suggested that the Covenanters were in actual fact a group of erstwhile Ephraimites who clashed with the repatriated Judeans and Benjaminites in the days of Nehemiah.[99] But a variety of palaeographical, historical, and scientific criteria make this early date untenable, *a fortiori* the dating of the Vorlage which underlies the Zadokite Documents in the fifth century B.C.E. Thus Brand's theory did not come under serious discussion.

S. Iwry's real-historical interpretation of the exile motif and the "return" vocabulary found in the Covenanters' literature is better attuned to the prevalent dating of the Qumran manuscripts and the emergence of the יחד in the second century B.C.E. He opines that the Covenanters were a group of Jews who, for reasons that are no longer ascertainable, had left the Land at some juncture after Nehemiah's days. Coming from Damascus where they had established their

---

98. See, int. al., C. Rabin, "The Historical Background of Qumran Hebrew" (ScrHier, ed. C. Rabin and Y. Yadin; Jerusalem: Magnes, 1958), 4. 144-61; R. Polzin, *Late Biblical Hebrew—Toward an Historical Typology of Biblical Hebrew Prose* (Harvard Semitic Monographs; Missoula, MT: Scholars Press, 1976), vol. 12; A. Hurvitz, *A Linguistic Study of the Relationship Between the Priestly Source and the Book of Ezekiel* (Cahiers de la Revue Biblique; Paris: Gabalda, 1982); E. Qimron, *The Hebrew of the Dead Sea Scrolls* (Harvard Semitic Studies; Atlanta, GA: Scholars Press, 1986), vol. 29.

99. J. Brand, "The Scroll of the Covenant of Damascus and the Date of Its Composition," *Tarbiz* 28 (1959) 13-39 (Heb.). More recently H. Stegemann has also argued in favor of dating the original composition of some Qumran works, foremost the Temple Scroll, in the third or even fourth century B.C.E. (See H. Stegemann, "The Origins of the Temple Scroll [11QT]," *Congress Volume, Jerusalem 1986,* ed. J. A. Emerton [VTSup; Leiden: Brill, 1988], 40. 233-52).

Covenant (CD viii 35), they actually returned to Israel in the first half of the second century B.C.E.[100]

This theory derives some support from the Wadi ed-Dâliyeh documents from which it can be deduced that the population of the province of Samaria, and possibly also of Yahud, experienced persecution and malevolence at the hand of the Persian authorities in the early fourth century B.C.E.[101] But there are no ancient reports of a voluntary or forced exodus of Jews from the Land of Israel at the height of the Persian rule which could eventually have triggered the actual return to the homeland of a group such as the יחד. The silence of the sources and the arguments presented above militate against the theories of Iwry, Brand, et al., which take the Covenanters' exile-and-return language and imagery at face value, investing them with a real-historical signification.

(4) *The Qumran Schema of Israelite History.* In the Qumran tradition the entire history of Israel is fitted into a schema of four major eras which, however, was adapted to the requirements of the secondary literary setting in which it is now found: the world epochs, קצי עולמים (cp. 1QS iv 16; ix 9) are no longer recorded in their chronological order. Their sequence is determined, rather, by the flow of the orator's arguments. However, a synoptic view of the texts leaves little doubt that the references in question were in fact extracted from a properly structured piece of historiography[102] in which the קצים in the Covenanters' history were detailed as follows:

(a) הראשונים קץ, the epoch of the former [i.e., the pre-destruction] generations (CD i 16; iv 6; viii 17, 31), when the first founders of the [divine] Covenant, באי הברית הראשונים (CD iii 10; iv 2; cp. i 4), established the fundamental tenets by which the יחד members were to be judged (CD xx 31).

---

100. Iwry, *EI* 9 (Jerusalem: IEJ, 1969) 80-88 (see above, n. 96).
101. See F. M. Cross, "The Discovery of the Samaria Papyri," *BA* 26 (1963) 110-21; idem, "Aspects of Samaritan and Jewish History in Late Persian and Hellenistic Times," *HThR* 59 (1966) 201-11; idem, "Papyri of the Fourth Century B.C. from Dâliyeh: A Preliminary Report on Their Discovery and Significance," *New Directions in Biblical Archaeology* (ed. D. N. Freedman and J. Greenfield; New York: Doubleday, 1971) 34-39.
102. The presumed structure and the content of that comprehensive schema can be given here only in bare outlines. A detailed treatment of the matter will be presented elsewhere. For the present see J. Licht ("The Doctrine of 'Times' according to the Qumran Sect and Other 'Computers of Seasons,' " *EI* 8, E. L. Sukenik Volume [Jerusalem: IES, 1967] 63-70).

Like the appellation הנביאים הראשנים, which in Zech 1:4; 7:7, 12 designates the prophets of the age of the monarchies, also קץ [הדורות] הראשונים in the Zadokite Documents refers to the First Temple Period,[103] possibly to the inclusion of the preceding times (CD iii 4) which are recorded in the Hebrew Bible. That age ended with the "destruction of the Land." At that time God punished "the transgressors of the [established] norms, מסיגי הגבול, who had led Israel astray" (CD v 20-21) and gave them up "to the sword" (CD i 3-4) because they had forsaken the divine covenant (CD iii 10-11).

(b) קץ הדורות האחרונים, the "epoch of the latter [rather than "last"][104] generations" (CD i 12; 1QpHab ix 4-5).

This expression defines the post-destruction generations who had returned from the exile with Zerubbabel, Ezra, and Nehemiah. It pertains also to their successors, the antagonists of the יחד in actual history, בהיותו.

The "latter generations" were in no way better than the "former." At first they steadfastly adhered to the divine commandments. But they soon went astray, misled by "the scoffers," אנשי הלצון (CD v 34), and the "latter [i.e., the "contemporary"] priests of Jerusalem," כוהני ירושלים האחרונים (1QpHab ix 4-5). That group was headed by the "Wicked Priest." He too had acted truthfully when he was appointed. But once safely installed in office he became haughty (cp. Deut 17:20) and forsook God (1QpHab viii 8-10). The postexilic period, viz., the days of "the return," which God had assigned as the קץ הברית, "the epoch of the [reconstituted] covenant" (CD i 4-8), became in fact a קץ חרון, another "epoch of wrath" (1QH iii 28).

The wrongdoings of the "latter generations" caused "all discerners of righteousness," יודעי צדק (CD i 1), viz., the followers of the Righteous Teacher, to separate themselves from their contemporaries. For them now opens

(c) הקץ האחרון, "the latter" [i.e., the present] epoch (1QS iv 16-17; 1QpHab vii 7, 12).

103. For the connotation of ראשונים and אחרונים, see Talmon (*Eschatology,* above, n. 86).
104. The translation "last" misconstrues the meaning of the Hebrew term. See Talmon, ibid.

This phase in the Covenanters' history coincides with the final stage of the קץ הדורות האחרונים. At that time עצת היחד established הברית החדשה (Jer 31:31), the "New [better, "reconstituted")" Covenant," from which all others are excluded. The Covenanters are the דור אחרון (CD i 12), the chosen ones who alone will be saved of all the sinful דורות אחרונים. Unlike the contemporary Jews who adhere to the "false temple" which their predecessors had erected, the יחד will build the true בית התורה (CD viii 33, 36), which is destined to become the fundament of the ultimate redemption of Israel.[105]

The term קץ האחרון designates the days of the actual existence of the יחד, when all the events detailed in the Qumran writings occurred: the Covenanters' initial dissension, the conflict with the Wicked Priest and his followers, the emergence of the Righteous Teacher, their retreat into the desert, and so on. During this span of time they had expected to experience the ultimate redemption, when they would assume the succession to biblical Israel and inherit its glory of old. This hope did not come true, and its realization was *nolens volens* deferred to an uncharted future, the

(d) קץ אחרית הימים (CD vi 11; 1QpHab i 5-6; ix 6; etc.), in which is set the appearance on the historical stage of the Twin Messiahs of David and Aaron (1QSᵃ i 1).[106]

This four-tiered schema brings to mind the vision of four successive empires presented in the latter part of the book of Daniel (chap. 11), in which are detailed four periods in the postexilic age. In comparison with the more comprehensive overview offered by the Qumran work, the scope of the Daniel text is chronologically limited. But their evident interdependence is pointed up by the shared basic concept of a tetrad of historical eras and by the culmination of both schemata in an account of the ultimate triumph of Israel (Dan 12:1-3),[107] respectively of the Covenanters, over their enemies (1QM) which will precede the establishment of the Messianic Eon (1QSᵃ).

105. The true בית התורה stands in opposition to the "illegitimate" temple, בית, which the returners with Zerubbabel, Ezra, and Nehemiah had built and which the Covenanters did not recognize for various reasons. See Talmon ("Calendar of the Covenanters," below, 147-85) and pertinent publications adduced there.
106. See Talmon, "Waiting for the Messiah," in this vol., pp. 273-300.
107. See Talmon, "Daniel," *The Literary Guide*, 343-56, above, n. 43.

The similarity is highlighted by the presence of a distinctive vocabulary in both the book of Daniel and in that מספר (as in Qumran literature generally): קץ (Dan 11:13, 27, 35, 40; possibly to be restored also at the end of vv 24 and 35); משכילים (Dan 11:33, 35; 12:3); חלק(לק)ות (Dan 11:21, 32), especially יחניף בחלקות (Dan 11:34), for which cp. דורשי חלקות (1QH ii 15, 32; iv 10-11; CD i 18, et al.); עוזבי ברית קודש (Dan 11:30); מרשיעי ברית (Dan 11:32); and cp. בקום רשעים על בריתך (1QH ii 12); et al.[108]

Chapters 1-11 of Daniel are attested at Qumran by fragments of eight manuscripts, of which 4QDan[a] "is closer to the time of the original composition of its text than any other extant manuscript of a book in the Hebrew Bible."[109] It stands to reason that in emulating the quadripartite Daniel schema of postexilic world history which affects Israel directly, the יחד members purported to integrate themselves into a late biblical historiographical pattern, thus once again emphasizing their spiritual, nay existential identification with the biblical people.

VII

The First Returners from the Exile

The Covenanters' self-integration into biblical Israel culminates in their assumption of the status of "the first returners to the Land" after the deportation which came in the wake of the destruction of Jerusalem. In retying the historical thread which was then severed, the Qumran authors completely disregard the "Returners from the Exile," of whom the postexilic biblical sources speak (Haggai, Zechariah, Malachi, Ezra, and Nehemiah). These biblical books, which pertain most directly to that period, are the most poorly represented in the Qumran finds of biblical MSS.[110]

---

108. Also the depiction of the כיתים in 1QpHab is presumably dependent upon the portrayal of the warring empires in Daniel 11 but was developed beyond the biblical text.

109. See Ulrich, *BASOR* 268 (1987), above, n. 43.

110. We have as yet no definitive roster of the biblical fragments from Qumran. Therefore the statement made here may need to be revised in the light of future information. No MS finds of Haggai, Zechariah, Malachi, Ezra, Nehemiah, and Chronicles were listed by J. A. Sanders ("Palestinian Manuscripts 1947-1972," [QHBT above, n. 28]). J. Strugnell has kindly informed me that MS fragments of these books were found in Cave 4 (4Q xii[a,b,c,e]). The book of Nehemiah, however,

The return of the Judeans to the Land and the leading figures of that period are passed over in silence in the Qumran writings. Those earlier generations had applied to themselves the honorific title זרע ישראל (Neh 9:2) and likewise had claimed for themselves the exclusive right to the auspicious designation הקדש זרע (Ezra 9:2), by which the prophet Isaiah had designated the remnant that will be divinely saved from the debacle which he foresaw (Isa 6:13).

The author of the Zadokite Documents pointedly appropriates that very title for the יחד members alone (CD xii 21-22). He ostensibly denies it to all other contemporary Jews and casts the Covenanters unhesitatingly in the role of the "holy seed" and of the "First Returners" to the Land after the exilation of 586 B.C.E.:

> For when they were unfaithful and forsook him, he [God] hid his face from Israel and his sanctuary and delivered them up to the sword. But remembering the covenant of the forefathers, he left a remnant for Israel and did not deliver them up to [utter] destruction [cp. Jer 5:18; 30:11; 46:28; Neh 9:31]. In the age of wrath . . . he remembered them [cp. CD vi 2-5] and caused the root he had planted to sprout [again] from Israel and Aaron to take possession of his land and enjoy the fruits of its soil [cp. Isa 6:11-13; Hag 2:18-19; Zech 3:10; 8:12].

Moreover there is no explicit reference in the יחד literature to Jeremiah's vision of a restitution of Israel's fortunes after 70 years (Jer 25:11-13; 29:10; Dan 9:2), which had been a source of (impatient) hope for the Judean exiles.[111] The repatriates who returned with Zerubbabel and Jeshua the High Priest, with Ezra and Nehemiah, saw this prophecy realized in the edict of King Cyrus (Zech 1:12; 7:5; Ezra 1:1; 2 Chr 36:21-22).

is not tangibly represented. The single (?) fragment of Ezra can attest to the presence of Nehemiah at Qumran only if we assume that Ezra-Nehemiah were already constituted there as one book. This question is discussed in commentaries and introductions. See also S. Talmon ("Ezra and Nehemiah [Books and Men]," *IDBSup* [Nashville, TN: Abingdon, 1970] 317-18).

111. The deportees of 597 B.C.E. refrained apparently from adjusting to the diaspora conditions, even for the span of the predicted "70 years." Their "impatient hope" caused Jeremiah to send a missive, in which he exhorts them to prepare for a longer stay in exile than they had expected (Jer 29:1-9). See S. Talmon ("Exil und Rückkehr in der Ideenwelt des Alten Testaments," *Exil, Diaspora, Rückkehr* [ed. R. Mosis; Düsseldorf: Patmos, 1977] 31-55).

The יחד substituted for Jeremiah's vision, and the cluster of pivotal texts connected with it, Ezekiel's prediction of a period of punishment for Israel destined to last 390 years for the Northern Kingdom and 40 years for Judah. The prophet is divinely commanded symbolically to carry the years of Israel's and Judah's castigation respectively, first by lying for 390 days on his left side and then for 40 days on his right side (Ezek 4:4-6).[112]

The author of the Zadokite Documents read a message of hope into Ezekiel's punitive oracle by construing the implied ending of the foreseen time of woe as the concomitant starting point of the redemptive history[113] of the יחד: 390 years after God had given Israel (actually Judah) into the hand of Nebuchadnezzar, he remembered his people and implanted them again in his [their] land (CD i 5-8).

The 40 years of Judah's punishment are captured in a statement about a period of 20 years during which the founders of the Covenant "groped like blind men" (CD i 9-10) awaiting the consummation of Ezekiel's prophetic vision. The reading "20" instead of the MT's "40" years (Ezek 4:6) may be an ancient variant which the Qumran tradition preserved or else an intentional textual emendation.[114] In any event, when examined against the background of the *Eigenverständnis* of the יחד, this reading becomes another witness to the Covenanters' intended self-integration into the framework of biblical history.

The summation of several schematic-symbolical data given in the Qumran literature results in the sum total of 490 years. This span of time is seen as intervening between the past destruction of Jerusalem and the future restitution of the Covenanters' "New World" in the eon designated אחרית הימים, after the vanquishing of all their enemies in the cosmic battle which is portrayed in the *War Scroll* (1QM):

112. In that passage were seemingly fused two biblical traditions drawn from the Exodus story, which in the primary account, however, pertain to two independent episodes. On the one hand the representation of one year by one day evidently reflects a pattern which ties the "40 years of wandering in the desert" to the 40 days in which the faithless scouts spied out Canaan: "your bones shall lie in this wilderness; your sons shall be wanderers [reading תועים for MT רועים] in the wilderness for 40 years, paying the penalty of your wanton disloyalty. . . . 40 days you spent exploring the country, and 40 years you shall spend—a year for each day—paying the penalty of your iniquities" (Num 14:33-34). On the other hand, the sum total of 430 years undoubtedly echos the statement in Exod 12:40-41 which gives that same figure for the duration of the Egyptian bondage.

113. See Talmon, "Waiting for the Messiah," in this vol., pp. 273-300.

114. See Talmon, ibid.

390 years of Israel's punishment
20 years of "groping" (CD i 9-10)
40 years of strife with their adversaries in history (CD viii 26-38)
40 years of the final cosmic war (1QM).

The sum total of 490 years is patently identical with the transition period of "70 [year] weeks" of which Daniel is advised in his vision that they "were marked out for [Israel] your people and [Jerusalem] your holy city; [when they will pass] rebellion shall be stopped, sin brought to an end, iniquity expiated, everlasting right[eous might], צדק,[115] ushered in, vision and prophecy sealed, and the most holy anointed" (Dan 9:24).

The three Hebrew terms, צדק, נביא, משח-למשח, are used here as catchphrases which announce the reinstatement of the public officeholders who in the First Temple Period had together constituted the pillars of the Israelite society: king, prophet, and priest. Like the predominant biblical vision, the Qumran *Vorstellung* of the future ideal eon foresees this same triad again becoming the fundament of Israel's renewed polity.

The future prophet (1QS ix 11) is conceived in the image of Elijah, who in the concluding passage of the biblical corpus of prophetic literature is portrayed as the harbinger of "the great and terrible day" which will precede the envisaged era of sublime reconciliation (Mal 3:22-24). That prophet will be the forerunner of "the Anointed of David and Aaron." The vision of Twin-Messiahs who are expected to arise in that future age, a prominent feature of Qumran theology, is most probably patterned after a postexilic biblical (prophetic) tradition. The book of Zechariah (Zech 3-4; 6:9-15) appears to propose this bicephalic system as a blueprint for the desirable structure of the Returnee's polity.[116]

Once again it can be shown that the Covenanters derived a pivotal facet of their spiritual universe directly from the world of ideas of the postexilic community, utilizing it as a sign and symbol testifying to the existential continuum of their own history with the history of biblical Israel.

115. For this understanding of צדק, see Talmon ("Biblical Visions of the Future Ideal Age," KCC [Jerusalem: Magnes, 1986] 147-61).
116. See Talmon, "Waiting for the Messiah," in this vol., pp. 273-300.

A Substitution Philosophy

The results of the foregoing examination of some central aspects of the יחד literature lend credence to the theses that were advanced at the outset:

(a) The specific יחד documents were produced by a particular Jewish community of the Second Temple Period. This community is not explicitly mentioned in the pertinent classical sources and thus was altogether unknown prior to the discovery of the hoard of manuscripts in the Qumran Caves. A renewed scrutiny of the ancient Jewish, Hellenistic, and early Christian literature may reveal veiled or implicit references which pertain to that community but which were hitherto not recognized as such.[117]

(b) In their totality, the Qumran finds mirror the Covenanters' *Eigenverständnis* and show the יחד to have been a socioreligious phenomenon *sui generis*. The particular spiritual profile of that community and its unprecedented social structure demand that the Qumran documents should first and foremost be appreciated on their own merits before the community that produced them is compared or identified with any other contemporaneous socioreligious Jewish entity known from the classical sources.

(c) An unprejudiced analysis of the Qumran literature brings to light the Covenanters' particular existential stance: the יחד members viewed their community as the direct and only legitimate heir of biblical Israel of the First Temple Period. They purged from their literature and their construction of Israel's history all memories of the generations of the Return documented in the postexilic biblical literature. Concomitantly they inserted their community into the resulting historical hiatus, appropriating for themselves the glorified status of "The First Returners from the Exile." In their eyes they were the divinely saved remnant of the deportees whom Nebuchadnezzar's army abducted to Babylon after the conquest of Jerusalem.

The Qumran Covenanters' *Eigenverständnis* constitutes the first instance in Jewish history of a *Substitution Theology*.

---

117. Echoes of the calendar dispute with the Covenanters, which were not recognized as such, presumably still reverberate in rabbinic literature. See Talmon ("The Calendar of the Covenanters," in this vol., pp. 147-85).

THE QUMRAN יחד — A BIBLICAL NOUN

I

One of the salient expressions occurring again and again in the Qumran Scrolls
is the term יחד, serving in noun clauses, such as אנשי היחד;[1] סר[ך] היחד;[2] עצת
היחד;[3] יחד אל;[4] etc. Similar expressions are found in CD, e.g., אנשי היחיד;[5]
מורה היחיד.[6] Schechter proposed to translate there: "Children of the men of the
Only" and "Teacher of the Only." Gressmann substituted "the One" for "the
Only." It is accepted that in the Qumran Scrolls this noun יחיד is but a different
spelling of יחד.[7] The references given above will suffice to indicate its
employment which necessitates its being rendered into English by "community,"
"congregation," "covenant," or similar nouns. In construct forms, such as סר[ך]
היחד and עצת היחד, יחד is coupled with other Hebrew equivalents of עדה, ברית
meaning "covenant" or "congregation."[8]

These construct forms appear to some scholars to be peculiar in form, יחד
being an adverb.[9] The adverbial quality of יחד cannot be contested, as any Bible
dictionary or concordance will prove. The same will hold true for the use of יחד
in rabbinic writings. But to infer from this that יחד as a noun is a faulty
translation of an obscure Arabic original is a rather hasty conclusion based on an
argument *ex silentio*.

1. 1QS v 1-2.
2. 1QS i 1, 16.
3. 1QpHab xii 4; 1QS iii 2; v 7; vi 10, 16; vii 2.
4. 1QS i 12; ii 22.
5. CD xx 32.
6. CD xx 1, 11.
7. S. Stern, "Notes on the Hebrew Manuscript Find," *JBL* 69 (1950) part 1. S.
   Zeitlin ("The Hebrew Scrolls: Once More and Finally," *JQR* 41 [1950-1951] 32-
   40) proposes to translate "the select" in contrast to the entire "community."
8. Regarding סרך with this meaning, consult talmudic dictionaries.
9. P. R. Weiss, "The Date of the Habakkuk Scroll," *JQR* 41 (1950) 140.

I wish to suggest that the word יחד is a true biblical noun which has not been recognized as such because of its external identity with the adverb יחד—יחדו. A close investigation of relevant Bible passages proves that there are indications of the employment of יחד in the meaning of "congregation, assembly." I shall endeavor to show, moreover, that in some instances יחד has a strictly technical quality, referring to the governing body of the community.

II

(1) In the introduction to the Blessing of Moses (Deut 33:5), the following passage is found: ויהי בישרון מלך ‖ בהתאסף ראשי עם ‖ יחד שבטי ישראל. Commentators deemed it unnecessary to deal with יחד, which was accepted as an adverbial addition to בהתאסף. The RV renders the clause "when the heads of the people were gathered, all the tribes of Israel together." But the metric structure of the sentence demands a different translation. The latter half of the sentence, according to the masoretic division, contains two parallel phrases. The verb בהתאסף in the first phrase is understood in the second as well. This arrangement is in accordance with biblical style.[10] The loss of length in *b* is made up by employing in it a three-fold subject instead of a two-fold in *a:*

בהתאסף ראשי עם
[בהתאסף] יחד שבטי ישראל

Alternatively we have here a quadruple structure in which the element בהתאסף יחד is divided up between the two parts of the sentence:

בהתאסף [יחד] ראשי עם
[בהתאסף] יחד שבטי ישראל

10. Gesenius-Kautzsch, *Hebrew Grammar* (28th ed.) 469.

Both these types of "incomplete sentences" are attested to in the Bible. The first will be found in an identical parallel (Isa 1:3a): ידע שור קנהו וחמור אבוס בימי שמגר בן ענת בימי יעל חדלו ארחות (Judg 5:6): or ;בעליו.[11]

The second type of structure is exemplified in Proverbs 31:24:

סדין עשתה ותמכר [לכנעני]
.וחגור [עשתה] נתנה לכנעני

Whichever structure we assume in our case, the parallel expressions are either יחד שבטי ישראל and יחד ראשי עם; or יחד שבטי ישראל and יחד ראשי עם. Both these nouns, שבטי ישראל and ראשי עם, refer to the leaders of the Israelite community who are otherwise called זקני ישראל (Exod 3:16; 1 Sam 8:4) *et sim.* יחד indicates here the constitutional body formed by these elders. The two phrases יחד שבטי ישראל and יחד ראשי עם are mere synonyms for this body-politic, named in other places קרואים (1 Sam 9:22); קראי מועד (Num 16:2); or simply עם (1 Sam 8:7, 10). Sulzberger styled this body "The Ancient Hebrew Parliament."[12]

(2) Three more passages will be adduced in order to substantiate the use of יחד as a noun in the Bible.

Seeing that the returning exiles had successfully started to rebuild the Temple, the neighboring tribes, presumably the Samaritans, approached Zerubbabel and the leaders of the Jewish community in order to offer their cooperation and to claim their share in the venture. Their claim was based on the assertion that they had worshipped the same deity since having been brought to Palestine by the Assyrian king (Ezra 4:1-3). Zerubbabel and his followers declined the offer in a definite manner, though evidently bent on not offending the petitioners. For political reasons (the apparent weakness of the new commonwealth) the Jews tried hard not to make enemies. The wording of their answer runs as follows: לא לכם ולנו לבנות בית לאלהינו כי אנחנו יחד נבנה ליהוה אלהי ישראל כאשר צונו המלך כורש מלך פרס.

---

11. Cp. also Deut 32:13b; 1 Sam 2:6, 7.

12. M. Sulzberger, *The Am-Haaretz, the Ancient Hebrew Parliament* (Philadelphia: J. H. Greenstone, 1909). Cp. also J. van der Ploeg ("Les chefs du peuple d'Israel," *RB* 57 [1950] 59).

The generally accepted interpretation of this passage is summed up by Batten:

"And for us" is wanting in Esd. and its omission gives force to the contrasting assertion, "we alone will build . . ." The impetus for the building operations is here derived from the royal order. It is possible to interpret the statement as the ground for the Jews' refusal of the Samaritan offer, "King Cyrus ordered us (not you) to build his temple." The reason commonly urged is that the Jews would have no dealings with this mixed race, being solicitous for a pure people and a pure religion. Such a consideration would have more force with Ezra than with Zerubbabel. The motive was probably political.[13]

But the motive was mainly religious or "communal." This is indicated in Zerubbabel's reply, which should be understood as: כי אנחנו [ה]יחד נבנה ליהוה אלהי ישראל.

יחד is plainly in apposition to אנחנו here and means "we, the community." The abbreviation יחד stands, presumably, for יחד בני הגולה (Ezra 4:1), or יחד הבאים מהשבי ירושלים (Ezra 3:8). This expression would be perfectly parallel to יחד אל in 1QS i 12, ii 22 and to the biblical יחד ראשי עם as we have just established (Deut 33:5).

This explanation gives a new insight into our passage and renders superfluous any emendation. It seems that neither the LXX nor the compiler of Esdras recognized the noun יחד in this phrase and therefore rendered יחד by ἐπὶ τὸ αὐτὸ (LXX); μόνοι (Esdr) = לבד, which is accepted by Batten as the better reading, since יחד usually means "together" and would instead imply the acceptance of the offer.[14]

(3) As in the former examples, the third instance to be cited contains an apparently colorless יחד where we expect a more definite expression. In 1 Chronicles 12:18 David addresses the men of Judah and Benjamin who come to his stronghold in the following manner: אם לשלום באתם אלי לעזרני יהיה לי עליכם לבב ליחד ואם לרמותני לצרי בלא חמס בכפי ירא אלהי אבותינו ויוכח. The RV renders the clause יהיה לי עליכם לבב ליחד, "my heart shall be knit unto you." And Curtis translates similarly: "Then shall mine heart be at one with you." But

---

13. L. W. Batten, *Ezra-Nehemia* (ICC; Edinburgh: T. & T. Clark, 1913) 128.
14. Ibid. That יחד[ו] indeed can mean לבד is proven by the parallelism לבדד ‖ יחדו in Ps 4:9.

this translation is unsatisfactory to the commentator himself. Therefore he remarks, "Only here is יחד used as a substantive."[15] That יחד is a noun in this case is obvious, and not in this case only, as I hope to have proved. David offers to accept the newcomers, provided their intentions are trustworthy: "My heart will be bent upon you for a covenant, if in peace you come to me, in order to help me." But if these men are intent upon delivering him into the hands of his enemies, "the God of our fathers look thereon and rebuke it." This last phrase contains a concealed threat.

Psalm 2:2: יתיצבו מלכי ארץ ורוזנים נוסדו יחד על יהוה ועל משיחו. The preceding as well as the following verse describe an insurrection against God and against his Anointed. "Nations and peoples" under the leadership of "the kings of the earth and the rulers" are striving to shake off the yoke imposed upon them. The clause נוסדו יחד in the second part of the sentence is parallel to יתיצבו in the first, where for reasons of style יחד is dropped. The two-fold מלכי ארץ, as against the one-fold רוזנים in the second half-sentence, makes good for the loss of metrical length. We assume therefore an apocopated chiastic structure:

יתיצבו [יחד] מלכי ארץ
ורוזני (ם) [ארץ] נוסדו יחד
על יהוה ועל משיחו

and translate:

> The kings of the earth present themselves (in council)
> And the rulers (of the earth) combine in a covenant
> Against God and his Anointed.

A strikingly parallel passage based on the equivalence of התיצב and בוא ביחד, instead of הוסד יחד, is found in 1QH iii 22: להתיצב במעמד[16] עם צבא קדושים ולבוא ביחד עם עדת בני שמים, "So that he might present himself in parade with

---

15. E. L. Curtis, *Chronicles* (ICC; Edinburgh: T. & T. Clark, 1910).
16. מעמד acquires the meaning of "division" in the scrolls, e.g., 1QS ii 22-23, איש ישראל איש בית מעמדו ביחד אל.

the host of saints and that he might enter into communion with the congregation of heavenly spirits [lit., the Sons of Heaven]."

To our list of constructions involving the word יחד should be added the phrase יסד יחד or הוסד יחד in the sense of "combine in a covenant."

III

It is a common feature of the Hebrew language to derive verbal forms from given nouns and vice versa.[17] It seems that we can prove the existence of a biblical verb יחד, covering the verbal aspects of the root, with the meaning "to covenant, to join a community."

(1) In Genesis 49:6 Jacob "blesses" his sons Simeon and Levi: בסדם אל תבא נפשי בקהלם אל תחד כבדי. It is well known that סוד[18] and קהל[19] may denote in Biblical Hebrew "tribal gatherings" or sessions of some social body. This applies to this passage as well. תחד is a future tense derived from יחד, parallel to תשב from ישב, with guttural influence on the vowel. The apposition is needed for the meter, though superfluous for the understanding of the passage. We thus obtain the equation יחד [בקהל] = בוא בסוד.

(2) The phrases האסף לעמיו (Gen 35:8, 17; 35:29; 49:29, 33; etc.), which the RV translates "to be gathered unto one's people," or שכב עם אבתיו (Deut 31:16), "to lie with one's fathers," serve in the Bible as standard metaphors for death. The notion involved is that of a passage from one social status to another, from the community of the living to the community of the dead. Isaiah 14:18 employs a slightly altered metaphor, כל מלכי גוים כלם שכבו בכבוד איש בביתו, which, being equivalent to שכבו איש עם אבתיו, should therefore be rendered "all the kings of the nations, all of them lie in glory, every one with his house" (i.e., family) and not "sleep in glory everyone in his own house" (RV). In contrast to all those nobles, the king of Babylon will be treated as an outcast. The comfort of becoming a member of that illustrious society after his death

---

17. Gesenius-Kautzsch, *Hebrew Grammar*, 97 ff.
18. Jer 6:11 and Ps 111:1. I have restored the noun סוד in this technical sense in 1QH ii 9: אשר בס]ודם ספר אל את כול הבאות]. The passage refers to the prophets who are mentioned in the context. See S. Talmon ("Notes on the Habakkuk Scroll," in this vol., pp. 142-46).
19. Neh 5:13. Cp. also קהלה, Neh 5:7.

will be denied him, לא תחד אתם בקבורה[20] (Isa 14:20), "Thou shalt not be joined with them in burial." Here again תחד is a future tense from יחד, which carries the meaning of "becoming a member of a community."

The same verb is employed several times in this technical sense in the Qumran Scrolls. In 1QS v 9 we read, להיחד בעצת אל (and not להוחד as transcribed by the editors), which is best translated "to enter God's community." The phrase is parallel to להיחד בעצת קודש (1QS v 20), "to enter the holy congregation." In the same manner I would interpret ליחד ברית עולם (1QS v 5) as a contraction of להיחד בברית עולם, meaning "to join the eternal covenant."

IV

It is quite feasible that an adverbial יחד, יחדו in the sense of "to be יחד-like, or "to behave in a יחד-manner" was derived from this noun and that its meaning was later diluted into "friendly/together." In those instances the root has lost its technical flavor and has become a standard, pale, and unspecific household word.

But in some passages which have a politico-social coloring, an apparent adverb יחדו might conceal a former noun יחד. I now submit some of these passages for consideration.

(1) Psalm 83:6, כי נועצו לב יחדו ‖ עליך ברית יכרתו, contains an equation of ברית and יחד. Bearing in mind David's words יהיה לי עליכם לבב ליחד (1 Chr 12:18), I would venture to read our passage כי נועצו לב יחד and to interpret לב יחד as a construct form with adjectival meaning, such as in הררי אל (Ps 36:7) or גבעת עולם (Gen 44:26). In that case הועץ לב יחד could be translated literally "to take counsel with a heart bent on [forming] a covenant." Similar notions might be embodied in ונועצה יחדו (Neh 6:7), ונועדה יחדו (Neh 6:2; Job 2:11), and so forth. This last expression is actually found in 1QH iv 24, הנועדים יחד לבריתכה.

(2) I suggest that the expression לב [ל]יחד is also embedded in the two halves of the sentence נהפך עלי לבי [ל]יחד נכמרו נחומי (Hos 11:8), which should be translated, "Mine heart is turned in me for a covenant; my compassions are kindled," and this in spite of the feelings of anger which would be expected as God's reaction to Israel's sins.

20. 1QIsa[a] reads: לוא תחת אותם בקבורה, which reading obviously originated from a mispronunciation of ד as ת.

(3) In order to appreciate the full significance of the picture contained in the words כי יאמר הלא שרי יחדו מלכים (Isa 10:8), I would suggest the slightly emended reading הלא שָׂרַי יַחְדָּי מלכים. The Assyrian king boasts of his might and strength. How could tiny Jerusalem hold out before the emperor whose very council is comprised of kings? And similarly I propose to read והלך מלכם בגולה הוא ושרי יחדו (Amos 1:15) instead of the MT הוא ושריו יחדו. In this case a diplography would easily explain the faulty שריו.[21]

CONCLUSION

This investigation was to show that the noun יחד, which is a striking linguistic feature of the Qumran Scrolls, is a biblical word. The expression is found in numerous passages of the Hebrew Bible, where it is employed as a synonym for ברית, קהל, עדה, exactly in the fashion of the scrolls. The term occurs in poetic passages which are accepted as presenting early Biblical Hebrew, as well as in books which are considered to be late, such as Ezra and Chronicles.

The majority of scholars have assigned the newly discovered scrolls to the last two centuries B. C. E. or to the first century C.E. We are thus able to trace the use of יחד as "covenant" from biblical times to the beginning of the Christian era.

It has been pointed out that, as is common in linguistic development, the technical noun יחד and its accompanying verb (and adverb) tended to assume less characteristic features, which in themselves might also be early, and to become a colorless description of any form of association. The last known instance of the purely technical employment traced in the Bible is to be found in the Qumran documents.

21. Further developments of this faulty reading may be observed in Jer 48:7 and 49:3.

A FURTHER LINK BETWEEN THE JUDEAN COVENANTERS AND THE ESSENES?

The last lines of CD xi (21-23) have baffled commentators, although the text is practically intact except for a lacuna at the very end of line 23. The words employed in the passage are by themselves easily understood. It is their combination which causes difficulties. Especially the latter part of the passage under review (xi 22b—xii 1a) has not been interpreted convincingly as yet. When editing CD for the first time, Schechter frankly admitted: "The meaning of the law is entirely obscure to me."[1] And with Rabin's painstaking edition at hand, Bardtke still maintains: "die Vorschrift Zeile 22b-23 kann nur unbefriedigend erklärt werden."[2] In view of this impasse, a new attempt at a solution may be permitted.

I

A proper evaluation of any law in the Covenanters' code, including the law under discussion, must take into account the specific meanings which are accorded in the Qumran literature to the salient expressions employed in those passages. Much caution is required in the employment of apparently related material in external sources such as rabbinic and N.T. literature for the purpose of clarifying issues particular to the Covenanters. The dissenting socio-religious ideology of the Covenanters often gave rise to a shift in the conceptual content of terms which they share with other contemporary or somewhat later religious groups. In many instances this shift stems from a conscious reinterpretation of

---

1.   S. Schechter, *Fragments of a Zadokite Work: Documents of Jewish Sectaries* (3 vols.; Cambridge: Cambridge University Press, 1910), 1. ad loc.
2.   H. Bardtke, *Die Handschriftenfunde am Toten Meer* (3d ed.; Berlin: Evangelische Haupt-Bibelgesellschaft, 1961) 269.

common terms, which was considered a *sine qua non* for the possibility of their application to the Qumranites' specific, cultic situations.[3]

Our proposal takes its departure from the assumption that the pertinent passage is of a composite structure and actually incorporates two, albeit materially related, subject matters. In this assumption we differ somewhat from scholars who discerned in the passage two independent commandments and also from Rabin, who takes it to contain one single law. In his view this law bars ritually unclean Covenant members from attending public worship and then goes on and commands them to come to the house of prayer either before or after the service so as not to make it void by their defilement.[4] However, such a qualification is hardly acceptable in view of the extreme segregation which they imposed on ritually unclean members (cp. 1QSa ii 3-11). It is highly improbable that they were at all admitted to the house of worship, even in private.[5] This seems to be the obvious implication of the first part of our passage: וכל הבא אל בית השתחות אל יבא טמא כבוס.

בית השתחות probably should be taken as an epithet of the sect's communal center, which served them as a substitute for the Temple from which they had dissociated themselves. It was the locus of communal activities: common meals, meetings, and public worship. The designation בית השתחות is presumably derived from the two mentionings in the Bible of the verb השתחוה with reference to worship in the house of God (2 Sam 12:20; Jer 26:2).[6] Members who were ritually defiled (טמא כבוס) quite naturally were excluded from this holy place.

Ginzberg postulated that the qualification of טמא by כבוס points specifically to the ritual uncleanness after seminal emission, basing this assumption on rabbinic legal traditions (*m. Ber.* 3:4-5; *b. Ber.* 22a).[7] He is followed by Rabin[8]

---

3. This aspect of the Covenanters' literature will be discussed in more detail in a separate publication. The present author has dealt with some instances of such a reinterpretation in "The Calendar of the Covenanters of the Judean Desert" (in this volume, pp. 147-85).

4. C. Rabin, *The Zadokite Documents* (2d ed.; Oxford: Clarendon, 1958) ad loc.

5. L. Ginzberg, *Eine unbekannte jüdische Sekte* (New York: Selbst Verlag) 101 = *An Unknown Jewish Sect*, Translated, Revised and Updated (New York: JTSA, 1976) 70-71.

6. But cp. also 2 Kgs 5:18; 19:17 = Isa 37:38, where the same terms are applied to idol worship.

7. Ginzberg, *An Unknown Jewish Sect*, 102.

8. Rabin, *The Zadokite Documents*, ad loc.

and other commentators of CD. However this explanation raises some doubts. The only other time the verb כבס occurs in CD (xi 3-4), it carries the technical notion of "washing ritually unclean garments." The same holds true for the only other recorded employment of the verb in Qumran literature, 1QM xiv 2. In contrast to this usage, ritual lustration of persons is always expressed by the verb רחץ (CD x 10-11; xi 1; 1QS iii 5; 1QM xiv 2-3). In both these usages the Covenanters pattern their terminology after Biblical Hebrew and more especially after the way these terms are employed in Leviticus (e.g., 14:8, 9; 15:8, 11, 27; 17:15, 16).[9] Only in biblical imagery is this technical preciseness loosened, and then כבס is sometimes applied also to the washing of persons (Jer 2:22; 4:14; Ps 51:4, 9).[10] Accordingly we presume that טמא כבוס in CD xi 22 must refer to a man whose clothes are ritually defiled and require purification. Until this is done he is excluded from the communal center: "Let no one enter the house of meeting who is [dressed in] unclean [garments] requiring [ritual] washing."

It may well be that in phrasing this law, its author had in mind the biblical passage which describes David's acts of purification: lustration (וירחץ ויסך) and change of clothes (ויחלף שמלתו) before entering the house of God to worship there (וישתחו) after the death of his first-born child by Bathsheba (2 Sam 12:20).

II

We have now to consider the following two lines of our passage, which also call for further clarification: ובהרע חצוצרות הקהל יתקדם או יתאחר ולא ישביתו את העבודה כולה [ ] [ת קודש הוא.

Let us first turn to the reconstruction of the lacuna. Both Schechter's conjecture to read [שב]ת and Segal's to read [עבוד]ת[11] emphasize the "prayer

---

9. The few sporadic instances in post-biblical literature adduced by Ginzberg (*An Unknown Jewish Sect*, 102) in which כבס designates ritual "washing with water," as against רחץ, "submersion in water," cannot match this obvious dependence.

10. In a few cases רחץ describes the washing of parts of sacrificial animals (Exod 29:17; Lev 1:19; 9:14).

11. M. H. Segal, "ספר ברית דמשק," *Haŝiloaḥ* 26 (1912), ad loc.; Schechter, *Fragments of a Zadokite Work*, vol. 1, ad loc.

situation" and arise out of the meaning "religious service," which they attach to the preceding words, את העבודה כולה. However, these reconstructions are doubtful. Rabin points out with apparent justification that the partly recognizable letter which precedes the preserved ת is probably a ו.[12] Hence he restores וימו]ת. This reading hardly recommends itself for internal reasons. The case dealt with here is not one involving capital punishment. Furthermore, by reading וימו]ת, the following two words (קודש הוא) are left hanging in the air. Rabin has therefore to assume that the "lacuna probably contained further purity laws." Accepting Rabin's epigraphical argument, we propose to restore עידו]ת.

The crucial point of our problem appears to be the interpretation of the expression: ישביתו את העבודה כולה. The verb שבת does not give much trouble. In the hifʿil it is used two times more in the scrolls, carrying the connotation "to stop, to discontinue" (1QS x 25; 1QH i 37).

As far as can be ascertained to date, the term עבודה in the Qumran literature never has the meaning "religious service," which, according to most commentators, it is supposed to have in the passage under review. In rabbinic writings, on the other hand, עבודה is widely used in precisely this sense, or more specifically in the sense of "sacrificial worship." It may well be that for this very reason the Qumranites abstained from employing the term in a manner which might recall associations with the temple and with sacrifice.

The nearest approximation to a "cultic" interpretation of עבודה in the scrolls may be its use as a designation of the "tasks" allotted to different categories of members (1QS i 13, 16-19, 22; ii 1). This does have some religious implications, since all deeds done by a Covenanter by definition are done in the service of God (1QH ii 32-33, 36). However, in none of these usages can the word be invested with the specific meaning "congregational," i.e., "public cultic service."

In the scrolls, as well as in biblical and in post-biblical Hebrew, the term עבודה is most commonly employed in the sense of "[physical] work." We find it, for example, in such salient expressions as אל יאות איש עמו בהון ובעבודה (CD xx 7) or ואשר לוא ייחד עמו בעבודתו ובהונו (1QS v 14). It is precisely this meaning that עבודה carries in the "Sabbath Laws" section which immediately precedes the passage discussed here: אל יתהלך איש בשדה לעשות את עבודת חפצו

---

12. *The Zadokite Documents*, ad loc. See S. Zeitlin (*The Zadokite Fragments* [JQRMS; Philadelphia: Dropsie, 1952] ad loc.).

השבת[13] (CD x 20). In that context the term is synonymous with מלאכה:
אל ידבר בדברי המלאכה והעבודה לעשות למשכים (line 19).

The combination of עבודה with the verb שבת is obviously derived from the
Bible, which uses similar terms in the treatment of the subject matter, namely
the cessation of work (cp. Neh 4:5; 2 Chr 16:5), especially at the beginning of
the Sabbath (cp. Gen 2:1-3; Exod 20:9-10; 31:13-17; Deut 5:13-14). It is this
proper observance of rest from work at specific times which is designated in our
passage ת קודש[עידו]. This same term recurs in CD iii 14-16, where the author
extols the exceeding theological importance of observing the festivals in their
appropriate seasons: שבתות קדשו ומועדי כבודו עידות צדקו ודרכי אמתו וחפצי
רצונו אשר יעשה האדם וחיה בהם (cp. further CD xx 31). The very same
expression presumably was found also in the original Hebrew of *Jub.* 2:32.

The reference to trumpet-blowing has similar implications. Outside the *War
Scroll* it is only in the passage under review that the technical term הרע חצוצרות
is found in the Qumran literature. In 1QM the trumpet-blows serve as signals for
the beginning or the cessation of particular military activities. These are
indicated once by the term עבודה: הצוצר]ות התרועה לכול עבודתם[(1QM ii 14;
cp. Num 31:6).

The combination חצוצרות הקהל, altogether a hap. leg. in the scrolls, is quite
clearly derived from Num 10:1-10 (cp. especially v 7). Some comparative
material may help to clarify its meaning in the present context. The Mishnah
(*m. Sukk.* 5:3; *Tamid* 7:3) and Josephus (*Ant.* 3.12.6 § 294) report that it was
customary in the Temple of Jerusalem to accompany sacrificial ceremonies on
the Sabbath and on festivals with trumpet-calls, in accord with prescriptions laid
down in Num 10:10.[14] However, since the Covenanters had discarded sacrifice,
it would appear that with them the trumpet-blows fulfilled a different purpose,
which is also mentioned in rabbinic literature. The priests in the Temple of
Jerusalem are reported to have blown trumpets on the Sabbath Eve "three [times]
to make people stop work and three [times] to distinguish between holy and
profane" (i.e., to announce the onset of the Sabbath).[15] Apparently the

---

13. *lege* חפצי השבת, and cp. CD vi 1; vii 5. חפץ may refer to the preparation of things,
especially food, needed on the Sabbath (cp. CD x 22). But see Ginzberg (*An
Unknown Jewish Sect*, 82-83).

14. It was a Samaritan custom to call for prayer with trumpet-blows. See R.
Kirchheim (כרמי שומרון [Frankfurt: Kaufmann, 1851] 20).

15. *m. Sukk.* 5:3; *b. Šabb.* 114b.

Covenanters used trumpet-signals in exactly the same fashion to announce cessation of all work and to ensure that their holy seasons would be observed at their appropriate times.[16]

The same intention also underlies the clause יתקדם או יתאחר. An identical combination of the two verbs (with קדם in the pi'el) recurs in 1QS i 14. There the Covenanters are admonished to observe the festivals strictly at their appointed times, i.e., according to their own special calendar, which differed from the lunar calendar which prevailed among the normative Jewish community. In 1QS i 14 the injunction is negatively phrased; it forbids a departure from the fixed times. Apparently this was the case also in our passage, since all the preceding laws on plates 10-11 are prohibitions too. These findings lead to the assumption that the negation ולא was misplaced in the passage by the medieval copyist of CD, who also most probably omitted it in some other passages.[17] Accordingly we propose to read the law discussed here as follows: ובהרע חצוצרות הקהל (ו)לא יתקדם או יתאחר וישביתו את העבודה כולה [עידו]ת קודש הוא, "And when the trumpets for assembly sound—and one should not do so earlier or later—they shall cease all work. This is a holy testimony."

This law was intended to ensure that no member would continue to work whenever a public function was about to be held. At the same time it restrained members from ceasing work individually by their own judgment, before the appointed time. Such a law is quite in keeping with the strict communal regulations to which the sect adhered, in ritual as well as in secular aspects of life. It is this situation which is mirrored in Josephus' account of the Essenes' daily routine, which has been compared with that of the Covenanters in other respects as well. Josephus states that after having uttered prayers at sunrise, the Essenes "are dismissed by their superiors to the various crafts in which they are severally proficient and are strenuously employed until the fifth hour, when they again assemble in one place" (*J.W.* 2.8.5 §129).[18] It is this cessation of work before assembly with which the law in CD xi 22b—xii 1a deals.

---

16. In some Jewish communities the usage prevails to this day.
17. CD v 5: נגלה, *lege cum* Schechter, Rabin: ולא נגלה. CD vi 16: ולגזול את עניי עמו, *lege cum* Rabin: ולא לגזול. CD vii 11: ימים אשר באו, *lege cum* Rost, Rabin: אשר לא באו (L. Rost, *Die Damaskusschrift* [Berlin: de Gruyter, 1933]). The contrasting phenomenon may be observed in 1QS ix 20, where ולהסר should be read, instead of ולא הסר (Rabin, *The Zadokite Documents*, 25; Wernberg-Møller, *The Manual of Discipline* [Leiden: Brill, 1957] 42).
18. H. St. J. Thackeray's translation in the Loeb edition.

Once this is recognized, we can fully understand the relationship of this law and the purity law which precedes it (CD xi 21b—22a). Josephus goes on to relate that among the Essenes, no one was admitted to the communal meals, in the morning or in the evening, until he had purified himself from the state of latent defilement which resulted from the unavoidable contact with impure matters throughout the day:

> After girding their loins with linen cloths, [they] bathe their bodies in cold water. After this purification, they assemble in a private apartment which none of the uninitiated is permitted to enter; pure now themselves, they repair to the refectory, as to some sacred shrine.[19]

We maintain that CD xi 21b—22 is the legal basis on which the Essene custom described by Josephus is founded. טמא כבוס defines the state of latent impurity as a result of which a member is enjoined to change his clothes before joining his fellows in their communal evening meal.

The foregoing analysis possibly furnishes one further link in the chain which connects the Judean Covenanters with the Essenes. By it we also gain one more illustration of the substitution of communal customs for the ritualistic and sacrificial acts which were common among their adversaries, the adherents of the Jerusalem Temple.

19. Ibid.

A NOTE ON 1QS VI 11-13

The interpretation of the passage 1QS vi 11-13 has caused considerable controversy among translators. Apparent syntactical irregularities and our insufficient knowledge of technical terms employed make it difficult to arrive at a proper understanding of ordinances outlined there.[1]

The text is given in Burrows' edition[2] as follows:

11 ובמושב הרבים אל ידבר איש כול דבר אשר לוא לחפץ[3] הרבים וכיא האיש

12 המבקר על הרבים וכול איש אשר יש אתו דבר לדבר לרבים אשר לוא
במעמד האיש השואל את עצת היחד

13 ועמד האיש על רגליהו ואמר יש אתי דבר לדבר לרבים אם יאמרו לו ידבר

Assuming that the terms רבים and יחד serve as equivalent connotations of one and the same institution,[4] the main difficulty to be explained is the meaning of the words וכיא and במעמד. Let us turn to וכיא first. With this word, a new sentence opens containing a temporal clause which rules the verbs ועמד and ואמר,[5] in line 13: "In case the supervisor . . . or any other man . . . stands up . . . and says. . . ." The sentence is closed with the conditional clause: "If they [הרבים] tell him [to do so], he may speak."[6]

1. Full references are given by R. Marcus ("*Mebaqqer Rabbim* in the Manual of Discipline vi.11-13," *JBL* 75 [1956] 298, n. 2).

2. M. Burrows, ed., *The Dead Sea Scrolls of St. Mark's Monastery* (2 vols.; New Haven: ASOR, 1950-51), 2. plate vi.

3. With the correction of להפץ to לחפץ.

4. Cp. Marcus (*JBL* 75 [1956] 298, n. 2). The equation was also proposed by H. Yalon ("מחקרים במגילות," *Kiryat-Sefer* 28 [1952] 66-68 = מגילת סרכי היחד [Jerusalem: Kiryat-Sefer, 1967] 72-76).

5. The two sentences are usually linked by translators, while the verbs ועמד and ואמר are severed from the temporal clause. This causes unnecessary complications. Cp. Marcus (*JBL* 75 [1956] 299-300).

6. A similar construction is sometimes employed in the *Zadokite Documents* = CD, e.g., in ix 2-4 (Rabin, ed., [Oxford: Clarendon, 1958] 45).

From this it follows that the מבקר who supervised many activities[7] of members of the Covenant had no prerogatives in sessions of the assembly. The restrictions incumbent upon ordinary members were incumbent upon him as well.

The passage contains, accordingly, two somewhat different ordinances. It begins with a general preamble stating that nobody is allowed to address the רבים without explicit permission. It then goes on to describe some special cases which are singled out by the clause אשר לוא במעמד האיש השואל בעצת היחד (line 12). It seems obvious that an offical is mentioned here, who is either identical with the פקיד mentioned in line 14, or else who occupies a position in the יחד congruent with the one held by that פקיד in the רבים (if those two terms are not equivalent). We cannot be far off the mark in assuming that the office referred to is that of a "speaker" who brought before the רבים members' requests, to be heard in the assembly. This speaker must be distinguished from the מבקר.

The term במעמד remains yet to be elucidated. The sense of either "office," "function," "rank," "delegation," or else of "position" or "standing," in which the word is often employed in the Qumran writings, does not fit the passage under review.

Now, as a rule, the speaker, who was usually present at sessions, would intervene between a member and the רבים. This seems to be understood implicitly in the preamble. But it apparently occurred that sometimes the speaker was unable to attend. In these exceptional cases, in the absence of the speaker (אשר לוא במעמד האיש ...[8]), a member would approach the רבים directly for permission to speak and would then proceed, if permission were granted.

Another possibility of an interpretation with some variation in meaning presents itself. The text of 1QS gives evidence to the fact that the scribe sometimes interchanged gutterals.[9] This phenomenon is sufficiently attested in rabbinic literature.[10] A striking case in 1QS may be observed in vi 7, in the paragraph adjoining the passage treated here. There the scribe exchanged ע for ח,

---

7. These activities are listed in CD xiii 7-19 (ibid., 65-67). The מבקר was approached by members without restrictions (ibid., xiv 11-12, pp. 69-71).

8. For references to מעמד in the sense of "presence," consult A. Kohut (*Aruch completum* [N. Y.: Pardes Pub., 1955], 5. 206).

9. The same holds true for the scribes of other Qumran Scrolls. Cp.:

Isa 54:11, MT:	סערה	1QIsa[a]:	סחרה
37:30, MT:	שחיס	1QIsa[a]:	שעיס
30:13, MT:	לפתע	1QIsa[b]:	לפתח

10. *b. ʿErub.* 53b.

writing על יפות instead of חליפות, "by turns." Now this may also have happened with the word במעמד, which should be read במחמד, i.e., "to the liking" or "with the consent," parallel with לחפץ in line 11. If this is accepted, the second clause in our passage would treat a case in which the מבקר, or any other member, tries to appeal to the רבים "against the will" of the speaker, לוא במחמד האיש השואל את עצת היחד אשר. The רבים could then overrule the speaker's decision and grant the petitioner permission to address the assembly.

We propose the following translation for the passage under review:

And in the session of the רבים no man shall speak a word which is not to the liking of the רבים. And if the man who supervises the רבים or one who has a word to speak to the רבים (not in the presence [or: without consent] of the man who asks [or: addresses] the council of the יחד [i.e., the speaker]) and the man should stand on his feet and say, "I have a word to speak to the רבים"; if they tell [allow] him, he shall speak.

ASPECTS OF THE TEXTUAL TRANSMISSION OF THE BIBLE IN LIGHT OF QUMRAN MANUSCRIPTS

I

The discovery of the scrolls from the Judean Desert added a new dimension to biblical text criticism. It goes without saying that these MSS which precede the oldest extant MSS of the MT by more than a millennium are, in view of their antiquity, of unsurpassed importance for an investigation into the early history of the Hebrew Bible. Much has already been learned from research carried out so far. More is to be expected from the edition of yet unpublished MSS and from an ensuing evaluation of their contribution to a better understanding of the processes by which the Bible text was transmitted.[1]

The new material often helps in elucidating the genesis and the history of individual variants in which one or more of the ancient VSS differ from the MT. They also open up new possibilities for the recovery or the reconstruction of the factors which underlie textual variation. The sifting of these cases, their classification, and a statistical assessment of the frequency of their appearance may make possible the systematic presentation of the processes which can be proved empirically to have been conducive to the emergence of *variae lectiones*.

---

1. A valuable summary of these aspects of the scrolls may be found in Frank M. Cross, Jr., *The Ancient Library of Qumran* ([revised edition; New York: Doubleday, 1961] 161-94) where pertinent earlier literature is quoted. See further F. M. Cross and S. Talmon (*Qumran and the History of the Biblical Text* [Cambridge, MA: Harvard University Press, 1975] hereinafter QHBT); H. M. Orlinsky ("The Textual Criticism of the Old Testament," *The Bible and the Ancient Near East, Essays in Honor of W. F. Albright* [ed. G. E. Wright; N.Y.: Oxford Univ. Press, 1964] 113-32); D. Barthélemy (*Les Devanciers D'Aquila* [Leiden: Brill, 1963]); W. H. Brownlee (*The Meaning of the Qumrân Scrolls for the Bible, with Special Attention to the Book of Isaiah* [New York: Oxford University Press, 1964]); Patrick W. Skehan ("Qumran and Old Testament Criticism," *ETL* 46 [1978] 163-82); E. Tov ("A Modern Textual Outlook Based on the Qumran Scrolls," *HUCA* 53 [1982] 11-27).

The pertinent information gained from these first-hand sources, because of their scope and their primacy, has enabled and should continue to enable scholars to improve on previous attempts along these line.[2]

Prior to the discovery of the Qumran Scrolls, observations on the skill and the peculiarities of the ancient copyists of the biblical text could be inferred only from the analysis of variants which are extant in medieval Hebrew MSS or had to be abstracted from deviating translations in the ancient VSS. With the pre-Christian Hebrew scrolls from Qumran at our disposal, we are now in a position to verify principles established by inference and to put them to a practical test. The scrolls afford us a completely new insight into ancient scribal craft and give us an unexampled visual impression of the physical appearance of the manuscripts in which the biblical *variae lectiones* arose. We can now observe at close range, *in situ,* so to say, scribal techniques of the Second Commonwealth Period, which left their impression on the Bible text in subsequent stages of its history. We can perceive the manuscript realities which were the breeding ground for the variants that crop up in the extant witnesses to the text of the Bible.

That the Qumran Scrolls indeed exhibit scribal conventions and techniques which were generally prevalent in Judaism of the Second Commonwealth is easily proven from the fact that the sectarian scribes followed rules which tally in many details with those laid down by the rabbis for Torah-scribes of mainstream Judaism.[3] There is obviously nothing specifically sectarian in the external appearance of most Qumran Scrolls, nor in the scribal customs to which their copyists adhered.[4] The same holds true for the majority of the deviating readings found in them. The impression of dissent that goes with the biblical

---

2. Cp. F. Delitzsch, *Lese und Schreibfehler im Alten Testament* (Berlin: de Gruyter, 1920) and E. Tov, "Criteria for Evaluating Textual Readings: the Limitations of Textual Rules," *HTR* 75 (1982) 429-48.

3. This was pointed out by the late E. L. Sukenik as early as 1947 in his first report on the scrolls: א.ל. סוקניק (*מגילות גנוזות* . . . *סקירה ראשונה* [ירושלים: מוסד ביאליק, י-יב [1948).

4. Notable exceptions are the enigmatic scribal marks or symbols found in the margins of 1QIsaᵃ, for which as yet no adequate explanation has been offered. See Burrows (*The Dead Sea Scrolls of St. Mark's Monastery* [2 vols.; New Haven: ASOR, 1950-51], 1. xvi). It appears that these signs are peculiar to 1QIsaᵃ. Only some of the simpler ones also turn up in other Qumran MSS. On the possibility of distinguishing MSS in the Qumran collection which were written at Qumran and those which were written elsewhere, see E. Tov ("The Orthography and Language of the Hebrew Scrolls Found at Qumran and the Origin of These Scrolls," *Textus* 13 [1986] 31-59).

scrolls from Qumran derives from the secession of their scribes from normative Judaism and has no roots in the MSS as such. That is to say, it must be attributed, not to their textual or manuscript character, but to sociohistorical processes which engulfed these scrolls. Genetically the biblical texts from Qumran are "Jewish." They became "sectarian" in their subsequent history.

What makes the evidence of the scrolls especially valuable is the fact that they do not present just one horizontal, cross-sectional view of a stabilized version, as, for instance, the masoretic *textus receptus* does. Because of their textual diversity, the kaleidoscope of the textual traditions exhibited in them—their concurrence here with one, here with another of the known VSS, or again in other cases, their textual exclusive individuality—the totality of the biblical MSS found at Qumran present in a nutshell, as it were, the intricate and variegated problems of the Hebrew text and VSS. The Qumran Scrolls comprise a comparatively small corpus of MSS in comparison with the bulk of Hebrew (masoretic and Samaritan), Greek, Aramaic, Syriac, Latin, etc. MSS which have to be sifted, collated and compared in the course of the critical work on the Bible text. The concentration of processes which obtain in the history of the Bible text in a small corpus such as this (a corpus which moreover is relatively homogeneous with respect to time and place of provenance) makes the Qumran Scrolls an ideal subject for a pilot-study on these processes. Although the results gained from an analysis of the Qumran material cannot be applied without qualification to the wider field of comparative research into the MT and the VSS, we may derive from them certain working hypotheses which then have to be verified by application to the wider problem.

Thus the situation at Qumran reflects on a basic issue in biblical textual research, namely the moot problem of the establishment of a Hebrew *textus receptus*. The coexistence of diverse text-types in the numerically, geographically, and temporally restricted Covenanters community; the fact that (some or most of) the conflicting MSS very probably had been copied in the Qumran scriptorium; and the fact that no obvious attempts at the suppression of divergent MSS or of individual variants can be discovered in that voluminous literature prove beyond doubt that the very notion of a biblical *textus receptus* had not yet taken root at Qumran. The superscribed corrections in 1QIsa[a], which in the majority of cases, though by no means in all, bring the deviant basic text in line with the MT[5] or with a proto-masoretic textual tradition (1QIsa[b]), cannot be adduced as evidence for a supposed tendency to revise 1QIsa[a] towards an established Qumran recension. This evidence is offset, is even neutralized by a Deuteronomy MS from Cave 5, roughly contemporary with 1QIsa[a].[6] Here the corrections run counter to the proto-masoretic tradition in practically every instance and align themselves with a Septuagintal text-type.

We have no reason to doubt that this "liberal" attitude towards divergent textual traditions of the Bible was prevalent also in the mainstream circles of Judaism of that period, i.e., in the second and first centuries B.C.E. It actually can be shown that according to rabbinic testimony even the model codices that were kept in the Temple precincts not only exhibited divergent readings, but represented conflicting text-types.[7] Phenomenologically speaking the situation that prevailed in the *ʿazarah* may be compared, though with qualifications, with the one that obtained in the scriptorium at Qumran. The difference consists in the fact that in the end the Temple codices were collated, probably in the first century C.E., and what is more important, that Rabbinic Judaism ultimately established a model text and strove to banish deviant MSS from circulation. However, at this stage the comparability of mainstream with Qumran practice breaks down. The active life span of the Covenanters community ends sometime in the first century B.C.E., although sporadic attempts at restoration vibrate into the first or possibly into the second century C.E. The latest MSS from Qumran, which give evidence to the local history of the Bible text in the crucial period, the last decades before the destruction of the Temple, do not present the slightest indication that even an incipient *textus receptus* emerged there, or that the very notion of a model recension ever was conceived by the Covenanters.[8]

The presentation of the sum total of the biblical documents from Qumran as a small-scale replica of the "MT and VSS" issue, derives further support from one more characteristic of that material. The Qumran finds exhibit, as stated, a basic homogeneity with regard to the time and the place of their provenance.

---

5. Cp. J. Hempel, "Beobachtungen an der 'syrischen' Jesajarolle vom Toten Meer (DSIa)," *ZDMG* 101 (1951) 149.
6. See M. Baillet, J. T. Milik, and R. de Vaux, *Les petites grottes de Qumrân,* (DJD; Oxford: Clarendon Press, 1962), 3. 169-71, pl. XXVI.
7. Cp. S. Talmon, "The Three Scrolls of the Law That Were Found in the Temple Court" (*Textus* 2 [1962] 14-27 [henceforth TSL]. Also the deviant readings in the Apocrypha and the NT point in the same direction).
8. Cp. P. W. Skehan, "The Qumran Manuscripts and Textual Criticism" (*QHBT*, 212-25).

There are no grounds to doubt that these MSS were written in Palestine and that a great majority of them, if not all, were copied at Qumran. It may also be considered as established that, some odd items excepted, the bulk of the MSS in the Qumran library was copied within a span of not more than 300 years, approximately from the middle of the third century B.C.E. to the middle of the first century C.E.[9] In view of these circumstances, the marked diversity of textual traditions which can be observed in these MSS presumably derives from the temporal and/or geographical[10] heterogeneity of the *Vorlagen* from which the Qumran MSS, or some of them, were copied. Thus, in addition to the horizontal cross-section view of the Bible text at Qumran during the last phases of the Second Commonwealth Period, the Qumran material also affords a vertical cross-section view of the transmission of the Bible text, in which are reflected various chronological layers and geographical or social-strata traditions.[11] These circumstances further enhance the similarity of the problems relating to the Bible text at Qumran to those adhering to the wider issue of the relations of the MT and the VSS.

The situation which obtains at Qumran holds out one more possibility of comparison with another phase in the history of the Bible text. In conformity with a basic characteristic of Second Commonwealth Judaism (mainstream and dissenters alike), the Covenanters' religious concepts were Bible-centered. Their original literary creations, such as the *War Scroll,* the *Hôdāyôt,* the *Manual of Discipline,* and the *Zadokite Documents* swarm with verbatim Bible quotations, paraphrases, and allusions.[12] Their most fundamental beliefs and practices reflect

9. Cp. Frank M. Cross, Jr., "The Development of the Jewish Scripts," *The Bible and the Ancient Near East. FS W. F. Albright* (ed. G. E. Wright; New York: Doublday, 1961) 133-202.

10. The case for an existence of local recensions of the Bible text in view of the Qumran evidence was argued by W. F. Albright ("New Light on Early Recensions of the Hebrew Bible," *BASOR* 140 [1955] 27-33); Cross (*The Ancient Library of Qumran,* 188-94 [see above, n. 1]). See also Cross ("The History of the Biblical Text in the Light of Discoveries in the Judean Desert," *QHBT,* 177-95).

11. For a discussion of these issues, cp. E. Y. Kutscher (*The Language and Linguistic Background of the Isaiah Scroll [1QIsaª]* [Leiden: Brill, 1974]), esp. pp. 61-89).

12. Basic information on the utilization of the Bible in these works is provided in the scholarly editions of the texts. A detailed discussion of the biblical quotations and allusions in 1QH i-iii is offered by P. Wernberg-Møller ("The Contribution of the *Hodayot* to Biblical Textual Criticism," *Textus* 4 [1964] 133-75).

the attempt to recapture and typologically to relive biblical Judaism.[13] It is this scripture-piety which produced the pesher technique so indicative of the Covenanters' system of Bible hermeneutics, by the aid of which biblical history was actualized and made existentially meaningful. In this unceasing process of quotation, interpretation, and adaptation, the Bible text at Qumran was exposed to a fate which is comparable to that which the *hebraica veritas* experienced on a wider scale in Rabbinic Judaism and in the orbit of Jewish and Christian communities that had recourse to translations of the Hebrew original. The deliberate insertion of textual alterations into scripture for various reasons of dogma, style, etc., and the uncontrolled infiltration of haphazard changes due to linguistic peculiarites of copyists or to their characteristic concepts and ideas which may be observed in the transmission of the Bible text at large, each have their counterparts in the "Qumran Bible." The study of these phenomena at Qumran again is facilitated by the comparative compactness of the material and by the decidedly more pronounced manner in which they become manifest. We thus encounter in the Qumran writings developments of biblical text-transmission which may be considered prototypes of phenomena that emerge concurrently and subsequently in the text-history of the Bible in Jewish and Christian tradition, albeit in less concentrated form and to different degrees of variation.

II

The foregoing general remarks will be illustrated here by an analysis of the manuscript conditions which, in the first stage, fathered the development of "double-readings,"[14] and ultimately were conducive to the masoretic techniques of

13. This aspect of Qumran sectarianism is often referred to in the voluminous literature on the סרך היחד. See S. Talmon,"The 'Desert Motif' in the Bible and at Qumran," *Biblical Motifs* ([in Studies and Texts, ed., A. Altmann; Cambridge, MA: Harvard University Press, Philip W. Lown Institute of Advanced Judaic Studies, 1966], 3. 31-63).

14. See the present writer's "Double Readings in the Massoretic Text" (*Textus* 1 [1960] 144-84 [henceforth DRMT]); and the notes on Exod 15:2 in "A Case of Abbreviation Resulting in Double Readings" (*VT* 4 [1954] 206-207) and on 1 Sam 15:32a in "1 Sam xv 32—A Case of Conflated Readings" (*VT* 11 [1961] 456-57).

variant-preservation in the *kethib-qere* system and in the midrashic *ʾal tiqrê* technique.

Two main types of conflation must be clearly distinguished. On the one hand a double-reading may result from the routine insertion into the main text of marginal or intralinear corrective notes and annotations together with the readings which they were meant to supersede. On the other hand, conflation will result from the premeditated intentional effort on the part of a scribe to preserve variant readings which he considered equal in value and worthy of preservation.[15] This type of conflation is a well attested trick-in-hand of the transmitters of the Bible text. It was widely practiced by scribes and copyists, Jews and Christians, throughout centuries, in the Hebrew original and in translations.

Lacking a universally recognized device of variants-notation, not to be confused with correction, the parallel readings either were recorded in the margins and between lines, or else were incorporated *prima manu (p.m.)* into the text-base, whenever this could be done without serious disruption of syntax or distortion of sense. But also when the variant initially had been noted *p.m.* outside the normal text-base, it easily could be transferred into the text by a subsequent copyist who used the annotated MS as his *Vorlage.* Although the practical results of variants-conflation will coincide with those of the routine conflation of a mistake with its correction, the two phenomena must be kept apart. Routine conflation is always due to a copyist's default and runs counter to the original corrector's intentions. Variants-conflation *secunda manu (s.m.)* indeed also results from scribal lapse, but it always puts into effect the purpose of the first-hand collator, namely the intentional preservation of variant readings.

Methodologically, therefore, the two types of conflation outlined above are different. But in practice we have no safe means of deciding in each case whether the marginal or intralinear notation from the outset was intended to replace a reading in the main text, whether it was meant to be added to the text-base, or whether it was considered a mere note, to be kept apart from the text proper at subsequent copyings also. The external similarity of emendation, restitution, and annotation, all of which were entered in the margins or between lines, could be conducive to conflation by mistaken interpretation of the collator's notation.

It is one of the great advantages of the biblical MSS from Qumran that in them we can yet perceive conflation in the different stages of its execution. The

15. On these see S. Talmon, "Synonymous Readings in the Textual Traditions of the Old Testament" (*ScrHier* 8 [1961] 335-83 [henceforth SROT]).

Qumran Scrolls furnish us with the means to trace step by step the intentional preservation of alternative readings on the one hand, and the perpetuation by default of scribal mistakes together with their corrections on the other hand.

III

Let us first consider the category of routine conflations which resulted from the mistaken insertion of superscribed or adscribed corrections into the text-base.

Superscription or marginal adscription as a means of correction was as familiar to the Qumran scribes as it is to the modern writer or copyist. It is unfortunate that in most cases, especially in 1QIsaᵃ, it cannot be decided whether the first hand is at work correcting a recognized and admitted mistake or whether a second hand thought fit to emend a text with which the initial scribe had found no fault. On the whole the corrections are towards the MT. Accordingly they are ascribed to a second hand who used a proto-masoretic MS as his *Vorlage*. However there are significant exceptions to this rule.

These two different types of correction make themselves manifest in the very first line of 1QIsaᵃ, in which we find three cases of superscribed single letters:

ישיהו, וירושלם, בימי

The first two seemingly are instances of corrected lapses which, at the same time, bring the text of 1QIsaᵃ in line with the (proto-) masoretic readings. In the third the opposite is the case: a normal MT-type reading (בימי) is (mis)corrected towards the Aramaic-determined morphology of the copyist. The first two may be ascribed to the initial scribe with much probability, the third with absolute certainty.

In 1QIsaᵃ iv 3 (Isa 3:25b) the insertion amounts to two letters. A typical variant reading, וגבוריך (2 f. pl. of גבור), supported by all VSS,[16] which is a better parallel to מתיך of the first stichos than is the masoretic וגבורתך (2 f.

---

16. Tg. Isa: ועבדי נצחנך; LXX: οἱ ἰσχύοντες ὑμῶν; Aq.: οἱ δυνατοί σου; Vg: *fortes tui*. See also A. Rubinstein ("Formal Agreement of Parallel Clauses in the Isaiah Scroll," *VT* 4 [1954] 200-201).

sing. of גבורה), was corrected towards the reading exhibited in the MT by the
superscription of ות:

ות
.וגבוריך

However no full identity with the MT reading was achieved. Here we seem to be
dealing not with a corrected mistake *p.m.*, but rather with a (subjective)
emendation *s.m.* based on a MT-type *Vorlage*.

Similarly, complete words were added to the basic text of 1QIsa[a] by
superscription. Again we can differentiate between omissions by default which
were filled in *p.m.* or possibly *s.m.*, and emendations of what a second hand
interpreted as a textual mistake perpetrated by the initial copyist. Thus the
superlinear סחריה in Isa 23:8 is for certain a correction *p.m.* of an obvious
omission in the basic text. The fact that by this correction 1QIsa[a] is brought in
line with the MT is an accidental corollary and is immaterial for the issue at
hand.

In Isa 8:17 the accusative particle את was inserted by superscription before
פניו, in accordance with the prevalent usage of 1QIsa[a]. Here the superlinear
correction goes against the MT, and most certainly stems from the original
copyist.

Much less clear is the situation with regard to the word צבאות, which is
added over מה יעץ ה' על מצרים in Isa 19:12. The basic text of 1QIsa[a], as it
stands, causes no difficulties. The correction makes it identical with the MT (=
Tg. Isa, LXX), which reads ה' צבאות in this verse, in vv 16, 18, 25, and
especially in v 17 where imagery is employed which is virtually identical with
the imagery of v 12. But on the other hand, the single tetragrammaton is also
well represented in this chapter (vv 19, 20, 21, 22). Accordingly it seems
preferable to ascribe the insertion of צבאות in v 12 to the emendatory activities
of the MT-oriented corrector and not to the first hand. The same goes for the
superlinear addition of אבני in Isa 14:19 to the basic reading of יורדי אל 1QIsa[a]
בור, which indeed may, but need not be, a simplified reading[17] of the somewhat

---

17. In the main tradition of Tg. Isa, אבני is not rendered נחתי לגוב בית אבדנא. MSS f, c
    insert אבני before לגוב, whereas in the First and Second Bomberg Bible (b, g), the
    word follows upon לגוב. Kimchi's commentary (ed. L. Finkelstein), as quoted in
    A. Sperber's edition of the Targum, has the interesting variant (גוב בית) אבדנא
    לסייפי. Could לסייפי be a miswritten לסיפי, which thus would tally with אדני that

cumbersome masoretic יורדי אל אבני בור (= LXX, Vg). Whatever the case may be, the restitution of אבני adjusts 1QIsaᵃ to the MT.

The random examples adduced so far clearly show that superscription was a technique recognized by the scribe and the corrector of 1QIsaᵃ as a means of restituting letters or words which had been omitted by default from the text-base. These interlinear and marginal notations contained a tacit, but nevertheless explicit, directive for future copyists to restore the superscribed or adscribed textual items into the text-base of their own copies, for which the annotated MS served as *Vorlage*. This restoration would be a mere mechanical retransfer from the margin or from between the lines into the line proper and would not require any readjustment in the text-base of the Vorlage. Since such *p.m.* or *s.m.* corrections of omissions and mistakes perpetrated *p.m.* most probably constituted the majority of marginal notations, they created a psychological readiness in copyists to restore into the main text of their own copy any superscriptions or adscriptions which they found in their *Vorlage*. Herein may be found the roots of routine conflation.

It is here that the Qumran Scrolls lend the support of manuscript facts to theoretical considerations. Let us first discuss some cases of hypothetical doublets which could have arisen but in fact did not arise from such a 1QIsaᵃ reading. An intriguing instance of correction by superlinear insertion is found in Isa 43:3. Here the basic text of 1QIsaᵃ has no equivalent for מושיעך of the MT. Its shorter reading אני ה' אלהיך קדוש ישראל is syntactically without fault, although metrically it lacks somewhat in length in comparison with the second half-verse. A second hand whose *ductus* is clearly distinguishable from that of the first, and who uses the normal as against the latter's elongated form (אלוהיכה), added גואלך between the lines. This is a good synonymous reading of the masoretic מושיעך.[18] Thus the difference between 1QIsaᵃ and the MT, which in the first stage consisted of the lack of one word, in the second stage developed into a *varia lectio*. A subsequent collator, not a mere copyist, of 1QIsaᵃ and the (proto-)MT easily could have combined the two readings into a non-extant doublet, אני ה' אלהיך קדוש ישראל מושיער (ו)גואלך, for which cp., e.g., Isa 49:26 (MT = 1QIsaᵃ), כי אני ה' מושיער וגואלך אביר יעקב (= LXX, Tg. Isa).

seems to underlie the Vg *ad fundamenta laci?* Cp. B. Kedar-Kopfstein's discussion of this reading ("Divergent Hebrew Readings in Jerome's Isaiah," *Textus* 4 [1964] 187).

18. Cp. SROT, 379-80.

The probability of routine conflation increases when we consider not restorative but corrective superscriptions which are meant to "replace" a component of the text-base. As a rule the tendency towards conflation will be checked by appropriate marks which prescribe the excision from the text [19] of the component that is to be replaced by the marginal notation. There are two instances of this kind, which hypothetically could have resulted in *conflatio*.

		נוראה
1) Isa 21:1	1QIsaᵃ:	ממדבר בא מארץ רחוקה
	MT:	ממדבר בא מארץ נוראה

The basic reading of 1QIsaᵃ is reflected in Syr, מן ארעא רחיקתא, which perhaps inadvertently substituted מארץ רחוקה, found nine times in the Hebrew Bible,[20] including one mention in Isa 39:3, for the hap. leg. נוראה מארץ[21] of the MT which underlies the LXX, φοβερόν, and Tg. Isa (?), חסינן. The superscription of נוראה with the concomitant deletion of רחוקה may confidently be attributed to a second hand by reason of the different *ductus*. Thus we deal here with the subjective emendation *s.m.* of a possibly bona fide reading *p.m.*

		יושבת
2) Isa 12:6	1QIsaᵃ:	צוהלי ורוני בת ציון
	MT:	צהלי ורני יושבת ציון

The basic reading of 1QIsaᵃ, בת ציון, presents what is to all intents and purposes a synonymous variant of the MT's יושבת ציון. Whereas the Syr, עמורתא דציון, clearly sides with the MT,[22] Tg. Isa's כנשתא דציון[23] appears to go with 1QIsaᵃ *p.m.*, although the evidence is not altogether decisive. Again it

19. Cp. Sifre (ed. Horowitz, 80): נקוד עליו מלמעלה ולמטה מפני שלא היה זה זה מקומו; R. Butin, *The Ten Nequdoth of the Torah or the Meaning and the Purpose of the Extraordinary Points of the Pentateuch.* (Reissue with a Prolegomenon by S. Talmon; New York: Ktav, 1969).

20. Seven times connected with the verb בוא: Deut 29:21; Josh 9:6, 9; 1 Kgs 8:41 = 2 Chr 6:32; 2 Kgs 20:14; and esp. Isa 39:3. Cp. Kutscher (*Language and Linguistic Background,* 287 [see above, n. 11]).

21. However twice מדבר ... נורא is found (Deut 1:19; 8:15).

22. Cp. Isa 10:24, MT: ישב ציון, Tg. Isa: יתיב ציון, Syr: דעמר בצהיון; Jer 51:35, MT: ישבת ציון, Tg. Isa: לכנשתא דציון, Syr: אשתביו דציון (probably resulting from an intentional or unintentional confusion of ישב with שבה).

23. Cp. Isa 1:8; 16:1; 52:2; 62:11 MT: בת ציון, Tg. Isa: כנשתא דציון, Syr: ברת צהיון.

81

would appear that a bona fide variant reading of the first hand was subsequently (*s.m.*?) corrected towards the MT by the superscription of יושבת. However, it seems that the concomitant deletion here affects only the second letter of the word בת,[24] thus creating the basis for a reading יושבת בציון, which indeed comes closer to the MT than 1QIsaᵃ *p.m.*, but is not identical with it. This reading is mirrored in the LXX^SA: οἱ κατοικοῦντες ἐν Σιων.

It does not require much imagination to reconstruct the reasoning of a copyist of 1QIsaᵃ who, in spite of the deletion mark in Isa 21:1, and because of the only partial deletion in 12:6, would have interpreted the superscriptions not as substitutions for components found in the text-base, but rather as faultily omitted, intrinsic parts of it, which he therefore restored to their proper place without altering the text-base. In both cases this could easily be done. In Isa 21:1 it would have resulted in the doublet מארץ רחוקה [ו]נוראה, for which cp. Deut 1:19, המדבר הגדול והנורא. In 12:6 the outcome would have been יושבת בת ציון, for which cp., e.g., בתולת בת ציון (Isa 37:22 = 2 Kgs 19:21).

Such a hypothetical development is even more probable in the following instance of hypercorrection:

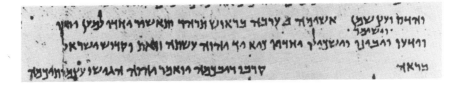

1QIsaᵃ 41:20

In Isa 41:20 a series of four synonymous verbs is used to describe the future recognition by the poor and the destitute of God's mighty deeds: למען יראו וידעו וישימו וישכילו יחדו כי יד ה' עשתה זאת. The MT is supported here by the verbatim rendition of the first two and the fourth verbs in Tg. Isa, ... דיחזון וידעון ויסתכלון, and by the latter's interpretative rendering of the crucial third, וישוון דחלתי על ליבהון. However, 1QIsaᵃ reads ויבינו here and has וישימו as a superscription, most probably introduced *s.m.* The basic ויבינו clearly is a variant reading. Whether it is due merely to an interpretation of the apocopated וישימו [לבם], or whether it is a true *varia lectio,* may be left undecided at present.

---

24. Kutscher (*Language and Linguistic Background,* 226 [see above, n. 11]) maintains that בת was struck out altogether.

The LXX translation ἐννοηθῶσιν, which may reflect ויבינו, possibly strengthens the latter proposition. But since this specific verb is a hap. leg. in the Greek translation of Isaiah, the evidence is not conclusive. Also the fact that the combination שים (לב)-ידע recurs in v 22 in inverted order, both in the MT and in 1QIsaᵃ, הגידו ונשימה לבנו ונדעה, makes us believe that ויבינו of 1QIsaᵃ, instead of וישימו in the MT, results from faithful adherence to a *Vorlage* which is yet mirrored in Syr, ונתבינן, and not from free word substitution.

Of more importance to the issue at hand is the fact that the superscribed emendation וישימו was subsequently disqualified by its enclosure within deletion-dots. Thus the basic non-MT ויבינו was restored to its original validity.[25] This two-stage correction might have led an imaginary copyist to consider the interlinear וישימו as a restituted omission and not as an emendation. As a result he would have conjoined this verb with ויבינו, thus creating the hypothetical doublet: . . . למען יראו וידעו וישימו ויבינו וישכילו יחדו.

It is obvious that the chances of an actual conflation will increase considerably in cases in which a variant reading is superscribed or adscribed without any accompanying critical symbols.

Isa 36:11   1QIsaᵃ: דברנא עם עבדיך עמנו ארמית
             MT: דבר נא אל עבדיך > ארמית

1QIsaᵃ 36:11

The redundant עמנו of 1QIsaᵃ, which has no equivalent in the VSS, was entered in the right-hand margin exactly in line with the following word ארמית. עמנו is a parallel reading of עם עבדיך, with which the preceding line ends.[26]

---

25. Cp., e.g., Isa 49:14, where the non-masoretic superscribed emendation ואלוהי is deleted by 'pointing' in favor of the basic ואדני (= MT).

26. Kutscher (*Language and Linguistic Background*, 539 [see above, n. 11]) assumes that עמנו in the first part of Isa 36:11 echoes עמנו in the second part of

Thus we have here a true variant-notation, a *qere*-type entry, which was registered alongside the *kethib*-type reading עם עבדיך, and was never meant to be integrated into the text proper. However the probability of its integration is much furthered by favorable manuscript conditions which could easily have induced a copyist of 1QIsaᵃ to take עמנו as an integral part of the original text-base.

We can now proceed from hypothetical to actual routine conflation. While in the preceding instances 1QIsaᵃ was presented as a possible basis for an ensuing doublet in an imaginary MS for which it might have served as the *Vorlage,* in the examples to follow, the faulty doublet actually occurs in 1QIsaᵃ.

We presume that a reading *cum* superscribed emendation lies at the basis of the following doublet in 1QIsaᵃ 51:11, which, however, was emended post facto by the erasure of one of its components.

The extant text of 1QIsaᵃ reads ופזורי ה' ישובו here, as opposed to ופדויי ה' ישובון of the MT which is supported by the VSS.[27] In the parallel, Isa 35:10, both the MT and 1QIsaᵃ read ופדויי ה'. Moreover, whereas the root פדה is represented twice more in the book of Isaiah (1:27; 29:22), פזר is not found in it at all. Even if one assumes that the Qumran scribe substituted ופזורי for ופדויי under the influence of scriptures which use פזר in reference to Israel's dispersion (Jer 50:17; Joel 4:2; Esth 3:8),[28] his reading still must be considered the *lectio difficilior,* with a fair claim at originality. Accordingly ופזורי may be deemed a synonymous reading of ופדויי and its textual equivalent. This equivalence is further indicated by the fact that ופדויי actually had also been written in the text-base of 1QIsaᵃ where it preceded ופזורי but was subsequently erased, possibly by a second hand. If indeed this was the case, the scroll initially contained the doublet ופדויי ופזורי ה', which, as we assume, resulted from a conflation of the main reading with a supralinear or marginal variant which the scribe of 1QIsaᵃ had found in his *Vorlage*.[29]

---

the parallel verse 2 Kgs 18:26: ואל תדבר עמנו יהודית. This supposition is highly improbable in view of the fact that in Isa 36:11b, 1QIsaᵃ altogether deviates from the MT and from the parallel reading in 2 Kings.

27. LXX: καὶ λελυτρωμένοις; Tg. Isa: ופריקא דיוי; Syr: פריקוהי דמריא.

28. Cp. Kutscher, *Language and Linguistic Background,* 274 (see above, n. 11).

29. Cp. ibid., 540. A similar situation may underlie the present text form of 1QIsaᵃ in Isa 2:4:

ל
ושפט בין הגואים והוכיח בין עמים רבים.

The crossing out of בין and the superscribed ל bring 1QIsaᵃ into conformity with the MT, whereas in the preceding instance, the erasure fortified the deviance of 1QIsaᵃ from the MT. The reading of 1QIsaᵃ may indeed be explained as a

IV

Now we can turn to the premeditated retention of parallel readings by conscious conflation, as reflected in Qumran biblical MSS.

We find in the scrolls, just as in the MT and the VSS, full-fledged doublets which have already been incorporated into the basic text. They may be arranged under the following two headings:

(1) *Doublets which are also reflected in extra-Qumran Bible texts,* and therefore obviously are rooted in an all-Jewish (not specifically sectarian) textual tradition.

(2) *Doublets which are found only in Qumran MSS.* These cases, which may be assumed with much probability to have arisen at Qumran, illustrate the collation activities of the sectarian scribes. At the same time Qumran MSS, and especially 1QIsa[a], present instances of interlinear or marginal critical notations, which in the MT or in one of the VSS have become part and parcel of the main text. Here the Qumran material fulfills two functions:

(a) It illustrates the manuscript conditions which are the basis of double-readings and enlightens us on the technical aspects of conflation.

(b) It assists in the discovery of presumed doublets in other extant text-traditions of the Bible.

We are not in all cases in a position to determine the sources from which the constituent variants of a doublet were culled due to the paucity of non-standardized textual traditions which survived the normalizing activity of scribes and revisers. Yet often one of the components of a *doublet* (e.g., in 1QIsa[a]) turns up as a *singlet* in the MT or in one of the extant VSS. This should cause no surprise in view of the diversity of the textual traditions of the biblical books which may be observed at Qumran. In the same fashion that the harmonization of variant readings by conflation was practiced by Greek or Aramaic translators and copyists, as well as by scribes of the MT, it was employed by the Covenanters. Furthermore, in this respect the atmosphere of scribal activities at Qumran resembles that which prevailed in normative circles.

---

conscious or unconscious harmonization with the first stichos of the verse (Kutscher, *Language and Linguistic Background,* 489), but in itself it is the *lectio difficilior.* הוכיח with the dat. pron. *lamed* is found in the parallel passage Mic 4:3 and prevails in the Hebrew Bible (Job 32:12; Prov 9:7, 8; 15:12; 19:25; and esp. Isa 11:4), whereas הוכיח בין is found only twice (Gen 31:37; Job 9:33).

At present our interest lies with the particular Qumran text-traditions and not with the text of a given biblical book as such. Accordingly, all the illustrations to be adduced quite naturally will be cases of textual deviations of a Qumran MS from the MT and/or from one or more of the ancient VSS. These may be subdivided conveniently as follows:

(1) *Double-readings in Qumran MSS which presumably derived from a Vorlage.*

(a) In Isa 37:9 the reading of 1QIsaᵃ   וישמע וישוב וישלח מלאכים
undoubtedly combines the MT wording in Isaiah   וישמע > וישלח מלאכים
with that of the MT parallel in 2 Kgs 19:9.   > ³⁰וישב וישלח מלאכים
Since the doublet is also reflected in the LXX, καὶ ἀκούσας ἀπέστρεψεν[31] καὶ ἀπέστειλεν ἀγγέλους, it may be considered as being derived from a text-type which was utilized both by the Qumran scribe and the Greek translator.

(b) Isa 51:23   1QIsaᵃ: ושמתיהו ביד מוגיך ומעניך אשר אמרו לנפשכי שוחי ונעבורה
            MT: ושמתיה ביד מוגיך > אשר אמרו לנפשך שחי ונעברה
            LXX: καὶ ἐμβαλῶ αὐτὸ εἰς τὰς χεῖρας τῶν ἀδικη-
                        σάντων σε καὶ τῶν ταπεινωσάντων σε
         Tg. Isa: ואמסרינה ביד דהוו מונן ליך
            Syr: ביד ממככניכי

Here, as in many other cases, it cannot be decided by any objective means whether the MT, probably supported by Tg. Isa (cp. Isa 49:26) and Syr (?), has a defective text or whether 1QIsaᵃ indeed presents a conflation. If, by rule of thumb, the shorter MT reading is taken to be original, the redundant ומעניך of 1QIsaᵃ may be explained as an interpretative gloss of the hap. leg. מוגיך, or else simply as a parallel reading. The two roots יגה and ענה are employed in *parallelismus membrorum* in Lam 3:33. Whatever the case, the doublet is proved to precede the text of 1QIsaᵃ by its appearance in the translation of the LXX.[32] It

---

30. Cp. DRMT, 133. The Qumran scribe's awareness of the MT readings in 2 Kings chaps. 18-20, which differ from those found in the parallel account of Isaiah chaps. 36-39, and his utilization of both text-traditions, illuminate the early textual history of the book of Isaiah.

31. In the Origenic tradition the word is shown to be an addition to the Hebrew text by means of an obelus.

32. This fact has fathered the suggestion (BH) to insert וביד מעניך (cp. Isa 49:26) after ביד מוגיך. In Isa 49:26 the LXX renders מוגיך as θλίψαντες. Accordingly we

is possible that the common *Vorlage* was influenced by the similarity of ideas and expressions in Isa 60:14: ו(א)הלכו אליך שחוח (כול) בני מנאצצך מעניך והשתחוו על כפות רגליך כ(ו)ל מנאציך.

(c) 1 Sam 2:24 4QSamᵃ: ‏[אל בני לוא טובה הש[מועה אשר אנוכי שו]מע
אל תעשון כן כי לו]א טובה השמעה[ות] אשר אני שומע
MT: אל בני כי לוא טובה השמעה אשר אנכי שומע
LXX: μὴ τέκνα ὅτι οὐκ ἀγαθὴ ἡ ἀκοὴ ἣν ἐγὼ ἀκούω μὴ ποιεῖτε οὕτως ὅτι οὐκ ἀγαθαὶ αἱ ἀκοαὶ ἃς ἐγὼ ἀκούω[33]

The Qumran text is very fragmentary. However, the restoration, as proposed by its editor F.M. Cross, Jr.,[34] may be considered almost certain, in view of its virtual identity with the Greek rendition. Again it can be stipulated that the doublet was found in one or more textual precursors of 4QSamᵃ, which both the Qumran copyist and the Greek translator used as their *Vorlage*.

(2) *Doublets which arose in the basic textual tradition of 1QIsaᵃ*. In the examples to follow, only one of the components of a presumed doublet in 1QIsaᵃ is yet extant singly in other textual traditions. Accordingly we assume that here conflation arose in the Qumran Scroll. In some cases this assumption can be supported, though not proved, by circumstantial evidence. The decision to classify these double-readings as intra-1QIsaᵃ conflations can be maintained only as long as the doublets are not found also in extra-1QIsaᵃ text-traditions.

(a) A clear case of an extended variants-combination may be found in Isa 38:19-20. The two verses actually are mere reiterations with only slight variations in spelling, and one possible sense-variant. At the same time it is obvious that 1QIsaᵃ adhered to a sentence division which differs from that of the MT and probably also underlies the LXX.[35]

---

may assume that the redundant (with regard to the MT) καὶ τῶν ταπεινωσάντων σε in Isa 51:23 indeed stands for 1QIsaᵃ ומעניך. The Greek words in question are absent from Aq., Sym., and Orig.

33. The second line is omitted in the Luc. tradition and in some late witnesses.

34. F. M. Cross, Jr., "A New Qumran Biblical Fragment Related to the Original Hebrew Underlying the Septuagint," *BASOR* 132 (1953) 15-26.

35. I have discussed some further concurrences of sentence-division between 1QIsaᵃ and the LXX against the MT in "1QIsaᵃ as a Witness to Ancient Exegesis of the Book of Isaiah," in this vol., pp. 131-141.

חי חי הוא יודכה כמוני היום אב לבנים יודיע אל אמתכה הי להושיעני: (a) 19
חי חי > יודך כמוני היום אב לבנים והודיע אלוה אמתך הי להושיעני: (b) 20

None of the extant witnesses to the book of Isaiah exhibits this doublet which thus is shown to be of particular Qumran vintage. It is obvious that the doubling could not have resulted from a scribal mistake for two reasons, as is suggested by Kutscher:[36]

Accidental dittography of complete syntactical units may be assumed only when evident manuscript reasons can be adduced to back up this assumption, mainly *homoioteleuton* or *homoioarkton*. Neither of these can account for the present doublet in spite of the phrase אל אמתך, which in the MT recurs at the ends of both v 18 and v 19. According to the proposed syntactical analysis, in 1QIsaᵃ the phrase does not close v 19 but is followed by הי להושיעני, with which the verse ends.

The assumption of accidental doubling is militated against by the even weightier fact that the textual peculiarities of the (b) reading were faithfully preserved, such as a defective spelling (אמתך, יודך), as opposed to the plene spelling of the (a) text (אמתכה, יודכה).

On the grounds of the spelling alone we can confidently state that the (b) variant stems from a text-type which differed from that of the 1QIsaᵃ text-base, where plene spelling prevails. On the other hand, the interlinear and marginal corrections in 1QIsaᵃ are often distinguished from the basic text by their defective spelling. Compare, e.g., the superscribed גאלך in 43:3 with the lower-case אלוהיכה. Thus we may surmise that variant (b) in 38:20 and some of the marginal or interlinear corrections were derived from the same extra-1QIsaᵃ text, or text-types.

Can this *Vorlage* of the (b) reading be further defined? The variant of (b) והודיע, as against יודיע of (a), is of no help. But the remaining *varia lectio* אלוה might point the way. It is evident that (b) here reads the divine epithet ʾeloah (אלוה) instead of the preposition אֶל in the MT.[37] The (b) reading is not supported by any other witness, whereas the MT variant is possibly, although only poorly, attested to in the Syr rendition of אל אמתך by the direct object ונחוה הימנותך, reflected also in the redundant paraphrase יחוון גבורתך of Tg.

---

36. *Language and Linguistic Background*, 541 (see above, n. 11).
37. Here we differ with Kutscher (ibid.), who maintains that אל was simply omitted in the (a) reading, as is the case in MS Ken. 96.

Isa.[38] Sym.'s περὶ τῆς ἀληθείας σου seems to mirror אל/על אמתך. The other VSS have preserved a medial stage between אל of the MT and אלוה of (b). Tg. Isa's main reading, דכל אלין קשוט, and possibly also the LXX's ἃ ἀναγγελοῦσιν τὴν δικαιοσύνην σου (which is clarified by the marginal καὶ τοῦτο ἀναγγεῖλαι in MS Q and the Syr. Hex.) reflect the consonantal base of the MT and a vocalized אֵל, which is the apocopated form of the demonstr. pron. אלה. For the Targum this was already recognized by Kimchi (ad loc.), who comments, "It appears that Jonathan translated this אל as if [it were pointed] with ṣere, like האל הארצות (Gen 26:3, 4)." He then goes on and quotes with disapproval Ibn Ezra, who, following Tg. Isa, interpreted אל אמתך to mean אלה האמונות, "these are the creeds/tenets." It seems, in fact, that Kimchi suspected Ibn Ezra of implying that he had based his comment on an actual variant vocalization אֵל, since he emphatically professes, "In no book have I seen אל pointed otherwise than with segol, and in the construct state with אמתך."[39]

The vocalization of אל as the pl. demonstr. pron., as it transpires from the Aramaic and Greek renditions and from Ibn Ezra's commentary, is now supported by the consonantal variant אלה found in the incomplete Isaiah Scroll (1QIsa[b]). However, we cannot be certain whether the scribe of 1QIsa[b], like Tg. Isa and the LXX, took אלה to represent the pl. demonstr. pron., or whether he considered it a defective spelling of אלוה, siding with (b). But it may be considered certain that the copyist of 1QIsa[a] thus interpreted the consonantal group אלה in his (a)-type *Vorlage* and transferred it to his own MS with the *waw* filled in, as a variant reading.

If the textual development indeed followed the above reconstructed pattern, the doublet in 1QIsa[a] 38:19-20 would give witness that the scribe of 1QIsa[a] collated a proto-masoretic with a (proto-)1QIsa[b] text with the resulting conflation of the present (a) and (b) variants.

From here follow some further considerations which will be discussed at a later stage.

38. I. L. Seeligmann (*The Septuagint Version of Isaiah* [Leiden: E. J. Brill, 1948] 69) considers אל/את אמתך of the MT the probable original reading.

39. ונראה כי יונתן תרגם אל זה כמו בצירי"י כמו הארצות האל שתרגם אבהן לבנן יחוון גבורת ויודן למימר דכל אילן קשוט. וכן פירש החכם ראב"ע, וזהו לשון פירושו: אב לבנים יודיע אלה האמתות, ואני תמה בזה כי לא ראיתי בשום ספר אלא אל נקוד סגולה וסמוך במקום עם אמתך. והמסרת אל אמתך שנים והם אלה השנים אשר הן בפסוק כי לא שאול תודך ובפסוק חי חי הוא יודך. Cp. S. Loewinger ("The Variants of DSI II," *VT* 4 [1954] 157, n. 3.)

(b) Isa 14:2   1QIsaᵃ: ולקחום עמים רבים והביאום אל אדמתם ואל מקומם

           MT: מקומם <   < אל והביאום > עמים ולקחום

         Tg. Isa (P): לאתרהון ויובלונונן

         Tg. Isa (R): ויובלונונן לארעהון

          LXX: εἰς τὸν τόπον αὐτῶν

The conflation of אל מקומם with אל אדמתם, smoothed over by the insertion of the conjunct. *waw,* is found only in 1QIsaᵃ. In this case both the conflated readings are preserved singly in extant textual witnesses: אל מקומם is the reading of the MT, LXX, and the Syr, and is reflected in one branch of the Tg. Isa tradition (Cod. Reuchlinianus, ed. de Lagarde), whereas another MS of Tg. Isa (Bibl. Nationale MS 1325) mirrors the parallel reading אל אדמתם.[40] This circumstance decisively weakens Kutscher's implied suggestion that 1QIsaᵃ merely harmonized אל מקומם of v 2a with על אדמת(ם) of vv 1 and 2b.[41]

(c) Isa 35:9   1QIsaᵃ: ופריץ חיות בל לוא יעלנה

            MT: ופריץ חיות בל < יעלנה

The double negation בל לוא, which has no equivalent in the MT or the VSS, suggests that the scribe of 1QIsaᵃ conflated two readings.[42] In view of the fact that 1QIsaᵃ faithfully retains the twenty-odd occurrences of בל in the book of Isaiah,[43] and by virtue of the plene spelling of לוא,[44] which is characteristic for the 1QIsaᵃ base, this latter variant should be deemed primary in the present setting. Thus בל must be considered a synonymous reading which was collated into the MS from a (proto-)masoretic-type text, such as, e.g., 1QIsaᵇ.

40. Not mentioned by Kutscher (*Language and Linguistic Background,* 537 [see above, n. 11]).
41. If one accepts Goshen-Gottstein's supposition, for which no manuscriptal evidence can be adduced, that Tg. Isa originally had the compound reading לארעהון ולאתרהון, the doublet in 1QIsaᵃ would have to be classified as derivative from a *Vorlage* ("Die Jeaja-Rolle im Lichte von Peschitta und Targum," *Biblica* 35 [1954] 35).
42. See also Kutscher (*Language and Linguistic Background,* 539). In Isa 33:21 the two words are employed synonymously in *parallelismus membrorum.*
43. Among these are found three cases of triple בל in one verse (33:20; 40:24; 44:9) and three of double בל (26:10, 14; 33:23).
44. One MS Ken: לא.

(d) Isa 62:7   1QIsaᵃ: עד יכין ועד יכונן ועד ישים / את ירושלים תהלה בארץ

              1QIsaᵇ: ע[ ]ם את]

              MT: עד יכונן ועד ישים את ירושלים תהלה בארץ

              Tg. Isa: עד דיתכין ועד דישוי

              Syr: עדמא דנתקנבי ועדמא דנעבדכי

              LXX: ἐὰν διορθώσῃ καὶ ποιήσῃ

The synopsis of all the extant witnesses to this verse reveals a typical case of textual expansion if the 1QIsaᵇ reading is considered original, or a case of contraction in 1QIsaᵇ if the MT or one of the VSS is chosen as a departure point for the textual comparison. Either way, 1QIsaᵃ exhibits a conflated reading.

The shortest reading, with only one verb in the sentence, is found in 1QIsaᵇ. Its preserved text is very fragmentary indeed but may be reconstructed as follows: [ירושלים ת[ה]לה בארץ[45] ע[ד ישי[ם את [46]ונו דמי לכם [ואל תת. The reading לכם, as opposed to לו in the MT and 1QIsaᵃ (= Tg. Isa: מן קדמוהי) which is supported by the LXX's ὑμῖν, proves that 1QIsaᵇ presents here a divergent text tradition, to which also the absence of תמיד in the preceding verse (found in all other VSS) gives evidence. Viewed against this background, the omission in 1QIsaᵇ of the MT's and 1QIsaᵃ's יכונן[47] (= LXX: διορθώσῃ; Tg. Isa: דיתכין) cannot be considered a *lapsus calami* resulting from *homoioarkton*.

The MT and all the VSS have two verbs, the first of which is obviously doubled in 1QIsaᵃ: עד יכין ועד יכונן. Since this duplication has no parallel in any other witness, it may be ascribed, with much probability, to the scribe of 1QIsaᵃ. What it amounts to is a combination of two forms of the causative of the hifᶜil formation יכין and the polel formation יכונן. Both formations are found in the book of Isaiah in the MT, as well as in 1QIsaᵃ: the hifᶜil in 9:6; 14:21; 40:20 (MT: להכין; 1QIsaᵃ: להוכין); the polel in 45:18; 51:13; 54:14 (MT:

---

45. Cp. Zeph 3:19: ושמתים לתהלה ולשם בכל הארץ. Nowhere in the Bible does כון carry a double object. May we assume two possible basic readings for Isa 62:7, namely עד ישים את ירושלים תהלה בארץ and עד יכונן את ירושלים?

46. The reading of 1QIsaᵇ in 62:6-7, אל דמי לכם [ואל תת]נו דמי לכם, leads one to suspect that in the MT and 1QIsaᵃ this obvious doublet was camouflaged by variation to read: אל דמי לו ואל תתנו דמי לכם. The LXX has preserved only the first component of the suspected doublet: οὐκ ἔστιν γὰρ ὑμῖν ὅμοιος. The main tradition of Tg. Isa exhibits the first variant in an apocopated form (MS K: להון; MSS b, g: לא פסיק לכון).

47. In the lacuna between the preserved ע of עד and the final ם of the following word, there is room for four to five letters at most.

תכונני; 1QIsaᵃ: תתכונני). Stylistically one cannot be preferred over the other, and they must be considered synonymous. One is inclined to presume that the scribe of 1QIsaᵃ culled them from two MSS that were at his disposal and conflated them in his copy.[48]

(e) Isa 40:19 1QIsaᵃ: הפסל ויעשה מסך חרש
MT: הפסל   >   נסך חרש
Tg. Isa: הא צלמא נגרא עביד
LXX: μὴ εἰκόνα ἐποίησεν τέκτων
Aq.: μὴ γλυπτὸν ἐχώνευσεν

The redundant ויעשה of 1QIsaᵃ which is reflected in Tg. Isa, עביד, Syr, דעבד, and the LXX ἐποίησεν is probably a variant of the MT נסך (miswritten in 1QIsaᵃ as מסך),[49] which was correctly rendered ἐχώνευσεν by Aq. More confident than Kutscher, and in spite of the garbled syntax of 1QIsaᵃ, we tend to propose that its scribe conflated a MT-type and an extra-masoretic reading in his copy.

(f) Isa 30:6 1QIsaᵃ: משא בהמות נגב בארץ צרה וציה וצוקה
MT: משא בהמות נגב בארץ צרה   >   וצוקה

All the VSS concur here with the MT in recording only two appositions to בארץ, as against three in 1QIsaᵃ. The word-pair צרה וצוקה is found again, though divided, in Isa 8:22 and once more, with a slight variation, in Zeph 1:15: יום צרה ומצוקה. In other formations the roots צרר and צוק also appear as pairs in Deut 28:53, 55, 57; Jer 19:9; Ps 119:143. Never is the redundant ציה of 1QIsaᵃ combined with either. This makes the 1QIsaᵃ reading a *lectio difficilior,* which can hardly be explained by Kutscher's contention that ציה, "parched land,"

48. A somewhat similar situation obtains in the MT to Isa 35:5. Cp. DRMT, 177.
49. For an interesting example of the otherwise abundantly documented interchange of נ-מ, see B. Kedar-Kopfstein's note on Isa 14:31 ("A Note on Isaiah xiv,31,"*Textus* 2 [1962] 143-45). Kutscher's supposition (*Language and Linguistic Background,* 258 [see above, n. 11]) that 1QIsaᵃ possibly substituted in 40:19 the rabbinic מסך for biblical נסך is ingenious but hardly warranted in view of the retention of נסך in 44:10. There Tg. Isa renders it אתיך; Syr: נסיכא; Theod.: χώνευσει; the LXX omits the word.

spuriously arose in the text under the influence of אין מים (MT: מהם) in the continuation of the verse.[50] Accordingly we are led to assume that ציה is a variant reading for either צרה or צ(ו)קה (possibly due to graphic confusion), which was incorporated by the scribe into his text.

(g) Isa 40:18 1QIsa^a: ואל מיא תדמיוני אל ומה דמות תערוכו לי

MT: ואל מי   תדמיון אל ומה דמות תערכו לו

Here the MT has the support of all the VSS. The variant reading of 1QIsa^a, which in fact constitutes a doublet, must accordingly be considered an inner-1QIsa^a development. It appears that the scribe combined two wordings of an idea which is found twice in chap. 40, in v 18 and again in v 25, and which are kept distinct in the MT and the VSS. The basic difference between them is in that one refers to God, the direct object, by the noun אל and the 3 pers. pron. לו, while in the other "He," being the speaker, refers to himself by the 1 pers. pron. לי and the pronominal suffix ני.[51]

	לו	תדמיון אל	
ומה דמות תער(ו)כו			אל מי(א)
לי		תדמיוני	

(h) A fairly obvious case of conflation of two interrogative particles may be found in:

Isa 36:19   1QIsa^a: וכיא ההצילו

MT: וכי הצילו

The VSS support the MT in that only one interrogative word is mirrored in them, but it is not possible to decide which of the two, כי or הַ, was in their respective *Vorlagen*.

---

50. Kutscher (ibid., 537) compares Ps 63:2. As a contrasting image Isa 41:18 = Ps 107:35 can also be adduced.
51. Kutscher (ibid., 76, 325, 560) assumes a mere contamination of v 18 by v 25, but this seems unlikely.

The non-MT variant ההצילו constitutes the retention of a form which had already been employed in the preceding verse (36:18, MT = 1QIsaᵃ), whereas כי is a variational form of interrogation.

(i) In a class by themselves are the doublets which result from a combination of parallel readings that present the same word-stock but differ in the word order.[52]

Isa 22:14 1QIsaᵃ: אם יכפר לכם העון הזה לכמה

MT: אם יכפר > העון הזה לכם

Tg. Isa: אם ישתביק חובא הדין לכון

Syr: לא תסבון לכון חטיתא

LXX: ὅτι οὐκ ἀφεθήσεται ὑμῖν αὕτη ἡ ἁμαρτία

In one of the readings conflated in 1QIsaᵃ, the pers. pron. לכם preceded the subject העון. This order, אם יכפר לכם העון הזה, which is also reflected in the LXX and the Syr, is well represented in a Yemenite textual tradition, as evidenced by the quotation of the verse in one Yem. MS of the Babylonian Talmud, *b. Taᶜan.* 11a, and in some MSS of the (Yem.) midrash ha-Gadol to Gen 37:29 (MSS ש, ד; ed. M. Margulies 637, 18), and to Exod 32:6 (MSS ב, ה, ס; ed. M. Margulies 681, 9). In the other reading the pers. pron. followed upon the noun. This is the arrangement of the MT, supported by Tg. Isa and by one MS of the LXX.[53]

The difference in spelling לכם, as against לכמה, may point to the derivation of the two readings from different text-types.[54]

(j) Isa 57:18 1QIsaᵃ: ואשלם לוא תנחומים לוא ולאבליו

MT: ואשלם > נחמים לו ולאבליו

Tg. Isa: ואשלים > תנחומין להון

Syr: ופרעה > בוייאא לה

LXX: καὶ ἔδωκα αὐτῷ παράκλησιν ἀληθινήν

---

52. Examples of inverted word-order in 1QIsaᵃ in comparison with the MT were assembled by Kutscher (ibid., 563-64).

53. Cp. J. Ziegler, ed., *Isaias* (Göttingen: Vandenhoeck & Ruprecht, 1939), ad loc.

54. Cp. Isa 38:20, above, pp. 87, 88.

The reading of the MT (= Tg. Isa, Syr), in which the dat. pron. לו follows upon the direct object, was conflated in 1QIsaᵃ with the reading presented by the LXX, in which it precedes it. The force of the LXX evidence is somewhat weakened by the omission in its translation of the second dat. object ולאבליו. This may have caused the transfer of the dat. pron. αὐτῷ. However the same word order is also maintained in MSS of the LXX, in Aq., Sym., Theod., and Orig., where the missing clause is restored.

(k) Isa 64:1 1QIsaᵃ: תבעה אש לצריכה להודיע שמכה לצריכה

MT: תבעה אש   >   להודיע שמך לצריך

LXX: καὶ κατακαύσει πῦρ τοὺς ὑπεναντίους καὶ φανερὸν ἔσται τὸ ὄνομα κυρίου ἐν τοῖς ὑπεναντίοις

Tg. Isa: להודעא שמך לסנאי עמך

In view of the exegetical difficulties inherent in this verse, it cannot be decided definitely whether the first (ה)לצריכ simply was omitted in the MT (followed by Tg. Isa, Sym., Theod.) or whether it accrued in 1QIsaᵃ (followed by the LXX). In the first case (ה)לצריכ would be the dat. object of both the verbs תבעה and להודיע. In the second, a conflation of the following two readings must be assumed:

לצריכה להודיע שמכה

להודיע שמכה לצריכה

Also the most closely amalgamated type of conflation found in the MT, the crossing of two variants in one word which results in hybrid readings, is not absent from 1QIsaᵃ.

(1) Isa 1:31 1QIsaᵃ: והיה החסנכם לנערת ופעלכם לניצוץ

MT: והיה החסן   לנערת ופעלו   לניצוץ

Here the 1QIsaᵃ reading results from the combination of a noun defined by the def. art. החסן (MT) with its parallel definition by the 2 pl. poss. suffix חסנכם,[55] which is reflected in the 3 pl. poss. suffix found in the main VSS.

LXX: ἡ ἰσχὺς αὐτῶν

Tg. Isa: תקפהון

Syr: עושינהון

(m) The enigmatic אייאמים of 1QIsaᵃ, as against איים of the MT in Isa 34:14, can possibly be explained as a hybrid reading.[56] We propose tentatively that the scribe combined the otherwise attested איים, some sort of desert being (Isa 13:22, 1QIsaᵃ: איים; Jer 50:39) with the hap. leg. יֵמִם (Gen 36:24), which carries a similar connotation. The VSS are of no help here, since the Hebrew synonyms would be similarly translated.

(n) An uncompleted case of hybrid reading of the same type may be found in Isa 30:23, where the present text of 1QIsaᵃ

ה
אשר תזרע את אדמה

has been super-imposed upon the variant אדמת[ך]. The ה at the end of the word אדמה clearly is a correction of an underlying ת. The initially intended definition by the 2 sing. poss. suffix אדמתך (= LXX: τῆς γῆς σου) was superseded by the definition with the aid of the def. art. האדמה (= MT; Tg. Isa: ית ארעא).

---

55. Cp. האהלי (Josh 7:21), החצי (Josh 8:33), ההרותיה (2 Kgs 15:16), and see DRMT, 178-79. After considering the possibility of conflation, Kutscher seems to prefer the doubtful explanation that the scribe of 1QIsaᵃ (inadvertently?) transferred from one determination to the other in the process of writing (Kutscher, *Language and Linguistic Background*, 557 [see above, n. 11]).

56. The possibility was suggested by Kutscher (ibid., 217—צורת כלאים), who tentatively explains the form as a combination of איי + אמ + ים (Kutscher, 165). My colleague A. Hurvitz has drawn my attention to a comparable case of proper nouns conflation in 1QapGen xxi 29 (ed. N. Avigad and Y. Yadin [Jerusalem, 1956]). Here a seeming combination of זוזים (Gen 14:5) with זמזומים (Deut 2:20) resulted in: מ
ולזוזמיא.

(o) Conflation may possibly explain the following reading of 1QIsaᵃ:

Isa 61:6 1QIsaᵃ: [57] חיל גואים תואכלו ובכבודם תתיאמרו

MT: חיל גוים תאכלו ובכבודם תתימרו

The phrase ובכבודם תתימרו is a *crux interpretum*. No satisfactory derivation for תתי(א)מרו has been proposed.[58] Tg. Isa, תתפנקון, Syr, תשתבחון, and LXX, θαυμασθήσεσθε[59] are of no help. But the 1QIsaᵃ reading in conjunction with Aq.'s rendition may point the way.

We assume for 1QIsaᵃ a combination of the MT spelling תתימרו (possibly reflected in Sym.'s στρηνιάσατε) with a spelling תתאמרו, which is mirrored in the renderings of Theod. and Aq.

Theod.'s ὑψωθήσεσθε clearly is derived from אמר in the meaning of "high," for which cp. Isa 17:6, 9, אמיר (בראש) = "branch," "tree-top" (?).[60] In a different connotation אמר appears to be reflected in Aq.'s rendition: πορφυρωθήσεσθε (faultily quoted by Hier. in his commentary as πόρφυρα ἐνδύσεσθε). We propose that here the translator had in mind the rabbinic "hem of a garment," which sometimes was made of purple (cp. *m. Neg.* 11:10: חלוק שנראה בו נגע אפילו הן ארגמן מציל את האמריות שבו,). In translating καὶ ἐν δόξῃ αὐτῶν πορφυρωθήσεσθε, Aq. probably took ובכבודם תתאמרו to mean, "You will put on their splendor [like] purple," thus exhibiting his familiarity with rabbinic language. We may assume that this same concept underlies the conflated reading תתיאמרו of 1QIsaᵃ.[61]

---

57. At first sight this could be explained as a plene spelling of תתימרו with the א serving as *mater lect.* for *patah.* Cp. Isa 30:31, MT, יכה; 1QIsaᵃ, יאכה.
58. Cp. E. Nötscher ("Entbehrliche Hapaxlegomena in Jesaia," *VT* 1 [1951] 300): מור—אמר—ימר.
59. Ziegler (*Isaias*, 168), following Fischer and Wutz, supposes that the influence of Aram. דמר, and of the similar passage Isa 60:5, may explain the use of θαυμάειν in the instance under review.
60. Theod.'s translation is not preserved here. The LXX is of no help.
61. Cp. Isa 3:22, MT: המחלצות והמעטפות; LXX (3:21): τὰ περιπόρφυρα καὶ τὰ μεσοπόρφυρα.

(p) Isa 57:17   1QIsaᵃ: ואהסתר ואקצופה

        MT: הסתר ואקצף

        LXX: καὶ ἀπέστρεψα τὸ πρόσωπόν μου ἀπ᾽ αὐτοῦ

              καὶ ἐλυπήθη

Tg. Isa, סליקית שכינתי מנהון, and Syr, ואתפנית ורגזת, do not bear on the issue.

Kutscher explains the redundant ה of 1QIsaᵃ אהסתר as due to Aramaic influence.[62] Thus both verbs would be (inverted?) imperfects.[63] However, a case can be made for the supposition that 1QIsaᵃ contains a fully developed doublet which may be observed *in statu nascendi* in the MT. The underlying alternative variants then would be ואסתר ואקצ(ו)(פ)(ה) and הַסְתֵּר וְקָצ(ו)ף.[64]

The assumption that in one variant וקצף was read as an absolute infin. is borne out by the vocalization of the ו with *shewa* in the MT and by the LXX's rendering it as a 3 sing., which points to a consonantal stock קצף without the prefixed א of the 1 sing. imperf.

(q) Isa 11:9   1QIsaᵃ: כי תמלאה הארץ דעה

        MT: כי   מלאה הארץ דעה

Here, as in similar cases in the MT,[65] we postulate that in 1QIsaᵃ the 3 f. sing. perf. מלאה (= MT) was conflated with the parallel imperf. form תמלא, which possibly is reflected in Tg. Isa, ארי תתמלי and Syr, דתתמלא.

(3) A. *1QIsaᵃ readings and corrections which constitute the basis of double-readings found in the MT.*

(a) In 1QIsaᵃ iii 20-25 (Isa 3:15-18) the tetragrammaton is recorded three times, accompanied by what in the MT is considered its *qere perpetuum*—אדוני. In v 18 the tetragrammaton is written in the line, with אדוני inserted on top of it. In v 17 the situation is reversed. In both cases the superscribed reading is presented as a correction by the "pointing" of the lower-case reading. Here the corrector quite clearly indicated the superiority of, or his preference for, the

---

62. *Language and Linguistic Background,* 198 (see above, n. 11). G. R. Driver construes the interpolated ה as an attempt on the part of the scribe to correct הסתר to אסתר ("Chronicles, OT, NT," *JTS* 2 [1951] 18).

63. Kutscher, ibid., 346.

64. Cp. Rubinstein, *VT* 4 (1954) 200-201 (see above, n. 16).

65. Cp. Isa 63:3, MT: אגאלתי; 1QIsaᵃ: גאלתי; below, p. 106.

superlinear variant. Obviously this is a matter of choice which is not rooted in the intrinsic primacy of one or the other reading, since the correction alternately goes both ways, but rather derives from the ideograph of the *Vorlage* used by the corrector, which was not identical with the MT. The MT reads in both verses אדני. In both these instances the substitution character of the superscription is made manifest by the pointing of the variant to be deleted. This is sufficient safeguard against the mistaken combination of the two by a later copyist. We encounter a different situation in the remaining instance, the first in the row of three, which has a direct bearing on the issue at hand, the emergence of double-readings. In v 15 the superlinear אדוני is added without the deletion of the lower-case tetragrammaton (cp. also 28:16; 30:15; 65:13). It is impossible to decide whether the omission of the deletion-points is due just to a *lapsus calami* on the part of the corrector, *p.m.* or *s.m.,* or whether the express purpose of the correction was the restoration of what the corrector considered to be an accidentally missing אדוני. Thus the superscribed word would constitute not a variant of the one in the line, but rather an addition to it. The latter assumption derives support, though not proof, from the MT, which in fact reads the double-name אדני יהוה. The doublet, and such it appears to be, accordingly did not arise in 1QIsaᵃ, but rather stems from a proto-masoretic text-type, which possibly preceded 1QIsaᵃ, but certainly is external to its textual tradition. Thus 1QIsaᵃ *p.m.* represents the earliest text-form of this specific case, 1QIsaᵃ *s.m.* the transitional stage, and the MT the ultimate doublet phase, also present in Aq.: κυριος κυριος (πιπι πιπι).

       (b) Isa 24:4 Mt: אמללו מרום עם הארץ

               1QIsaᵃ: אמלל מרום ᵉᵐ הארץ

As Kutscher correctly observed, the reading of the verb in the sing. (אמלל) proves that the lack of עם in the text-base of 1QIsaᵃ is not just a case of faulty omission, subsequently corrected. The shorter text of 1QIsaᵃ underlies also the renditions of the LXX (οἱ ὑψηλοὶ τῆς γῆς) and Syr (רומה דארעא), which have no equivalent for עם. This is, moreover, also missing in one MS Ken. Tg. Isa follows the MT: תקוף עמא דארעא. Accordingly, the reading (הארץ) עם may be conceived of as a parallel of מרום (הארץ), which in 1QIsaᵃ was collated between the lines from a text-type which is no longer extant. At a subsequent copying, for which a MS of the 1QIsaᵃ type served as *Vorlage,* the superscribed variant was misconstrued as a corrected omission and was inserted in the text proper. This resulted in the doublet, as exhibited by the MT.

In passing we may observe that a similar conflation of עם (הארץ) with דלת (הארץ), the very opposite of מרום (הארץ), occurred in the MT of 2 Kgs 24:14, לא נשאר זולת דלת עם הארץ. Here again the word עם is not translated in the LXX, οἱ πτωχοὶ τῆς γῆς. It appears that in this case the two basic readings may still be found singly in parallel passages:

2 Kgs 25:12:	ומדלת הארץ	cp. Jer 52:16:	ומדלות הארץ
Jer. 39:10:	ומן העם הדלים	cp. Jer 52:15:	ומדלות העם[66]

(c) Isa 21:17   MT: ושאר מספר קשת גבורי בני-קדר ימעטו

                     בני

         1QIsa[a]:   גבורי   קדר

The shorter basic reading of 1QIsa[a], without the (redundant?) בני, underlies the main targumic tradition, גיברי ערבאי, and Theod., . . . τῶν ἰσχυρῶν κηδάρ. It is also found in one MS Ken.[67] The parallel reading בני קדר, which was interpolated between the lines in 1QIsa[a], is found singly in the LXX: . . . υἱῶν Κηδάρ. The MT, followed by the LXX, τῶν ἰσχυρῶν υἱῶν Κηδαρ; Syr, גברא דבנו קדר; and some witnesses of Tg. Isa (L[RN]), גברי דבני ערבא; presents the double-reading which resulted from the integration of the superscribed variant into the text proper.

(d) Isa 56:12   MT: וחיה כזה יום מחר גדול יתר מאד

                          יתר

         1QIsa[a]: מאוד   גדול ומחר היום כזה ויהי

The shorter basic reading here has the support of Tg. Isa, ותהי שירותנא דמחר טבא מדיומא דין סגיאה לחדא, and possibly of Syr, ונותר לן סוגאא דטב. One MS and some printed editions of Tg. Isa (bogf), however, mirror the MT, סגיאה לחדא רבא. The LXX does not render the verse at all. Aq., Theod., and Sym.

---

66. These instances will be discussed separately.
67. Cp. Kutscher (*Language and Linguistic Background*, 549 [above, n. 11]), who fails, however, to mention the evidence of Tg. Isa and Theod., which supports the basic 1QIsa[a] text.

restored the missing passage in complete agreement with the MT. The same pertains to Orig.[68]

In view of Tg. Isa's (and Syr's) concurrence with the base of 1QIsaᵃ, we are inclined to assume that the superscribed גדול constitutes a variant-notation which at a subsequent stage of copying was embodied in the main text, thus creating the doublet found in the MT.

(e) Isa 61:1 MT: יען משח ה׳ אתי לבשר ענוים שלחני לחבש לנשברי-לב
לקרא לשבוים דרור ולאסורים פקח-קוח

שלחני
1QIsaᵃ: יען משח ה׳ אותי לבשר ענוים ולחבוש לנשברי לב
לקרוא לשבויים דרור ולאסורים פקח קוח

The MT is supported by all VSS. The shorter 1QIsaᵃ text may well have resulted from the omission of שלחני which subsequently was restored as a superscription. However the ו prefixed before לחבוש makes it quite clear that שלחני cannot have been an integral component of the basic 1QIsaᵃ reading, unless it is conjoined with לבשר ענוים (שלחני), against the masoretic sentence division. It may therefore be surmised that the superscribed שלחני represents a variant reading שלחני לנשברי לב, not otherwise attested, which the writer or corrector of 1QIsaᵃ collated into his copy. If that is the case, the MT would exhibit a faulty conflation of the two variants. While לחבוש לנשברי לב appears to be the smoother expression (cp. Ezek 34:4, 16), the reading שלחני לנשברי לב can be maintained by its comparison with 2 Sam 10:3, כי שלח לך מנחמים and Ps 111:9, פדות שלח לעמו. In the first reading the whole series of infinitive constructs, לבשר, לקרא, לחבש, etc., would be dependent on the finite verb משח אתי. In the second, only לבשר would be dependent on משח, while the finite שלחני would open a new series of infinitive constructs.

(3) B. One more category of double-readings in the MT on which the Qumran Scrolls throw light remains to be mentioned. These are readings in which a Qumran MS will exhibit only one component in its text-base, without any superlinear or marginal variant-notation, as against a fully fledged doublet in the MT. I discussed some such instances in a previous publication in which the MT served as the point of departure.[69] Further suggestions are made in what follows.

68. Cp. Kutscher, ibid., 552.
69. DRMT, 162 (Isa 14:12), 163 (12:2), 168 (35:8), 169 (37:18), 177 (25:5).

It goes without saying that in many cases of a supposed doublet in the MT, the single reading in the 1QIsaᵃ which serves as the controlling standard can be interpreted as a defective reading resulting from faulty omission. The situation is comparable to the choice between a dittography in one text or a haplography in another, where either decision would result in a satisfactory reading. A good example of such a situation may be seen in:

Isa 3:22 MT: המחלצות והמעטפות והמטפחות והחריטים
1QIsaᵃ: והמחלצות והמעטפות > והחריטים

Here the Greek and the targumic evidence appear to support the MT, and a haplography in 1QIsaᵃ is as good an assumption as a variant conflation in the MT. It is possible, however, to present מטפחות (widely used in Rabbinic Hebrew but found only once in the Hebrew Bible, Ruth 3:15) as an interpretative reading of the hap. leg. מעטפה/ת, which is also extremely rare in rabbinic language (*t. Kelim* 5.4; ed. Zuckermandel, 595).

The scales can be tipped in favor of the doublet assumption whenever it is supported by one of the following: (1) concurring evidence of an independent ancient version; where no such support is forthcoming, when (2) one component of the double-reading can be shown to be redundant on grounds of metrical, syntactical, or sense considerations, or else can be explained as a harmonizing intrusion from a parallel passage.

We shall open this series with the analysis of an MT reading which already on some previous occasion was presented as arising from conflation by its comparison with a parallel MT reading and with its rendition in the LXX. Its doublet nature can now be further substantiated with the aid of Qumran evidence.

(a) 2 Sam 5:11 MT: וחרשי עץ וחרשי אבן קיר[70]
4Q Samᵃ: וחרשי > קיר

We propose that the redundant אבן in the MT represents the reading וחרשי אבן which is yet extant in the LXXᴮ: καὶ τέκτονας λίθων, and for which cp.

---

70. This passage was published by Cross ("The History of the Biblical Text," *QHBT*, 177-95).

also 1 Chr 22:15, וחרשי אבן ועץ (LXX: οἰκοδόμοι λίθων καὶ τέκτονες ξύλων).

The synonymous Qumran variant וחרשי קיר turns up in the MT and the LXX of the parallel passage, 1 Chr 14:1[71] and in the Lucianic tradition (oc_2e_2): καὶ τέκτονας τοίχου. The MT doublet underlies two Greek minuscules: καὶ τέκτονας τοίχου λίθων. Tg. Isa paraphrases וארדיכלין דאומנין בבנין כותליא.[72] It is feasible that בבנין arose out of the Heb. אבן, which in MS y possibly turns up as ואבנין after the rendition of עץ וחרשי: ונגרי דאומנין למקץ אעין ואבנין.

(b) Isa 26:6 MT: תרמסנה רגל רגלי עני   פעמי דלים

תרמסנה >   רגלי עניים פעמי דלים

The redundant רגל (sing.) of the MT, which is the reading of the Syr, רגלא, has no equivalent in the Greek tradition and is also absent from one MS Ken. It is probably a variant of רגלי (pl.), which was inserted into the text-base (= Tg. Isa).

(c) The following is probably a case of conflation, possibly involving a misreading:[73]

Isa 59:13   MT: דבר עשק וסרה הרו והגו מלב דברי-שקר

1QIsaᵃ: הגוא מלב דברי שקר   <   ודברו עושק וסרה

The VSS support the consonantal base of the MT as it stands and follow also the masoretic sentence division, which has a break after וסרה, taking הרו together with הגו as the *verb. reg.* of דברי שקר. All the Greek sources and the Syr (בטנן) derive הרו from הרה "to conceive, to become pregnant." The LXX and Sym. render it by κύειν, Theod. and Aq. by (ἐν γάστρι) λαμβάνειν. Thus understood, הרו makes a poor parallel for the remaining verbs דבר and הגה, and at the same time clearly shows the translators' dependence on an earlier verse in the same chapter, 59:4. There הרה parallels ילד and is again rendered by κύειν in the LXX,[74] these being the only two instances in which the LXX employ this

---

71. In inverted order: וחרשי קיר וחרשי עצים.
72. Cp. Syr: ואומנא דראפא דאסתא.
73. If הרו is seen simply as a miswritten dittography of הגו; cp. BH.
74. Theod.: ἐν γάστρι ἔλαβον.

verb in the Hebrew Bible.[75] It is feasible that הרו intruded into MT 59:13 from v 4, possibly due to the correspondence of ideas expressed in those two verses and the further similarity of the phrases employed in them (v 4: דבר שוא; v 13: דבר עשק). If that be the case, the combination הרו והגו would not constitute a true doublet.

However, with some grammatical license, הרו can be, and probably should be, derived from ירה, "to teach, to instruct," as was done, and correctly so, by some medieval commentators, e.g., Kimchi (in his father's name) and Rashi (as a second proposition to its derivation from ירה, "to shoot, to throw," for which he quotes Exod 15:4). הרו[76] ... דברי שקר thus would make an excellent alternative reading to הגו ... דברי שקר[77] and could well be taken as a variant notation which was conflated with the basic reading. The restored two variants individually make for a better metric structure than the present doublet:

$$\text{(ו)הרו}$$
דבר ע(ו)שק וסרה מלב דברי שקר
$$\text{(ו)הגו}$$

(d) Isa 57:18   MT: ואנחהו ואשלם > נחומים לו ולאבליו

1QIsaᵃ: > ואשלם לוא תנחומים לוא ולאבליו

The renditions of the LXX, καὶ παρεκάλεσα αὐτόν, Tg. Isa, וארחים עליהון, and Syr, וביאתה[78] convincingly show that MT ואנחהו[79] probably should be emended to read ואנחמהו (cp. BH). In that case ואנחמהו could well be a parallel variant of ואשלם נחמים לו,[80] which in this combination is not found again in the Hebrew Bible,[81] whereas the piʿel of נחם is recurrently employed in the book of Isaiah and elsewhere to describe God's reconciliatory intentions for

---

75. The noun κύησις is used in Ruth 4:13.

76. Cp. Isa 9:14; Hab 2:18, שקר (ו)מורה).

77. Cp. Isa 33:18, לבך יהגה אימה; Prov 24:2, et al.

78. The ensuing noun נחומים is translated by the same root, and so is לנחם in 61:2.

79. Retained, however, by Aq.: καὶ καθοδήγησα.

80. The LXX translate ואשלם, ἔδωκα and שים in 61:3, δοθῆναι. Did they read the same verb in both verses? An interchange between שלם and שים can be observed also in 1 Sam 2:20, MT: ישם ה' לך; 4QSamᵃ: ישלם (= LXX: ἀποτείσαι). See F. M. Cross, Jr. ("A New Qumran Biblical Fragment Related to the Original Hebrew Underlying the Septuagint," *BASOR* 132 [1953] 22).

81. The noun נחומים is found twice more in: Hos 11:8 and Zech 1:13. In Isa 66:11 תנחמים is employed, for which cp. Jer 16:7 and Job 15:11; 21:2 (תנחמות). None of those is construed with שלם.

Israel (49:13; 51:3, 12; 52:9; 61:2; 66:13; further 40:1; 54:11; 12:1). Thus the redundant ואנח(מ)הו would have to be considered a variant-gloss which intruded into the text-base of the MT (but is missing from two MSS Ken.) and resulted in a cumbersome lengthening of the second half-verse.

(e) Isa 24:22 MT: ואספו אספה אסיר על בור וסגרו על מסגר
1QIsa[a]: אספו אספה > על בור וסגרו על מסגר

On the grounds of the lopsided parallelism and the unwieldy structure of the MT, and in view of the fact that the LXX renders only ואספו. . . על בור of the first half-verse,[82] Seeligmann raised doubts as to the original authenticity of the words אספה אסיר.[83] He then hesitatingly, although to my mind correctly, suggested taking אסיר as a corrupted variant gloss of ואספו, namely ואסרו. This assumption derives further support from the Origenic and Lucianic traditions which do render אספה, but again omit אסיר: καὶ συνάξουσι συναγωγὴν αὐτῆς[84] εἰς δεσμωτήριον καὶ ἀποκλείσουσιν εἰς ὀχύρωμα. The Hebrew original of this reading, which is also reflected in Tg. Isa, ויכנשונון מכנש לבית אסירי ויעגנונון לבית עגנא (where לבית אסירי appears to equal בור), has now been recovered in 1QIsa[a], whose text at the same time witnesses to the originality of אספה.

We can therefore endorse, with only a slight adjustment, Seeligmann's conclusion that the variant notation אסרו] > אסיר[85] "must have crept into the Hebrew text during the centuries that elapsed between the composition of the Septuagint and that of the later (Greek) version," since Sym.'s rendition, as quoted by Euseb., already reflects the word in question: καὶ ἀθροισθήσονται ἀθροισμὸν δεσμίου εἰς λάκκον καὶ συγκλεισθήσονται εἰς συγκλεισμόν.

---

82. καὶ συνάξουσι καὶ ἀποκλείσουσιν εἰς ὀχύρωμα καὶ εἰς δεσμωτήριον, with על בור transferred to the end of the verse.

83. Seeligmann, *The Septuagint Version of Isaiah,* 63 (see above, n. 38).

84. The additional phrase obviously stems from Theod., as maintained by Seeligmann, ibid.

85. Possibly representing אספו אספה אסרו אסורה) or some reading like it.

In the following two instances the doublets assumedly found in the MT occur in the form of hybrid readings:

(f) Isa 63:3	MT:	וכל מלבושי אגאלתי
	1QIsaᵃ:	וכול מלבושי גאלתי

The phrase is missing in the LXX and is rendered paraphrastically in Tg. Isa, וכל חכימיהון אסלעים. Sym. and the Luc. revision restore: καὶ πάντα τὰ ἐνδύματά μου ἐμόλυνα. The queer form אגאלתי has been explained as a possible Aramaism or simply as a miswritten גאלתי (BH),[86] which latter we find now in 1QIsaᵃ.

We suggest explaining אגאלתי as a combination of אגאל (which is no longer extant) with the alternative variant גאלתי (= 1QIsaᵃ and Syr: פלפלת). The former would take up the 1 pers. imperf., which is mirrored in ואדרכם . . . . ואראמסם of the MT (cp. also . . . ויז). These words are omitted from 1QIsaᵃ, whose text here is much shorter. The latter (גאלתי) would follow the 1 pers. perf. found in דרכתי at the opening of the verse.

An identical conflation of a perf. with an imperf. form is found in the scroll reading to Isa 11:9, תמלאה; MT, מלאה.[87]

(g) Isa 23:11	MT:	ה' צוה אל כנען לשמד מעזניה
	1QIsaᵃ:	ה' צוה אל כנען להשמיד מעוזיה
	LXX:	ἀπολέσαι αὐτῆς τὴν ἰσχύν
	Tg. Isa:	לשיצאה תוקפהא

Kutscher offers the learned but unconvincing explanation of the unusual MT reading as possibly being an attempt on behalf of the prophet to employ a characteristically Phoenician pl. ending נם instead of the usual ם ending. He admits, however, that the נם ending is never found in inscriptions with an appended 3 pl. f. poss. pron.[88]

---

86. Cp. Kutscher, *Language and Linguistic Background*, 344 (see above, n. 11).
87. Cp. above, p. 98.
88. Kutscher, *Language and Linguistic Background*, 445 (see above, n. 11).

We suggest that מעניה in the MT arose from a conflation of מעוזיה[89] of 1QIsaᵃ (for which cp. in this context Isa 17:9; 23:4, 13) with a parallel reading מעוניה,[90] which is not extant for the passage under review. The synonymity of מעוז and מעון as an epithet for God can be proved:

(1) from their serving alternately in combination with a third synonym, מחסה

Joel 4:16: וה' מחסה לעמו ומעוז לבני ישראל

Ps 91:9: כי אתה ה' מחסי עליון שמת מעונך

(2) from their being employed alternately in one and the same context

Jer 16:19: ה' עזי ומעזי ומנוסי[91]

Ps 90:1: אדני מעון אתה היית לנו[92]

(3) from their being used alternately in a recurring passage

Ps 31:3: היה לי לצור מעוז

71:3: היה לי לצור מעון

In both passages a noun derived from עזז is found in the continuation: in 31:5, ואתה מחסי עז, and in 71:7, כי אתה מעוזי.

V

The coexistence at Qumran of varying text-formations of the Bible and the absence of any noticeable attempt at establishing one universally recognized recension of binding force must have confronted the Qumran scribes with the problem of what attitutde to take towards these conflicting, but not yet assessed or rated, textual traditions. The individual scribe could solve this problem by adhering faithfully to the MS which he had chosen, or had been assigned, as the *Vorlage* for his own copy. In a reasonable number of instances, such as were discussed above, he could perpetuate parallel readings which he found in other

---

89. The pl. of מעוז is found only in Dan 11:19, 38, 39.

90. The pl. מעונם from מעון is not extant in the Bible. מעונות occurs in Jer 21:13; Nah 2:13; Job 37:8; 38:40; Cant 4:8.

91. Cp. further Isa 25:4; Nah 1:7; Ps 27:1; 28:8; 37:39; et al.

92. Some MSS of the MT read here מעוז. Also a graphical confusion of ז-נ may have caused the interchange. Cp. Josh 15:29, where the MT reads ובזיותיה for the patently correct ובנותיה (= LXX, ad loc. and MT, Neh 11:27).

MSS at his disposal by noting such readings in the margins or between the lines of his own copy or, sometimes, by integrating them into his text-base. Now these devices, which were a common stock-in-trade of the ancient Bible scribes regardless of their socioreligious affiliations, are mere practical expediences that may work fairly well up to a certain point for the individual copyist but cannot satisfactorily solve the problem of the community's disposition towards divergent but equally well documented readings. In Bible MSS which are intended for public use, critical annotations must be kept to a practical minimum. In fact even these relatively few marginal entries will tend to disappear at subsequent copyings by sheer routine omission, unless they are absorbed into the text proper. Even where authoritative guidance is absent, we may find a spontaneous tendency towards the simplification and the stabilization of the textual traditions of the Holy Writ and other hallowed books. This process cannot be expected to culminate in complete unification,[93] but it will effectively circumscribe the scope and reduce the number of textual types which are allowed a continued existence until, if ever, conscious official redactional activities set in.

The impending gradual disappearance of variant readings, which on objective grounds could not be declared to be intrinsically inferior to those which happened to have taken root in the predominant textual traditions, may well have been viewed with misgivings by those concerned with the preservation of scripture. The practical advantage of perpetuating a fairly standardized text-type for communal-cultic purposes was offset by an understandable apprehension for the unrecoverable loss of what were, to all appearances, valid and venerated textual traditions of the biblical books, which per force would result from the above-outlined process.[94] Contradictory as it may sound, such pro and con deliberations seem to have produced diverse techniques of non-manuscript variant preservation. This helped to balance the lopsided weight given to the favored text-tradition(s) which had become increasingly predominant, to the exclusion of, and even complete suppression of, less-favored *variae lectiones*. Here again a comparison with the attitudes and techniques that were current in the normative community is in order.

93. Cp. DRMT, 146-50.
94. In all languages one perceives a tendency to conserve spelling and pronunciation habits and also textual formulations in the face of modernizing trends. This tendency may have religious or nationalist motivations or may result from scribal inertia. Cp. L. Bloomfield, *Language* (8th edition; New York: Holt, Rinehart, & Winston, 1961) 291 ff.

The prevalence of trends of thought in rabbinic circles, such as were outlined above, may have been responsible for the sages' perceptible latitude about the employment of a Bible text in scholarly discussion which contrasted conspicuously with their unceasing efforts to establish an exclusive *textus receptus* for public worship and for official text-transmission. Whereas deviant readings were banned from books which were earmarked for these latter categories, they were readily accepted and used as bases for midrashic exposition.[95] In fact at times it appears that such an officially discarded variant was not employed merely as a convenient peg upon which to hang a midrash that was on hand, but rather that the midrash in question was constructed on a variant that had been barred from the *textus receptus* in order to give it a non-manuscript lease on life. This supposition especially applies to the specific type of the midrash,[96] in which an established text is suspended, as it were, and another reading becomes the point of departure for an ensuing midrashic comment, by means of the introductory formula: "do not read . . . , but rather read. . . ." A famous case in point is the *'al tiqrê* midrash (*b. Ber.* 64a), which hinges on reading in Isa 54:13, בוניך, "your builders," instead of the MT, בניך, "your sons" (cp. LXX: τέκνα; Tg. Isa: בנך), a variant which now has turned up in 1QIsaᵃ as an emended reading: נ̇יכי̇ב.[97]

Similarly the midrash, זרעו (בשר) זרועו אלא (בשר) אל תקרי (*b. Šabb.* 33a),[98] can be anchored in the different textual traditions of Isa 9:19. Here the MT (= 1QIsaᵃ) reading, איש בשר זר(ו)עו י(ו)אכלו, "they shall eat every man the flesh of his own arm" (LXX: τοῦ βραχίονος αὐτοῦ), is abandoned, as it were, for a variant זרעו, "his offspring," which underlies Tg. Isa's paraphrastic rendering, גבר נכסי קריביה ייבזון, and Sym.'s rendition τοῦ πλησίου αὐτοῦ. Both readings

---

95. Cp. TSL, 14-15.
96. נ״ה טורשינר, אל תקרי, אשכול, אנציקלופדיה ישראלית ב' (1932) 386-94.
97. Cp. Kutscher (*Language and Linguisic Background*, 225 [see above, n. 11]), who points out that the midrash appears to echo the reading of 1QIsaᵃ and stresses the fact that the first בניך in the MT of Isa 54:13 was retained in 1QIsaᵃ. Again in 49:17 1QIsaᵃ reads בוניכי instead of MT, בניך. But there the copyist may have been influenced by the context. See H. M. Orlinsky ("של מחקרים במגילת ישעיהו מנזר סאנט מארק," *Tarbiz* 24 [1954] 4-9). Cp. further the midrashic comments in *b. Soṭa* 12b on 1 Chr 2:18 and in *Cant. Rab.* 137 on Cant 1:5, where בוניה respectively בונות is implied instead of the MT, בניה, respectively בנות. See also D. Flusser ("The Text of Isa. xlix,17 in the DSS," *Textus* 2 [1962] 140).
98. Cp. Yalqut on Isaiah, ad loc. (ed. J. Spira, 75), et al.

seemingly were conflated in the mainspring of LXX^{AB}, τοῦ βραχίονος τοῦ ἀδελφοῦ αὐτοῦ.

We do not propose that every extant *ʾal tiqrê* midrash can be shown to have arisen from a textual variant which is still identifiable. This certainly is not the case. *Variae lectiones* which supposedly triggered the emergence of many a midrash of this type have been lost to us, together with the (suppressed) MSS which exhibited them.

Here is a possible example. Isa 2:22 (missing in the LXX) warns against reliance on man, "for wherein is he to be accounted of," כִּי בַמֶּה נֶחְשָׁב הוּא. The Masoretic Text reading בַמֶּה is reflected in Tg. Isa, וכלמא חשיב הוא; Syr, מטל דאיך מנא חשיב; and Aq., ἐν τίνι ἐλογίσθη αὐτός. Now this phrase, among others, is employed in an *ʾal tiqrê* midrashic comment on Prov 16:5 (*b. Soṭa* 4b) as proof that "everyone that is proud in heart is an abomination to the Lord: 'Ula said [he is considered] as if he had built a *bamah*,'" and then goes on to quote Isa 2:22, winding up with, אל תקרי במֶה אלא בָמָה. At first glance it appears that here a mere different vocalization of the same consonantal group is involved.

But the fact that the point of departure for the exposition in question is a biblical proverb which castigates "the proud in heart," suggests another possibility: an interchange between ב and ר, with the resulting reading רמה in Isa 2:22. This word can be construed as a (synonymous) parallel of במה (Ezek 16:24, 25, 31, 39) and in fact sometimes is textually confused with it (Judg 4:5 MT, רמה; G^B, βαμα; 1 Sam 22:6 MT, רמה; G^{BL}, במה; cp. DRMT, 157-58). Or else רמה can be derived from רום, "to be exalted." In an association with גבה לב (Prov 16:5), this would bring to mind the expression רום (לב), *hybris,* which is recurrently referred to in Isa 2:11, 12, 17, adjacent to במה in 2:22. Interestingly this latter concept emerges in the V rendition of Isa 2:22, *excelsus reputatus est ipse,* which accordingly may also be based on a reading רמה.[99]

Moreover this specific type of midrash progressively degenerated, and ultimately the *ʾal tiqrê* formula often was employed, even when the midrash in question could not be related to an actually extant reading, by definition originally a *sine qua non* requirement, and had become a mere exegetical

---

99. Cp. B. Kedar's remarks in "Divergent Hebrew Readings in Jerome's Isaiah" (*Textus* 4 [1964] 183).

Spielelement.[100] Vice versa, the introductory formula of a genuine *ʾal tiqrê* midrash often was dropped, so that now the same exposition is sometimes preserved in parallel versions, both with and without that formula.[101]

These short remarks which are intended but to sketch cursorily the genesis and some phases of development of the *ʾal tiqrê* midrash lead one to presuppose the existence of a transition stage from manuscript notation to extra-manuscript midrashic preservation of biblical variant readings. It appears that these aspects of text-transmission can still be traced in Qumran writings.

A few comments on the textual character of the variants which assumedly underlie the *ʾal tiqrê* midrash, and many a midrash not so designated, are called for before we enter into a discussion of the pertinent Qumran material.

In a majority of cases the textual variations involved are of the simplest and most common types: interchange of graphically similar letters or of auricularly close consonants; haplography or dittography; continuous writing of separate words or division of one word into two; plene or defective spelling; metathesis, differences of vocalization, sometimes entailing a change of verb conjugation. Some cases of more complicated textual phenomena do not affect the overall impression.

With respect to the issue at hand, we note that only under exceptionally favorable circumstances can we hope to find the very same reading recorded both as a variant-notation in a Hebrew manuscript that is still extant or as a double-translation in one of the VSS, and at the same time also in its non-manuscript form as the basis of an *ʾal tiqrê* midrash. Such a propitious concurrence of independent evidence characterizes the following instance, although in the midrashic factor the *ʾal tiqrê* formula is not present.

100. This and related techniques of variation on biblical themes in midrash exegesis were discussed and illustrated by I. L. Seeligmann in his valuable study "Voraussetzungen der Midraschexegese" ([VTSup; Leiden: Brill,1953], 1. 150-81, esp. 159-60).

101. The Sam. variant in Num 11:32, (ה)שחוטו להם וישחטו (ed. Blayney), as against the MT, שטוח להם וישטחו, is reflected in an *ʾal tiqrê* midrash in Sifre Num. § 98 (ed. Friedmann, 26b), which is adduced *in extenso* without the introductory formula in *b. Yoma* 75b; *y. Nazir* 4 53c, and in Yalqut Shimʿoni I, 635 on Num 11:32. Another Sam. variant in Exod 12:17, המצוה את ושמרתם (= LXX: καὶ φυλάξεσθε τὴν ἐντολὴν ταύτην), as against the MT, המצות את, appears to underlie the *ʾal tiqrê* midrash (cp. Rashi, ad loc.) in Mekilta d'Rabbi Ishmael, Tractate Pisḥa, chap. 9 (ed. Horowitz-Rabin, 32; ed. Lauterbach, 74), which again is quoted without the formula in Mekilta d'Rabbi Shimʿon b. Yoḥai (ed. Epstein-Melamed, 22:3); cp. further Rashi to *b. Yoma* 33a; *Meg.* 6b.

In this case a double-translation of the two letters אל in the LXX (and possibly also in Tg. Isa) to Ps 29:1 is involved. The crucial passage in the MT, הבו לה׳ בני אלים, is rendered by the Greek translator (28:1):

$$\text{ἐνέγκατε τῷ κυρίῳ υἱοὶ θεοῦ}$$
$$\text{ἐνέγκατε τῷ κυρίῳ υἱοὺς κριῶν,}$$

and by Tg. Isa: הבון קדם י״י תושבחתא כתי מלאכיא בני אלים.

Here the first line in the LXX and the first phrase in Tg. Isa conceive of the underlying Hebrew text as of an invitation to divine beings, υἱοὶ θεοῦ, כתי מלאכיא, to praise God (תושבחתא), taking אלים (בני) in the vocative as a pl. of the common noun אל = "god" (cp. Exod 15:11; Ps 89:7; Dan 11:36; et al.). In its general meaning the passage thus may be compared, e.g., with Ps 97:7 and Job 38:7, to which latter also Ibn Ezra (ad loc.) alludes. This most natural explanation is further reflected in the rabbinic tradition which identifies בני אלים as "angels," מלאכי שרת.[102] However the second rendition of the LXX, υἱοὺς κριῶν, clearly derives from the plene spelling בני אילים = "(young) rams" (for which cp. בן ראמים in v 6), construed as the syntactical object and paralleling כבוד ועז in the second half-verse. The same possibly also applies to the redundant בני אלים in Tg. Isa, and certainly to Jerome's translation, *adferte filios arietum.*

The above evidence indicates that the variant spelling אילים at some time or other was extant in manuscripts and was retained in the extra-masoretic Greek tradition in the form of a variant-notation (cp. also Tg. Isa). In the masoretic manuscript tradition, with the exception of some odd copies, this variant-reading אילים was discarded. But it did enjoy a midrashic after-life. Shoḥer Tov (ed. Buber, 116, ad Ps 29:1) relates בני אלים to Israel, who are likened to helpless sheep over whom God will appoint David as shepherd; or again, and this time more in line with the Greek-Latin conception, presents Israel as "the sons of men slaughtered like sheep. Abraham said: I slaughter; Isaac said: I am slaughtered."

As already stated this example is a rare case in which are yet preserved both ends of the transition process: the textual variant-notation in the form of a doublet in one (set of) extra-MT witness(es), side by side with the rabbinic

---

102. Cp. Seder Eliahu Rab., chap. 2 (ed. Friedmann, 12).

tradition in which the variant that was ejected from the MT was made the basis of a midrash. However, ordinarily we shall have to content ourselves with illustrating the transition from one phase to the other by drawing on examples which individually reflect only one of them but which, if viewed in conjunction, typologically represent the transition-process *in toto*.

We can now revert to the double-reading in 1QIsaᵃ 38:19, which was discussed above (p. 88) and in which we seem to discern the typical characteristics of a potential *ʾal tiqrê* midrash. Again the pregnant consonant combination אל is involved. As noted, 1QIsaᵃ here records in its text-base the variant והודיע אלוה אמתך alongside יודיע אל אמתכה, which is the reading found in the MT.

The transition from MT אֶל to 1QIsaᵃ אלוה, or vice versa, may be considered as textually exceedingly simple, especially since a potential intermediate stage, אלה, is yet extant in 1QIsaᵇ. Thus we may take as certain the manuscript coexistence, towards the end of the Second Temple Period, of the above three readings which most probably derived from one another, either in the order אל → אלה → אֱלוֹהַּ or אלוה → אלה → אל or אלה ← אלוה → אֶל. The problem of the actual historical development is of no relevance to the present issue. The scribe of 1QIsaᵃ obviously did not feel competent to decide on the respective merits of אל and אל(ו)ה, or else deemed both worthy of preservation and therefore, rather than choosing between them, integrated the two readings in the text of his copy.

At this juncture we are well within the phase of manuscript variants-notation, which, however, took place in one witness only, viz., 1QIsaᵃ, whereas in our other Hebrew sources and in the ancient VSS, a decision was reached as to the retention of one reading and the rejection of the other(s). Now it does not require much imagination to visualize the discarded variant אלוה cropping up in midrashic literature in the formulation: אל תקרי אל אלא אלוה. True, such a midrash, to my knowledge, is not extant, but it would have been in the very best tradition of the type to embark on an exposition which utilizes the simple graphic or linguistic variation אלוה—אלה—אל, which was found in biblical MSS for the fashioning of an exegetical comment with theological or ideological undertones.

This pattern of development can indeed be observed in Qumran writings of the pesher-type which share many features with the Rabbinic midrash, without being identical to it. In this setting we can perceive the simultaneous utilization of variant readings for expository purposes when only one of the given possibilities is quoted as actual scripture. Here are three illustrations of the phenomenon in question.

(a) Hab 1:11, MT, אז חלף רוח ויעבר וְאָשֵׁם זו כחו לאלהו, is quoted as וישם זה כוחו לאלהו in 1QpHab iv 9,10. The MT reading, which derives אשם from אשם, "to be guilty," is supported by the LXX, ἐξιλάσεται and Tg. Isa, וחב. In the ensuing comment, which is based on the first part of the above scripture, 1QpHab clearly shows acquaintance both with its own biblical reading and also with that of the MT (LXX, Tg. Isa) and with the masoretic sentence division: (a) פשרו על מושלי הכתיאים אשר בעצת בית אשמ[תם] יעבירו איש מלפני רעהו ... [?]. (b) מושלי[הם אחר זה ז]ה אחר זה יבואו לשחית את ה[ארץ]. The second pesher, (b), in which the salient word is לשחית, "to despoil, to lay waste," in all probability mirrors וישם of the *Vorlage* from which 1QpHab quoted, the verb being understood as derived from שמם. The first exposition (a), in which בית [אשמ]תם, "[their] house of guilt," is the pivotal expression, obviously is based on אָשֵׁם, found in the MT, which reading, however, is not explicitly quoted. Nevertheless, it is possible that this very reading actually was subsequently adduced in 1QpHab iv 14-15,[103] where another pesher is introduced but was lost for us in a lacuna: ז]ה אחר זה יבואו לשחית את ה[ארץ?   ז]ה כוחו לאלהו פשרו .... If this indeed can be maintained, we would have here what amounts to a variant-notation, in quotation, together with two midrash-like expositions which are based alternately, first on the one and then on the other of the parallel variants.

(b) Hab 2:16, MT, שתה גם אתה והערל, "drink, and *uncover* yourself,"[104] is quoted in 1QpHab xi 9 as שתה גם אתה והרעל, "drink, and become *intoxicated*," a change of concept which may have resulted from a simple metathesis. Here the MT is supported by Tg. Isa, and 1QpHab by the LXX,[105] Aq., and Syr.

---

103. Unless we assume that in this instance the Qumran author quoted only the second part of the verse, starting with [וישם] (unlike the masoretic sentence-division) and now deriving the word from שים.

104. This appears to be the required translation of the phrase, rather than RV "and be as one uncircumcised." ערל here should be taken in the meaning of ערם. The metaphor is rooted in a situation like the one described in the tale of Noah's drunkenness (Gen 9:2), which may well have been in the back of the prophet's mind. In addition to the above similarity, cp. Hab 2:17, יכסך, with Gen 9:23, ערות אביהם לא ראו. Cp. Hab 2:15, למען הביט על מעוריהם, with Gen 9:23, ויכסו; further Lam 4:21.

105. Which presents a double-translation, διασαλεύθητι καὶ σείσθητι. Cp. M. Stenzel, "Habakuk II," *VT* 3 (1953) 97-99.

The interesting feature of this example is that, notwithstanding his own reading, והרעל, the author of 1QpHab sets his pesher to the tune of the MT variant, והערל, in its obvious (but in Hab 2:16, unsuitable) derivation from the root ערל, "uncircumcised": כי לוא מל את ערלת לבו, "he did not circumcise (the foreskin of) his heart." Without employing the exact formula, the pesher exhibits here the technical intricacies which characterize the rabbinic ʾal tiqrê midrash. We observe a similar suspension of an explicit Qumran reading in favor of an extra-Qumran variant which becomes the departure point for a midrashic exposition.

The same factors seem to have been at work in the following instance, in which, however, the actual biblical quotation was lost in a lacuna and has to be restored by inference.

(c) The first word of 1QpHab ii 1, יסופר, preceded by a lacuna at the lower margin of col. i, is the end of a quotation of Hab 1:5, a verse which in the MT opens, ראו בגוים והביטו, "Behold among the *nations,* and regard. . . . " The pesher, which is only partially preserved, never mentions the word בגוים, "nations," but instead refers three times in a row to *"the traitors,"* הבוגדים. It certainly can be postulated, as is done by I. L. Seeligmann,[106] that the biblical *Vorlage* with which the author of 1QpHab was familiar in fact contained the *varia lectio* הבוגדים. But one could also postulate that 1QpHab presents here a typical variant-midrash. Bypassing the reading בגוים, which he actually may have quoted, the author anchored his actualizing paraphrase in a parallel variant, בבוגדים, which he found in a manuscript of the text-type that seems to underlie the LXX's οἱ καταφρονηταί.[107] Thus the emerging situation would be comparable to what we encountered in the previous example.

The foregoing analysis leads us to conclude that the category of the variant-midrash which in rabbinic literature is best, though not exclusively, represented by the ʾal tiqrê type, is exemplified in the Qumran writings by the variant-pesher. The Qumran material thus offers proof for the high antiquity of this midrashic category. At the same time the combined evidence of Qumran and rabbinic techniques proves the contention that variant readings in the biblical

---

106. In his review of K. Elliger, *Studien zum Habakkuk Commentar vom Toten Meer* (Tübingen: Mohr, 1953) in *Kiryat-Sefer* 30 (1954) 40.

107. It is of interest to notice that a similar pair of variants may be observed in Prov 10:3, where the Ben Chayim edition and some MSS read בוגדים instead of רשעים, which is found in other MSS and printed editions and also underlies the VSS.

textual traditions were viewed with relative equanimity by both groups and even were perpetuated by diverse manuscript and non-manuscript devices.

This conclusion opens up a new avenue of approach to the problem of the genesis and the early history of the *kethib-qere* variants, an issue which we hope to discuss in a separate publication.

OBSERVATIONS ON VARIANT READINGS IN THE ISAIAH SCROLL (1QIsa^a)

I

The discovery of the first scrolls from the Judean Desert, especially those containing biblical texts, immediately raised the problem of the textual relationship between the newly found MSS and the MT. The attention of scholars was drawn particularly to 1QIsa^a[1] on account of its completeness and the large number of variant readings it presented. The antiquity of the scroll, which on paleographic grounds was dated to before the destruction of the Second Temple, naturally enhanced the interest of this MS. It certainly provides us with enlightening material on the form—or on one of the forms—of the text of Isaiah as it was then known, before it assumed the textual structure which was later standardized as the "Masoretic Text."

We can distinguish two modes of approach to the study of 1QIsa^a:

(1) In order to understand the character of the new scroll, a close scrutiny and classification of the variant readings was needed to determine which were important and which were merely trivial. The aim was to differentiate those variants which were to be regarded as mere corruptions or errors from those which were variant readings in the full sense of the term, i.e., readings peculiar to 1QIsa^a which could claim consideration equal to their parallels in the MT.

(2) Since 1QIsa^a, and likewise all the other biblical MSS discovered, were soon recognized as texts which had been produced outside the orbit of mainstream Judaism, it was quite natural to compare them with other known witnesses to the biblical text which diverged from rabbinic tradition and preserved linguistic, stylistic and textual peculiarities which were not to be found in the MT.

---

1. M. Burrows, *The Dead Sea Scrolls of St. Mark's Monastery* (2 vols.; New Haven: ASOR, 1950), vol. 1.

A preliminary classification of the differences between the scroll and the MT was undertaken by the editor of the MS, M. Burrows,[2] who summarized the results of his examination as follows: "Differing notably in orthography and somewhat in morphology, it agrees with the MT to a remarkable degree in wording. Herein lies its chief importance, supporting the fidelity of the Masoretic tradition."[3]

Burrows' conclusions must indeed carry some weight, but his sweeping generalization does not do justice to the matter. It is just because both texts are so similar that their divergences arouse special interest.[4] As in any other case of comparative textual criticism, one can distinguish in 1QIsa[a] two principal categories of variant readings:

(1) those variants which appear to have a conscious and systematic character;

(2) those arising from inadvertence, which lack any consistency or legitimacy.

Under the first head we can subsume several sub-groups, each of which is to be further divided into various branches, viz.:

(1) textual differences and additions[5] containing exegetical or explanatory matter;

(2) variants which reveal the scribe's ideological or societal idiosyncracies, the tendential nature of which is evident at a glance;

(3) differences in morphology and syntax which yield information about linguistic phenomena characteristic of the copyist's period or of the social stratum to which he belonged.

Concerning these phenomena, general principles can be established which pertain to a number of particular cases. Sometimes one can even anticipate a certain variant in a given context. Generally speaking the scribe's practice is not consistent, since he owes allegiance to two masters. In matters of language, for example, he is obliged to follow the ancient text as it is placed before him or dictated to him, but at the same time he is under the influence of the linguistic

2. "Variant Readings in the Isaiah Manuscript," *BASOR* 111 (1948) 16-24; *BASOR* 113 (1949) 24-34.

3. Burrows, *BASOR* 111 (1948) 16, 17.

4. P. Kahle, *Die hebräischen Handschriften aus der Höhle* (Stuttgart: Kohlhammer, 1951) 26-30.

5. "Additions" from the standpoint of the MT. It is, of course, possible that the additional matter may be merely an indication that something has been omitted in the MT.

usages familiar to him in everyday speech. For this reason, 1QIsa[a] is not a homogenous MS. It exhibits a mixture of distinctive traits, which are the result of "hobbling on two sticks," or sometimes even more than two.

Also the second category can be divided into sub-classes. The actual determination of the variants included in it as products of inattentiveness requires that such classification must always be empirical, without the possibility of drawing inductive conclusions.

What is the issue at stake? It can be assumed that the scribe who is accustomed to using an unabbreviated form of the imperative and future of the verb, e.g., דרושו[6] ותחפיורו,[7] will do so in most cases when the verb occurs in the future tense.[8] This does not apply to cases in which the verb has been misspelled as a result of having been misheard or miscopied, where the copyist's memory has been at fault, or where the copyist wrote carelessly. This area is completely reduced to blind chance. Even if one can classify such errors according to their presumed causes, such a classification does not allow the deduction of a principle applicable to the example or examples being considered at any given moment.

A feature common to both these categories is their disqualification as evidence for the original form of the book of Isaiah, since they are not primary but secondary sources, the result of a development or of conflation which distorted the original text on which they were based. Textual variants in 1QIsa[a] of the kinds under review certainly cannot be given priority over MT readings.

So far scholars will not disagree either over the principle or over the contention that there are many variant readings in 1QIsa[a] which fall under these headings and bear no relation to the MT. But from here it is still a far cry to the pronouncement that 1QIsa[a] has no textual value whatever. H. Orlinsky's description of the scroll as "an unreliable oral variation on the theme of what came to be known as the masoretic text of Isaiah" would hardly seem to be a well-considered opinion, since it is based only on partial evidence, namely the two kinds of variants which we have indicated above, or, more precisely, on the

---

6.   Isa 1:17. Cp. also אמורו (3:10); שפוטונה (5:3); and many other such instances.

7.   Isa 1:29. Cp. also יחלופו (2:18;); ימשולו (3:4); ויסקולהו (5:2). All these occur in the middle of a verse and not at its end.

8.   It should be stressed once again that the scribe's practice is not completely uniform. An abbreviated form is frequently found alongside unabbreviated forms, even in the same passage. Thus, e.g., ויקו alongside ויעשה (5:2); or ויט ידו alongside ותהיה נבלתם (5:25).

second of them. But not all the variants which occur in 1QIsa[a] can be explained by the statement that

> in addition to faulty copying and spelling, faulty memory was at work. That is to say, the Hebrew text of St. Mark's is utterly unreliable not because it was copied from memory, but because the memory of the person who brought it into being (as well as of the scribes who did the writing and copying) was faulty.[9]

Apparently Orlinsky himself withdrew somewhat from his original uncompromising stance and softened his judgment by saying: "the masoretic expression must be regarded as the preferred and original reading unless and until the St. Mark's variant is demonstrated on quite independent grounds (e.g., on the basis of style, content, versions) to be a) a legitimate variant and b) the superior reading."[10]

It is therefore appropriate that we should examine each particular variant in 1QIsa[a] on its merits and not judge all variants on the basis of general preconceptions as a ragbag of the copyists' slips of memory or of scribal errors. We should first investigate whether all those textual variants in 1QIsa[a] which cannot be explained as being tendentious do indeed fall under the description of "scribal errors and copyists' mistakes." Perhaps we shall find that some kinds of variant readings cannot be grouped under either of the two principal categories mentioned above. The result of this inquiry seems to us to be positive, so that our discussion will turn upon the third category of textual variants, which we shall henceforth call "synonymous readings." We begin by excluding from our study all those variants which were introduced into the MS in order to correct or improve a passage which appeared to the scribe to require correction or improvement. Likewise we shall not deal with all those variants which can be recognized at a glance as scribal errors. Errors of this kind can, generally speaking, be summed up either as inversion, or as omission of letters or words or even whole parts of sentences. All such readings are quite definitely excluded from serving as evidence for the original form of the book of Isaiah.

9. H. M. Orlinsky, "Studies in the St. Mark's Isaiah Scroll," *JBL* 69 (1950) 165.
10. Ibid., 166, n. 8.

The case is different with regard to the many instances in which one phrase is substituted for another without detriment to the sense of the passage or to its syntactical and logical integrity. It is highly probable that in this area also the scribe was influenced by current linguistic usage to alter the text before him, either intentionally or unintentionally. Nevertheless, it would seem that one cannot legitimately assume that all these instances of phrase-substitution are due to the faulty memories of the scribes, as Orlinsky holds, and on this ground discount the value of the scroll as independent evidence for the textual form of the book of Isaiah.

Even if one accepts Orlinsky's view that the scroll was written from memory, one must necessarily admit that this assumption alone does not explain all the variant readings which occur in it. Slips of memory may also work according to certain principles. Anyone who alters a phrase as a result of incorrectly remembering the text which he is writing or quoting will replace an uncommon word by one more commonly used or a rare grammatical form by its more current equivalent, or he will impose a uniform pattern on phrases which recur in the text—the phenomenon usually termed "harmonization."

Anyone who alters the text, especially if he does so inadvertently, will tend in the direction of what is normal and accepted. Hence it follows that whenever we find cases in which the scroll has a rare word or phrase in place of a more usual one in MT, we can conjecture that it is not a "lapse of memory" that has caused the divergence.[11] It is preferable to assume that in such a case the copyist was not misled by his faulty memory, but that objective factors caused him to write what he wrote, i.e., that he copied his *Vorlage* correctly. If so, then variants of this kind are not attributable to the copyist's faulty memory; they are more likely to be a faithful reflection of an early text. We must therefore accept such a reading as parallel in authenticity to that of MT, carrying equal weight and having equal value. One cannot determine *a priori* which reading is the original and which the derivative. Borrowing a term from the study of biblical

11. The decision about what is rare and what is common, what is usual and what is unusual for the scribe of 1QIsaᵃ can be determined by a study of the actual text of the book of Isaiah and in relation to the language of the social circle in which the scribe lived and worked, insofar as this is revealed in the writings of the Covenanters. See below.

style, we have given the name "synonymous readings" to this particular phenomenon.

This term is used to denote parallel variants in two witnesses to a biblical text, which differ over the choice of certain elements in synonymous phrases that are interchangeable in Hebrew.[12] The class of synonymous readings will include only those variants which do not affect the subject matter of the text, are derived correctly according to Hebrew grammatical and stylistic rules, cannot be accounted for as being deliberate or due to slips of the pen or lapses of memory, and (as far as our knowledge goes) do not spring from different linguistic strata distinguishable from one another in point of time, place, or class in society.

It would seem that the synonymous readings in 1QIsa[a] are remains of parallel forms of the text which were current at a period prior to the establishment of an official, uniform text of the book of Isaiah. They belong to the early stages of the text-tradition and originated when the essential core of the of the content and wording of the book of Isaiah had already been determined. At that point the scribe or oral tradent was still free to make alterations in details, especially to choose at will synonymous words or phrases where they did not make any substantial difference to the meaning.

II

In order to prove the soundness of his contention that 1QIsa[a] is merely "an oral variation of the text-tradition known as MT during the second half of the first millennium B.C.E.," Orlinsky discusses at length the verse, "The vile person will speak villainy and his heart will work [יעשה] iniquity" (Isa 32:6), where the scroll reads, "The vile person will speak villainy and his heart will devise [חושב] iniquity." Many scholars had proposed to restore this alternative reading in the Hebrew text before the discovery of the scroll confirmed it, on the strength of the LXX reading, νοήσει, and the Aramaic Targum, which reads מתעשתין. The scroll text is thus borne out *prima facie* by two important sources of evidence, as well as by the sense of the passage. This would mean that the

---

12. We are restricting the use of the term "synonymous readings" to the sphere of lexis, although its meaning is wider and can also be applied also in the fields of morphology and syntax.

scroll text is ancient, most probably older than the strange reading, "his heart will work iniquity," preserved in the MT.

Here Orlinsky actually succeeds in giving convincing proof that the MT reading is, after all, to be preferred.

(1) A study of biblical style shows that the phrase "his heart will work iniquity" is merely an abbreviated form meaning "his heart will plan to work iniquity," as we find it in Ps 58:3, "in your heart you work wickedness."

(2) It was naturally difficult for translators to render the phrase "his heart will work iniquity" into other languages, and they therefore gave it various interpretations. Hence LXX has νοήσει and the Targum מתעשׂתין. So too 1QIsa[a] gives the interpretation חושב.

(3) Thus the ancient versions did not translate an ancient variant reading but were simply "explaining" the MT. Proof of this can be found in the fact that the LXX always render the verb חשב in the book of Isaiah as λογίζομαι, while the Targum uses the root חשב. This means that if in the present case they found it necessary to vary their usual practice by translating νοήσει and מתעשׂתין, we have here evidence that they did not read "his heart devises [חושב] iniquity" in the Hebrew original before them.[13] This being so, it is probable that "his heart will devise iniquity" is not an ancient, independent reading but a gloss or explanation which found its way into the LXX, the Targum, and also 1QIsa[a].

In his discussion of the above example, Orlinsky correctly points out that, when we come to examine a reading which diverges from the MT, we must not be satisfied with merely considering the passage in isolation, but must take into consideration all the parallel linguistic usages in the book under discussion, in order to understand the ancient translator's *modus operandi*. It is only in the light of such an examination that we shall be able to decide whether the divergent reading in the version springs from a need to explain the original, or whether it originated in an ancient Hebrew reading.[14]

In order to determine the factors that caused the MT reading to be changed in 1QIsa[a], we are required to examine the use of the phrase employed by the writer of the scroll, as well as that of the parallel phrase in the MT which he apparently rejected, both in the book of Isaiah and in Qumran literature, so as to understand the place of such phrases in the scribe's linguistic tradition.

13. Orlinsky, *JBL* 69 (1950) 152-55.
14. Ibid., 154.

III

Among the "substitution" group of parallel phrases and other variants to be attributed to "lapses of memory," M. Burrows cites the verse, "This people I created for myself that they might recount [יספרו] my praise" (Isa 43:21),[15] which appears in the scroll in the form: "that they might tell [יומרו] my praise."[16] According to Orlinsky, this passage serves as a further proof of his assumption that the scroll was written from memory as an oral variation on the MT.[17]

But is this really the case? Is it permissible to draw an analogy between the previous example and the present one? An investigation shows that the scribe of 1QIsa^a introduced an unusual reading into the text, whereas the MT uses a common and normal biblical expression. We find the phrase ספר תהלה four times in the book of Psalms: 9:15; 78:4; 79:13; 102:22. Of similar phrases one may cite (twice each): הגיד תהלה (Isa 42:12; Ps 51:17); שיר תהלה (Ps 106:12; 149:1); and (once each) the following phrases: הזכיר תהלה (Isa 63:7); הגה תהלה (Ps 35:28); הביע תהלה (Isa 60:6); בשר תהלה (Ps 119:171); and דבר תהלה (Ps 145:21).[18]

Hence we learn that Biblical Hebrew offered an extremely variegated choice of verbs to govern the object "praise," and these occur interchangeably in psalmodic literature. But among all these we have not once found the combination אמר תהלה. This means that if the scribe of 1QIsa^a suffered a lapse of memory, he was not distracted by remembering normal biblical phraseology, but rather departed from it to choose an expression which has no parallel in the biblical writings. If we are to assume that these readings are not independent of one another but that one was developed from another, then it is correct to give preference to 1QIsa^a according to reasoning employed by Orlinsky in reference to another variant in the scroll: "since יריע and יודיע[19] are scarcely independent

---

15. M. Burrows, *BASOR* 111 (1948) 27.
16. This reading also occurs in 1QIsa^b. See A.L. Sukenik, *Megillot Genuzot* (Jerusalem: Bialik, 1948),1. 43. The text of this scroll approximates to the MT.
17. Orlinsky, *JBL* 69 (1950) 156-57.
18. The phrase השתבח [ב]תהלה comes close to these expressions. See Ps 106:47 and 1 Chr 16:35.
19. Isa 42:13, MT, "He will cry [יריע]; he will shout aloud"; 1QIsa^a, "He will make known [יודיע]; he will shout aloud."

variants, it is much more likely that the rarer יריע became the far more common יודיע than vice versa."[20]

Furthermore, it is a surprising fact that the scribe of 1QIsa[a] apparently suffered a lapse of memory in the case of the common phrase ספר תהלה, substituting for it אמר תהלה inadvertently or on his own initiative. In three other passages he gives the actual reading of the MT: "יגידו his praise in the islands" (Isa 42:12); "יבשרו the praises of the LORD" (Isa 60:6); "אזכיר . . . the praises of the LORD" (Isa 63:7). We should further stress that two of these combinations, viz., הזכיר תהלה and בשר תהלה are peculiar to the author of the book of Isaiah and do not occur elsewhere in the Bible.[21] Can one attribute to the scribe of 1QIsa[a] such carelessness and forgetfulness of a common phrase as to replace it by a collocation which has no parallel in biblical literature, when he "remembers," and reproduces correctiy three other passages in which the author of the book of Isaiah chose to employ an especially rare expression which does not occur anywhere in the Hebrew Bible?

It is impossible to draw definite conclusions about the Hebrew language and its phraseology from the biblical writings that have been preserved, since this corpus is only a part of the ancient Hebrew literature and does not afford conclusive evidence for the style of Hebrew, spoken or written, in those days. It is therefore advisable to seek additional sources which may help us in solving the problem of whether, in the substitution of יומרו תהלתי for יספרו תהלתי, there may be a tendency to follow a locution current at the time of writing.

The most promising course is to examine other Qumran documents for such linguistic peculiarities. This examination does not yield a rich harvest, since to the best of my knowledge a combination including the word תהלה occurs only once in the Qumran writings, viz., in a fragment of 1QM.

There we find another expression which is also without parallel in Scripture: ירננו כולם את תהלת המשיב.[22] This phrase provides a new verb which we may add to the list of those used in the Bible in connection with תהלה.

But words approximating to תהלה and synonymous with it are to be found in the Qumran writings in conjunction with the very verb ספר. Instead of תהלת

20. Orlinsky, *JBL* 69 (1950) 166, n. 22.
21. All the examples cited above are taken from the second part of the scroll. Kahle, as is well-known, distinguished two "hands" in the scroll; the former wrote as far as chap. 33, and the latter continued from this point. Kahle, *Die hebräischen Handschriften,* 72-76.
22. Sukenik, *Megillot Genuzot* 1, 24.

אלהים, the Qumran writings sometimes have the phrase צדקות אל.²³ Thus in the psalm with which 1QS concludes, we find, "my tongue shall continually recount [תספר] the just deeds of God."²⁴ So also, by way of antithesis, "the priests recount God's just deeds," while "the Levites recount the iniquities of the children of Israel."²⁵ Such expressions confirm the assumption that the technical term "to recount [ספר] praise/just deeds/iniquity" in a cultic recital was current among the Covenanters, who, to judge by all indications, were nurtured in the language of the Bible, especially that of the book of Psalms.²⁶ Hence it is inconceivable that the scribe of 1QIsaᵃ, through a fault of memory, could have changed the familiar phrase ספר תהלה into אמר תהלה, which has no parallel either in biblical literature or in the Qumran writings.

We have here, rather, a case of "synonymous readings" which may have originated when the text of the book of Isaiah came into existence and persisted separately in the MT and in 1QIsaᵃ. There is no question here of two readings, one of which evolved from the other, nor is either dependent upon the other. It is impossible to determine which of the two is the earlier or is to be preferred. Two textual traditions of equal value have been preserved for us. When the archetypal text of the MT came to be accepted officially, and MSS containing deviating readings were rejected, some vestiges of the rejected texts were preserved among certain independent, sometimes even hostile, social units that did not submit to the decisions of the mainstream authorities.

The passage under discussion may offer some insight into an important group of textual discrepancies between the Masoretic Text and other witnesses to biblical books, such as 1QIsaᵃ. Among a tangle of errors, corruptions, and attempts at correction, we can find remains of textual traditions which go back to the earliest period in the history of the biblical text. These alternative

---

23. We find the terms צדק[ה] and תהלה used synonymously in the Bible. See Ps 35:28. This is also suggested by the fact that the verb רנן, which is linked with תהלה in 1QM, a combination which has no parallel in biblical literature, occurs occasionally in conjunction with צדקה: Ps 51:16, "so shall my tongue sing aloud of your צדקה," and Ps 145:7, "they shall sing of your צדקה." The same combination is to be found in the Targum to Ps 35:28, לישני תרנן צדקת, where MT has ולשוני תהגה צדקתך, "and my tongue shall speak of your צדקה."

24. M. Burrows, *The Dead Sea Scrolls of St. Mark's Monastery* (2 vols.; New Haven: ASOR, 1950-51) vol. 2, plate X, line 23. Cp. plate I, line 21.

25. Ibid., plate I, lines 22-23. Cp. Ps 71:15, "my tongue shall recount your צדקה."

26. Sukenik, *Megillot Genuzot* 1, 27-28.

readings are not really "variants," since they originated at a time when there was not yet a standard text from which they could be said to have deviated. The fixed authoritative pattern of a single received and sanctified text had not yet been determined. These alternative readings are rooted in a period prior to the formation of the archetypal text, a period in which the process of composition of what was later to become the basis of the Masoretic Text had not yet been concluded.

Synonymous readings such as have been preserved in various MSS of a particular biblical text are frequently mirrored in the freely varied use of such expressions in the MT itself. Take the examples cited above, and you will find that the variety of verbs connected with תהלה concerns not only the relation between the MT and 1QIsaᵃ, but recurs repeatedly in biblical literature. Thus we find the noun used in conjunction with various verbs: הגיד,[28] שיר, ספר,[27] השתבח.[31] הביע, הזכיר,[30] השמיע, הגה,[29] דבר.

This multiplicity of verbs would seem to suggest that there was no fixed linguistic tradition in the use of these phrases, and this fact has a bearing on the text of any particular passage. It is therefore not at all surprising that the scrolls of the Judean Desert add two new items to those we already knew from the books of the Bible, viz.: אמר תהלה (1QIsaᵃ 43:21); and רנן תהלה (1QM).[32] Nor is it a cause for wonder that one of these combinations is preserved in a parallel passage in the text of 1QIsaᵃ.

27. Ps 71:15.
28. Isa 57:12; so also Ps 22:32.
29. Ps 71:24.
30. Ps 71:16.
31. It should be noted that in two parallel cola of one verse, the verb sometimes governs two objects. Occasionally the expression synonymous with תהלה determines the character of the verb which is common to both clauses. Thus, e.g., in Ps 149:1: "Sing [שירו] to the LORD a new song; [sing] his praise in the assembly of the pious ones." So also Ps 35:28: "My tongue shall speak [תהגה] your צדק; it shall [speak] your תהלה all the day."
32. See above.

IV

33למען ציון לא אחשה :Isa 62:1

ולוא אחריש :1QIsa^a

(1) The two verbs חשה and החריש are synonymous and therefore interchangeable in biblical literature and are frequently used in the two cola of a parallelism.[34] It was this fact that resulted in the emergence of alternative synonymous readings. In the case before us, the scribe of 1QIsa^a presumably perpetuated an established reading and did not vary the text as a result of forgetfulness or carelessness. It is appropriate to mention that in all other instances in which the author of the book of Isaiah uses either of these verbs, 1QIsa^a invariably agrees with the MT.[35]

(2) The general principle of "synonymous readings" applies equally to all parts of speech. Here are two examples of nouns interchanged.

אשר לא הראם חזקיהו בביתו ובכל ממשלתו :Isa 39:2

.בביתו 36ובכל ממלכתו :1QIsa^a

ממלכה and ממשלה are interchangeable terms, like the expressions ממלכה and מלכות, which appear in two parallel accounts of the same matter in the MT.

2 Sam 5:12: ממלכתו

1 Chr 14:2: מלכותו

In this class we can also include the interchange of מושיע and גואל which constitutes the difference between the MT and 1QIsa^a in:

---

33. See Burrows, *The Dead Sea Scrolls*, 1. 28: "practically synonyms; either a slip of memory or possibly a conjectural restoration."

34. Thus, for example, Isa 42:14.

35. חשה, Isa 57:11; 64:11; 62:6; החריש, Isa 36:21; 41:1.

36. So also in the parallel passage, 2 Kgs 20:13. The words בכל ממלכתו ‖ ממשלתו are not rendered in the major codices of the LXX; in the Hexapla they are marked with an asterisk.

MT, Isa 43:3: קדוש ישראל מושיעך
1QIsa^a: גואלך קדוש ישראל

The scribe of 1QIsa^a did not originally have an apposition to the words קדוש ישראל. גואלך was added between the lines, above the word נתתי, which is joined directly with קדוש ישראל without any space being left before it on the line. Apparently this copyist sometimes left a blank space when he could not read a passage in the exemplar before him. Hence many words have been filled in subsequently in the MS, sometimes p.m., sometimes by one or more correctors.[37] In any case it may be said that most of the words filled in between the lines, or in the margins, are closer to the MT readings than those in the main text. Some scholars assert that these additions were already worded in accordance with the readings of the MT. For this reason it is difficult to accept the suggestion that גואלך was inserted by a corrector on the strength of a faulty oral tradition. It is more probable that it originated in the *Vorlage* used by the corrector, which would thus represent an intermediate stage in the development of the text between 1QIsa^a and the MT. Once again, we can conclude that the two readings מושיעך and גואלך were in existence concurrently before one of them, מושיעך, was declared the authorized reading and was incorporated in the proto-MT, which caused the alternative reading גואלך to be rejected, and, as a result, lost.

V

The "synonymous readings" enable us to understand an important and interesting stage in the history of the textual tradition of the biblical books. This stage preceded the promulgation of one text as the officially recognized and only binding one. An examination of the synonymous readings, not only in 1QIsa^a, but in all witnesses to the biblical text, may reveal remains of early text-forms which were suppressed and of which traces have remained only in the ancient versions and in dissident traditions, such as the Samaritan text of the Pentateuch

---

37. It is not easy to decide between these two possibilities on the strength of real or conjectured peculiarites in the shape of the letters. See J. C. Trever, "A Palaeographic Study of the Jerusalem Scrolls," *BASOR* 113 (1949) 15-16. Cp. Burrows, *The Dead Sea Scrolls*, 1. xv.

and the scrolls of the Judean Desert. Further vestiges may be found even in the masoretic tradition itself—for example in parallel passages in the Masoretic Text, in quotations from biblical books in early rabbinic writings, or in *kethib* and *qere* readings.[38]

38. See S. Talmon, "Synonymous Readings in the Textual Traditions of the Old Testament," *ScrHier* 8 (1961) 335-83.

1QIsaᵃ AS A WITNESS TO ANCIENT EXEGESIS OF THE BOOK OF ISAIAH

I

In the very first attempt to clarify systematically the readings deviating from the MT which were discovered in 1QIsaᵃ, Millar Burrows defined the textual relationship between the scroll and the MT as follows:

> Differing notably in orthography and somewhat in morphology it agrees with the Masoretic text to a remarkable degree in wording. Herein lies its chief importance, supporting the fidelity of the Masoretic tradition. There are minor omissions, but nothing comparable with those found in the Septuagint of some of the books of the Old Testament. Words repeated in the MT are sometimes not repeated in our manuscript: e.g. vi 2 כנפים שש; vi 3 קדוש (repeated once); viii 9 התאזרו וחתו; xxxviii 11 יה; lvii 19 שלום; lxii 10 עברו. Such omissions may have been made deliberately by a scribe who did not have the modern scholar's concern for meter.[1]

This definition expresses a rather high estimate of 1QIsaᵃ as a witness to the text of the book of Isaiah. It was followed by similar statements voiced by other scholars who set out to prove the antiquity and the authenticity of the MT by drawing attention to the basic resemblance between its textual tradition and that of 1QIsaᵃ.

A basic identity exists between the MT, which is preserved to us only in comparatively late manuscripts (none of them from before the ninth century C.E.), and 1QIsaᵃ, which beyond any doubt stems from the pre-Christian era.

---

1. M. Burrows, "Variant Readings in the Isaiah Manuscript," *BASOR* 111 (1948) 16-17.

This surely implies that the scribe of 1QIsa[a] must be considered a fairly reliable workman who took great care to transmit somewhat mechanically, but faithfully, the intricacies of a textual tradition held holy in his community. Just as did the scribes who handed down the MT, he sometimes copied passages in his manuscript which were faulty and, no doubt, without sense even to him.

As opposed to this remarkable basic concurrence of 1QIsa[a] with the MT, the former differs from the latter textually in a fair number of instances, as is well known. Now these deviations from the MT are often quoted by the same scholars to prove the scribe's laxity and the unreliability of the text of 1QIsa[a].

It appears to us that this two-edged reasoning comes dangerously near to juggling of evidence. There cannot be two measures by which to judge and evaluate this ancient manuscript. It is methodically unsound to give credit to 1QIsa[a] where its tradition coincides with that of the MT, while condemning it as unworthy of trust whenever it goes its own way, unless its direct dependence on the MT or on its prototype has been conclusively proved. It is in this respect that, wittingly or unwittingly, scholars have failed by taking recourse to an unproven conjecture as if it were an established fact: the MT is applied as a yardstick to measure the textual tradition of 1QIsa[a], with the tacit assumption that Isaiah's prophecies were handed down in one single formulation which moreover was preserved most faithfully in the MT. But actually this question of whether all versions of the Bible were derived from one ancestor or whether we have to assume a manifold textual tradition in the latter half of the Second Temple Period, or even in the very first stage of literary biblical composition, has constituted the bone of contention between two schools of textual scholars since the beginning of the twentieth century. Instead of judging 1QIsa[a] by the axioms of an *Urtext* theory, we should use the new finds from the Judean Desert as a test for this theory. By stating matters in this manner we are widening the scope of a mere investigation into the impact of 1QIsa[a] on the study of the book of Isaiah. This will call for further comments at a later stage.

Before proceeding we have to consider some additional factors. In spite of the alleged general textual integrity of 1QIsa[a], it cannot be denied that in many instances the scroll is demonstrably faulty. By processes which sometimes can be retraced to a reasonable degree of certainty, errors of various types were incorporated in the text of the scroll. Again, in some cases we can observe in the scroll attempts at improving imaginary or real misreadings which the scribe or copyist found in his *Vorlage* and which often remained unchanged in the MT. These errors have already been assembled and roughly categorized by

Burrows in the article mentioned previously. They drew the special attention of E. Y. Kutscher[2] and H. M. Orlinsky,[3] who, more than others, became convinced of the inferiority of 1QIsa[a] as compared with the MT.

It must be conceded that erroneous readings due to failings of the copyists are more numerous in the scroll than in the MT. The same holds true for the number of attempts at correcting obviously faulty readings. But it should be stressed, on the other hand, that his process of textual revision is far from being complete. Many cases of a *crux interpretum* in the Hebrew Isaiah were left to stand unchanged in 1QIsa[a], as they are in the MT. Statistically speaking we may say that only a minority of difficult passages in the book were smoothed over in 1QIsa[a], while the great majority were transmitted in their unsatisfactory wording. In those cases where 1QIsa[a] presents a better reading than the MT, it is difficult to determine whether this is due to a secondary attempt at improvement or whether it is due to the scroll's occasional preservation of an original, straight-forward text. The maxim that the *lectio difficilior* should usually be given preference over a parallel smooth reading is a valid safeguard against hasty textual emendation. But it should not be considered an inviolable rule by which to decide the relative value of variants.

From the foregoing discussion arises a rather multicolored picture of 1QIsa[a] as a witness to the text of the book of Isaiah. Even if the scroll should ultimately be judged to be inferior to the MT, this does not rule out the possibility that in many individual instances it has preserved readings superior in sense to those of the MT, and textually more original than their parallels in the MT. In order to form a balanced opinion of 1QIsa[a] and the trustworthiness of its scribe, the discussion should begin with an evaluation of the scroll by itself without setting the MT as a standard for comparison. This should be done first so as to decide whether the scroll has any intrinsic value. At the second stage of such an investigation, 1QIsa[a] should be compared with other extra-masoretic versions, with the Septuagint, the Peshitta, and to a lesser degree with the targum, which probably perpetuate other independent textual traditions. Only after such a procedure is a comparison with the MT called for.

2. E. Y. Kutscher, *The Language and Linguistic Background of the Isaiah Scroll (1QIsaᵃ)* (Leiden: Brill, 1974).
3. Cp. his "Studies in the St. Mark's Scroll, I-IV," *JQR* 43 (1952-53) 329-40; V, *IEJ* 4 (1954) 5-8; VI, *HUCA* 25 (1954) 85-92.

This comparison will often result in a deadlock, both versions presenting equally acceptable readings. Again, in other instances we may arrive at the conclusion that neither parallel reading can be considered original but that both were derived from a common ancestor, which sometimes can still be restored conjecturally.

Finally we should submit all the variant readings of a given passage to a synoptic analysis. This synopsis will often reveal a striking resemblance between, even an identity with, 1QIsa^a and one or more of the extra-masoretic versions. These textual concurrences are of great value, since they point to an ancient Jewish tradition current in Israel in the latter half of the Second Temple Period.

II

The diversity of textual tradition which can still be observed in our sources makes it sufficiently clear that at some stage or other in the history of the book of Isaiah different avenues were leading to its interpretation.

Our modern concept of the prophet's words is decisively influenced by the system of vowels and syntactical symbols, the *ta'amim*, with which the Masoretes endowed the biblical text during the ninth and tenth centuries C. E. This system embodies exegetical reflections which undoubtedly are deeply rooted in Jewish tradition. Yet they convey only one possible approach to the Bible. 1QIsa^a presents to us a text devoid of the masoretic aids to its explanation. But on the other hand, it is free from those explanatory symbols which transmit a historically dated interpretation of the Bible text. This interpretation constituted the tradition of only one, however important, sector of the Jewish people.

Here the exegetical importance of 1QIsa^a becomes apparent. It bears witness to a phase in the Jewish interpretation of the book of Isaiah independent from that embodied in the MT. Furthermore, it often provides us with an excellent tool for a novel approach to the interpretation of Isaiah's prophecies. If we succeed in reading the text of the scroll without unconsciously providing it with the vowel signs and text-divisions to which we have become accustomed, we sometimes will arrive at a new interpretation of a given passage which assumedly was in the mind of its scribe even where its consonantal text does not differ from that preserved in the MT.

We shall now adduce some examples to test these theoretical considerations. We shall start with instances in which only a difference in pointing of a single word is assumed to constitute the variant and go on to deal with cases of identical consonantal texts which were divided syntactically in different ways.

(1) Different vocalization of single words. We shall first adduce an example in which the scroll most probably contains faulty pronunciation of a crucial word. However it is important to show that this same pronunciation is mirrored partly in the translations of the Septuagint, the Peshitta, and the Isaiah Targum.

(a) Isa 19:10, MT: והיו שתתיה מדכאים כל עשי שכר אגמי נפש

        LXX: καὶ ἔσονται οἱ διαζόμενοι αὐτὰ ἐν ὀδύνῃ καὶ
                           πάντες οἱ τὸν ζῦθον ποιοῦντες λυπηθήσονται
                           καὶ τὰς ψυχὰς πονέσουσιν[4]

        1QIsa[a]:   והיו שותתיה מדכאים כל עושי שכר אגמי נפש

        Tg. Isa: ויהון אתר בית שתי מהא כבישין אתר דהוו
                           עבדין סיכרא וכנשין מיא גבר לנפשיה

The RV translates the verse under review: "And her pillars shall be broken in pieces, all they that work for hire shall be grieved in soul." Here, as in the LXX rendering, אגמי נפש is tacitly equated with עגם, probably on the basis of Job 30:25: עגמה נפשי לאביון, "was not my soul grieved for the needy?" The root עגם is a hap. leg. This may have been conducive to the substitution of א for ע, both in the MT and 1QIsa[a]. Tg. Isa, however, seems to have thought of אגם, "pond."

But we are mainly concerned with two other words in the verse. In translating "her pillars," the RV obviously connected שתתיה with שתת, from which also שת, "base, foundation," is derived. שָׂכָר was taken as just a variant pronunciation of שָׂכָר, "wages."

---

4.   The last passage in the LXX is apparently a *Doppelübersetzung* influenced by Isa 53:10: ἀπὸ τοῦ πόνου τῆς ψυχῆς. Cp. J. Ziegler, *Untersuchungen zur Septuaginta des Buches Isaias* (Göttingen: Vandenhoeck and Ruprecht, 1934) 65.

The ancient versions, however, ascribed to these words a quite different meaning. The LXX's οἱ διαζόμενοι, which is preserved only in some MSS but is nevertheless considered original (the main tradition reads ἐργαζόμενοι), takes שתתיה as a technical term which does indeed fit the context. The same verb is used to translate the Hebrew root ארג in Judg 16:14. It has been suggested that the Hebrew שתת is of Egyptian origin and that it carries the meaning of "weaver, ropemaker."[5]

Tg. Isa's בית שתי מהא definitely connects שתתיה with שתה, "to drink." Now it appears that 1QIsaᵃ's reading שותתיה points to the same concept. שתת alongside שתה is employed by both the MT and 1QIsaᵃ in Isa 22:13: אכל בשר ושתות יין . . . כי מחר נמות. Hence 1QIsaᵃ concurs with Tg. Isa in the interpretation of the first half of the verse under review.

This leads to the assumption that 1QIsaᵃ's reading differed from that of the MT also in the second half of the verse as well, though their consonantal texts are identical. Here the LXX translation contains the clue. שכר was rendered by the LXX ζῦθον, i.e., "beer," the Hebrew word obviously being read שֵׁכָר. We suggest that this was also the reading of the scroll and that accordingly its text is to be translated: "And her drunkards [lit. drinkers] shall be downcast [depressed]; all makers of beer [shall be] grieved in soul."

The argument advanced here goes to show that in the verse under discussion, 1QIsaᵃ presents an ancient attempt at Jewish exegesis, one part of which is also reflected in the targum, while another part underlies the Greek translation. As already stated, we think that in this case 1QIsaᵃ represents a misinterpretation of scripture. In the following example, however, we feel strongly that 1QIsaᵃ contributes to a better understanding of the biblical text.

(b) Isa 26:9, MT: כי כַאֲשֶׁר משפטיך לארץ צדק למדו ישבי תבל

Tg. Isa: כמא דדינך מתקנין לארעא

LXX: διότι φῶς τὰ προστάγματά σου ἐπὶ τῆς γῆς

This is a case of an assumed variant which ordinarily would not attract the attention of a reader of the scroll since its consonantal text is identical with that

5.   S. L. Koehler and W. Baumgartner, *Lexicon in Veteris Testamenti Libros* (Leiden: Brill, 1953) 1015, s.v. שתת.

of the MT (excepting the *plene* writing of יושבי which is written defective in the MT). The difference seems to lie in the second word, which in the MT is obviously taken as a particle and is pointed כַּאֲשֶׁר. The RV consequently translates the passage in a rather forced manner: "for when thy judgements are in the earth, the inhabitants of the world learn righteousness."

The ancient translators had before them essentially the same text as that preserved in the MT. But they could not make head or tail of it. The targum inserted a verb מתקנין, which nicely completes the relative clause introduced by כמא, but is patently secondary.[6] The LXX turned the particle into a noun, φῶς, reading intentionally or unintentionally כְּאֵשׁ for כאשר. It appears that this is a step in the right direction. A noun seems to be required after the comparative כ. Retaining the consonants of the MT כאשר, we propose to point the word כְּאֹשֶׁר or כְּאֹשֶׁר and to translate the phrase "like happiness [sweetness] are your statutes to the [dwellers of the] earth, the inhabitants of the world learned justice." Thus the parallelism of the verse is restored and is now in full accord with the other verses in the passage Isa 26:7-10.

The idea that God's precepts (משפטים) produce happiness or sweetness (אֹשֶׁר) for their observers recurs in Isa 30:18: "for the Lord is a God of righteousness [משפט], happy [אשרי] are all they that wait for him." And again in Isa 56:2: "Happy [אשרי] the man that doeth this . . . that keepeth the Sabbath, from profaning it, and keepeth his hand from doing any evil." We may further compare Ps 106:3: אשרי שמרי משפט עשה צדקה בכל עת, "Happy are they that observe the laws [and] he that doeth righteousness at all times." Here we have the same combination of (י)אשר—משפט—צדק(ה) that supposedly is also to be found in the verse under review (Isa 26:9).

Our argument may be strengthened by a further consideration. We assumed that the restored noun אֹשֶׁר—אֹשֶׁר carries the sense of "happiness" or "sweetness" and that this sensation is bound up with the notion of justice and righteousness. Now is it mere coincidence that in contrast to this, injustice is compared to bitterness? We venture to propose that Isa 26:9 is the very antithesis of Amos 5:7: ההפכים ללענה משפט וצדקה לארץ הניחו, "Ye who turn justice to bitterwood and cast down righteousness to the earth," are bound to come to grief. The

---

6. We tend to assume that this translation is molded after the pattern of a similar expression in Isa 42:4, עד ישים בארץ משפט, where Tg. Isa translates עד דיתקין בארעא דינה.

incompatibility of God's intentions and man's acts is forcefully brought out in these mutually opposed scriptures by the employment in both of them of the salient terms משפט—צדק(ה)—לארץ, modified by the antithetic concepts of אשר and לענה.

We wish to emphasize that the reading of Isa 26:9 that was proposed here adheres to the consonantal text as transmitted both in the MT and 1QIsaᵃ. However, availing ourselves of the flexibility inherent in the unpointed text of 1QIsaᵃ, we achieved two results: (a) We were able to restore the hitherto only presupposed noun אֶשֶׁר—אֶשֶׁר, from which באשרי in Gen 30:13 may also have been derived. Accordingly we may expect to find some further instances in the MT in which this noun was erroneously taken as the relative pronoun and was pointed אֲשֶׁר.[7] (b) We could interpret satisfactorily the verse under review and place it in proper relationship with other scriptures which express similar ideas.

(2) Erroneous pointing coupled with the additional interchange of two very similar letters, י and ו, seems to have resulted in the following variant:

| (a) Isa 19:9, MT: | ובשו עבד   פשתים שריקות וארגים חורי |
| 1QIsaᵃ: | יבושו עובדי פשתים שריקות ואורגים חורו |

The substitution of י for ו in ובשו—יבושו—ו(ו)בשו is just another case of the alternate employment of the perfect and the imperfect and does not affect the sense of the verse. However, the interchange of חורי and חורו is of a different nature. Let it be stated that the reading of the MT is supported by Tg. Isa's translation מצדן, "nets," which points to a derivation of חורי from חור, "hole." The LXX also renders חורי as a noun, βύσσον, probably deriving it from חור (Esth 1:6; 8:15). The weavers of that material (ארגים חורי) would be put to shame (αἰσχύνη λήμψεται) like the flax workers mentioned in the first part of the verse. This is approximately the rendering of the RV: "Moreover they that work in combed flax, and they that weave white cloth, shall be ashamed." לחדותא of the Pesh. is inconclusive since its meaning cannot be ascertained.

---

7.   Prof. G. R. Driver has kindly drawn my attention to some of his notes in which he dealt with the root אשר and its occurrences in the Hebrew Bible ("Studies in the Vocabulary of the Old Testament," *JTS* 38 [1933] 37-43; "Mythical Monsters in the Old Testament," *StudOr* 1 [1956] 234-35; "Problems in Job," *AJSL* 52 [1935-1936] 160).

In contrast to these, 1QIsaᵃ's reading חורו must obviously be explained as a perfect form (3 pl.) of the verb חור and should probably be pronounced חָורו (or חָוֵרו, if pausal forms were employed in 1QIsaᵃ). This reading was already tentatively proposed by some commentators (cp. BH) prior to the discovery of 1QIsaᵃ. The second member of the verse thus contains a verb parallel to יבושו in the first member: "Ashamed shall be they that work in combed flax and weavers [of flax] shall wax pale."

(b) The same parallelism of בוש—חור recurs in Isa 29:22: לא עתה יבוש יעקב ולא עתה פניו יחורו, "Jacob shall not now be ashamed, neither shall his face now wax pale."

It could be argued that the scroll's reading in this verse should be viewed as an attempt to explain away the hap. leg. חורי of the MT. By employing the rule of *lectio difficilior* the MT should then be given priority over 1QIsaᵃ. But we shall immediately see that this rule cuts both ways. If it were to be applied categorically it would, for example, prove the superiority of 1QIsaᵃ over the MT in the following instance:

(c) Isa 11:6, MT: ועגל וכפיר ומריא יחדו ונער קטן נהג בם

1QIsaᵃ: ועגל וכפיר ימרו   יחדו ונער קטן נהג במה

Instead of the noun מריא, "fatling," in the MT, 1QIsaᵃ has a verb in the perfect form, ימרו, which like מריא is derived from the same stem מרא with elision of the א. Again, this reading had already been restored conjecturally before the discovery of the scroll. Now, the noun מריא is found several times in the Hebrew Bible (2 Sam 6:13; 1 Kgs 1:9, 19, 25; Isa 1:11; 11:6; etc.), but there is not one single instance of the verb מרא being used. Therefore it is 1QIsaᵃ that in this case has preserved the more difficult reading.

The same division of the MT and 1QIsaᵃ can also be observed in the translation. Tg. Isa's ופאים mirrors the MT's מריא. On the other hand, the rendering of the Pesh., נרעון, "they will graze," concurs with 1QIsaᵃ's ימרו. Surprisingly, the LXX has conflated both interpretations, translating: καὶ μοσχάριον καὶ ταῦρος καὶ λέων ἅμα βοσκηθήσονται.

The reading of 1QIsaᵃ is stylistically better suited than that of the MT. In that reading the verse contains four syntactically complete parts (a-b; a-c) each with its own predicate.

This stylistic superiority of 1QIsaᵃ over the MT deserves serious consideration. But of even more importance is the exegetical and textual concord of 1QIsaᵃ, the Pesh. and one Greek tradition. There is not sufficient evidence to explain this as being due to the same trend of emendation conceived independently in the Hebrew, Greek, and Syriac traditions. Similarly no direct interdependence between these three witnesses to the text of the Bible can be established. It therefore appears that their combined evidence points to an ancient source from which all three were derived. This admittedly hypothetical source represented an exegetical tradition based on a text varying from that of the MT, which must have been firmly established in Jewish circles in the period of the Second Temple.

(3) Different pointing coupled with an interchange of non-similar letters.

Isa 14:11, MT:	הוֹרַד שְׁאוֹל גְּאוֹנֶךָ הֶמְיַת נְבָלֶיךָ
1QIsaᵃ:	[הו]רד שאול גאונך המית נבלתך

The translation of the MT, "Thy pomp is brought down to hell [and] the noise of thy viols," shows that here we are confronted with a parallelism in which the words הורד שאול are tacitly applied also to the second apocopated member. הֶמְיַת נְבָלֶיךָ can be taken with some imagination as a parallel to גאונך. But 1QIsaᵃ's reading נבלתך, "thy corpse," can by no means be combined with הֶמְיַת. The scribe obviously read the word as הֵמִית, conceiving it as a parallel to הורד שאול. Though "he killed your corpse" sounds somewhat unusual, this exegetical tradition is also witnessed to by the rendering of Sym.: ἐθανατώθη τὸ πτῶμά σου. A reference to death is also contained in Theodotion's translation, that apparently reads the noun הָמֵוֹת instead of the verb הֵמִית, ὁ θάνατος κατέρρηξέν σε; Tg. Isa, תושבחת זמרך, and the LXX, ἡ πολλή σου εὐφροσύνη, mirror the MT; while the Pesh. presents elements of both interpretations, ומית כנרך, "and thy viol will die."

(4) In some cases slight differences in the consonantal text of 1QIsaᵃ suggest a syntactical arrangement that differs from the one indicated by the masoretic accents.

Isa 26:16, MT:	ה׳ בצר פקדוך צקון לחש מוסרך למו
1QIsaᵃ:	ה׳ בצר פקדיך צקון לחשו מוסריך למו
Tg. Isa:	ה׳ בעקא הוו דכירין לדחלתך בעקתהון הוו
	מלפין אולפן אוריתך ב[ו]ן[ו]חשי

The *atnach* under פקדוך indicates that in the MT the second stichos opens with the word צקון. The second half of this verse is admittedly difficult. The apparent noun צקון is usually derived from צוק, "distress," but is registered in the most recent dictionary of the Bible (Koehler) as "unexplained." The RV took it as a verb from the stem יצק, and translated accordingly: "Lord, in trouble have they visited thee, they poured out a prayer when thy chastening was upon them." The first half of this translation corresponds roughly to the ancient versions. But instead of interpreting מוסרך in the second half as "chastening, affliction," the LXX and Tg. Isa take it as a reference to God's commandments, the LXX, ἡ παιδεία σου; Tg. Isa, אוריתך. This is the sense which the word מוסר usually carries in the Bible (e.g. Jer 17:23; 32:33; Zeph 3:27; Prov 8:33; 12:1; etc.), and this is obviously also the meaning of the plural מוסריך of 1QIsaᵃ.

In contrast to the MT and the versions which take לחש as a noun (the LXX μικρᾷ read πικρᾷ; Tg. Isa בחשי), 1QIsaᵃ has here a verb, לחשו. It seems that this is paralleled by צקון, which in 1QIsaᵃ is probably a contraction of צעקון. That צקון was understood as a verb by the writer of the scroll may also be deduced from his reading פקדיך, "thy precepts," a noun parallel to מוסריך in the second stichos, instead of the verb פקדוך in the MT. The noun פקדים is frequently used in the Psalms and is, so to speak, the catchword of Psalm 119, where it is paralleled by חוק, תורה, *et sim.*

All this results in a different verse division in 1QIsaᵃ, and in a perfect parallelism of members: ה׳ בצר פקדיך צ[ע]קון, לחשו מוסריך למו. We suggest the following translation: "Lord, in distress they call out your precepts, they whisper your commandments unto themselves."

We are fully aware that the few examples analyzed here can only indicate the line of approach to the scroll of Isaiah which was advocated. A full investigation will result in proper appraisal of the scroll as a witness to ancient Jewish exegesis and of its writer as an exegete of no mean achievement. In conclusion we wish to state that the exegetical tradition underlying the scroll is reflected not only in ancient translations, as we set out to prove in this essay, but also in talmudic and midrashic literature. But this problem should be dealt with separately.

NOTES ON THE HABAKKUK SCROLL

W. H. Brownlee published a translation of the Habakkuk Scroll[1] which he subsequently improved in several places in two further articles.[2] Further emendations of his readings and translation were proposed by S. Stern and I. Rabinowitz.[3] These suggestions were only tentative, being based on preliminary prints and transcriptions. Since then a full photographic reproduction of the scroll on which Dupont-Sommer based his translation and notes[4] has been published in *The Dead Sea Scrolls of St. Mark's Monastery.*[5] Some further suggestions are made here.

1QpHab ii 4. His first improbable translation, "to the gates of the needy and upright," was dropped by Brownlee himself, and Sukenik's suggestion to fill the lacuna את ש[ם קו]דשו was accepted.[6] This seems to be a more convincing reading than Stern's ש[בת קו]דשו.[7] Brownlee would like to have this phrase preceded by the verb הלל (either in the perfect or the imperfect).[8] But the MS certainly allows for more letters, presumably some nine to twelve. The clause should be read: כיא לוא האמינו בברית אל [וגדפו ויחרפו]את ש[ם קו]דשו. The verbs

1. W. H. Brownlee, "The Jerusalem Habakkuk Scroll," *BASOR* 112 (1948) 8-18.
2. Idem, "Further Light on Habakkuk" *BASOR* 114 (1949) 9-11; "Further Correction of the Translation of the Habakkuk Scroll" *BASOR* 116 (1949) 14-16.
3. S. Stern, "Notes on the New Manuscript Find," *JBL* 69 (1950) 25-29; J. Rabinowitz, "The Second and Third Columns of the Habakkuk Interpretation Scroll," *JBL* 69 (1950) 31-50.
4. "Le Commentaire d'Habacuc, découvert près de la Mer Morte, Traduction et Notes," *RHR* 2 (April-June 1950) 129-71.
5. Millar Burrows, ed., *The Dead Sea Scrolls of St. Mark's Monastery* (2 vols.; New Haven: ASOR, 1950-51), vol. 1.
6. Brownlee, *BASOR* 116 (1949) 15. See also Rabinowitz (*JBL* 69 [1950] 33). Dupont-Sommer reads את ש[מו קודשו], an unnecessarily complicated construction (*RHR* 2 [1950] 140).
7. Stern, *JBL* 69 (1950) 25.
8. Dupont-Sommer (*RHR* 2 [1950] 129-71) reconstructs the perfect, Rabinowitz (*JBL* 69 [1950] 33) the imperfect.

employed are again used in a similar context, in exactly the same form, x 13:
אשר גדפו ויחרפו את בחירי אל.

1QpHab ii 7. Stern suggested the reading: את כל ה[באות על]הדור האחרון.[9]
This is better than Brownlee's restoration which is much too long. It should be
added that the same expression appears in vii 1-2, though connected there with
Habakkuk and not with the מורה הצדק. Compare ii 9 as well.

1QpHab ii 9. Brownlee's reading, [אשר ב]ידם ספר אל את כל הבאות על עמו,
is awkward but was nevertheless accepted by Dupont-Sommer and Rabinowitz.
However, בס[ודם] seems to be intended.[10] One is reminded of expressions such
as סוד בחורים (Jer 6:11) or סוד ישרים (Ps 111:1). A similar conception is
implied in vii 5: פשרו על מורה הצדק אשר הודיעו אל את כל רזי דברי עבדיו
הנביאים.

After על עמו, I would read ועל ל ארצו]. Rabinowitz admits that the reading
ו[על הגואים] crowds the available space.[11]

1QpHab ii 12. Stern was puzzled by Brownlee's reading פשרו על הכתיאים
א[שר מחנה]?[קלים וגבורים but made no alternative suggestion. א[שר המה] seems
to be the obvious solution.

1QpHab iii 1: ... ובמישור ילכו לכות ולבוז does not imply a characterization of the Kittim, as Brownlee suggests: "and in uprightness. They come to
smite and to despoil the cities of the land. . . ." The clause ובמישור ילכו is
intended to convey a notion of the ease with which the enemy conquers the
country. It is parallel, in a way, to א[שר המה] קלים וגבורים. The sentence starts
at the beginning of the line and should be rendered: "By level road will they
come," i.e., unimpeded by obstacles. This conforms with the general description
of the enemy in the corresponding passage of Hab 1:6-10.[12] Compare אשים
העקוב למישור (40:4); והיה העקוב למישור (Isa 42:16); מחשכים לפניהם לאור ומעקשים למישור
תנחני בארץ מישור (Ps 143:10).

---

9. Stern, *JBL* 69 (1950) 26. Rabinowitz and Dupont-Sommer have the same
reading.

10. ו and י, as well as ד and ר, are nearly indistinguishable in this scroll.

11. Rabinowitz, *JBL* 69 (1950) 42-43.

12. Compare Rabinowitz, *JBL* 69 [1950] 45). Dupont-Sommer's translation, "la
plaine (liquide)," meaning "sea," is much too metaphorical (*RHR* 2 [1950] 140-
41).

1QpHab iv 1. The printed text transcribes וקלס ורוזנים מישתק לו. The parallel in Hab 1:10 reads: במלכים יתקלס ורוזנים משתק לו. Accordingly we should prefer a verbal form in the MS as well, viz., יקלס,[13] which means a pa‘al or pi‘el form instead of the hithpa‘el of the MT, without affecting the meaning. See line 3: וקלסו.

1QpHab iv 8. The text is obviously בעוון היושבים בהם[14] and should be corrected accordingly in the transcription[15] and translation.

1QpHab iv 10. The passage should be read: פשרו על מושלי הכתיאים אשר בעצת בית אשמ[תם] יעבי/ורו איש מלפני רעהו מושלי[הם ז]ה אחר זה יבואו לשחית את הארץ,[16] "Its meaning concerns the rulers of the Kittim who, upon the advice of their [governing] house of guilt,[17] remove one man before his fellow-man. Their rulers come one after the other to destroy the country."

1QpHab v 12. אשר מאס את התורה בתוך כול ע] [ם, whatever the lacuna conceals, the final ם seems to indicate a possessive pronoun, as otherwise the article would be required before the word. Accordingly "their" should be inserted in the translation. Besides Brownlee's and Dupont-Sommer's attempts to read "peoples," עדתם or עצתם suggest themselves, referring back to lines 9-10.

1QpHab vii 7. פשרו אשר יארוך הקץ האחרון ויתר על כול אשר דברו הנביאים, which Brownlee translates: "Its meaning is that the final end (goal time)[18] delays and is left for all of which the prophets spoke."[19] Dupont-Sommer renders the passage, ". . . c'est que le temps ultime sera long et qu'il dépassera tout ce qu'ont dit les prophètes."[20] Neither of those translations do justice to the phrase ויתר על כול. I suggest, " . . . that the end-time will be delayed even more than the prophets said." This would be justified by the commentator's contention that the end of time was not revealed to Habakkuk, though he was told to write down the

13. See Stern, *JBL* 69 (1950) 26 (above, n. 3).
14. Ibid.
15. Burrows, *The Dead Sea Scrolls*, pl. 56. This reading is accepted by Dupont-Sommer (*RHR* 2 [1950] 141-42).
16. The commentator hints presumably at the gods of the Kittim. שמרון הנשבעים באשמת (Amos 8:14) suggests a possible comparison.
17. Dupont-Sommer translates: "avec le parti de leur maison coupable," (*RHR* 2 [1950] 142-43).
18. *BASOR* 116 (1949) 15.
19. *BASOR* 112 (1948) 12.
20. *RHR* 2 (1950) 135.

"events of the latter generation" (lines 1-2). A similar uncertainty about the time of the last days is indicated in Hab 2:3, although there is no doubt that come they will. These lines point to hopes for an imminent messianic age amongst the members of the New Covenant which the commentator saw fit to check. A parallel structure with ויתר is apparently employed in Dan 8:9. BDB compare this structure with the Syriac יתיר מן.[21]

1QpHab ix 12. The transcription runs: הוי הבוצע בצע רע, while the MT has הוי בצע בצע רע (Hab 2:9). The more probable reading הוי הבוצע can easily be traced in the photoprint of the MS.[22]

1QpHab x 9. "Oracle of lies" for מטיף הכזב is rather impersonal. "Preacher of lies" would be better. He is accused of having induced people, לבנות עיר שוו בדמים ולקום עדה בשקר.[23] A shortened hiphʿil form ולקים, dependent on התעה as לבנות depends on התעה, seems preferable. Compare hiphʿil forms with dropped ה in ix 11 and xi 15.

1QpHab x 11. בעבוד כבודה is presumably a misprint (misreading?)[24] and should be emended to בעבור כבודה. The personal pronoun refers back to עיר or עדה. There should be a period at the end of the preceding line. שוו, here as in the line before, does not carry the poss. pron. of the 3 sing. The consonantal ו is indicated by a double letter.[25]

1QpHab xii 1. Brownlee dropped his first reading of יחתה, as a verb,[26] in favor of וחתה, as a noun,[27] "and terror of the blood of men." But though his second spelling is better, a verbal form is required here. I read וְחִתָּה from חתת,

21. Brown, Driver, Briggs, *Hebrew-English Dictionary of the Old Testament*, (1906) 452.
22. Burrows, ed., *Dead Sea Scrolls,* pl. 59 (see above, n. 4). See Dupont-Sommer, *RHR* 2 (1950) 147.
23. Both Brownlee (*BASOR* 112 [1948] 14) and Dupont-Sommer (*RHR* 2 [1950] 138, 147-48) failed to recognize this hiphʿil form, which resulted in a queer conception of עדה as "a court" or "par témoigner," when it should be understood as "community." We have here a sentence based on two parallel half-lines: לבנות עיר שוו בדמים ‖ ולקים עדה בשקר. A strict congruency is observed.
24. See note 10.
25. Brownlee and Dupont-Sommer apparently failed to recognize this.
26. *BASOR* 112 (1948) 14.
27. *BASOR* 114 (1949) 9.

(cp. Isa 7:8; 8:9; 20:5; Jer 48:20), meaning: "you will be afraid because[28] of the blood of men (which you spilt) and the violation of country, city, and all that dwell therein." This idea is elaborated in lines 6-7, where the quotation קריה מדמי indicates that in our verse דמי governs two constructs.

1QpHab xii 9. המה ערי יהודה אשר גזל הון אביונים . . . . Brownlee, who translates "They are the cities of Judah which robbed the wealth of the poor,"[29] misunderstood the construction because a pers. pron., referring to ערי, is missing. The robber is the priest; the robbed are the cities of Judah.[30]

1QpHab xii 15. Again a case where it is possible to read either ד or ר. The line is fragmentary but easily restored with the aid of the MT: הוי ה[אומר לע]ץ הקיצה [עורי לאב]ן דומה (Hab 2:19).[31] Brownlee translates "lofty stone,"[32] which makes no sense. The MT has דּוּמָם, which is intelligible but grammatically irregular, being either an adverb, where we would have expected an adjective, or a wrongly pointed adjective דּוּמֵם, after אָבֶן, instead of דּוּמְמָה. Our text apparently spelled the word[33] דּוּמָה, omitting a מ, for דּוּמְמָה. The translation should read: "Alas, woe unto him who says to (the) wood, 'Awaken'; 'Arise,' to a dumb stone."

28. For מ . . . מן in this sense, cp. W. Gesenius, (Hebrew Grammar, 28th ed. [1948] 383).
29. BASOR 112 (1948) 15.
30. Dupont-Sommer's translation is correct (RHR 2 [1950] 139).
31. Burrows, The Dead Sea Scrolls, pl. 60.
32. BASOR 112 (1948) 15.
33. Dupont-Sommer wants to read דומם, as in the MT (RHR 2 [1950] 151), maintaining that the bottom line of the final מ has disappeared in the lacuna. This is definitely not the case, as a close investigation of the reproduction proves. The last letter in this word is a ה.

THE CALENDAR OF THE COVENANTERS OF
THE JUDEAN DESERT

I

Discussion of the Qumran Covenanters has tended to concentrate upon comparison with other trends of thought which led to secession from normative Judaism. Students of the Qumran Scrolls have set out to prove their authors' affinity of thought with Christianity at various phases of its development, or even with Karaism, though the latter emerged hundreds of years later than the יחד. But actually it is imperative to trace the roots of that group within the Jewish community of the Second Temple Period, for it was from this society that the יחד emanated, and upon its tradition the main precepts of the Covenanters were grounded. Upon this common foundation the Qumranites reared a superstructure of beliefs and ideas in respect to which they parted company with mainstream Judaism. As is the habit of dissenters, the founders of the יחד held themselves to be the genuine representatives of Israel, "the true keepers of the Law," if we may use a definition applied by the Samaritans to their own community. In their view the Torah had been distorted by their opponents, who, in their eyes, were traitors to the Covenant between the nation and its God.

The arguments of the Sons of Light were aimed at the major group of the Jewish people of that time, from whom they had seceded. The dispute between the two factions is reflected in the Qumran writings in a one-sided fashion. Hence we are obliged to seek in the literature of the main community, i.e., in early rabbinic writings, elements which may balance the picture. The open, as well as the disguised, polemics in the writings of the Sons of Light will not be sufficiently comprehended until we discover the opinions against which they were directed. The essence of a deviation in ideas is often fully understood only after the meaning of its parent thought has been adequately established.

We are not called upon to elucidate the characteristics of the Jewish people and their traditions during the Second Commonwealth. Suffice it to stress in this context one essential feature of the Jewish society of the late Second Temple Period, viz., the large measure of indulgence in discussion that it allowed even on matters of הלכה. Freedom of opinion and the freedom of voicing an opinion in the בית המדרש were rarely curbed. But once a verdict had been given and a הלכה established, the holders of differing concepts were expected to conform without reservation. Thus we learn from the Mishna that a teacher was held to be a "rebellious elder" when he instructed others to *act* in accordance with his view in opposition to a decision reached by the majority of the court of his town and continued contumacious even after his argument had been overruled by the High Court in the Hall of Hewn Stones, לשכת הגזית. If after the decision of that court "he returned to his town, and taught as he taught before, he was innocent. But if he *instructed [others] to act [accordingly]*, he was culpable" (*m. Sanh.* 11:2).

Hence we must seek the reasons for the overt breach between the normative community and the adherents of the Teacher of Righteousness first and foremost in the sphere of action rather than in ideas, i.e., in facts that constituted a tangible barrier between the parties in daily life. When the Teacher of Righteousness began to teach *action* running counter to rulings accepted by the Jewish body politic and its leaders, he passed from the status of an antagonist in halakic dispute to the status of a "rebellious elder," and his deviation from the mainstream tradition was declared to constitute a heterodoxy (*t. Ber.* 7:20).[1] From that moment he became liable "to death by strangulation by the sentence of the court," as befits a rebellious elder (*m. Sanh.* 11:2).[2]

Among the acts which estranged the Sons of Light from mainstream Judaism, special importance attaches to their adherence to a calendar not identical to that of the mother-community. No barrier appears to be more substantial and fraught with heavier consequences than differences in calendar calculation, to quote the French sociologist E. Durkheim, since a common calendar "expresses

1. *Tosefta Kifshutah,* Ed. S Liebermann (New York: JTSA, 1955) 39; idem, "Light on the Cave Scrolls from Rabbinic Sources," *PAAJR* 20 (1951) 395-404.
2. It is to be assumed that they also cast upon him the slur of being a "false prophet who prophesies what has not been heard and what he has not been told, whose death is at the hands of men" (*m. Sanh.* 11:5). In the eyes of their opponents, the Teacher of Righteousness and his followers forfeited their part in the world to come by reading extraneous—that is heretical—books (*m. Sanh.* 10:1), and by writing books of that category. The Covenanter's retort may be found in 1QH iv 9-10, 16, 20; CD i 14-15; viii 13 et al.

the rhythm of collective activities."[3] An alteration of any one of the dates that regulate the course of the year inevitably produces a breakup of communal life, impairing the coordination between the behavior of man and his fellow, and abolishes that synchronization of habits and activities which is the foundation of a properly functioning social order. Rather than making theoretical statements, the sages voiced their own appreciations of these facts of which they were fully aware by telling an episode, reported with slight variations, in reference to Tannaitic rabbis of the first, second or third generation: "Once a pagan [גוי] asked R. Joḥanan ben Zakkai [end of first century C.E.], saying: 'We have our festivals and you have your festivals. We have kalenda, saturnalia, and kartosis; and you have Pesaḥ, Aṣeret [Šebuʿot], and Sukkot.[4] And when do we both together rejoice?' Said R. Johana ben Zakkai to him: 'On a day on which rains fall' " (*Deut. Rab.*, כי תבוא, 7).[5] Whoever does not observe the festivals of the year at the same time as the community in which he lives, ceases to be a member of the social body to which he hitherto belonged.[6]

One may venture to say that the deviation from the calendar of the mainstream community was for the Covenanters, as for other dissident groups such as the Samaritans and later the Karaites, a sign and symbol of their thwarting the authority of the contemporary public Jewish leadership, and of their dissidence from the body politic.[7] Their opponents rightly interpreted this act as a proclamation of civil revolt.

In this essay we shall attempt to present the calendar controversy as a decisive factor in the process of the formation of the יחד as a self-contained socioreligious entity cut off from the mother community. We shall first discuss the influence of a separatist calendar-reckoning on the cult. The structure of the

---

3. *The Elementary Forms of Religious Life* (trans. S. W. Swain; London: Allen and Unwin, 1915) 11.

4. Instead of this enumeration of festivals, the version which involves R. Joshua (probably ben Korḥah, middle of second century C.E.) in the episode reads: "When you rejoice we do not rejoice, and when we rejoice you do not rejoice" (*Gen. Rab.* 13:6 [ed. Theodor-Albeck; Jerusalem: Wahrmann, 1965] 116).

5. ([Ed. S. Liebermann; Jerusalem: Bamberger Wahrmann, 1940] 121). An attribution of the episode to R. Joshua ben Ḥananiah (early second century C.E.) may be found in *Midr. Ps.* 117:1 ([ed. S. Buber; New York: Om, 1947] 479).

6. This rule also applies to other attempts in Jewish history to introduce changes in calendar calculations, the first being attributed to Jeroboam ben Nabat (see S. Talmon, "The Cult and Calendar Reform of Jeroboam I," *KCC* [Jerusalem: Magnes, 1986] 113-39).

7. Cp. A. Dupont-Sommer, "Exégèse du Manuel de Discipline," *VT* 2 (1952) 230.

Qumran calendar will then be described, as well as the principles wherein it differed from the current Jewish calendar. It will be demonstrated that allusions to the calendar controversy are scattered throughout Qumran literature. The examination of the writings from this point of view will produce new interpretations of several passages whose connection with the issue under review has previously not been realized. Also various sayings in rabbinic literature will be shown to reflect polemics against that deviating calendar. The information gathered from rabbinic sources and from the Qumran writings induces the conjecture that the Covenanters differed from other Jews, not only in the timing of the festivals, but also in the calculation of the day. We shall endeavor to adduce evidence for the hypothesis that the Qumranites reckoned the day, including the Sabbath, from the morning and not from the evening, as was the practice in mainstream Judaism.

II

The basic difference in calendar calculation caused the Covenanters to withdraw from the Temple and its cult. This withdrawal did not result from their opposition to the offering of sacrifices on principle, as is often suggested,[8] but from the fact that the dates on which the holidays were observed in the Temple of Jerusalem were "those in which all Israel were in error" (CD iii 14).[9] The juxtaposition of passages shows that this error originated with the fall of the "angels of heaven" (CD ii 18, reading עירי for עידי), as a result of which the secrets of the lunar period were revealed to mankind (*1 Enoch* 8:3). "In this erred the sons of Noah and their families" (CD iii 1), and most of the Israelites until the recent generation.[10] It therefore stands to reason that whoever followed them and did not keep the festivals at their appointed times would "not obtain repentance nor be purified in the waters of *expiation*" (1QS iii 4). This was the

---

8. See int. al., G. Vermes (*Discoveries in the Judaean* Desert [New York: Desclée, 1956] 39, 212).
9. Y. Yadin, *The Scroll of the War of the Sons of Light against the Sons of Darkness* (trans., C. and B. Rabin; Oxford: Oxford Univ. Press, 1962) 198, 210. We should no doubt also take into consideration the illegitimacy of priests of non-Zadokite descent serving in the Temple as a factor in the Covenanters' abstention from offering sacrifices (ibid., 181-84).
10. I.e., down to the time of the author of the scroll. God had warned Noah of this error (*Jub.* 6:32-38 and see below).

fate of most Jews who had failed to keep the Holy Covenant, whereas "from those who are left that hold God's commandments," that is, the members of the יחד, "God has established His Covenant for Israel for ever" (CD iii 12-13). By virtue of this Covenant, God has condescended "to reveal to them[11] mysteries in which all Israel has erred," these being "the Sabbaths of His holiness, the appointed days of His glory, the holidays of His righteousness, the ways of His truth, and the desires of His will which man shall do and live by" (CD iii 14-16). Therefore everyone who joins the Covenant undertakes "not to enter the Temple to kindle the fire on God's altar in vain" (CD vi 12-13), not to offer untimely and, therefore, useless sacrifices. He also pledges "to make himself one with God's counsel and to walk before Him pure in accordance with all that has been revealed to him on their destined and appointed days" (1QS i 8-9). That is to say, he undertakes to keep the festivals and their determined times according to the יחד calendar, "to make announcement of the distinction between the sacred and the profane and to keep the Sabbath-day as it is interpreted, and the appointed days and the days of fasting according to the commandments [reading כמצות] of those who have entered the new [better: renewed] Covenant in the Land of Damascus to offer up sacrifices according to the [authorized] interpretation" (CD vi 17-20) "nor to depart from all [emend בכול to מכול] God's words at their appropriate time, nor to advance their times, nor to delay any of their appointed days" (1QS i 13-15).[12] It may be presumed that every Covenanter renewed this pledge annually at the ceremony of his reconsecration (1QS i 11—ii 25). Therefore "he shall be accepted for his fragrant [of the יחד] offerings [of] atonement before God and it shall be reckoned to him as a perpetual Covenant" (1QS iii 11-12).

It is almost self-evident that it became difficult for the members of the יחד to live side by side with other Jews, especially so in Jerusalem, in the orbit of the Temple. At communal festivals their abstention from the official ceremonies became most apparent and caused friction and bodily assaults. Their opponents rose against them, "banding together against the life of the righteous man, they abominated all that walked in innocence, and pursued them with the sword and lusted for a feud among the people" (CD i 20-21).[13] Although we readily admit

---

11. In contrast to the secret of the lunar period revealed to mankind by the angel Sahariel on the eve of the flood (*1 Enoch* 8:3).
12. Cp. 1QS iii 10-11. See also "A Further Link Between the Judean Covenanters and the Essenes?" (in this vol., pp. 61-67).
13. Cp. *1 Enoch* 46:7.

that considerations of conceptual differences have to be taken into account, it appears that the members of the יחד realized increasingly that they could "no longer be a part of the house of Judah but each side must mount guard for itself; the fence has been rebuilt, and the bounds are farflung" (CD iv 11-12), mainly as a result of deviations in everyday life. Therefore they decided "in these times [circumstances] to separate themselves from the abode of wicked men and go to the desert, there to prepare the way [of God?] to do all that has been revealed from time to time" (1QS viii 13-15).

These men believed that in the wilderness of the Judean Desert their foes would not interfere with their observing the festivals according to their own calendar. But it proved to be otherwise. For in the *Pesher on Habakkuk* (1QpHab xi 4-9) we are told that the Wicked Priest "pursued the Teacher of Righteousness . . . unto the abode of his exile," i.e., Qumran, "to devour him in the wrath of his anger," and just "at the time of the appointed repose of the Day of Atonement he appeared unto them to confound them and to cause them to transgress on the day of fasting, the sabbath of their rest." This passage refers to a conflict which arose between the rival factions on the Covenanters' actual Day of Atonement.[14] We must perforce conclude that the priest had set out to put an end to the observance of the Day of Atonement by the supporters of the Teacher of Righteousness on the day of their own reckoning. For even if that (High) Priest had been a wicked man, he would not have undertaken a journey from Jerusalem to the Judean Desert on the Day of Atonement observed by all Israel, thus desecrating the holiest Jewish festival.

The account under review brings to mind the episode concerning R. Gamaliel and R. Joshua adduced in *m. Roš. Haš.* 2:8-9. R. Gamaliel, then the head of the Sanhedrin, proclaimed the beginning of the new month on the evidence of two witnesses whom R. Dosa ben Hyrcanos and R. Joshua considered to be unreliable. It would appear that while R. Dosa differed from R. Gamaliel only on principles, R. Joshua disagreed with him also on the practical issue. Since the argument supposedly concerned the fixing of the first day of the month of Tishre, there arose the apprehension that R. Joshua might proclaim a date of his own for the Day of Atonement, which falls on the tenth of that same month, and that owing to his prominence, many would be inclined to follow him, thus causing a division in the nation. Therefore Rabban Gamaliel sent to

14. I have discussed this matter in "Yom Hakippurim in the Habakkuk Scroll," in this vol., pp. 186-99.

R. Joshua, saying, "I decree that you come to me with your staff and money on the Day of Atonement as it falls according to your reckoning." Although conditions are not identical, the issue resembles to some degree the controversy between the High Priest and the Teacher of Righteousness.[15]

In both instances, the leaders of the respective communities, Rabban Gamaliel and the High Priest, sensed that if they were to pass over in silence the deviation of their antagonists from the calendar dates established by them, they would condone anarchy and precipitate a breakup of the national unity. They had reason to fear that confusion would prevail in the nation and that a day that was regarded as an ordinary working day by one would be deemed a holiday by his neighbor.[16] Now, while R. Joshua submitted to Rabban Gamaliel's decree, and "taking his staff and money in his hand, went to Jamnia to Rabban Gamaliel on the day on which the Day of Atonement fell according to his own calculation," the Teacher of Righteousness continued contumacious. Therefore the contemporary High Priest was compelled to coerce him and his supporters to profane "the fast-day, *their* day of rest" (1QpHab xi 4-9).

III

The immediate failure did not induce the יחד members to despair of success in the future. After the manner of all eschatologically-minded men, they envisioned the time in which the *reign of wickedness* would pass and their own concept of truth would prevail. Their rich and complex literature, as yet only partly published, served them as a means of preparation for the final and decisive battle against their adversaries.[17] They visualized Jerusalem as it would be after their victory, when the יחד would constitute "the abode of the Holiest of Holies of Aaron," when their priests would be summoned "to offer fragrant odours . . . and will be accepted to atone for the Land" (1QS viii 9-10). It goes without saying that worship would then be conducted in accordance with the canons of

15. It had never been my intention to identify the Wicked Priest with Rabban Gamaliel or R. Joshua with the Teacher of Righteousness, as H. H. Rowley assumes (*The Zadokite Fragments and the Dead Sea Scrolls* [Oxford: Blackwell, 1952] 58, n. 1). The comparison aimed at pointing out a resemblance in the two episodes and in the social setting of the occurrences described in the Mishnah and in 1QpHab.

16. See above, pp. 2-3.

17. Portrayed in 1QM.

the Covenanters and according to the calendar which they had computed. With this end in view, they composed tables of the priestly families and of their order of service in the Temple.

A "genealogical list of priestly families" was found Cave 6. In my opinion this list is probably alluded to in CD iv 4-5, as "the account of their names according to their generations." That part of CD contains a kind of short catalogue of as yet mostly unknown יחד writings: "Account of their Woes" refers, it would seem, to books in which were described the persecutions of the Sons of Light by their foes, such as the *Pesher on Habakkuk* (1QpHab), the *Hôdayôt* (1QH), the *Pesher on Psalms* (4Q 17) et sim. "The [account of the] years of their sojournings" alludes to parts of CD and to similar works which have not yet been discovered (or published), in which the theme of the Covenanters' exile was treated. The "explanation of their acts" may denote the *Manual of Discipline* (1QS) or the *Book of Hagu/i* (1QS x 6), i.e., the statutes of the יחד. Along the same lines we may be permitted to interpret the words "[explanation of] the period[s] of their office" as referring to the *Book of the Priestly Courses*, fragments of which were found in Cave 4 and have been published in part by J.T. Milik.[18]

Records of the priestly courses are also found in rabbinic tradition and cannot be considered a novelty.[19] The innovation lies in the number of courses and in the calculation of the period of service of each course. According to *b. Taʿan.* 27 a; *y. Taʿan.* 4:2 (67 d), Moses had originally established eight courses, "four of Eleazar and four of Itamar. Samuel increased them to sixteen, David came and increased their number to twenty-four" (Cp. 1 Chr 9:22 and 2 Chr 24:6-18). This last figure formed the basis for the arrangement of the priestly courses in the Second Temple (*m. Sukk.* 5:6-8). This is to be deduced from *m. Taʿan.* 4:2 and parallels, where it is said that "the first prophets set up twenty-four courses" (so also *b. ʿArak.* 12b). The regulation is based upon 1 Chr 24:1-18 (see also *m. Mid.* 3:5; Josephus, *Ant.* 7.14.7; *Ag. Ap.* 2.8).

Differing from this arrangement, the Covenanters divided the cycle of the sacred service into twenty-six courses. This is explicitly stated in 1QM ii 1-2:

18. J. T. Milik, "Le travail d'edition des manuscrits du Désert du Juda" (VTSup; Leiden: Brill, 1957), 4. 24-26.
19. Yadin, 1QM 202-28; P. Winter, "Twenty-six Priestly Courses," *VT* 6 (1956) 215-17; E. Schürer, *A History of the Jewish People in the Time of Jesus Christ* (trans. from the German; New York: Scribner's Sons, n.d.), Second Division, vol. 1. 216-22.

"The fathers of the community are fifty-two. The major priests shall be appointed after the High Priest and his deputy in twelve courses to serve constantly before God. And the twenty-six heads of courses shall serve in their appointed turn." Each course was appointed over two out of the fifty-two weeks of the year, serving one week in each half-year comprised of twenty-six weeks. Rabbinic sources confirm the changing of the courses each week (see *m. Sukk.* 5:8; *Tamid* 5:1).

The fragment of the *Book of the Priestly Courses* at Qumran records in detail the names of the courses and the periods of their service in relation to the main festivals of the year. We thus obtain a notion of the working of the יחד calendar and its principles. The fragment reads:

The First Year, its appointed seasons	השנה הרישונה מועדיה
On the 3rd[20] [in] Maoziah[21] (MT: Maaziah), the Passover	ב 3 [ב] מעוזיה הפסח
[On the 1st] in Jeda[iah], the raising of the Omer	[ב 1] ביד[ע]יה הנף ה[עומר]
On the 5th in Seorim, the [Second] Passover	ב 5 בשערים הפסח [השני]
On the 1st in Jeshua, the Festival of Weeks	ב 1 בישוע חג השבועים
On the 4th in Maoziah, the Day of Remembrance	ב 4 במעוזיה יום הזכרון
[On the] 6th in Joiarib (MT: Jehoiarib), the Day of Atonement	[ב] 6 בייריב יום הכפורים
[On the 4th in Jeda]iah, the Festival of Tabernacles.	[ב] 4 ביד[ע]יה חג הסכות

The table lists the courses of "the first year" only. We may therefore deduce that this was not necessarily a permanent arrangement, i.e., the same courses did not necessarily take over every year at the periods indicated. Hence it follows that

20. Milik did not publish the Hebrew text but only a transcription and a translation. Nor did he tell us in what way the figures are indicated in this MS.
21. I.e., in "the week of" the respective course.

twenty-six tables were required, corresponding with the twenty-six weeks in which a given course could perform the sacred service within a complete and comprehensive cycle.

Tables of this sort apparently were also used in rabbinic circles. This can be inferred from a fragmentary inscription discovered in Caesarea, which lists the priestly courses in their order. Unfortunately only that part of the inscription is preserved in which the serial numbers of the courses were inscribed. The names are missing:

The fif[teenth cour]se	‎[משמר]ת חמש ע[שרה]
The sixtee[nth co]urse	‎[מש]מרת שש עש[רה]
The seve[nteenth c]ourse[22]	‎[מ]שמרת שב[ע עשרה]

Fragment of a Table of Priestly Courses from Caesarea

As already stated, the Qumran table is fragmentary. The names of several courses are missing, before Maoziah is mentioned again in the second round of service. But it is not difficult to restore the list almost completely, since it copies in effect the enumeration of the priestly courses given in 1 Chr 24:7-18. In both rosters Joiarib and Jedaiah are listed in the same order. Seorim is separated from them by Harim. In 1 Chr 24:8-10 four courses intervene between

22. Prof. Y. Yadin directed my attention to this inscription, and Mr. Y. Aviram put a photograph at my disposal. The photograph is published with the kind permission of Mr. A. Wagmann of Caesarea. The inscription itself has since been lost.

Seorim and Jeshua. The two lists differ in one respect: Maaziah takes first place in the Qumran fragment, whereas in 1 Chronicles the list concludes with Maoziah, the first place being given to Joiarib,[23] who comes second in the Qumran fragment.

It should be noted that, while in the Jewish calendar the cycle of the courses begins in the seventh month, Tishre, in the Qumran calendar the roster of courses starts in the first month, Nisan. It would appear that this difference reflects the two Beginnings of the Year recognized in Jewish tradition. By beginning their festal calendar in Nisan, the יחד is perpetuating a tradition recorded in *m. Roš. Haš.* 1.1 (mentioned by Josephus, *Ant.* 1.3.3): "On the 1st of Nisan is the New Year for kings and festivals." The beginning of the order of courses in Tishre is based on another system, which is also is mentioned there: "On the 1st of Tishre is the New Year of [reckoning] years, Sabbath Years and Jubilees."

We may now ask how the Covenanters adapted the system of 24 courses underlying Chronicles to their calendar of 52 weeks, which required 26 courses. In the Qumran fragment not one name is mentioned which does not occur in Chronicles. It appears, nevertheless, that we can still determine the technique which the יחד employed to solve the problem.

An examination of the roster shows that the course of Maoziah takes over for a second spell of duty 23 weeks after its first tour of service. The same is the case with Jedaiah and, by analogy, also with Joiarib. But we should expect that in an order of courses based on two half-years of 26 weeks each, the cycle would repeat itself after 25 weeks. This discrepancy leads to the conclusion that the יחד basically accepted the system of courses which obtained in the mainstream tradition but added two courses to the roster that together served four periods, whether in weekly alteration or each for a fortnight continuously. Two of these

---

23. In the list of priests who reportedly returned with Zerubbabel (Neh 12:1-7), Jehoiarib is placed seventeenth (12:6). His promotion to the head of the roster in 1 Chr 24:7 is sometimes presented as corroborating the assumption that this second version was composed in the Maccabean Period, since the Hasmonean family was related to the priestly course of Jehoiarib (1 Macc 2:1). (See Schürer, *History*, 224 [see above, n. 19].) But if the order of the courses in the Temple was founded on rotation (see above p. 156), this cannot be considered evidence. Hence it is also quite possible that "when the Temple was destroyed for the first time on the 9th of Ab, it was both the end of the Sabbath and the end of the Sabbatical Year, and (the order of) Jehoiarib was serving his course." There is no need to stamp this report as late and unreliable (Schürer, *History*, 274).

courses were placed at the head of the list, serving in the weeks from the 29th day of the 12th month to the 4th of the 1st and from the 5th to the 11th of the 1st month, while the remaining two courses brought up the rear, serving from the 15th to the 21st and from the 22nd to the 28th day of the 12th month. This arrangement may serve as a proof of the secondary nature of the יחד order of priestly courses, which was taken from a framework fashioned for a different time-reckoning and was adapted to their own requirements by a simple process of patching.

The Qumran table opens with a new cycle. It deals exclusively with "the solemn seasons of the first year." Therefore only such courses as serve at one of the festivals are enumerated. This excludes the anonymous courses at the head and at the end of the list. One may surmise that the table was drawn up for the purpose of organizing the priestly service during the first year after the expected victory of the Sons of Light over all their adversaries, that is, at the beginning of that future eon in which the Temple service would eventually be conducted according to their calendar.

On the strength of these arguments, we can now complete the arrangement of the priestly courses in that same first year:

Month	Days	Name of Course	Month	Days	Name of Course
Twelfth	29—4	?		29—4	Maoziah
First	5—11	?	Seventh	5—11	Joiarib
	12—18	Maoziah		12—18	Jedaiah
	19—25	Joiarib		19—25	Ḥarim
	26—2	Jedaiah		26—2	Seorim
Second	3—9	Ḥarim	Eight	3—9	Malkijah
	10—16	Seorim		10—16	Mijamin
	17—23	Malkijah		17—23	Hakkoṣ
	24—30	Mijamin		24—30	Abijah
Third	1—7	Hakkoṣ	Ninth	1—7	Jeshua
	8—14	Abijah		8—14	Shekaniah
	15—21	Jeshua		15—21	Eliashib
	22—28	Shekaniah		22—28	Jakim
	29—4	Eliashib		29—4	Ḥuppah
Fourth	5—11	Jakim	Tenth	5—11	Jeshebeab
	12—18	Ḥuppah		12—18	Bilgah
	19—25	Jeshebeab		19—25	Immer
	26—2	Bilgah		26—2	Ḥezir
Fifth	3—9	Immer	Eleventh	3—9	Happiṣṣeṣ
	10—16	Ḥezir		10—16	Pethaḥiah
	17—23	Happiṣṣeṣ		17—23	Jeḥezkel
	24—30	Pethaḥiah		24—30	Jakim
Sixth	1—7	Jeḥezkel	Twelfth	1—7	Gamul
	8—14	Jakim		8—14	Delaiah
	15—21	Gamul		15—21	?
	22—28	Delaiah		22—28	?

The proposed restoration is confirmed by a fragment apparently torn from a Book of Priestly Courses which reads: ב. 6 ביחזקאל ל 29 ב 22 לעשתי עשר. We are told here that the 6th day of service of the course of Jeḥezkel fell on the 22nd of the 11th month. This calculation agrees with the above list. Milik's assumption that the additional number "ל 29" is to inform us that the day fell on

159

the 29th of the lunar month and that the author intended to synchronize the two different calendars,[24] requires further examination.

The names of the courses recur in parallel order in both parts of the table. Its first half is opened by Maoziah, serving on the festival of Passover. This same course also opens the second half at "the day of Remembrance," i.e., at New Year. Thereafter Joiarib serves, the Day of Atonement falling to its portion. In the first part of the list that same course is apportioned the last days of the Mazzot Festival. In both cases the course of Jedaiah relieves Joiarib. Once the Raising of the Omer (with which the counting of the 50 days between Passover and Pentecost begins) falls to their share, and once the Festival of Tabernacles.

From this list we can deduce the dates of two festivals, the Raising of the Omer and the Festival of Weeks, which in their turn will help us to understand the structure of the Qumran calendar. Attention should be paid to the fact that the dates of these two festivals are not fixed in the Pentateuch by month and day. The second, the Festival of Weeks, is dependent on the first, since it is to be celebrated 50 days after it (Lev 23:15-16); and the first, the Raising of the Omer, depends on Passover and on the interpretation of the words ממחרת בשבת (Lev 23:11).

For the sake of clarity, let us once more survey the dates of service of the first three courses enumerated:

Maoziah serves from the 12th to the 18th day of the 1st month, and the Festival of Passover falls on his 3rd day, the 14th of the month.

Joiarib serves from the 19th to the 2th of the 1st month, and the last day of Passover falls on their 3rd day, the 21st of the month.

Jedaiah serves from the 26th day of the 1st month to the 2nd day of the 2nd month, and the Raising of the Omer falls on their 1st day.

On this basis the following conclusions may be drawn:

(1) The יחד began the counting of the Omer on the 26th day of the 1st month.[25] This means that, like the Sadducees, Boethusians, and Samaritans, they interpreted the expression ממחרת השבת as referring to the first day of the week, Sunday, and not to the day following the first day of the Passover (m. Menaḥ. 10:3). But contrary to the Sadducees and Samaritans, they started counting on the first Sunday *after* Passover and not on the Sunday in the middle of the festival.

---

24. VTSup 4 (1957) 25.
25. See D. Barthélemy, "Notes en marge des publications récentes sur les manuscrits de Qumrân," *RB* 59 (1952) 200-201.

(2) The Raising of the Omer fell on a Sunday coinciding with the first day of the course of Jedaiah. From this it follows that all the other courses, officiating each for one week, began their spell of service on Sunday as well.

(3) The date of the Festival of Weeks is conditioned by the Raising of the Omer: it is always celebrated 50 days after it. Hence it too will always fall on the 1st day of the week, on a Sunday.[26]

(4) The beginning of the cycle of the courses does not coincide with the beginning of the counting of the months. The first day of the year falls in the middle of the spell of service of a priestly course.

Let us now turn to the second part of the roster. Jedaiah is relieved by the course of Ḥarim that serves from the 3rd to the 9th day of the 2nd month and is followed by Seorim that serves from the 10th to the 16th of that month. The "Second Passover" falls on their 5th day, the 14th of the month.

From the day of the Raising of the Omer to the Second Passover, 19 days pass, comprising 7 days of Jedaiah, seven of Ḥarim, and the first 5 days of Seorim. Up to the Festival of Weeks we are therefore short of 30 days: 2 days of Seorim and 28 of the four courses of Malkijah, Mijamin, Hakkoṣ, and Abijah. We then reach the course of Jeshua, which serves from the 15th to the 21st of the 3rd month, the Festival of Weeks falling on its first day, a Sunday. This shows that the author of the book of *Jubilees* was not in error when he placed the Festival of Weeks on the 15th of the 3rd month (15:1; 16:13; 44:1-5). I. Epstein tried to explain the apparent anomaly by arguing that the author of *Jubilees* inserted 2 lunar months (Nisan-Iyyar) into his solar year and thus successfully crammed 50 days between the day following Passover, ממחרת השבת, according to his understanding (the 22nd of the 1st month), and the Festival of Weeks which fell on the 15th of the 3rd month.[27] J. Morgenstern, on the other hand, ascribed to the author of *Jubilees* a simple error of calculation and decided that he should have fixed the Festival of Weeks on the 11th day of the 3rd month.[28] It now transpires that the author of *Jubilees* based himself on a calendar calculation that was current at Qumran. The apparent problem has ceased to exist and the conjectures entertained have become redundant.

In order that the Raising of the Omer, and consequently also the Festival of Weeks, should always fall on the first day of the week, it is essential for the days

26. Cp. Qirqisani, "Account of Jewish Sects," *HUCA* 7 (1930) 326, 364, 389-90.
27. "Le livre des Jubilées," *REJ* 22 (1891) 8-10.
28. "The Three Calendars of Ancient Israel," *HUCA* 3 (1926) 93, 96.

of the months always to be attached to fixed days of the week. Otherwise there could be no assurance that the 26th of the 1st month would fall permanently "on the morrow after the Sabbath." Once this is achieved the dates of all the other festivals will also remain unchanged. Thus, for example, calculation shows that the first day of Passover (15th of the 1st) will always fall on a Wednesday, since the Passover lamb was sacrificed on the third day of Maoziah, which is also the third day of the week. The same result is attained by counting back 11 days (4 of Maoziah and 7 of Joiarib) from the Raising of the Omer, always celebrated on a Sunday.

The first day of Passover (15th of the 1st month), being bound to fall on a Wednesday, the first day of the year, i.e., the first of Nisan, would also coincide with a Wednesday. This fact was undoubtedly appraised by the יחד as a portent, since on that day the two great luminaries had been created (Gen 1:14-18), and only thereafter the counting of the days, months, and years might fittingly begin.

The Qumran calendar, which probably obtained also in other groups, had the advantage that its festivals did not "wander" as they do in other calendaric systems. The principles underlying this arrangement were established by A. Jaubert in a study of the calendar pertaining to the book of *Jubilees*. It can be shown that in each set of three months the serial days are coupled with fixed days of the week, as the following table demonstrates:[29]

29. A. Jaubert, "Les Calendrier des Jubilés et de la Secte de Qumran," *VT* 3 (1953) 250-64. The criticism of the proposed system raised by J. Morgenstern ("The Calendar of the Book of Jubilees, Its Origin and Its Character," *VT* 5 [1955] 34-76) was successfully refuted by A. Jaubert ("Le Calendrier de Jubilés et les Jours Liturgiques de la Semaine," *VT* 7 [1957] 35-61).

DAYS OF THE WEEK

		Sun.	Mon.	Tues.	Wed.	Thur.	Fri.	Sat.
					1	2	3	4
MONTHS	I	5	6	7	8	9	10	11
	IV	12	13	14	15	16	17	18
	VII	19	20	21	22	23	24	25
	X	26	27	28	29	30	1	2
MONTHS	II	3	4	5	6	7	8	9
	V	10	11	12	13	14	15	16
	VIII	17	18	19	20	21	22	23
	XI	24	25	26	27	28	29	30
MONTHS	III	1	2	3	4	5	6	7
	VI	8	9	10	11	12	13	14
	IX	15	16	17	18	19	20	21
	XII	22	23	24	25	26	27	28
		29	30	31				

The fragment of the Book of Priestly Courses discovered at Qumran completely confirms A. Jaubert's conclusions.

IV

We may now ask in what way the Covenanters' calendar actually differed from the current Jewish calendar. It may be stated at the outset that some elements of the liturgical calendar of the יחד were known before the discovery of the Qumran manuscripts. From allusions and explicit statements it can be inferred that the same method of calendation was also known to the compilers of some apocryphal and pseudepigraphal writings such as *Jubilees, Enoch,* and the *Testaments of the Twelve Patriarchs.*[30] It is therefore not surprising that the author of CD praises the book of *Jubilees* and holds it up to his readers as a model of calendaric accuracy: "And the exact account of their epochs [קציהם],[31] . . . behold, it is accurately defined in the Book of the Divisions of Times into their Jubilees and Weeks" (xvi 2-4).

30. Cp. S. Talmon, "Yom Hakippurim," in this vol., pp. 186-99.
31. The possessive pronoun in קציהם should be understood as referring to an unspecified noun, such as מאורות. The words following are an interpolation disrupting the proper sequence of the sentence and should be translated approximately: "Israel being blind to all these [appointed epochs]."

The assumption that the Qumran calendar is identical with the one that underlies some apocryphal and pseudepigraphal works has received considerable support from the discovery at Qumran of fragments of *Jubilees* and remains of eight MSS of the book of *Enoch*. In three of these copies the extant text of *Enoch*, especially of chaps. 72-82 (the Book of Celestial Physics) is extensively expanded. In addition there were found remains of a composition which is still unidentified, which resembles the book of *Jubilees* and which was apparently written in vindication of the peculiar Qumran calendar.[32]

The essence of that calendar is explained by the author of *Jubilees* when he reports the commandment given by God to Noah after the flood: "Instruct the children of Israel that they observe the years according to this reckoning, three-hundred and sixty-four days, and [these] will constitute a complete year, and they will not disturb its time from its days and from its feasts" (6:32). The reference is to the solar year, as is stated explicitly: "And God appointed the sun to be a great sign on the earth for days and for sabbaths and for months and for feasts and for years and for sabbaths of years and for jubilees and all seasons of the year" (*Jub.* 2:9).

A year of 364 days was accepted also by the author of the Book of Celestial Physics (*1 Enoch* 72-82). The first chapter of that work is devoted to an account of the solar period. It was the practice to divide the year into 2 halves, which in turn were subdivided into secondary divisions of 3 months. Each month numbered 30 days. At the end of each quarter 1 day was added. The 3rd, 6th, 9th and 12th months therefore numbered 31 days each.[33] Hence 364 days constituted a solar year.[34] The same tradition was followed by the יחד. This is not stated explicitly but is obviously implied in some of its writings. At the beginning of the 10th column of 1QS, the heavenly luminaries are mentioned, and their influence on the order of the festal days, the months, years, and sabbatical years is described.[35] It is stated that the reckoning of the months and the fixing of the

32. J. Strugnell, "Editing the Manuscript Fragments from Qumran," *BA* 19 (1956) 93 = *RB* 63 (1956) 65.
33. Cp. *1 Enoch* 82:4-8.
34. It should be noted that the author was acquainted also with a year of 360 days, comprising 12 months of 30 days each, without intercalary days at the end of every quarter (*1 Enoch* 74:10-12).
35. The language employed in this passage is very similar to that of the Book of Celestial Physics. It may be surmised that it is the remnant of a larger work on the celestial luminaries, of which a further fragment has been preserved in 1QH

festal days must be based on the solar period: "The great [luminary][36] for the Holy of Holies and a trustworthy sign,[37] for the beginning of His eternal graces, for the commencement of appointed days at every time that occurs, at the beginning of the months at their appointed seasons and the holy days in their established order, for a reminder of their destined times" (1QS x 4).[38]

The authors of these books based their calendar on the course of the sun, deciding arbitrarily that 364 days constitute one complete year,[39] which meant a deficiency of approximately a day and a quarter as compared with the true solar year on which was founded the Julian calendar introduced in 46 B.C.E.

The Jewish calendar, on the other hand, is calculated by lunar months, 12 of which amount to 354 days only. This fact is discussed at length by the author of the Book of Celestial Physics (*1 Enoch* 78:15-16):

And three months he makes of thirty days, at her [the moon's] appointed time, and three months he makes of twenty-nine days each, at which she accomplishes her waning in the first period of time, and in the first portal in one hundred and seventy-seven days. And in the time of her going out, she appears for three months [of] thirty days each, and she appears for three months [of] twenty-nine each.

xii 3-11 (cp. especially *1 Enoch* 82:15-20; 41:5). See "The Emergence of Institutionalized Prayer," (in this vol., pp. 200-243).

36. המ[אור ה]גדול is the required restoration, in the present author's opinion. Cp. 1QH xii 5. M. Burrows (*The Dead Sea Scrolls of St. Mark's Monastery* [2 vols.; New Haven, CT: ASOR, 1950-1951], vol. 2) reads גדול הם; A.M. Habermann (*'Edah we'Eduth* [Jerusalem: Mahbarot Lesifruth, 1952] 83), המגדול. Y. Yadin ("Three Notes on the Dead Sea Scrolls," *IEJ* 6 [1956] 160-62) proposed to read זו (1QM, pp. 208-9), where others transcribed ה, thus arriving at the reading גדול זום בהתחדשם. Habermann's suggestion to close the sentence with בהתחדשם and to begin the next sentence with המ[אור ה]גדול is to be recommended. Abbreviations are apparently used on several other occasions in this same manuscript: א[ל] (1QS x 1) and נ[אמ]ן (x 4). המאור הגדול is also referred to in 1QH xii 5 and in 1Q *34* bis (D. Barthélemy, O. P. and J. T. Milik, *Qumrân Cave 1* [DJD; Oxford: Clarendon, 1955], 1. 154). See further: Dupont-Sommer (*VT* 2 [1952] 230 [see above, n. 7]) and W. H. Brownlee (*The Dead Sea Manual of Discipline* [BASORSS 10-12; 1955]). H. E. del Medico ("La traduction d'un texte démarqué dans le Manuel de Discipline [DJD, 10. 1-9]," *VT* 6 [1956] 26-29) interprets the poem in an imaginary fashion which can hardly be accepted.

37. Habermann's restoration, ibid., and see below.

38. Cp. *1 Enoch* 74:12.

39. *1 Enoch* 72:32, "And the year amounts to exactly three hundred and sixty-four days."

This means that in every half year the moon was to complete her revolutions three times in 29 days and three times in 30 days.

Hence the lunar year was shorter than the solar year by 10 days. This difference, of course, did not escape the notice of the author of *Jubilees* (6:34-36), who warned Noah to beware of such miscalculations:

> And all the children of Israel will forget and will not find the path of the years, and will forget months [sic.] and seasons and sabbaths, and they will go wrong as to all the order of the years. . . . For there will be those who will assuredly make observations of the moon how [she] disturbs the seasons and comes in from year to year ten days too soon.[40]

Similar contentions were voiced by the author of CD: "In it erred the sons of Noah and their families . . . the sons of Jacob erred in them" (iii 1-4),[41] until God raised up the Teacher of Righteousness and his followers and revealed to them the secrets of the calendar (CD iii 13).[42]

The examination of the roster Priestly Courses has shown that the dates of all the festivals detailed in the Pentateuch by day and month were strictly retained in the Qumran calendar. However, the Raising of the Omer and The Festival of Weeks, whose dates are not explicated but were settled in relation to Passover, were fixed in that calendar by calculations which differed from the general Jewish time reckoning.

But even when the יחד accepts dates given in the Pentateuch by day and month, the synchronization of their festal days with those of mainstream Jewry is not yet guaranteed. For example, while the10th day of the 7th month, the Day of Atonement, is permanently fixed in the calendar of the יחד and always falls on the 6th day of the week, the 10th day of the seventh lunar month changes every year in comparison with the date fixed in accord with the sun's course. The actual

---

40. Cp. *1 Enoch* 79:5. There the difference in respect to the half-year is given: "She falls behind the sun and the order of the stars exactly five days in the course of one period." In *1 Enoch* 74:9-17 the author sums up the discrepancy in respect to three, five, and eight years (R. H. Charles, *The Book of Enoch* in *The Apocrypha and Pseudepigrapha*, [Oxford: Clarendon, 1913], vol. 2. ad loc.).

41. Cp. 1Q 27 1 i 3-5 (DJD, 1. 103): "They know not the mystery that was and did not consider ancient things," etc. This interpretation is required by the juxtaposition of the chapters and by the internal affinity of theme to the book of *Jubilees*.

42. The same applies to 1Q 34 bis ii 3 (DJD, 1. 154).

difference depends on the degree of distance of the year in question from the nearest leap year, which was designed to synchronize the lunar calendar with the solar period. If that year were the first of an intercalary unit (two to three years), the discrepancy would amount to 4 or 5 days. Where a second non-intercalary year is concerned, the discrepancy would amount to 14-15 days, and in the third year to as many as 24 to 25 days. If the second year of the cycle were a leap year, the Day of Atonement of the lunar calendar would precede that same day in the solar calendar by 8-10 days. If the third year were a leap year, it would precede it by 3-5 days only. This gives us the key to understanding the dispute between the Wicked Priest and the Teacher of Righteousness and his faction over the observation of the Day of Atonement (1QpHab xi 4-8). It would appear that an echo of that episode may be discerned also in the fragmentary *Pesher on Psalms*, published by Allegro. Commenting on the text "The meek shall inherit the earth and shall delight themselves in the abundance of peace" (Ps 37:11), the author says, "This refers to the poor who accept the appointed time of fasting and who will be delivered from all the snares of Belial."[43] His purpose is to hearten the יחד members who had been discouraged and scared by the act of the Wicked Priest.[44]

V

The Covenanters' contention against basing the calendar calculation on the lunar period customary in mainstream Judaism did not go unanswered by the sages. Traces of the dispute are discernible in rabbinic literature.

The disputation had two aspects. Each side was convinced that its method approximated to astronomical accuracy and that the use of the rival system would inevitably lead to miscalculation of the days appointed for the festivals.[45]

43. J. M. Allegro, "A Newly Discovered Fragment of a Commentary on Psalm XXXVII from Qumran," *PEQ* 68 (1954) 29-75 = 4Q*171* ii 8-10: פשרו על עדת האביונים אשר יקבלו את מועד התענית ונצלו מכול פחי בליעל .

44. The "Day of Fasting" plays a cardinal role in the Covenanters' thinking and is recurrently mentioned in their compositions. In 1Q *34* bis, a part of a "Prayer for the Day of Atonement" has been preserved. See "The Emergence of Institutionalized Prayer" (in this vol., pp. 200-243).

45. In a later epoch R. Abraham ibn Ezra defined the problem in his *Book of Intercalation* in this manner: "Know that if the time-calculation of Samuel is true, our entire intercalation system is wrong and all our festal days and fasts are

Simultaneously the leaders of the two factions were also fighting for the exclusive right of regulating their followers' pace of life and of functioning as supreme authority over the Jewish people. The prerogative of calendar calculation, on which depended the proclamation of the new months and consequently the fixing of the festivals, served as a prominent and effective sign of sovereignty in the community. The Covenanters' rejection of the official calculation was therefore deemed tantamount to repudiation of the civil and religious authority.[46]

It is for these reasons that the rival factions could not reach a compromise. The members of the יחד argued that God had created "the great [luminary][47] for the Holy of Holies . . . for the beginning of appointed days at every time that occurs . . . at the new years and at the period of their appointed times" (1QS x 4-6). Anyone who opposed this fundamental principle confounded the dispositions of creation and had no portion in the world to come.

The rabbis, counterattacking, quoted against the Qumranites the words of the psalmist (Ps 28:5):[48]

> "Because they regard not the works of the Lord, nor the operation of His hands, He shall destroy them and not build them up". . . "the operation of His hands," these are the new moons, as is written, "And God made the two great luminaries" (Gen 1:16); it is also written, "He appointed the *moon for seasons'"* (Ps 104:19). These are the heretics,[49] who do not reckon either appointed days or periods; "He will destroy them, and not build them up"; He will destroy them in this world and He will not build them up in the world to come.[50]

false, heaven forbid" (Cited by A. A. Akavia, "The *Sefer Haʿibbur* of Abraham ibn Ezra," *Tarbiz* 26 [1957] 305). Ibn Ezra disputed the Amora Samuel's reckoning which he considered to be inaccurate. Yet Samuel said of himself, "I am as familiar with the paths of the heavens as I am with the paths of Nehardea."

46. For this reason R. Dosa sought to appease R. Joshua and to induce him to yield to Rabban Gamaliel's decree. Anyone disobeying his command impaired the unity of Israel, since "if someone is appointed warden over the community and be he the unworthiest, he is considered master of masters" (*b. Roš. Haš.* 25b).

47. Cp. *Jub.* 2:9 and supra.

48. See *Midr. Ps.*, ad loc. (ed. Buber) 230.

49. The mode of explanation resembles that of the Qumran *pesharim:* a Bible verse is quoted and then interpreted with reference to topical matters.

50. M. Friedländer (*Der Antichrist in den vorchristlichen jüdischen Quellen* [Göttingen: Vandenhoecks Ruprecht, 1901] 144) seizes upon this midrash in

The emphasis on the heretics' failure in this world and in the next, in itself a normal thematic development in rabbinic literature,[51] gains added significance in light of the Covenanters' tendency to console themselves for their bitter fate in their days, when evil is reigning, with the hope of victory in a fervently expected future age.

In the course of the controversy, both sides drew support from scripture. Sometimes they even seized upon the same text and interpreted it in opposite and conflicting ways, either by combining verses, as in the above instance (*Midr. Ps.* 104:19), or else by emending the biblical text (an illuminating example will be adduced below). Thus fared the verse Isa 30:26, "Moreover the light of the moon shall be as the light of the sun, and the light of the sun shall be sevenfold as the light of the seven days." Jewish tradition referred these words to the days of the Messiah (*b. Pesaḥ.* 68a; *Sanh.* 91b), when "there will be in the world only the brilliance of splendour and the sight of the Holy Spirit.[52] In the days of the Messiah the light of the moon shall be as the light of the sun" (Rashi, ad loc.).

This future equality of the moon with the sun can be inferred from the first clause in Isa 30:26. The second clause, on the other hand, "and the light of the sun shall be sevenfold," seems to indicate that the relative strength of the luminaries will not be changed. While the moon will attain the present strength of the light of the sun, the latter's strength will increase sevenfold as compared with its present strength. This interpretation is, however, ruled out by the final clause of the verse. The word "sevenfold" is not referred anymore to the light of the sun in the world to come as compared with its light in this world, but to the concluding words of the verse: "as the seven days." This implies that in the future world the sunlight of one day, as well as the moonlight of one night, will equal the volume of light of seven times seven days in the present world,[53] or of the days of creation (Rashi ad Zech 4:2). The theme is further elaborated in *Ex.*

his endeavor to discover in rabbinic writings polemics against an antinomian sect allegedly called *Minim*.

51. Cp. especially *m. Sanh.* 10:3, which treats of evildoers who have no portion in the world to come.

52. Cp. Isa 60:19-20.

53. According to the text of 1QIsaᵃ: שבעת ימים. The ה" (הימים) is entered there in the margin; whether by the scribe himself or s.m. cannot be determined.

Rab. (15:21) and in *Tg. Psalm*, ad loc.: ". . . and the light of the sun shall be three-hundred and forty-three fold [7 X 7 X 7] like the light of the seven days."[54]

It is obvious that the future equality of the luminaries could not be acknowledged by the Covenanters, who emphasized the priority of the sun over the moon in this world and in the world to come, בהסגר מולדי עולה,[55] "when the wicked [periods of reckoning by the] moon's risings shall end" (1Q 27 1 i 5; DJD, 1. 103).[56] Then "the great [luminary] shall become . . . a [true] sign for the commencement of his graces" (1QS x 4).[57] "For wickedness shall cease forever and righteousness shall be revealed like the sun [which is the] foundation of the world" (1Q 27 1 i 6).

It is therefore interesting to note that in 1QIsaᵃ 30:26 the crucial third clause, כאור שבעת הימים, upon which the rabbinic explanation hinges, was at first omitted and was inserted *post factum,* probably by a corrector. It is altogether missing in a quotation of that verse in *1 Enoch*. The author of the Book of Celestial Physics informs us that "in the circumference of the sun there is a seventh portion of light wherewith additions are made to the moon" (*1 Enoch 78:4*), "and when her [the moon's] light is uniform [i.e., full] it amounts to the seventh part of the light of the sun" (*1 Enoch* 73:3). He is, doubtless, relying for his authority on the text quoted above, "and the light of the sun shall be sevenfold" (Isa 30:26). In order to eliminate the notion that the moon's light would at some time equal that of the sun, as apparently implied by the beginning of that verse, "the light of the moon shall be as the light of the sun," it is further explicated that verily "his [the sun's] light is sevenfold brighter than that of the moon; but as regards *size* they are both equal" (*1 Enoch* 72:37).

The shorter version of Isa 30:26, which assumedly underlies the paraphrase in *1 Enoch*, is preserved also in the LXX, which ends the verse with the words: καὶ τὸ φῶς τοῦ ἡλίου ἔσται ἑπταπλάσιον, and omits the last clause of MT.[58] We are not in a position to decide whether the author of *1 Enoch* deleted the last

54. Thus also Rashi in his commentary, ad loc. Kimchi dissociates himself from this interpretation.
55. Cp. *Midr. Ps.* 28:5: אלו המולדות.
56. A different interpretation of the passage was proposed by I. Rabinowicz ("The Authorship, Audience and Date of the de Vaux Fragment of an Unknown Work," *JBL* 71 [1952] 25-26).
57. למפתח חסדיו in contrast to בהסגר מולדי עולה. This reading rules out the interpretations of Brownlee, Dupont-Sommer and del Medico (see above, n. 36).
58. The text of Lucian's recension and of the Hexapla have been adapted to the MT by the addition of: ὡς τὸ φῶς τῶν ἑπτὰ ἡμέρων.

clause from his *Vorlage,* or whether the words "as the light of the seven days" were added in the MT. If they are an addition,[59] we are concerned not with a mere midrashic expansion,[60] but with a polemical argument against adherents of the solar calendar, an argument which was embodied in the MT of Isaiah.

VI

The opposition to the lunar calendar hallowed in the normative Jewish community and the acceptance of calendar calculations based on the solar year furnish us with an explanation of the recurring exhortations in the Qumran writings that the festivals must be observed as they had been established, "and that their times must not be advanced nor may any of their appointed days be delayed" (1QS i 14-15). It is easily understood that the Covenanters accused their opponents of erring in their calendation and of misleading others. But to all appearances the differences in calendar-calculation do no explain the repeated association of "Sabbath and appointed days" in this context (CD iii 14-15; vi 18-19; xii 3-4). The Sabbath is permanently fixed in both calendars, since they do not differ in the order of the days of the week. This being so, we are inclined to think that the concern over the observation of the Sabbath pertains to a problem which differs from the one connected with the festivals. The profanation of the Sabbath, against which the Covenanters inveigh, does not result from changed dates but rather from certain actions permissible in the Jewish community but forbidden in the יחד laws. For this reason the author of CD found it necessary to devote an entire part of this work to the Sabbath commandments (CD x-xi). Most of the rules listed in that passage deal with a man's acts pertaining to himself or to his fellowmen. Only one regulation of specifically public character is recorded (CD x 17-18): "Let no man offer on the altar on the Sabbath, except the burnt-offering of the Sabbath; for thus it is written 'apart from your Sabbath offerings' (Lev 23:38)."[61] Desecration of the Sabbath by transgression of this

---

59. As may be held on ground of the LXX evidence.
60. I. L. Seeligmann, *The Septuagint Version of Isaiah: A Discussion of Its Problems. Ex Oriente Lux nr. 9* (Leiden: Brill, 1948) 63.
61. The prohibition against offering sacrifices on Sabbath except the Tamid was observed by other dissenters such as the Samaritans and the supporters of Anan the Karaite. For references consult C. Rabin (*Qumran Studies* [Scripta Judaica; Oxford: Oxford University Press, 1957], 2. 58).

prohibition could have been linked with the desecration of the festivals by changing their established times.

From the wording of the prohibition in CD, and particularly from the prominence given to the words "Let *no man* offer up," one could infer that the legislator was referring primarily to the Passover sacrifice offered by each individual.[62] But at the same time this precept also provides an explanation for differences in opinion between the יחד and the mainstream community on Raising the Omer and the interpretation of "on the morrow after the Sabbath." As said, rabbinic halakah took the word *Sabbath* to refer to the first day of Passover, which could sometimes fall on a Friday. Consequently the Omer would then have to be raised on the Sabbath "on the morrow after," as explicitly stated in *m. Menah.* 10:9: "The rule is to harvest it at night, but if it is done by day it is valid, and it overrides the Sabbath." The Covenanters had to prevent this possibility; if the offering of festal sacrifices was prohibited on Sabbath, so was the Raising of the Omer. By explaining "[on the morrow] after the Sabbath," as referring to the actual Sabbath, i.e., to the seventh day of the week, the danger was removed. Now the Omer would always be raised on a Sunday.

In open dispute with the ruling of the יחד and similar dissenters, the rabbis emphasized that the Omer must be cut even on the Sabbath. Following upon the description of the preparations for the cutting, the *m. Menah.* 10:3 reads: "On a Sabbath [the harvester] says to them, 'On this Sabbath?' And they answer, 'Shall I cut?' And they answer him, 'Cut.' They repeat each word thrice. Why? Because of the Boethusians who used to say that the Omer may not be reaped at the close of a festival."

Here then, the problem of keeping the Sabbath and that of keeping the festivals at their established times were mutually involved. But not only this. The conclusion of the Mishna is surprising. According to the prominence of the instruction to observe the commandment of the Omer even on a Sabbath, contrary to the opinion of the Boethusians, the phrasing should have been: "because of the Boethusians who used to say that the Omer may not be reaped *on the Sabbath.*" For from what preceded we learn that the Boethusians prohibited

---

62. Ibid. The present author prefers to assume that the shot was aimed at the priests whom also Jesus of Nazareth charged with profaning the Sabbath (Matt 12:5). The parallels in Mark 20:23 ff and Luke 6:1 ff.do not record this complaint. Cp. D. Daube (*The New Testament and Rabbinic Judaism* [1956] 67-68); also G. Vermes (*Discovery*, 104, n. 104).

the cutting of the Omer on every outgoing of a festival, even if it fell on a weekday.

Is it possible that we are confronted here with another controversy? Could it not be that the Boethusians also opposed the Pharisaic regulation that "it is the rule to harvest it [the Omer] at night" (*m. Menaḥ.* 10:2) and therefore also to harvest it at the close of a festival? The reason is that the Boethusians did not accept such a reaping as a proper execution of the commandment to cut the Omer "on the *morrow* after the Sabbath." That this was actually the case, also in reference to the יחד, is proven by the table of priestly courses discovered at Qumran, supplemented by information from rabbinic sources. In the Jerusalem Temple the courses changed on the Sabbath, after offering the additional (מוסף) sacrifice.[63] But the analysis of the "roster of priestly courses" indicates that with the יחד the courses changed on the first day of the week, evidently in the morning. Now, since the Raising of the Omer coincided with "the first[64] day of Jedaiah," it inevitably follows that it was raised on a Sunday.

The dispute may have gone even deeper. We may assume that the Covenanters did not reckon the beginning of the day from sunset, as is Jewish custom, but rather from sunrise, like the Christians. If this assumption can be proved, it would explain the association of the Sabbath with the festivals in the calendar controversy. For in this case the Sabbath rest of mainstream Jewry did not overlap with that of the יחד. Friday night, regarded as sacred by the former, would be considered profane by the latter, the converse being the case with Saturday night.

No clear deductions can be drawn from the above Mishna passage. The opposition of the Boethusians and the יחד to cutting the Omer at the close of a festival may have arisen from a punctilious interpretation of the word ממחרת ("on the morrow after") and may have applied only to the Raising of the Omer. But the extreme dependence of these dissidents on the course of the sun for their calendar calculation, their prayers, and the fundamentals of their belief, induces the conjecture that the Mishna alludes to an additional difference of principle between the calendar calculation of the Boethusians and the יחד, and the current calendar of the mainstream community.

---

63. *M. Sukk.* 8:8; *Tamid* 5:1; Josephus, *Ant.* 7.14.7. Cp. 2 Kgs 11:6-9.
64. The number was restored by Milik (*Qumran Cave 1*), since after fifty days the Festival of Weeks will fall on the first day of service of the course of Jeshua.

We shall derive indirect support for this supposition from an analysis of the Covenanters' order of prayer.

VII

The different system of calendation and the resulting divergences in the dates of the festivals not only necessitated the compilation of a special roster of the priestly courses, but also produced the growth of other works bound up with the Covenanters' code of worship. Among the scrolls and fragments that have been unearthed, there are scattered pieces of a sort of "Order of Benedictions" for each day of the year.[65] For the present we shall content ourselves with the analysis of the structure of one section in this "Order of Benedictions," viz., "The Song of the Seasons" embodied in 1QS ix 26—x 17.

In this song the poet describes the sequence of his prayers from the time he rises in the morning: "From the moment that I put forth my hands and feet I shall bless Thy name" (x 13). It would appear that his words refer to the blessing of the Creator on the passing of the night, of the type "O God, the soul which Thou hast given me" (*b. Ber.* 60b). Next the second paragraph of the *Shema^c* prayer is listed. The words "at the beginning of [my] going and coming,[66] to sit and to rise up" are in the nature of a paraphrase of "You shall say them over when you are at rest in your house, when you walk on the road, [when you lie down,] and when you rise" (Deut 6:7).

The poet then mentions the Eighteen Benedictions beside the *Shema^c*, the principal morning prayer.[67] The number of benedictions is not complete, nor are they detailed in the established order in Jewish tradition. Nevertheless the resemblance is sufficiently close to prove that the poet did depend on the Eighteen Benedictions. These prayers are to be uttered before the petitioner touches food, "and before I raise my hand to fatten on the delicacies of the world's fruit,"[68] words which allude at one and the same time to the "blessing of

---

65. For a detailed analysis see "The Emergence of Institutionalized Prayer" (in this vol., pp. 200-243).

66. Reading ‏צאת[י] ובוא[י]‎ .

67. See J. Elbogen (*Der Jüdische Gottesdienst in seiner geschichtlichen Entwicklung* [2d ed.; Frankfurt/M: Kauffmann, 1935] 15-49).

68. Cp. ‏"[לה]רשן בעד[נ]י שמים ובנובת ארץ"‎ (1Q 34 bis; DJD, 1. 153) and also the *Pesher on Psalm 37* (4Q*171A* ii 10; DJD, 5. 43).

the years" in the Eighteen Benedictions and to saying grace before meals. There is a further reference to the evening *Shema* prayer, "and as I lie down on my couch I shall sing unto Him."

In this liturgy the festival prayers are adjoined to the daily blessings. A Prayer for the Day of Atonement has been partly preserved. Preceding it there may be discerned traces of prayers for the seasons of the year.[69]

We may suppose that a liturgy of this sort was used by members of the יחד (הרבים) when they met "on the third part of all the nights of the year to read in the book . . . and to make the benedictions together" (1QS vi 7-8). This same composition was probably mentioned in 1QM xv 5 as The Book of the Order of Times (ספר סרך עתו), in which was also recorded the Prayer for the Time of War (תפילת מועד המלח[מה]).[70]

A comparison of the Order of Benedictions with the order underlying the Mishna tractate *Berakot* will elucidate the bearing of this inquiry on our main problem, viz., whether the Covenanters reckoned the day from sunset to sunset (as was the custom in rabbinic tradition) or from sunrise to sunrise.

The Mishna opens by noting the times of the principal benedictions repeated daily and by discussing how they should be uttered in normal and in unusual situations (*m. Ber.* 1-8). Afterwards the benedictions for special occasions are quoted (*m. Ber.* 9). Prayers for festivals are not recorded within this framework.

It is important to stress the sequence of benedictions at the beginning of the tractate. First of all the evening prayer is discussed: "When should the *Shema* be said in the evenings?" Only afterwards does the tractate concern itself with the reading of the *Shema* in the morning (1:2).[71] The rabbis wondered at the precedence of the evening prayer over the morning prayer (*b. Ber.* 1a). They found authority for it in the wording of a Bible verse: "since it is written, and when thou liest down and when thou risest up" (Deut 6:7). Thus they based their practice of reckoning the day from the evening on Pentateuchal evidence.

The Covenanters' order of prayer, however, begins with the morning benedictions: "With the coming of the day and night I shall enter into the Covenant of God" (1QS x 10). "From the moment I put forth my hands and feet I shall bless Thy name" (x 13). They too base their prayers on a paraphrase of Deut 6:7 but with a noteworthy change in the arrangement of its components,

---

69. Cp. 1Q 34 bis; DJD, 1. 152-53.
70. As suggested by Yadin, 1QM ad loc.
71. The periods of the day are listed in the same sequence in the מודים prayer of the Eighteen Benedictions: ועל נפלאותיך שבכל עת ערב ובוקר וצהרים.

which is certainly intentional. The mere juxtaposition of the two versions will prove the point.

Deut 6:7:	ובקומך	בשכבך	ובלכתך	בשבתך
1QS x 14:	ועם משכב יצועי	וקום	ובוא[י] לשבת	צאת[י]

The reversal of the order of the verse cannot be by chance. The Covenanters certainly were aware that Scripture places "sojourn at home in the evening" and "going to bed" before "rising in the morning" and "departure." And even if they themselves might not have regarded this order to establish the commencement of the day from sunset, the mainstream tradition (later) embedded in *b. Ber.* 1a emphatically drew attention to this interpretation. They had no choice, therefore, but to reverse the sequence of phrases in the biblical verse in order to make it a *point d'appui* for their view that the day was to be reckoned from sunrise. They surely found supporting evidence for their concept in the creation pericope, in which the fashioning of the sun preceded that of the moon (Gen 1:16).

A similar inversion can be discerned in the definition of pivotal terms which are regularly used in connection with the celestial luminaries. In biblical and mishnaic language, the verb בוא always denotes the setting of the sun, whereas the verb יצא denotes its rising. In the language of the scrolls, the opposite is the case: [עונתו ממן אור מבוא][72] stands for sunrise, whereas מוצא אור corresponds to בפנות ערב,[73] "on the turn of the evening" or nightfall. This may be considered additional proof for the supposition that the Covenanters based the reckoning of the day on a method contrary to that accepted in rabbinic tradition.[74]

---

72. 1QH xii 4-5. This restoration appears to be preferable to del Medico's suggestion (*VT* 6 [1956] 35), [ממ]זרח, which is unsupported by parallels. Cp. 1QH xii 6-7: עם האספו אל מעון חוקו ;1QS x 2: ובקץ האספו אל מעונתו; 1QS iii 19: במעון אור תולדות האמת, et sim.
73. 1QH xii 5-6. Cp. 1QH xii 7, where מוצא לילה is equivalent to עם האספו אל מעונתו in 1QS x 2, referring to the setting of the moon; cp. further 1QM xiv 13.
74. These matters may have prompted the rabbis to assemble in the tractate *Berakot* several decrees against heretical sects (*m. Ber.* 9:5), including one most probably directed against the יחד (*t. Ber.* 6:20; ed. Liebermann, p. 39; *b. Ber.* 12d); cp. S. Liebermann's notes on this passage in his *Tosefta Ki-fshuṭah*, ([1955] part I, p. 123) and his remarks in "Light on the Cave Scrolls from Rabbinic Sources" (*PAAJR* 20 [1951] 395); further, I. Lévi ("Le Tetragrammaton et l'écrit Zadokite de Damas," *REJ* 68 [1914] 119-25).

The reading of 1QS x 13-14, בראשית צאת[י] ובוא[י] לשבת וקום, must be viewed, as said, as a deliberate inversion of the MT of Deut 6:7 (= 11:9), בשבתך ... ובלכתך ... בשכבך ובקומך, and cannot be dismissed as just a case of poetic license. The author of 1QS preserved indeed the antithetical pair of verbs שכב—קום, although in reversed order.[75] But instead of ובלכתך,[76] which the MT employs in Deuteronomy in antithesis to בשבתך, he substituted the verb combination צאת ובוא, most probably under the influence of a literary reminiscence. This supposition can be underpinned by recalling that in Biblical Hebrew, as well as in the language of the scrolls, the expression בוא ויצא has a technical military connotation, serving as a sort of hendiadys,[77] whereas in 1QS x 13 it carries a more general meaning. In this context, the phrase צאת ובוא is apparently conceived as a kind of compound verb which constitutes one member in the quadruple arrangement צאת ובוא ... [ל]שבת ... [ו]קום ... משכב. Or else the two verbs צאת ובוא can be construed singly as individual parallels of שבת וקום, completing a triple clause with עם משכב יצועי .

Now the combination of the four verbs, צאת, בוא, שבת, קום, is not extant at all in the MT. It is therefore noteworthy that this singular combination may be found in a Qumran variant which has attracted the attention of scholars and has been proclaimed one of "the occasional, rare readings which are original and seem superior both to the received Hebrew and the Greek."[78] In Isa 37:28 (= 2 Kgs 19:27), ושבתך וצאתך ובואך ידעתי, 1QIsaᵃ opens the verse with an additional verb, reading: קומכה ושבתכה וצאתכה ובואכה ידעתיא. It may be safe to conclude that this reading was in the mind of the author of 1QS when he replaced the ובלכתך (Deut 6:7) with the synonymous expression צאת ובוא. Since the additional [ה]קומכ is not attested in any of the versions of either Isa 37:28 or its parallel 2 Kgs 19:27, this peculiar variant may serve as proof that the author of

75. Whenever קום is coupled in Biblical Hebrew with שכב in the meaning of "to rise—to lie down," it is preceded by this latter verb for obvious reasons. Cp. Gen 19:33, 35²; Num 24:9; 2 Sam 12:16-17; 2 Kgs 19:5, 7-8; Jonah 1:6-7; Job 7:4; Ruth 3:14. (Cp. also Isa 43:17; Ps 41:9; Job 14:12.) קום may precede שכב when it is employed as an auxiliary verb (Gen 19:35¹).

76. For הלך denoting activities preceding שכב, "lying down," cp. Prov 3:23-24; 6:22.

77. Deut 31:2; Josh 14:11; 1 Sam 18:13; 29:6; 2 Sam 5:2; 1 Kgs 3:7; 2 Kgs 11:8 (Ps 121:8)—1Q 28 i 17; DJD, p. 23.

78. M. Greenberg, "The Stabilization of the Text of the Hebrew Bible, Reviewed in the Light of the Biblical Materials from the Judean Desert," *JAOS* 76 (1956) 164, n. 51. This verdict was accepted and substantiated by S. Iwry ("The Qumran Isaiah and the End of the Dial of Ahaz," *BASOR* 147 [1957] 27-29).

1QS was conversant with the text of Isaiah in a form similar to, or identical with that perserved in 1QIsa[a]. The introduction of this paraphrase into his loose quotation of Deut 6:7 enabled him to adjust that verse to his requirements without incurring the onus of wilfully altering scripture.

To take up again our main line of thought. If, as assumed, the association of "Sabbath and appointed days" in the writings of the יחד dealing with the calendar dispute shows the יחד to have differed from other Jews in the reckoning of days, and therefore also of the Sabbaths, it is likely that the impact of the debate will have left traces also in rabbinic literature. This is indeed the case.

The tone of derision introduced by the Covenanters into their arguments against their opponents was captured by the midrash: "The insolent have made great jest of me . . . how have they made jest . . . again and again they say to me: You do not circumcise,[79] and you do not *keep the Sabbaths* nor read the Torah" (*Midr. Ps.* on Ps 119:20; ed. Buber, p. 495).[80]

The sages answered in kind. Their counterattack is delivered with a certain reserve, which bears the stamp of historical authenticity. They could not ignore or conceal the fact that these dissenters, like the "Cuthaeans" (Samaritans), kept "every commandment which they kept . . . more strictly than Israel" (*b. Ḥul.* 4a). There was no point, therefore, in heaping indiscriminate abuse upon the dissidents. They needed a specifically determined proof of offences with which to charge them, such as could justify their conviction and excommunication, although to all appearances they behaved like other Jews. Polemics of this type are transmitted, in the name of Eleazar of Modiᶜin: "He who profanes Sabbaths[81]

79. Referring perhaps to halakic differences concerning the procedure of circumcision or the time of its performance. The Samaritans, e.g., rule that a newborn child shall be circumcised on the eighth day, without allowing exceptions recognized by the rabbis, such as illness or weakness of the infant.

80. Probably a charge directed against basing *halakot* on the Oral Law instead of deriving them exclusively from the Written Law. Cp. Rabin (*Qumran Studies*, 55-56).

81. According to the correct reading of *Aboth d'Rabbi Nathan* ([ed. S. Schechter; New York: Feldheim, 1945], text A., chap. 26, p. 82). See L. Finkelstein (*Introduction to the Treatises Abot and Abot d'Rabbi Natan* [New York: JTSA, 1950] 74). Cp. CD xii 3: וכל אשר יתעה לחלל את השבת ואת המועדות לא יומת. Parallels of the quotation from *Ab. d'R. Nathan* in *m. ᶜAbot.* 3:11; *b. Sanh.* 99a; and *Sipre Num.* 6:112 ([ed. H. S. Horowitz; Jerusalem: Wahrmann, 1966] 121) record the saying with some alterations, the most important of which is the reading המחלל את הקדשים [התורה]. These changes may have been introduced deliberately, so as to apply that saying to halakic differences between the and dissenting groups in

and despises festivals and desecrates the Covenant in the flesh and reads into the Torah what is not there, notwithstanding that he has [observance of] Torah and good works to his credit,[82] has no portion in the world to come." This saying, in all probability, is attacking Jewish dissenters who excelled in their devotion to the commandments, who had "observance and good works" to their credit, but were at odds with the sages on issues of circumcision, the interpretation of the Torah and the observance of the Sabbath and the festivals. The latter were, in the present author's view, the members of the Qumran community, who rejected the dates of the Jewish festivals and fixed them according to their own calendar and desecrated the eve of the Sabbath, which was not considered holy according to their system of reckoning the day from the morning. Support for this inference may be derived from the last section of the book of *Jubilees*, which is devoted to Sabbath regulations (50:6-13). In this section the author stresses once and again the prohibition against engaging in work on the *Sabbath day*, relying for authority on a paraphrase of the Sabbath commandment (Exod 20:8; Deut 5:13): "Six days you shall labor, but the seventh day is a Sabbath for Yhwh your God. You shall do no work that day, neither you, nor your son, nor your daughter, nor your men-servants, nor your maidservants, nor your cattle, nor the sojourner who lives with you." There is not the slightest hint here of a prohibition of work on any part of the sixth day, on which preparations for the Sabbath are made: "You shall do no work whatever the *Sabbath day*, save what you have prepared for yourself on the sixth day, so as to eat and to drink and to rest, and keep the Sabbath from all work on that day . . . and every man who does any work thereon . . . who shall do any of these things on the Sabbath shall die" (*Jub.* 50:9-13).

regard to laws of chastity, especially in regard to restrictions concerning the menstruant. Cp. *y. Yebam..* 2:4 (3d): א'ר יודי בן פזי ולמה סמך הכתוב פרשת עריות. לפרשת קדושין ללמדך שכל מי שהוא פורש מן העריות נקרא קדוש. It is probable that the author of CD had this issue in mind when he counted "conveying uncleanness to the sanctuary" among the apparent "three kinds of righteousness" which are actually "the three nets of Belial" (iv 17-18). In *Odes. Sol.* 8:13 the accusation is levied against the Sadducees that they "trod the altar of the Lord, [coming straight] from all manner of uncleanliness; and with menstrual blood they defiled the sacrifices." Cp. L. Ginzberg, *An Unknown Jewish Sect* (trans. from the German; New York: JTSA, 1976) 18.

82. This definition prevents the application of these words to the Christians. See Finkelstein's refutation ("Introduction," p. 79) of the argument in favor of this hypothesis, put forward by A. H. Weiss in *Dor Dor we-Dorshaw* ([Hebrew; Vilna: Romm, 1904], 1. 237).

It would seem that on the ground of this cumulative evidence one may be justified in suspecting the authenticity of the wording of CD x 14-15, which contradicts our supposition: "Let no man do any work on the sixth day from the time when the orb of the sun is distant from the gate by its own diameter [lit., fullness], for that is what He said, 'Guard the Sabbath day and keep it holy' " (Deut 5:12). This is the only application in CD of the prohibition of work to a part of the sixth day. This extension is derived from a Pentateuchal verse not quoted in *Jubilees*: "Observe/remember the Sabbath day and keep it holy" (Exod 20:8; Deut 5:12). Should we regard it as mere coincidence that this very text served the rabbis as authoritative base for the inclusion of the Sabbath eve in the Sabbath law? Thus R. Juda ben Bathyra in *Mek. d'R. Šimʿon bar Yoḥai* 20, 8:[83] "[From the wording of the commandment, 'observe] the [Sabbath] day,' it follows that it applies to the day only. Whence therefore [do we include] the night? This is taught by [the additional phrase] 'to keep it holy.' [If so,] why does it say 'the day'? Because the day commands more respect than the night."[84]

This extension of the Sabbath law so as to include in it the night preceding the Sabbath is conspicuously out of place in a legal framework associated with the solar calendar[85] and is unsuited for a community whose members derived from that calendar the honorific title of Sons of Light. But this extension is most appropriate in the framework of a lunar calendar by which abided the Sons of Darkness. For this reason the extension was accepted by mainstream Jewry in the Second Temple Period (cp. Josephus *BJ*. 4.9.12) and later by both the Rabbanites and the majority of Karaites in the Middle Ages.[86] It seems reasonable to suppose that the copyist of CD, who lived in the 10th-11th centuries (or one of his predecessors), whether a Karaite or a Rabbanite, altered

83. (Ed. N. Epstein; Jerusalem: Mekize Nirdamim, 1955) 148-49.
84. Ginzberg (*An Unknown Sect*, 108) correctly discerned that the "Extension of the Sabbath," as prescribed in CD x 15, points to a certain resemblance between the Qumran halakah and that of the rabbis. However, differing from his opinion, the present author holds that this resemblance is not original, but resulted from a change introduced into the preserved MS of CD by a medieval copyist.
85. S. Zeitlin (*The Zadokite Fragments* [JQRMS; 1952] 17-18) relies on this halakah for differentiating between the law of the book of *Jubilees* and that of CD, and also as a basis for his opinion that the יחד from the Judean Desert (in his view, the Karaites) "followed a lunar-solar calendar."
86. S. Poznanski, "Meswi al-Okbari, Chef d'une Secte Juive du IXe Siècle," *REJ* 34 (1897) 161-91.

the ancient wording,[87] which originally had been similar to that of *Jubilees*, and adjusted the text to the current laws prevailing in his community.

The supposed alteration of the text of CD was not effected simply to correct an apparent distortion which the copyist considered he had found in that ancient work, but was imperative for immediate reasons. Beginning with the second half of the 9th century, we witness a renewal of the debate as to whether the day was to be reckoned from sunrise or from sunset.[88] According to the report of the Karaite historian Al-Qirqisani[89] (second half of the 10th century), the dissident Meswi al-Okbari (ca. 850) began the reckoning of the day from sunrise. Supporters of his view are mentioned down to the middle of the 12th century at least. Benjamin of Tudela (1160-1173) was apparently referring to them when he wrote:

> There [in Cyprus] are to be found both Rabbanites and Karaites. And there are as well Jewish-Cypriot sectaries who hold the Law in contempt and are excommunicated by Israel[ites] everywhere. *They profane the eve of Sabbath and observe the night preceding Sunday.*[90]

Against Jews of this type R. Abraham ibn Ezra is still arguing in his commentary on Exod 16:25: "many faithless people have been led astray on account of this verse and have said that we are ordered to keep the *Sabbath day and the night following it*. For Moses said, 'for *today* is a sabbath unto the Lord,' and *not the night before it*."[91]

---

87. A suspicion has already been entertained that the scribe of CD on several occasions made additions to the text which he had before him. See, e.g., Ginzberg (*An Unknown Sect*, 279-80).

88. It is probable that the revival of the old controversy was associated with the discovery of the "Cave Writings" at the end of the 8th century, as related by Timotheus, Bishop of Seleucia. See O. Braun ("Der Katholikos Timotheos I und seine Briefe," *Oriens Christianus* 1 [1901] 138); O. Eissfeldt ("Der Anlass zur Entdeckung der Höhle und ihr ähnliche Vorgänge aus älterer Zeit," *ThLZ* 74 [1949] 597-600).

89. *Kitāb al-Anwār*, 1. 2. Cited by Poznanski (*REJ* 34 [1897] 165); L. Nemoy, "Al Qirqisani's Account of the Jewish Sects and Christianity," *HUCA* 7 (1930) 330, 389. The author's thanks are due to Prof. Z. Ankori for advice in matters of Karaite calendation.

90. *The Itinerary of R. Benjamin of Tudela* ix 5-8, (ed. Grünhut-Adler; London, 1907) 23, reprinted from *JQR* OS 16-18 (1904-1906).

91. Prof. Yadin drew my attention to this passage.

The linking of the Sabbath with the festivals in the "Calendar Dispute," both in the writings of the יחד and of the sages, furnishes us with evidence for the hypothesis that the Covenanters differed from normative Judaism on two main principles: a) in the calculation of the year, employing respectively the solar period and the course of the moon as basis of their computations, and b) in the method of reckoning the day, from sunrise or from sunset. The controversy over the priority of the sun or the moon in calendation continued in later generations within the Jewish community, as well as between mainstream Judaism and dissident groups. The impact of this debate may be discerned in medieval literature, Jewish, Christian, Karaite, and Moslem. The "Sabbath controversy," on the other hand, died down, either because the great majority of Jews yielded to the practice of reckoning the day from the evening, or because those who disagreed with that system had severed their links with the Jewish community. As a result of this process, reports of the profanation of the Sabbath owing to differences of time calculation are rare. The problem is only hinted at here and there in the margins of the never-ending debate on the calendar.

The above saying in *Aboth d'Rabbi Nathan* is transmitted in the name of R. Eleazar of Modiᶜin, who participated in the Bar Kokhba revolt and figured prominently in the leadership of that period.[92] It bears the recognizable imprint of problems which were typical at the time of the man to whom it is ascribed, and who, being a priest, would have clashed with dissenters in everyday life, though he encountered them in the period of their decline.[93]

With the disappearance of the Covenanters of the Judean Desert, detailed information on the יחד, its way of life, and its code of laws, comes to an end. Later generations preserved its memory in vague fashion. Polemics aimed in the past directly at certain conspicuous actions of the Covenanters, were now diverted to other dissident movements that are not always clearly identifiable.

92. Tradition presents him as the uncle of Simon Bar Kokhba. See A. Hyman (*The History of the Tannaim and Amoraim* [Jerusalem: Boys Town Publishers, 1964], 1. 215). S. Yeivin (*The Bar Kokhba War* [Jerusalem: Bialik, 1946] 56) holds that R. Eleazar of Modiᶜin was identical with Eleazar the Priest, in whose name coins were struck during the revolt.

93. According to one view, the scrolls were deposited in the caves during the Bar Kokhba War. See H. H. Rowley (*Zadokite Fragments*, 88). The majority of scholars concur with the opinion that the יחד disappeared from the historical scene only after the destruction of the Second Temple. (R. de Vaux, Fouilles aux Khirbet Qumrân. Rapport préliminaire sur la deuxième campagne," *RB* 61, 229-36).

This assumption may readily explain the rewording of the saying cited above in a later tradition: "R. Sheshet said in the name of R. Eleazar ben Azariah,[94] that every man who despises the festivals is like an idolater, as it is written, 'You shall make no molten gods,' and next to it, 'The feast of unleavened bread you shall keep' "[95] (Exod 34:17-18). It may be conjectured that originally the saying was ascribed to R. Eleazar ben Azariah,[96] in exactly the same phrasing, or in a similar form, as that in which it was transmitted in the name of R. Eleazar of Modi'in. However, in the time of R. Sheshet, who belonged to the third generation of the Babylonian Amoraim (4th century), the saying had lost precision, because the dissenters at whom it had been aimed had meanwhile become obsolete. In its new version, both vague and lacking in distinctiveness, it is adjusted to serve in the dispute with new dissidents who did not distinguish themselves any more by strict adherence to the Law or by good deeds, but yet adhered to a calendar calculated differently from that current in Judaism.

VIII

The great importance attaching to the calendar controversy in the life and laws of the Covenanters of the Judean Desert prompts us to present this issue as a pivotal criterion for testing propositions to identify the Sons of Light with one of the other dissident Jewish groups that left an imprint in rabbinic literature or in Hellenistic writings.

More than one dissident faction adopted a particular calendar calculation which differed from the calendar current in the wider community from which it had split off. The Samaritans, Sadducees, Boethusians, and Karaites[97] were all

---

94. R. Eleazar ben Azariah, too, came of a priestly family and belonged to the second generation of Tannaim. For some time he took Rabban Gamaliel's place at the head of the Sanhedrin at Jamnia. One may be tempted to surmise that in the first place the saying was transmitted in the name of only one of the two rabbis and that eventually it also became attached to the other, owing to similarity of name and (priestly) status.

95. *b. Pesah.* 118a; *Mak.* 23a.

96. See n. 94 above.

97. A telling definition of the importance of the calendar in the history of Jewish sectarianism has been preserved by the Karaite al-Qirqisani (10th century). In describing the sect led by Abu 'Isa, Qirqisani relates that despite the fact that

distinguished by deviations from the calendar reckoning of the main community. Therefore, we cannot avail ourselves of this criterion in order to identify positively the Sons of Light with one of those other dissident groups.[98] But in a negative way we may state that the Sons of Light can only be identified with a movement one of whose distinguishing marks was a calendar calculation varying from that accepted in rabbinic tradition.

Of all the dissident groups with whom the יחד has been compared, the Essenes certainly show the greatest similarity. The subject has been treated profusely, and there is no need here to rehash the discussion. But neither the supporters of the identification of the יחד with the Essenes, nor those who accept it with reservations, seem to have taken note of the fact that our sources do not report that the Essenes adhered to a calendar which differed from that of other Jews.[99] Some thought should surely be given to this phenomenon. Until proof is adduced that also in this matter the Essenes resembled the "Sons of Light," the proposed identification becomes questionable. Therefore, one must ask whether the missing link may possibly be found by some further investigation. Rabbinic sources note that the Boethusians differed from the Pharisees on matters of calendation. According to the reading of the Erfurt MS of the Mishna, it was because of them that the rabbis abolished the custom of lighting bonfires to signal the onset of a new month. When the Boethusians created confusion by lighting fires on their part to proclaim the new moon, "they [i.e., the sages] enacted that messengers should go forth" (*m. Roš. Haš.* 8:2). And, as already stated, the Boethusians used to say, "The Omer may not be reaped on the closing [night] of the [Passover] festival" (*m. Menah.* 10:3), but only on the Sunday following upon the Sabbath that falls in the week of Passover. Because of the Boethusians and in accordance with their own interpretation of the verse "on the

they had parted from the Rabbanites in matters of opinion and belief, they were not boycotted by them. He adds, "I asked Jacob ibn Ephraim al-Shāmi, 'Why do you encourage association with the followers of ʿĪsā and intermarry with them, although they attribute prophecy to men who are not prophets?' He answered me: 'Because they do not differ from us in the keeping of the festivals.'" Qirqisani reacts to this reply with mockery concerning the Rabbanites, who valued the calculation of festive seasons more than beliefs and ideas (L. Nemoy, *HUCA* 7 [1930] 382).

98. Cp. S. Liebermann ("The Discipline, etc.," *JBL* 71 [1952] 205-206).

99. The point was already raised by the present author in a review of Y. Yadin's book, *Hamegilloth Hagenuzoth* (published in the Hebrew daily *Haaretz*, Feb. 15, 1957). See now Rabin (*Qumran Studies*, 81).

morrow after the Sabbath,"[100] the rabbis laid triple emphasis on the ordinance to cut the Omer after the first day of Passover, even when this involved a desecration of the Sabbath. Now, if we were to accept the suggestion of Y. M. Grintz[101] to equate the enigmatic name "Boethusians" with *Beth (E) sin,* who are none but the "Essenes" of Hellenistic literature,[102] the missing link would have been found. We could then conclude that also the Essenes adhered to a calendar calculated differently from that of the Pharisees, thus gaining a further clue in support of the identification, or at least the association, of the Sons of Light with the Essene community.

Whatever the decision in this matter, the quest for a new criterion for identifying the יחד, undoubtedly a matter of exceeding significance in the study of the scrolls, should not obscure the importance of an elucidation of the calendar controversy itself. The abidance by a divergent method of calendation served as an effective indication of aspirations to attain social and religious independence and was seized upon by nonconformists in Israel from the time of Jeroboam I[103] down to the sectarian secessions at the height of the Middle Ages. The יחד of the Judean Desert provides a characteristic and enlightening example of this phenomenon.

---

100. *t. Roš. Haš.* 1:15, ed. Liebermann, p. 309; *m. Ḥag.* 2:4; *b. Menaḥ.* 65a; *y. Roš. Haš.* 2:1, 57d.
101. "The Yaḥad Sectarians, Essenes, Beth(e)sin," *Sinai* 32 (1954) 11-43 (Hebrew).
102. This supposition was already entertained by Azariah di Rossi (*Me ʾor ʿEnayim,* chap. III, 90-97). For further references see Grintz (*Sinai* 32 [1954] 38).
103. See Talmon ("The Cult and Calendar Reform of Jeroboam I," *KCC,* 113-39).

YOM HAKIPPURIM IN THE HABAKKUK SCROLL

At this stage of our knowlege of the Qumran Scrolls, when not all of the material found in the caves has been published, it seems precarious to attempt a final solution to the problems connected with that find. Caution is moreover demanded because of the fact that even the material published has not yet been evaluated sufficiently. The suggested identifications of the community which produced the scrolls and the fixing of the date of their produciton are therefore based on partial evidence only, archaeological, epigraphic, linguistic or historical. But no solution, offered until now, will answer all queries and silence all objections raised by opposing scholars.[1] A satisfactory determination of that community is the more complicated as the salient features of the scrolls and the circumstances of their discovery, if taken one by one, allow the identification of the New Covenanters with several other dissident groups known, more or less, to the students of Jewish history.[2]

I

We should therefore view with suspicion Dupont-Sommer's attempt to assign to the compilation of one of the manuscripts, the Habakkuk Scroll

1. P. Kahle, "Der gegenwärtige Stand der Erforschung der in Palästina neu gefundenen hebräischen Handschriften," *ThLZ* 9 (1950) 528-530; G. R. Driver, "New Hebrew Scrolls," *The Hibbert Journal* 49 (1950) 11-21; S. Zeitlin, "The Hebrew Scrolls: Once More and Finally," *JQR* 41 (1950) 1-58; R. P. R. de Vaux, "La grotte des manuscrits hébreux," *RB* 56 (1949) 586-609; S. A. Birnbaum, "The Date of the Isaiah Scrolls," *BASOR* 113 (1949) 33-35; idem, "The Leviticus Fragments from the Cave," *BASOR* 118 (1950) 20-22.
2. See Kahle, Driver, Zeitlin, op. cit.; R. P. R. de Vaux, "A propos des manuscrits de la Mer Morte," *RB* 57 (1950) 417-29; P. R. Weiss, "The Date of the Habakkuk Scroll," *JQR* 41 (1950) 125-54.

(1QpHab), a date as precise as the year 42-41 B. C. E.[3] This scholar's argument culminates with the assumption that a well-known historical event is hinted at in the scroll. This point is taken as a clue to the solution of the main problem, namely the date of its composition. Dupont-Sommer maintains that in the passage, פשרו על הכוהן הרשע אשר רדף אחר מורה הצדק אבות [אבית ?] גלותו לבלעו בכעס חמתו ובקץ מועד מנוחת יום הכפורים הופיע אליהם לבלעם ולהכשילם ביום צום שבת מנוחתם (1QpHab xi 4-8), the author refers to the conquest of Jerusalem by Pompey in 63 B. C. E. He quotes Josephus (*Ant.* 14.3.4) in order to prove that this event took place on a Yom Kippurim.[4] According to Dupont-Sommer's interpretation of that passage in Josephus it was because of the Fast, which hampered the Jews in the defence of the city, that the Roman attack was successful.

This theory is plausible, but is actually without foundation. Dupont-Sommer's interpretation of the relevant passage in Josephus, apparently drawn from Strabo,[5] is extremely doubtful.[6] But even if this part of Dupont-Sommer's argument were tenable, there is no reason to assume that the phrase in the Habakkuk Scroll, discussed here, contains any reference to that historical event. It is hardly conceivable that a notion of this kind can be read into the text with which we are concerned. Although the phrase אבות גלותו is somewhat strange,[7] the sentence as a whole makes good sense. We are told that the Wicked Priest, the major opponent of the New Covenanters, appeared at the Righteous Teacher's abode, where the latter had taken refuge together with (some of) his followers. The pursuer intended to harm the Covenanters, literally "to devour them and the Righteous Teacher." Dupont-Sommer refers the adjoining passage הופיע אליהם לבלעם ולהכשילם to God, who appears "tout resplendissant pour les engloutir et pour qu'ils trébuchassent," bent on destroying the wicked people. The proposed change of subject is completely unwarranted. By הופיע אליהם none but the Wicked Priest is meant. It requires some imagination to regard these words as a reference to a Roman attack on Jerusalem. A comparison with the beginning of

---

3. A. Dupont-Sommer, "Le Commentaire d'Habacuc découvert près de la Mer Morte. Traduction et Notes," *RHR* 137 (1950) 159, 169-70.
4. Ibid. 169.
5. Strabo, *Geography,* 16.2.40.
6. See M. Dagut, "The Habakkuk Scroll and Pompey's Capture of Jerusalem," *Bib* 32 (1951) 542-548.
7. W. M. Brownlee, "The Jerusalem Habakkuk Scroll," *BASOR* 112 (1948) 15. Dupont-Sommer's reading אבות נלותו is possible, but his translation "tu as osé le dévètir" is far-fetched (*RHR* 137 [1950] 138, 149-50).

the scroll suffices to prove that the compiler of this work was not at a loss for stronger and more suitable words for the description of a battle or the depiction of an enemy. And as he was presumably acquainted with the War Scroll (1QM), he could easily have borrowed more appropiate terms to describe an attack of the Roman army than, "he appeared upon them to devour them and make them stumble," in order to confer a notion of the fierce battle in which Jerusalem was taken. It is, moreover, most unlikely that he would not have expressly mentioned the Roman troops. Though Hyrcan II, the aspirant to the office of the High Priesthood, whom Dupont-Sommer identifies with the Wicked Priest,[8] attached himself to the Romans, it was not he who played the major role in the conquest of Jerusalem. The absence of any reference in the above passage to external forces involved in the struggle between the Righteous Teacher and the Wicked Priest proves sufficiently that the author of 1QpHab had no such factors in mind.

Dupont-Sommer's theory should therefore be dismissed as unwarranted. With the refutation of his main argument, his reconstruction of the Covenanters history becomes a mere assumption.

II

But although the passage in question contains no direct evidence leading to the determination of the date of the Habakkuk Scroll, it constitutes a rather interesting and important contribution to our knowlege of the יחד. If correctly interpreted, the phrase הופיע אליהם ביום צום שבת מנוחתם shows that the בני צדוק employed a calendar calculation which differed from the one adopted by the official authorities, the Wicked Priest, and his followers.[9] A close investigation of the text of the scroll will substantiate this explanation.

The Wicked Priest is reported to have come to the teacher's abode on a "Yom Hakippurim," obviously not being bound to observe this day as a Holy Day. If this priest were a non-Jew there would be no problem. But it is generally thought that no such basic differences existed between the opposing factions. The יחד בני צדוק or יחד בני האור, as I suggested elsewhere the group be called,[10]

8. Dupont-Sommer, *RHR* 137 (1950) 169.
9. P. Lagrange, "La Secte Juive de la Nouvelle Alliance aux Pays de Damas," *RB* 9 (1912) 328, 333-34.
10. "The Qumran יחד—A Biblical Noun," in this vol., pp. 53-60.

were dissenters who differed from the mother-community in many issues but not on fundamentals.[11] Their hatred of the Wicked Priest and of his partisans is the hatred of protesting co-religionists who had interpreted differently the common heritage. The Wicked Priest is not reported to have violated basic rules of the Law. Therefore, his activities on that Yom Hakippurim cannot be explained as a flagrant violation of the Holy Fast.

The solution suggested here offers a satisfactory explanation. The Covenanters' Day of Atonement did not coincide with the official Fast and had therefore no binding force for the Wicked Priest. We might even conjecture that the Righteous Teacher and his adherents repaired to a place in the desert so as to keep their Fast in the proper fashion, unmolested by their opponents. The exclusiveness of that Holy Day, incumbent only upon the Covenanters is possibly expressed in the personal pronoun of יום צום שבת מנוחתם, "on the Fast-day, the Sabbath of *their* rest."

But the priest pursued the dissenters even to their place of refuge, bent on barring them from the observance of their heterodox Yom Hakippurim. This is the obvious meaning of the verbs בלע and כשל which describe the Priest's intentions. כשל may be viewed as a technical term meaning "to transgress a law," and is used in this connotation in Hos 4:5: וכשלת היום וכשל גם נביא עמך לילה. Sometimes the verb appears in conjunction with עון, as in Hos 5:5: ואפרים יכשלו בעונם וכשל גם יהודה עמם,[12] "Ephraim will stumble in their sin and together with them will stumble Judah."

From the qal a causitive hiphᶜil is derived which describes the inducement, either by persuasion or by force, to transgress a command. A parallel passive hophᶜal form is extant in Mal 2:8, הכשלתם רבים בתורה, and Jer 18:23, והיו מכשלים לפניך בעת אפך עשה בהם, "let them be deemed transgressors [lit. stumbled ones] before thee; in the time of thy wrath deal with them."[13] A noun with a similar notion is quite common in Ezekiel (7:19; 14:3, 4, 7; 18:30; 44:12).[14] In a completely parallel manner כשל and הכשיל are employed in Rabbinic Hebrew.[15] b.Giṭ. 43a (Ḥag 14a): אין אדם עומד על דברי תורה אלא אם

---

11. P. Lagrange, *RB* 9 (1912) 330, 345.
12. Cp. Hos 14:2; Jer 6:21; Ps 31:11.
13. Cp. Jer 18:15; Ezek 36:14-15; 2 Chr 28:23.
14. Cp. 1 Sam 25:31; Jer 6:21.
15. See J. Levy, *Neuhebräisches und Chaldäisches Wörterbuch über die Talmudim und Midraschim* (Leipzig: Brockhaus) 1876-89, s.v. כשל.

כן נכשל בהם,[16] "one is not aware of the words of the Torah, but after transgressing them"; *b. Roš. Haš.* 21b: אם מעכב אתה את הרבים נמצאת מכשילן. בלע.[17] לעתיד לבוא is used in a like sense, pointing to moral or ritual transgressions. Prov 19:28: ופי רשעים יבלע און; or Isa 3:12: עמי מאשריך מתאים. Isa 28:7,[18] וגם אלה ביין שגו ובשכר נבלעו.ודרך ארחתיך בלעו, contains features strikingly reminiscent of Hab 2:15, on which the author of 1QpHab based the *pesher* under discussion here.

That he indeed interpreted and understood בלע in this technical sense can be proven from yet another passage in his exposition. His comment on Hab 1:13, פשרו על למה תביט בוגדים תחריש בבלע רשע צדיק ממנו, runs as follows: בית אבשלום ואנשי עצתם אשר נדמו בתוכחת מורה הצדק ולא עזרוהו על איש הכזב אשר מאס את התורה בתוך כל עדתם. One seems to be on safe ground in suggesting that איש הכזב אשר מאס את התורה is the explanation of בבלע רשע צדיק, in which case בלע would be equivalent to מאס.

Lastly, it should be pointed out that the interpretation of ביום צום שבת מנוחתם as referring to the Covenanters' particular Yom Hakippurim makes obvious the connection between the *pesher* and the basic text in Hab 2:15: הוי משקה רעהו מספח חמתך ואף שכר למען הביט על מעוריהם. The meaning of that verse is not very clear,[19] but the author interpreted it, apparently, as dealing with the "Wicked Man" who forces his neighbor to drink when drinking is forbidden, or in other words, forces him to transgress a ritual law. The reading למען הביט אל מעוריהם,[20] instead of מועדיהם, constitutes the key word from which יום הכפורים and יום צום שבת מנוחתם can be derived rather easily. In his usual manner, the author identifies the hostile agent with the Wicked Priest who intended to force the יחד בני צדוק to desecrate their holiest day: מנוחתם לבלעם ולהכשילם ביום צום שבת .

---

16. *b. Ber* 28b.

17. Cp. *b.Yoma* 77b; *b.Giṭ.* 33a; *b. ʿAbod. Zar.* 2a 11b; *b. B. Qam.* 16b.

18. Cp. Num 14:20.

19. See commentaries. T. H. Robinson, F. Horst propose to read ומסביא הברו ואף שָׁבָר (*Die Zwölf kleinen Propheten* [HAT; 1938] 178). J. Wellhausen's emendation מסף חמתו is accepted by H. Ward ("A Commentary on Habakkuk," [ICC; Edinburgh: Scribner, 1912] 17) and by Kittel in *Biblia Hebraica.*

20. This variant is not borne out by the VSS nor has it been suggested by modern scholars. It is doubtful that the variant was in the author's text. We may assume that the reading מועדיהם constitutes an improvement which facilitated his commentary.

The text in 1QpHab xi 7-8 which describes the interference by official authorities with the special duties of an exclusive group, reminds one of two similar passages in the Hebrew Bible. The prophet Amos, predicting the calamities to befall Israel, cites as one of the people's sins their preventing the Nazirites from observing abstention from wine (2:12): ותשקו את הנזרים יין ועל הנביאים צויתם לאמר לא תנבאו. Amos speaks in rather general terms, but Jeremiah tells of a singular event in parallel circumstances. Fleeing before Nebuchadnezzar's army, the Rekhabites had taken refuge in Jerusalem, although their statutes forbade settling in permanent settlements. Furthermore, like the Nazirites, they were not allowed to drink wine. Jeremiah's invitation that they should avail themselves, nevertheless, of the wine offered to them is firmly declined (35:1-11). The prophet cites the Rekhabites' steadfastness as an example of adherence to a command, even though not divine (35:12-16). Here again, the forcing of a drink on somebody who by his exclusive laws is forbidden to partake of it, is symbolic of coercion to transgress a ritual command. We are obviously concerned with a standard metaphor.

This would explain the associations aroused immediately in the mind of the author of 1QpHab when reading Hab 2:15: הוי משקה רעהו. His deduction, לבלעם ולהכשילם ביום צום שבת מנוחתם, is instantaneous and was most probably accepted by his audience as completely natural.

At this stage of our investigation two further passages will be brought under scrutiny which bear witness to the fact that the New Covenanters adhered to a special calendar-calculation. Amongst the statutes enumerated in the Damascus Documents, we find the prescription: ולהודיע בין הקודש לחול ולשמור את יום השבת כפרושה ואת המועדים ואת יום התענית במצא]'[באי הברית החדשה בארץ דמשק (CD vii 17-19). Furthermore, the author dwells on the especially strict observance of the Sabbath (x 16; xi 18). But the festivals and the Day of Atonement are not treated so elaborately. The Covenanters' mode of observance of these days apparently did not differ from that prescribed by the official authorities. The phrase "to observe the festivals and the Day of Fast in compliance with the command[21] of those who entered the New Covenant in the Land of Damascus" should therefore be understood as stressing the necessity of

---

21. [.]במצא is read by most scholars במצו[ת]. (See C. Rabin, *The Zadokite Documents* [Oxford: Clarendon, 1953] ad. loc.). This reading corroborates our interpretation.

keeping these days in accordance with the particular time-table of the dissenting community.

The importance of keeping the festivals at their appointed time is furthermore laid down in 1QS (v 13-15). The Covenanters are exhorted there "not to depart from all the words of God (to keep them) at their times and not to antedate them and not to be late in (one of) all their fixed times."[22] These recurring admonitions are fully understood when considered in the light of the thesis proposed here, namely that the Covenanters employed a calendar differing from the one prevalent at the time in the mother community.

And finally, CD xx 1-4 mentions the book of *Jubilees* in a fashion which leaves no doubt whatsoever that this book ranked very highly with the בני צדוק. It is, as a matter of fact, equivalent in merit to the Law alone. The Torah of Moses and the "Book of the Division of Time according to *Jubilees* and Cycles [of seven years]" are deemed to be very "accurate" and completely sufficient for the knowlege of divine ordinances and time-calculations respectively. It is therefore not suprising that fragments of the book of *Jubilees* have been discovered in the Qumran Caves.[23]

The book of *Jubilees* and its content and character need not be described here. But in order to make its value for our investigation explicit, we shall quote definition of this work given by Charles:[24] "In the forefront, as its name suggests, stands the question of the calendar. . . . The writer's aim seems to have been nothing less than a reformation of the Jewish calendar. The prevailing system has led to the nation forgetting new moons, festivals and sabbaths, in other words it has produced grave irregularities in the observance of matters which were of divine obligation."

III

The thesis put forward here opens up new aspects in the religious and social background of the Qumran Covenanters and offers a new understanding of the passage in 1QpHab from which we originally started. The Wicked Priest's sole purpose, when "appearing" at the Teacher's place of refuge, was the wilful

---

22. ‏ולוא לצעוד מכול דברי אל בקציהם ולוא לקדם עתיהם ולוא להתאחר מכול מועדיהם‎. Cp. also "A Further Link," in this vol., pp. 61-67.
23. R. de Vaux, *RB* 56 (1949) 586-609.
24. R. H. Charles, *The Book of Jubilees* (Oxford: Clarendon, 1902) §18.

interruption of the Covenanters' unauthorized Day of Atonement. The importance of this action should not be underrated. The adoption of a different calendar by any dissenting group evidences an intention to dissociate themselves definitely from the social and religious entity in the midst of which they were living. This step is a far-reaching decision in the process of alienation, affecting not only the cultic issues such as feasts and fasts, but the whole web of social organization. The fixing of a different date for so significant a day as Yom Hakippurim constitutes therefore a disregard for the official religious rules as well as a manifestation of civic insurrection. Some examples, taken from Jewish history, will illustrate the social importance of alterations in the calendar.

(1) A very early instance of this kind is recorded in 1 Kgs 12:32-34, where the division of the Davidic-Solomonic kingdom is described. One of the first actions of Jeroboam I, after having been elected king of Israel in the wake of the rebellion against Rehoboam, was the introduction of a cultic time-table differing from the one valid in Jerusalem. He transposed the Feast of Tabernacles from the 15th day of the seventh month to the 15th day of the eighth month (12:32). The writer remarks that this dating was an unwarranted innovation intended to apply to the Northern Kingdom exclusively (12:32-33). Jeroboam chose the Feast of Tabernacles as the starting point for his new calendar, because it was, apparently, the first of the Pilgrimage Festivals to occur after the founding of his new state. The pilgrimage to Jerusalem on these festivals was of singular importance in the creation of a nation-wide feeling of unity and kinship. Therefore, by his action, Jeroboam erected a most formidable barrier between the populace of Judah and Israel. The changed date of the Festival of Tabernacles affected subsequently the calendar as a whole and caused a most decisive difference in social organization between the Northern and the Southern Kingdoms.[25]

(2) The importance of unanimity in calendar-timing as a tangible means of establishing a coherent society becomes more and more evident in later periods of Jewish history. Three main factors may be adduced to explain this development:

(a) The transition from a predominantly agricultural society, such as Israel was in the period of the First Temple, to a partly urbanized society, Jewry in the Second Commonwealth, estranged sizable groups of the population from the natural time-reckoning according to the seasons of the year. The agricultural context of the festivals became almost meaningless for townspeople who,

---

25. See S. Talmon, "The Cult and Calendar Reforms of Jeroboam I," *KCC* 113-139.

presumably, constituted an influential section of the populace in the Second Commonwealth. The natural rhythm of tilling, sowing and harvesting had no meaning in the time-calculations of artisans, priests, and merchants. An authoritative determination of periods and festivals was therefore a *conditio sine qua non* of the regulation of social life.

(b) The diminution of tangible power wielded by the leadership compelled the leaders to use with rigor any means which would enforce their authority. The prerogative of the fixing of the calendar became a mighty and useful weapon in the hands of those who knew how to use it.

(c) The dispersion of the Jewish community after the destruction of the First Temple brought about a dissimilarity of life-styles which could have dissipated the sense of social and religious kinship were it not mitigated and checked by tangible, unifying factors.[26] Jews in the Diaspora lived in climatic and civic conditions which could have estranged them completely from their brethren in Palestine. A common calendar, the synchronization of festivals, independent of the natural course of seasons, served as a unifying bond and restored the feeling of communal interdependence.

The endeavor of Jewish religious and civil authorities to establish one exclusive legal calendar should therefore be viewed as a fight for national self-preservation. Any diversity in the calendar constituted a danger to the continuity of Jewish society as a whole.

This will explain the action of the Wicked Priest, resented so much by the New Covenanters. Their keeping of a separate Yom Kippurim, as a vindication of a separate calendar, was a direct negation of his authority and a dangerous precedent which had to be stifled.

We might conjecture that the challenge to his personal authority, probably not a solitary incident, enhanced the priest's fury and anxiety and produced his immediate action. In the eyes of the Righteous Teacher and his followers this was one more "wicked" deed and was deplored as such.

(3) A similar combination of priestly rivalry and heterodox attitude of some social entities in Jewry of that time whose historical experiences differed from those of the mainstream community constituted one of the causes of the Samaritan schism. It explains the Samaritans' insistence on following a separate

---

26. See S. Talmon, "The Emergence of Jewish Sectarianism in the Early Second Temple Period," *KCC* 165-201.

calendar.[27] The priesthood of the community took over this important privilege from their Jewish colleagues when, after the final split from the mother-community, their status changed from pretenders to the high priesthood to actual holders of this office.

How far the changed time-calculation ultimately affected the social intercourse between Jews and Samaritans can be gleaned from the Tractate *Kuthim*.[28] The different date of Passover in the two communities, for example, raised the question whether Samaritan bread may be used by Jews on the first day after Passover. As their Feast of Unleavened Bread does not necessarily coincide with the Jewish Feast this must be ruled out, because the Samaritan bread might have been baked during the days of the Jewish Passover. The Samaritans are known to adhere to all the prescriptions concerning the preparation of the Unleavened Bread and the ritual observance of the Festival.[29] In this case, therefore, the problem caused by Samaritan Mazzot and their ultimate rejection, arises from different timing alone.

(4) This line of thought will shed new light on yet another legal ruling connected with the Samaritans. In *m. Roš. Haš.* 2:1-2 we are told that the proclamation of the New Moon was made known to the entire country by lighting bonfires and swinging torches on the Temple Mount. The signs were taken up, in a prearranged order, by neighboring locations and flashed from there to the next posts. But this comparatively rapid means of communication had to be abandoned משקלקלו הכותים. After that time a relay of messengers was established. Those כותים, presumably the Samaritans,[30] are accused of having wilfully caused confusion amongst the members of the Jewish community by kindling fires at wrong times. The geographic position of Shechem and the mountain range of Gerizim and Ebal in the central part of Palestine facilitated this interference and made it most effective.

But it seems to be doubtful that the Samaritans' actions should be seen as a wilful act of hostility on their part. I am inclined to assume that the confusion caused by their torches was accidental and not intentional. The Samaritans, like

27. J. A. Montegomery, *The Samaritans* (Philadelphia: Winston, 1907) 38, 312; M. Gaster, "The Samaritans" (Schweich Lectures; London: Milford, 1925) 65-67.
28. R. Kirchheim, ed., *Septem libri Talmudici parri Hierosolymitani* (Frankfurt/M: Kauffmann, 1851) 31-37.
29. See *b. Ḥul.* 4a: כל מצוה שהחזיקו בה כותים הרבה מדקדקים בה יותר מישראל.
30. This identification is accepted by traditional Jewish commentators as well as by modern scholars. See H. Danby, *The Mishna* (Oxford: Oxford University Press, 1933) 189.

the Jews, employed this traditional way of proclaiming the New Moon. The Mishnah refers to the final stage of the Second Commonwealth, when the rabbis discarded that time-honored custom and introduced a new system.[31] At that time Samaritan communities already existed in diverse towns in Palestine and probably also in Syria and Egypt. As in the case of the Jews, the Samaritans made use of the torch-system to announce the renewal of the moon from their religious center in Shechem to the daughter communities. Abulfath, the Samaritan Chronicler, relates that his coreligionists used to light bonfires on their mountain ridges on the first day of the seventh month. According to one tradition this was done in memory of the initial victory of Baba Rabba, their national hero. Another tradition connects this custom with Baba Rabba's last days.[32] This uncertainty induced Geiger to suppose that Abulfath's story contains but a reminiscence of facts related in our Mishnah.[33]

The term employed in *m. Roš. Haš.* 2:1, משקלקלו [הכותים], is often used in talmudic literature as a technical expression denoting sectarianism.[34] In the beginning of the relevant passage (*b. Roš. Haš.* 14b), we are told that משקלקלו האפיקורסים,[35] witnesses who came to give evidence of the appearance of the New Moon, were accepted only if they were personally known to the Sanhedrin. Formerly no such distinction existed. According to the traditional explanation,[36] this had become necessary because of false witnesses, hired by sectarians, who tried to mislead the court. But Rashi was justified in his interpretation of the occurrence,[37] namely that the misleading of the official authorities was

---

31. In y. *Roš. Haš.* 2:1 the discontinuation of the torch-system is attributed to Rabbi Jehuda who lived at the end of the second century C. E. But Z. Frankel (*Darke Hamishnah* [Leipzig: Hunger, 1859] 205) proved that the Mishna must be referring to the days of the Temple; B. Zuckermann, "Materialien zur Entwicklung der altjüdischen Zeitrechnung im Talmud," *Jahresbericht des jüdisch-theologischen Seminars in Breslau* (Breslau: Schottländer, 1882) 31.

32. E. Vilmar, *Abulfathi annales Samaritani* (Gotha: Perthes, 1865) lxviii, lxx 16ff, 134, 142.

33. A. Geiger, "Neuere Mittheilungen über die Samaritaner," *ZDMG* 20 (1866) 145.

34. E.g., b. *Sanh.* 108b; y. *ʿAbod. Zar.* 5.4.

35. In ed. Wilna, בייתוסים is substituted for אפיקורסים; y. *Roš. Haš.* 2:1 reads מינים. Other sources identify אפיקורסים with the Sadducees. Danby (Mishnah, p. 189) gives "sectaries" as a possible translation of the term. This proves that אפיקורסים was not always just a freethinker, but served often as equivalent to "Sectarian" (מין). Cp. *m. Sanh.* 10:1; y. *Sanh.* 11:27.

36. Cp. b. *Roš.Haš.* 24b; y. *Roš. Haš.* 2.1 and the traditional Jewish commentaries on the Mishna cited.

37. See his comment on y. *Roš. Haš.* 2.1.

incidentally caused by the sectarians' intention to proclaim the New Moon on a date conforming with their calendar calculations.

The examples adduced will suffice to indicate the ever-growing social importance of calendar calculations. The problems of civil authority connected with this issue will explain the steps taken by the Wicked Priest against the New Covenanters on their Yom Hakippurim. It may be said that the less real power is given to communal authorities by force of circumstances, the stricter the insistence on their prerogative of fixing the calendar. On the other hand, rival forces will always strive to appropriate for themselves this prerogative as a manifestation of social independence. This tendency was evidenced in biblical times in the split between political entities, the Northern and Southern Kingdoms, and later in the Samaritan dissent. The process was carried on inside those communities. On the Samaritan side we may point to Dustan and his faction who aimed to introduce a calendar similar to the one accepted by the compiler of the book of *Jubilees*.[38] In the Jewish community, the Sadducees, the Boethusians, and the New Covenanters may be cited as typical examples.[39]As in the case of the Sadducees, a clash between the priestly class and competing spiritual leaders may have aggravated the tension between the mainstream community, viz., the Wicked Priest and his followers, and the New Covenanters under leadership of the Righteous Teacher.[40]

(5) This ever-growing tendency during the last centuries of the pre-Chrisitan era and the first centuries C. E. to vindicate dissident inclinations by the adoption of a separate calendar conveys new meaning to a well-known episode related in *b. Roš. Haš.* 25a-b. We are told that Rabban Gamaliel,[41] the head of the Sanhedrin, and Rabbi Joshua differed with regard to the beginning of the New Month. Rabban Gamaliel made his official proclamation on the strength of a statement by two witnesses that they had seen the New Moon. R. Joshua denied the acceptability of the statement since it was disproved by his own astronomical calculations. The end of the story proves that Rabban Gamaliel obviously estimated his colleague and his scholarship very highly. He nevertheless ordered

---

38. M. Gaster, *The Samaritans*, 66-67.
39. See "The Calendar of the Covenanters," in this vol., pp. 147-85.
40. Lagrange, *RB* 9 (1912) 327: "Les prêtres sont donc respectés mais sont confinés dans leur domaine. Dans les conseils composés de dix membres, ils n'ont que quatre voix contre six, ce qui est toujours la minorité. Si tout ne nous trompe, l'admnistrateur de chaque groupe et l'administrateur général sont toujours des laïques" (CD xii 5-6; xiv 8-14; x 4-7).
41. End of first to beginning of second century C. E.

him to appear before his seat, carrying staff and purse, on the day which according to Rabbi Joshua's calculation would be the date of Yom Hakippurim. He was not satisfied with coercing his opponent to observe the Holy Fast on the day fixed by him, the head of the community, but made him publicly desecrate the day appointed by Rabbi Joshua in accord with his calculation, as the Day of Atonement. The incident constitutes a striking parallel to the episode related in the Habakkuk Scroll.

The harshness of Rabban Gamaliel's action cannot be explained as a mere sign of his domineering personality and vindictive character.[42] His action can be fully appreciated only if considered against the background of the communal conditions described above.[43] Rabban Gamaliel employed those stern measures since he could not tolerate any deviation from official legal rulings. For the sake of communal unity even Rabbi Joshua's personal prestige and scholarship must be sacrificed. A lax handling of this affair could have resulted in Rabbi Joshua's behavior being interpreted by the public as a separatist move, showing his disregard for the central authority. Rabban Gamaliel's action stemmed from ulterior motives as pointed out by Rabbi Akiba who tries to comfort Rabbi Joshua on his way to Yavneh. Rabbi Akiba states very clearly that the importance of the fixing of New Moons and festivals by the Sanhedrin does not lie in the scientific correctness of the assumed dates. Rabbi Joshua's calculation might indeed be superior to Rabban Gamaliel's reckoning, based on a statement by eyewitnesses. But the importance of the latter's proclamation lies in its becoming communal law by command of one, generally accepted, legal authority. R. Dossa b. Horkinas carries this point even further: "Whosoever was appointed head of the community, be he unworthiest amongst the unworthy, his appointment automatically makes him noblest of noble." Rabban Gamaliel's decision must therefore be considered final and binding, regardless of its objective merits.

42. L. Finkelstein (*Akiba, Scholar, Saint and Martyr* [Cleveland/New York: Meridian, 1962]) represents the discussion between Rabban Gamaliel and his contemporaries as the result of the latter's personal ambitions. This view was successfully refuted by G. Alon in his review of the book, *Tarbiz* 9 (1939) 262-65 (Heb.).

43. After having imposed the ban upon Rabbi Eliezer, in another dispute, Rabban Gamaliel is reported to have said in prayer: "Master of the world, it is well known before you that not for my honour nor for the honour of my father's house did I act as I acted, but for your honour, (namely) that disputes may not increase in Israel" (*b. B. Meṣ.* 69b).

IV

Our point of departure was the refutation of Dupont-Sommer's explanation of the Yom Hakippurim incident in the Habakkuk Scroll. We put forward a different interpretation of the passage concerned. The linguistic and thematic investigation revealed interesting aspects of the יחד. The New Covenanters deviated from mainstream Judaism, not merely in spiritual and legal matters, but also by the employment of a different calendar calculation.

It was thought worthwhile to enlarge upon this point. The suggested reinterpretation of the one passage in the Habakkuk Scroll acquires new significance when seen against a wider background. Viewed in comparaison with other separatist movements, in biblical as well as post-biblical times, deviation from the official calendar is found to constitute a standard feature in Jewish heterodoxy, especially during the last centuries B. C. E. and in the first centuries C. E.[44]

Pesher Habakkuk column xi, referring to the Wicked
Priest's interference with the Covenanters' observance of
Yom Hakippurim; Courtesy of the Israel Museum, Jerusalem

44. See S. Talmon, "The Calendar of the Covenanters of the Judean Desert," in this vol., pp. 147-85.

THE EMERGENCE OF INSTITUTIONALIZED PRAYER IN ISRAEL IN LIGHT OF QUMRAN LITERATURE

The scholarly investigation of Jewish prayer, its origins and development, has tended to concentrate on the clarification of historical and philological issues, i.e., on the textual criticism of individual prayers and the reconstruction of their original forms. Only recently has the scope of inquiry widened under the impact of new discoveries, especially from the Cairo Genizah and the liturgical material from Qumran, and due to the influence of techniques and methods developed in the field of comparative liturgy. Special reference should be made to the work of Joseph Heinemann who added a new dimension to this field of investigation by applying to it the tools which had been forged in biblical research by the *Gattungsforschung* school.[1] This approach has opened up new possibilities for our understanding of the development and employment of diverse liturgical forms and patterns in the setting of the synagogue.

It appears, however, that the use of the term *Sitz im Leben* in almost exclusive application to the immediate sphere of cultic practice (a severe handicap to the classical *Gattungsforschung*) does not satisfactorily illuminate the sociological dimension of prayer as an institution. Warned of both the possibilities and dangers, we shall present some new lines of thought concerning the genesis and history of Jewish prayer, which can be perceived through an analysis of pertinent Qumran literature, as well as present some wider methodological ramifications.

I

In its most basic aspect, *prayer* in Israel as elsewhere may be described as a spontaneous act of the individual which gives expression to his awe of and

---

1.   J. Heinemann, *Prayer in the Talmud—Forms and Patterns* (StJud, trans. S. Sarason; Berlin: de Gruyter, 1977), vol. 9.

thankfulness toward a superhuman being, to whose superior power he submits by choice or by necessity, and by whose will he abides. Initially prayer is offered not in the normal course of events but rather erupts at prominent occasions of joy or sorrow in the life of the individual. This type of prayer must be as old as thinking man. Its emergence may be considered to be bound up with his initial experience of the supernatural and with the very beginning of his contemplation of man's place in the universe. Spontaneous prayer has no fixed forms, nor can it be offered at preordained times. It is determined exclusively by the individual's needs or by the stirring of his soul. It is an expression of a preexisting personal emotion formulated ad hoc, not a means for the creation of an emotion. It is intimately bound up and correlated with the situation out of which it arises. The worshipper expects, or at least hopes for, an immediate response from the deity to whom the prayer is offered, whatever form this response may take.

In contrast, *institutionalized prayer* is a prayer in which the spontaneous, the individual, and the sporadic are replaced by the conventional, the universal and the periodic. Institutionalized prayer does not arise directly out of a specific human situation in which man yearns for a perforce intermittent high-tension communion with God. It is rather a means toward the achievement of a stabilized, unbroken bond with God. Institutionalized prayer does not aim at bringing about an immediate response from the deity with regard to a specific situation, but rather at safeguarding the continuous, slow-flowing relationship between the worshipper and his God. This basic, even relationship, however, also entails a promise for the communicant of achieving at given times the desired intense spiritual tension which is inherently possible in the belief in God.

By its standardization, its fixity, and its recurrence, institutionalized prayer serves as an expression of what is common to a congregation (or to mankind), not of what determines the individuality of man. Thus the very institutionalization of prayer reveals a communal spirit and at the same time strengthens this spirit. In the words of F. Heiler, "prayer is a social phenomenon . . . it is, as a whole, the reflex of human relations."[2] We may go further and conclude that it is a prime socializing factor of a given group. As such it can easily replace sacrificial forms of worship, since it retains under a different form of

2. Cp. F. Heiler (*Prayer* [trans. McComb; New York: AJS, 1958] 58). Our discussion is heavily indebted to Heiler's pioneering work.

devotional practice, the communal, standardized, nonindividualistic aspects of sacrifice.

The salient points of difference between individual-voluntary and communal-institutional prayer can be summarized as follows:

	Individual-voluntary	*Communal-institutionalized*
Time:	Occasional, unpredictable	Recurring at fixed interludes
Wording:	Situation-conditioned, spontaneous	Stereotyped formulations
Place:	Undefined	Specifically appointed locales

The precise beginning of institutionalized prayer in Judaism, i.e., the establishment of a definite order of prescribed prayers in fixed formulations which are to be uttered according to a detailed time-schedule, still escapes the knowledge of scholars.

In the worship of the people, prayer was indeed already present in the First Temple Period. It was, however, predominantly offered in conjunction with sacrifice. This sacrifice-*cum*-prayer situation is reflected in Isaiah's castigation of his fellow Jerusalemites who profusely offer animal-sacrifices together with lip-service-prayer, while their actions prove that these do not arise out of sincere, personal belief and do not express a commitment to God's laws (Isa 1:10-17). The reference to prayers (1:15) refers specifically to prayers offered in conjunction with sacrifices on holidays: Sabbaths, New Moons, Assemblies, and Festivals (1:13-14). But there is no mention of daily prayers. It may have been the custom to spend such festive days in the paternal house, to participate in the sacrifice with one's family, as, e.g., David was wont to do (1 Sam 20:29), in a setting similar to that prescribed for the offering of the Passover lamb (cp. Exod 12:1ff.). Otherwise one would go to see a prophet on such a day (2 Kgs 4:23), a rule which may have applied only to people residing too far from Jerusalem to allow for participation in the Temple service. Solomon's prayer at the dedication of the Temple, offered in combination with appropriate sacrificial acts (1 Kings 8), may be taken as representative of the same attitude and concepts, with special emphasis on their communal-national setting.

In Hannah's supplication (1 Sam 1:11) and in the thanksgiving psalm attributed to her (2:1-10), we can perceive prayers of the individual that were not intimately connected with sacrifice but seemingly were self-contained forms of devotion. This type of nonsacrificial invocation becomes prominent in the prophetic writings and especially in the book of Jeremiah (see, e.g., Jer 14:11; 29:12ff.). It is to be found in the psalmodic literature (Ps 55:17; 69:14), as well as in the postexilic historiographies such as the books of Daniel, Ezra and Nehemiah. Situations are presented there in which prayer without sacrifice is offered by an individual on behalf of the community (Dan 9:4-19; Ezra 9:5-15; Neh 9:5-37).

However in all these instances we deal with extraordinary circumstances, not with prayer that constitutes an integral part of an established worship pattern. For this reason these prayers exhibit individual forms and wordings which are unique and never reiterated, although they obviously contain stock phrases which were forged by a cultic-literary tradition.[3]

One can think of only one prayer which appears to have been couched in a fixed phraseology already in early biblical times. It is the text often referred to in scholarly literature as the "little credo" which accompanied the offering up of firstfruits to the priest (Deut 26:5-10). By its wording it can be characterized as a short recital of the main events in Israel's history from the days of the patriarchs to the conquest of Canaan, rather than as a prayer or invocation.

It is commonly agreed that in biblical times, as long as the Jerusalem Temple functioned and probably for some time after its destruction, communion between the individual and his Creator, as between the nation and its God, was based primarily on sacrificial worship over which the priests presided, without accompanying invocations. "The distinctive characteristic of the Israelite priestly sanctuary is the holy silence which reigned within it. The priestly sanctuary of Israel may be described as the realm of stillness." Thus Kaufmann, who goes on to explain that in contrast to other peoples of the Ancient Near East for whom incantation and recitation constituted the very core of ritual life, "in the cultic ceremony of the priestly code, all functions of the priest are carried out in silence without the accompaniment of any utterance, song, or recitation . . . there also is no room for prayer. The priestly sanctuary is not a place of prayer. Not only does the priest not offer supplication but neither does he offer a prayer of

---

3.   See M. Greenberg ("On the Refinement of the Conception of Prayer in Hebrew Scriptures," *AJSR* [Cambridge, MA: AJS, 1976], 1. 57-92, esp. pp. 87ff.) on the development of fixed liturgical formulae and Kaufmann's observation quoted there.

thanksgiving during the holy service. . . . Words spoken by the priest never are part of the cultic act and always are uttered outside the sanctuary."[4]

If we follow the sequence of cosmic creation, human evolution, and the national development of Israel, as depicted in the Bible, we may well assume that the biblical writers gave sacrifice precedence in time over prayer. Cain and Abel offer firstfruits of fields and flocks (Gen 4:3-4); Noah sacrifices beasts and birds (8:20); and Abraham erects altars to God (12:7-8) before the first mention of his "pronouncing the name of God" (13:4) is made. The technical term for prayer, התפלל, is found in the Bible for the first time in Gen 20:7, 17, where Abraham intercedes for Abimelech before God. (ברכה, which sometimes describes devotional glorification of God, also is not used earlier in this sense.)

The community-directed nature of sacrifice, as opposed to the predominantly individualistic character of prayer in the Bible, is also brought into relief by the contrasting definition of the appropriate places at which these two forms of devotional practice should be carried out. Kaufmann correctly emphasizes that the proper place for sacrifice is always *a* or *the* sanctuary of YHWH. In contrast to this, prayer has no distinctive or restricted locus.[5] It may be offered anywhere in the land of Israel or outside of it (Lev 26:40; 1 Kgs 8:46ff.; Dan 2:17ff.); from the belly of a fish as Jonah did (2:2ff.); or from the top of a mountain as Elijah did (1 Kgs 18:37). This does not exclude the Temple from becoming a place of prayer. A postexilic prophet, taking his cue from Solomon's prayer (1 Kgs 8:41-43), if an early date can be assumed for that composition, actually portrays the future temple as "a house of prayer for all peoples" (Isa 56:7).

The cessation of sacrifice which resulted from the destruction of the first Temple gave rise to the need for a new concept of worship. As long as the hope for a restitution of the Temple in the immediate future was still alive, sacrifice was thought of as being suspended only temporarily, not as being abolished. The story of the pilgrims from Shechem, Shiloh, and Samaria who went up to the house of God with frankincense and offerings in the days of Gedaliah when the Temple lay in ruins, implies that a skeleton sacrificial cult was still being maintained there by the Israelites after the capture of Jerusalem (Jer 41:4-5; cp. Ezra 4:2). Moreover the destruction of the Jerusalem Temple probably did not affect the continuation of sacrifice at other centers of worship. The mere existence of such centers is evidence that their adherents had not subscribed to the

---

4.   Y. Kaufmann, *Toledot HaEmunah HaYisraelit* (Tel Aviv: Dvir, 1927), 2. 476-77.
5.   F. Perles, "Prayer," *Encyclopedia of Religions and Ethics*, ed. J. Hastings (Edinburgh: Scribner, 1918) 192.

exclusiveness of the Temple in Jerusalem (the prevailing idea since Josiah's reform) and that they may have been built in open defiance of that sanctuary. Animal sacrifice may have continued in Egypt at the temple of Elephantine and later at Leontopolis, as well as at the Samaritan sanctuary on Mt. Gerizim. These splinter-groups, the earliest Jewish "sectarians," demonstrated their deviation from the main community not by introducing new forms of devotion, but rather by transferring to independent sanctuaries the sacrificial service that had developed in Jerusalem.

Scholars have aften assumed that new forms of worship sprang up among the Judean exiles in Babylonia. Their steadfast insistence on the exclusive legitimacy of the Jerusalem Temple made it impossible for them even to consider the erection of a substitute sanctuary and the introduction of a makeshift sacrificial cult.[6] When the hope for an immediate return to Israel and for the restoration of the Temple in the appreciably near future reached a low ebb, it became imperative to find adequate compensation for the apparently indefinite loss of the sacrificial institutions. Then and there liturgical worship consolidated to fill the existing void. Thus the synagogue and communal prayer came to replace the Temple and animal sacrifice.[7]

The evidence adduced in support of this theory is pitifully slim; one might say that it is nonexistent. Its proponents seem to have taken refuge in this line of reasoning because they could not visualize a community, and a Jewish community at that, which existed for an appreciable length of time (at least several generations) without any tangible form of institutionalized worship. Indeed the theory appears to have arisen from the modern amazement over a seemingly unprecedented historical phenomenon: a pious community lacking

6. The refusal of the Judean captives to normalize their lives in exile, on the personal as well as on the communal level, is reflected in the letter of guidance which Jeremiah dispatched to the deportees of 597 B.C.E., persuading them to adjust to a situation in which they were destined to live for seventy years, i.e., two or three generations (Jer 29:1-10, 24-32).

7. K. Kohler, *The Origins of the Synagogue and the Church* (New York: MacMillan, 1929) 3ff. L. Finkelstein, "The Origin of the Synagogue," *PAAJR* (1928-1930) 49-59. This transition was reduced *ad absurdum* by S. Blank ("Some Observations Concerning Biblical Prayer," *HUCA* 32 [1961] 75-90).

any system of religious paraphernalia. This deficiency, says Kaufmann, already made the ancients wonder:

> The diaspora which lived without a cult was an altogether new phenomenon in that period. Never had there been a group of people that remained faithful to a god and did not "worship" him; a group of people that remained faithful to the god who had deprived them of his cult; a group of religious men who actually did not worship any god. There can be no doubt that all this perplexed and amazed the pagan world. The vast cleavage between this people and the heathen nations was exemplified most distinctly by this wondrous fact.[8]

Even if we were to subscribe to the above-mentioned theory, there is no indication that the transfer from sacrifice to prayer in post-exilic Judaism resulted from a conscious and determined substitution of the one for the other. If it occurred at all at such an early stage, it must have been a spontaneous and uncontrolled process. There is not even a hint in our exceedingly meager prerabbinic sources to show that this transition ever was codified or attained legal force. The fact is that the law codices of the Bible (embedded in the Pentateuch and the books of Ezekiel, Ezra, and Nehemiah) contain not even one precept referring to *praying* or to the manner in which *prayer* should be offered. This conspicuous absence of nonsacrificial cultic legislation in all strata of biblical literature stands in glaring contrast to the plethora of statutes and instructions pertaining to sacrificial worship. Sacrificial cult laws pervade virtually all biblical legal writings, including those prophetic and historiographic books of postexilic composition and most notably the Priestly Code, which the majority of scholars consider to have achieved its final form only after the Return from the Exile. One is forced to conclude that "the theory that the synagogue—as a house of prayer, not of assembly or sacrifice—originated in Babylonia during the Exile is quite without foundation; all the pertinent biblical, intertestamental and early rabbinic literature, together with the results of archaeology, rule this out."[9]

---

8. Kaufmann (*Toledot* [above, n. 4], 2. 34). However Kaufmann himself then proceeds to make a case for the assumed replacement of sacrifice by prayer in the Babylonian Exile.
9. H. Orlinsky, "Nationalism-Universalism and Internationalism in Ancient Israel," *Translating and Understanding the Old Testament* (New York: Abingdon, 1970) 255, n. 15 and literature cited there. Cp. R. de Vaux, *Ancient Israel: Its Life and Institutions* (trans. McHugh; London: McGraw Hill, 1961) 343.

In short, until the end of the Persian, and probably the Hellenistic period, prayer had not yet become a cultic institution whose place and function in communal life could be compared with that of sacrifice in the time of the First and Second Temples.[10]

The absence of codification, definition, and binding formulations may account for the fact that not even one text of a Jewish public prayer was preserved from before the destruction of the Second Temple, or for that matter from before the middle of the first millenium C.E.[11] This lack of information certainly may derive from incidental circumstances. Our written sources for the time period in question, especially for the period from 300 B.C.E. to 150 C.E., are extremely limited. These were turbulent times for the Jewish people, during which manuscripts were often accidentally destroyed or fell prey to persecutors who submitted them to fire. However, the complete absence of documented knowledge of the exact wording of early Jewish prayers, even as quotations in rabbinic literature, cannot be explained solely as having resulted from historical vicissitudes. There are indications which suggest that this state of affairs was brought about, at least partially, by intent. In some striking pronouncements of the early sages, one senses an opposition to committing prayers to writing. In contrast to the regulations about biblical manuscripts, the rescue of prayer books from a fire on the Sabbath is not permitted, even though they contain the Divine Name and biblical verses (since such an attempt would involve transgressing the Sabbath laws). Due to the possibility of desecration which would result from letting such books be consumed by fire, it follows that "those who commit blessings to writing are like those who burn the Torah" (*t. Šabb.* 13.4).[12] We are

---

10. Cp. I. L. Seeligmann ("Cultic Tradition and Historiography in the Hebrew Bible," *Religion and Society in Israelite History. The Eighth Historical Congress* [Jerusalem: Magnes, 1955] 141-61 [Heb.]). Indeed, against all expectations one may observe that in times of national duress (e.g., the enslavement in Egypt or the persecutions described in the book of Esther), no reference is made to individual or communal prayers. Cp. S. Talmon ("'Wisdom' in the Book of Esther," *VT* 13 [1963] 429ff.).

11. I. Elbogen, *Studien zur Geschichte des jüdischen Gottesdienstes* (Frankfurt/M: Kauffmann, 1924).

12. Ed. Zuckermandel, pp. 128-29; ed. S. Lieberman, p. 58. A variant reading of הלכות for ברכות is extant; cp. *b. Tem.* 14b. For a complete discussion of the passage, cp. S. Lieberman (*Tosefta Kifshutah,* part III, *Shabbat-Eruvin* [New York: JTSA, 1962] 205-6); Elbogen (*Der jüdische Gottesdienst* [2d ed.; Frankfurt/M: Kauffmann, 1924] 7); D. Goldschmidt (*The Pesach Haggadah* [Jerusalem: Bialik, 1948] 8, n. 1).

further told that when it was reported to R. Ishmael (second half of the first century C.E.) that someone had written a tome of prayers, he went to check on the report, obviously intending to censure the man. Aware of R. Ishmael's approach, the owner of the volume threw it into a pail of water so as not to be caught *in flagrante* (*t. Šabb.* 13.4ff.].

The sages' apparent objection to prayer books may disclose their intention to maintain a distinct difference between the canonical Hebrew Bible[13] and other literature which was not considered sacred or binding, and was only to be transmitted orally. They strove to keep prayers from attaining the fixity of wording which would result from committing them to writing. The above *dicta* reveal the sages' endeavor to maintain the occasional-private character of prayer and to ensure that it not become a full-fledged substitute for sacrificial worship. The opposition to such replacement no doubt existed as long as the Temple functioned and may have endured for some time after the destruction, so long as the hope for an immediate return was nourished. Whereas repetitiveness and exact similarity are imperative for the proper execution of the ritual act, stereotyped wording in prayer was rejected: "Whoever makes his prayer fixed [or prays at preordained times]—his prayer is not [any more in the nature of] supplication" (*m. Ber.* 4.4).[14]

We are led to believe that the lack of information on the early history of Jewish prayer results to some degree from the intentional suppression of evidence, triggered by an opposition to the institutionalization of prayer. If this be the case, then it follows that the chances for discovering any early prayers of mainstream Judaism in the period of the Second Temple are very slim indeed.

---

13. Translations of biblical books into Aramaic should not be written down. R. Gamliel's discarding of a targum of Job should be judged (*t. Šabb.* 13.2-3) in light of the action of R. Ishmael mentioned above.

14. אל תעש תפילתך קבע אלא רחמים ותחנונים. Cp. *m.* ʾAbot 2.13: העושה תפילתו קבע אין תפילתו תחנונים, "Do not make your prayer fixed, but [let it retain the free form of] beseeching and supplication." The variant "does not fulfill his obligations," לא יצא ידי חובתו, which occurs in *b. Ber.* 40 b, reveals a later development. This ruling stands in glaring contrast to the injunction of Shammai (*m.* ʾAbot 1.15): עשה תורתך קבע, "Make your [study of] Torah [a] fixed [duty]." It should be noted, however, that the opposite trend also appears in rabbinic literature, e.g., *t. Ber.* 4.5: כל המשנה מטבע שטבעו חכמים בברכות לא יצא (ed. Zuckermandel, p. 9; ed. Lieberman, p. 19; cp. Lieberman, *Toseftah Kifshutah,* part I, *Berakhot-Terumoth* [1955] 61). This attitude may be reflected as well in Ben Sira's dictum (7:14): "Do not enter into the meeting [or "conversation"] of princes [LXX, "elders"], and do not repeat [Syr., "change"] a word of [your] prayer."

However the situation is altogether different with regard to dissident groups who defied the authority of the sages and did not consider their pronouncements and rulings as binding. The discovery of the writings of such a group in the Judean Desert which inform us directly of their ideas and practices and provide some information on suppressed trends in Judaism, offers new insights into the beginnings of institutionalized Jewish prayer. The importance of these writings for the clarification of the issue at hand lies in the following:

(1) they are witnesses from the "dark age" of documentation of Jewish history and literature;

(2) they derive from a secessionist group that did not necessarily heed rabbinic injunctions;

(3) they reflect historical, sociological, and religious circumstances which promoted an early development of institutionalized prayer.

II

The life of the Covenanters of Qumran was regulated by a calendar-reckoning which differed from that to which mainstream Judaism adhered.[15] Due to the concomitant divergencies in the timing of the festivals, the Covenanters were cut off from the cultic institutions of contemporary Judaism, foremost from participation in the Temple service where sacrifices were offered in accord with the common Jewish calendar, i.e., not at times appointed in their solar calendar (CD vi 11-14). The resulting voluntary abstention from Temple rituals created a situation within this group which was similar to the circumstances that were to determine the socioreligious development of "normative" Judaism after the destruction of the Temple. In both instances the lack of the medium of sacrifice promoted the emergence of institutionalized prayer. As in normative Judaism, so apparently in the Qumran community "prayer [times] derived from the daily sacrifices," תפילות מתמידין גמרו (b. Ber. 26b).

Soon after the discovery of the first Qumran scrolls, attempts were made to investigate the liturgical elements in them, especially in the *Thanksgiving Scroll* (1QH), and to evaluate their evidence for the beginnings of Christian liturgy. In 1952 J. A. Jungmann could point out some similarities between the

---

15. S. Talmon, "The Calendar of the Covenanters of the Judean Desert" (in this vol. pp. 147-85). In addition, see B. Jongeling (*A Classified Bibliography of the Finds in the Desert of Judah, 1958-1962* [Leiden: Brill, 1971] 105-10).

early Christian order of prayer and the Qumran materials.[16] In 1953 Baumgärtel added further insights.[17] In 1960 the present author tried to show that in the Covenanters' *Manual of Discipline* (1QS) we may discover references to fixed prayer times and to formulated prayers which are later mirrored in the prayer book of the synagogue.[18] Since then additional liturgical materials from Qumran have been published by Baillet,[19] Strugnell,[20] and Milik.[21] To these must be added the *Psalms Scroll* from Cave 11 (11QPs^a), edited by J. Sanders.[22]

Of special interest for our investigation is the extra-canonical piece, which, together with one or two other apocryphal compositions, follows upon Psalm 150 and is in turn followed by Psalm 140 and David's autobiographical song preserved as Psalm 151 in the Septuagint and the Syro-Hexapla. That piece (11QPs^a xxvii) is in fact not a psalm at all but rather a summary roster of David's songs composed under prophetic inspiration (11QPs^a xxvii 11), which are said to have amounted to 4050 *in toto*. In addition to 3600 "psalms" of an apparently general nature, David is also said to have composed 364 songs to be sung at the altar with the daily sacrifices, 52 songs to accompany the Sabbath offerings throughout the year, and an additional 30 songs for the New Moons and all the festivals.

16. J. A. Jungmann, "Altchristliche Gebetsordnung im Lichte des Regelbuches von ʿEn Fescha," *ZKT* 75 (1952) 215-19.

17. E. Baumgärtel, "Zur Liturgie in der 'Sektenrolle' vom Toten Meer," *ZAW* 65 (1953) 263-65.

18. "The 'Manual of Benedictions' of the Sect of the Judean Desert," *RQ* 2 (1959-60) 475-500. The main conclusions presented in that paper were integrated in the present essay. Other studies in this vein are by H. Haag ("Das Liturgische Leben der Qumrangemeinde," *ALW* 10 [1967] 78-109) and M. Weinfeld ("Traces of Kedushat Yotzer and Pesukey De-Zimra in the Qumran Literature and in Ben-Sira," *Tarbiz* 45 [1976] 15-26 [Heb.]).

19. M. Baillet, "Un Recueil Liturgique de Qumrân Grotte 4: 'Les Paroles des Luminaires,' " *RB* 68 (1961) 195-250.

20. J. Strugnell, "The Angelic Liturgy at Qumran, 4QSerek Širôt ʿOlat Haššabāt" (VTSup; Leiden: Brill, 1960), 8. 318-45; C. Newsom and Y. Yadin, "The Masadah Fragment of the Qumran Songs of the Sabbath Sacrifice," *IEJ* 34 (1984) 77-88; C. Newsom, *Songs of the Sabbath Sacrifice: A Critical Edition* (Missoula, MT: Scholars Press, 1985).

21. J. T. Milik, "Milki-Sedek et Milki-Rešaʿ dans les anciens écrits juifs et chrétiens," *JTS* 23 (1972) 95-144.

22. J. Sanders, *The Psalms Scroll of Qumrân Cave 11* (DJD; Oxford: Clarendon, 1965), vol. 4. See further: E. M. Schuller, *Non-Canonical Psalms from Qumran: A Pseudepigraphic Collection* in *Harvard Semitic Studies* (Atlanta, GA: Scholars Press, 1986), vol. 28.

There remains the question whether the *širôt ʿolat haššabāt* published by Strugnell are to be identified with the 52 songs for the Sabbath sacrifices composed by David or whether they should be viewed as liturgical substitutes for (rather than accompaniments to) the nonexisting sacrificial service in the historical period in which the New Temple had not yet been established. In view of the Covenanters' abstinence from the Temple service and the fact that there is scope for attempting the reconstruction of their prayer book (see below), I would opt for this second interpretation of the purpose and meaning of the *širôt ʿolat haššabāt*.[23]

The exact nature of the *Psalms Scroll* (11QPs[a]) is still under debate. The question of whether it should be viewed as a copy of the canonical book of Psalms, as its editor and many others hold, or rather as a "psalter," i.e., a compilation for liturgical use, as M. H. Goshen-Gottstein and the present writer have suggested, has not yet been settled.[24] However there can be no objection to including this scroll and other pre-masoretic psalmodic compositions in our present investigation.[25]

These clearly defined materials and some less-obvious references and quotations in other scrolls make possible the reconstruction of the Covenanters' Manual of Benedictions, the oldest Jewish prayer book, viz., a roster of bles-

---

23. This understanding of the *širôt* is now borne out by new information which can be gained from the halakic treatise *mqṣt mʿśy* (or *dbry*) *htwrh* (4QMMT, unpublished). For an attempt to identify and possibly to reconstruct some of these unknown Davidic compositions, see J. Strugnell ("More Psalms of David," *CBQ* 27 [1965] 207-16).

24. See M. H. Goshen-Gottstein ("The Psalms Scroll (11QPs[a])—A Problem of Canon and Text," *Textus* 5 [1966] 22-33); S. Talmon ("Extra-Canonical Hebrew Psalms," in this vol., pp. 244-73). Sanders has of late reaffirmed his opinion concerning the canonical nature of the scroll in "Cave 11 Surprises and the Question of Canon," *New Directions in Biblical Archeology* ([ed. D. N. Freedman and J. Greenfield; New York: Doubleday, 1971] 113-30) and "The Qumran Psalms Scroll (11QPs[a]) Reviewed," *On Language, Culture and Religion: in Honor of Eugene A. Nida* [ed. Black and Smalley; The Hague: Mouton, 1974] 79-99). In the latter article (pp. 96ff.) Sanders has overstressed my willingness to consider his point of view, a willingness not to be construed as full assent.

25. For an updated catalogue of all pre-masoretic psalter materials from Qumran, see J. A. Sanders (*The Dead Sea Psalms Scroll* [Ithaca, N.Y.: Cornell University. Press, 1967]) and his comprehensive list of "Palestinian Manuscripts" (*Qumran and the History of the Biblical Text,* hereinafter QHBT [eds. Frank M. Cross and S. Talmon; Cambridge, MA: Harvard University Press, 1975] 401-13). DJD 7 (ed. M. Baillet; Oxford: Clarendon, 1983) contains further Psalms fragments.

sings arranged according to the calendar, containing daily prayers side by side with festival prayers after the manner of the *Maḥazorta* still used in the Syrian Church. We shall endeavor to restore the main outlines of this compendium.

It has rightly been pointed out that the concluding section of the *Manual of Discipline* (1QS) forms a separate literary unit.[26] This section begins[27] on the last line, 26, of column ix: "[In every period that][28] is to be he shall bless his Maker, and wherever he is, he shall [tell of his righteousness. With an offering] of the lips he shall bless him throughout the periods which G[od] has decreed."[29] The passage ends on the words: "What will clay reply, a thing formed by hand? What counsel will it understand?"[30] However this unit is not all of one piece. It is made up of three clearly recognizable subunits, which, though written in the same characteristically psalmodic style, are quite distinct from each other in content. By this criterion it can be established that the beginning of the second subunit is at col. x, line 8: "As long as I exist a decree shall be engraved on my tongue for fruit of praise and for a gift of my lips. I will sing with knowledge," etc. And, though with less certainty,[31] it can be said that it ends at col. xi, line 15: "Blessed art thou, O my God, who openest to knowledge the heart of thy

---

26. See A. M. Haberman, *ʿEdah weʿEduth* (Jerusalem: Maḥbarot Lesifrut, 1952) 82-83; H. E. del Medico, *L'énigme des manuscrits de la Mer Morte* (Paris: Plon, 1957) 320; P. Wernberg-Møller, Review of C. Rabin's *Qumran Studies* in *RevQ* 1 (1958) 139-44.

27. As opposed to Haberman (*ʿEdah weʿEduth*), who holds that 1QS col. x is not continued directly from col. ix.

28. Haberman's reconstruction.

29. אשר חקק א[ל]. On this reading see Talmon ("The Calendar of the Covenanters," in this vol., pp. 147-85); Brownlee (*The Dead Sea Manual of Discipline* [BASORSS 112 (1951)], 10-12. 88, n. 2).

30. The scribe left the lower half of col. xi blank, thus marking the end of the scroll.

31. This conjecture finds confirmation in the rabbinic dictum (*t. Ber.* 6.20): "He who opens [a benediction] by *yod he* [the holy name] and closes with *yod he* is a wise man; [he who opens] with *yod he* and closes with *ʾaleph lamed* is a boor; [he who opens] with *ʾaleph lamed* and closes with *ʾaleph lamed*—this is heterodoxy" (see the comments of S. Lieberman in his edition of the Tosepta and idem, "Light on the Cave Scrolls from Rabbinic Sources," *PAAJR* 20 [1951] 395ff.). A similar, albeit fragmentary, closing phrase is found at the end of the *Prayer for the Day of Atonement* (D. Barthélemy and J. T. Milik, *Qumran Cave I* [1955] 153, 1Q 34bis i 7). Moreover in Psalm 119, which served the Qumran author as a prototype in other matters also, the first stanza ends (119:12) with the formula: "Blessed be thou, O Lord; teach me thy statutes" (cp. 119:26, 64, 68, 108, 124, 135, 141).

servant."[32] The third subunit begins accordingly at col. xi, line 16: "Direct in righteousness all his works," etc.[33]

As already stated the three subunits are all written in the same psalmodic style which is especially pronounced in the similarly patterned opening and closing verses of each of them. However closer study reveals that the first two units are quite different from the third. While in the present writer's opinion, the first two form an integral part of the *The Manual of Discipline* (1QS),[34] the third must be regarded as a hymn of praise, a kind of poetic epilogue to a work which has an essentially legal character.

The first subunit (ix 21—x 8) has been named by Y. Yadin The Psalm of the Appointed Times.[35] This title is appropriate to its subject matter: the marking of the times of the prayers to be said every day and on each day of the year. The second subunit, which will henceforth be referred to as The Psalm of Benedictions, contains a list, albeit incomplete, of prayers to be said at the times specified above. Thus the Psalm of Benedictions is simply a continuation of the Psalm of the Appointed Times. Together they provide a fitting conclusion to the *Manual of Discipline* (1QS). The third subunit (xi 15-22) is a work belonging in the same class as the *Thanksgiving Hymns* (1QH) and has no intrinsic connection with the subject matter of 1QS.

The true nature and purpose of these passages can best be understood by studying them side by side with parallel passages from other writings of the Covenanters of Qumran. This comparison will confirm our assumption that all these texts are derived from a single prototype, a Manual of Benedictions drawn up by the members of the יחד. Furthermore the comparison will dispose of both the crypto-historical interpretation given by del Medico to the Psalm of the

---

32. Brownlee (*The Dead Sea Manual of Discipline*, 45 [see n. 29]) attaches xi 15 as a new heading to the following unit. So also P. Wernberg-Møller (*The Manual of Discipline, Translated and Annotated with an Introduction* [STDJ; Leiden: Brill, 1957], 1. 153, nn. 41-42), who explains the two points after the word תפארתו as verse dividers.

33. Possibly we should read "My works" (מַעֲשַׂי).

34. In contrast to the opinion of many scholars who would detach cols. x-xi from the rest of the scroll. See Haberman's remark: "Perhaps the next column [x] is in fact the conclusion of another book" (*'Edah we'Eduth*, 1952, 82-83 [see above, n. 26]).

35. Y. Yadin, *The Scroll of the War of the Sons of Light against the Sons of Darkness* (trans. C. and B. Rabin; Oxford: Clarendon, 1962) 321.

Appointed Times[36] and the mystical explanation of parts of the same psalm propounded by Brownlee,[37] Dupont-Sommer,[38] and others.

The five parallel columns of the accompanying Table A contain the Psalm of the Appointed Times (col. 1),[39] an excerpt from the *Thanksgiving Hymns* (1QH xii 3-11) (col. 2),[40] two fragments which were discovered in the first cave (cols. 3 and 4),[41] and a section from *Jubilees* (col. 5). It will be seen that the Thanksgiving Psalm exhibits great similarity with the Psalm of the Appointed Times, in structure and in wording. Both open with a song of praise and thanksgiving (1QH xii 3-4; 1QS ix 26—x 1; cp. 1Q *34bis* i 2, 4), then proceed to a listing of the appointed prayer times (1QH xii 4-10; 1QS x 1-5), and conclude with a devotional ode (1QH xii 11ff.; 1QS x 6-7; cp. 1Q *34bis* iii 6-7). The two compositions are not identical, however, and a closer analysis may help to establish their internal relationship.

The Thanksgiving Psalm provides the shorter version of the two. It lacks the details of the Psalm of the Appointed Times which refer to the appointed prayer times for the festivals, the seasons of the annual cycle and their "leaders," the sabbatical and jubilee years, for all of which special songs were available, as detailed in "David's Compositions" (11QPs^a xxvii). These omissions result in the loss of much of the enumerative quality which adheres to the Psalm of the Appointed Times. The Thanksgiving Psalm is a free rendition for poetic purposes of that normative-liturgical composition which was incorporated into a work which is of an essentially individual rather than public character. Its author appears to have paraphrased a *Vorlage* which had achieved an authoritative, almost canonical rigidity.

If this interpretation is correct, some further conclusions of wider application present themselves. Here, as in many other instances, the Qumran materials may enlighten us regarding the techniques of ancient Hebrew liturgical compositions, especially the relationship between the "individual" song or psalm

---

36. H. E. del Medico, "La traduction d'un texte démarqué dans le Manuel de Discipline" *VT* 6 (1956) 34-35; idem, *L'énigme des manuscrits de la Mer. Morte* 316 (see above, n. 26).

37. W. H. Brownlee, BASORSS 10-12 (1951) 38ff. (see above, n. 29).

38. A. Dupont-Sommer, "Exégèse du Manuel de Discipline," *VT* 2 (1952) 229-43.

39. Del Medico conjectured that the Psalm of the Appointed Times was copied from the *Thanksgiving Hymns*.

40. E. L. Sukenik, *Otzar Hammegilloth Haggenuzoth,* (Jerusalem: Magnes, 1957) Heb.

41. 1Q 27 ([DJD; Oxford: Clarendon, 1955], 1. 103); 1Q *34bis* (pp. 145-52).

and the "communal." The paraphrastic, derivative nature of the Thanksgiving Psalm may be compared with the free arrangement of excerpts culled from the canonical book of Psalms in the book of Chronicles (e.g., 1 Chr 16:8-36; cp. Ps 96; 105:1-15) or for that matter in the book of Jonah (chap. 2).

The author of the Psalm of the Appointed Times assigns six times of prayer to every period of twenty-four hours, one in each of the six parts into which the day was divided in Jewish[42] and also in ancient Christian[43] tradition: three for the period of daylight and three night watches, each one lasting for four hours.[44]

Of the six periods specified, three belong to the hours of daylight:

(a) The Early Morning Prayer, which is to be recited "at the beginning of the dominion of light"[45] or "with the coming of light from [its dwelling]," i.e., just before dawn, as defined in the Mishna (*Ber* 1.2).

(b) The Midday Prayer, מנחה—"at its (the sun's) circuit" (orbit)

(c) The Evening Prayer, i.e., ערבית—"at its (the sun's) ingathering to its decreed dwelling" or "at its turn [at evening] and the outgoing of light."

The prescription of three prayer times during the hours of daylight patently derives from a biblical tradition which relates that Daniel "got down upon his knees three times a day and prayed and gave thanks before his God" (Dan 6:10; cp. *t. Ber.* 3.6). The same inference can also be drawn from the words of the psalmist, "But I call upon God; and the Lord will save me. *Evening* and *morning* and *at noon* I utter my complaint and my moan, and he will hear my voice" (Ps 55:16-17), which is paraphrased in the thanksgiving section of the ʿAmidah prayer, "We will give thanks unto you and relate your praise . . . at all times, evening and morning and at noontide."

---

42. *m. Ber.* 1.1-2.

43. Jungmann, *ZKT* 75 (1952) 215-19 (see above, n. 16).

44. Dupont-Sommer assumes that the Covenanters had only two times of prayer (*VT* 2 [1952] 232 [see above, n. 38]). He bases his view on the Psalm of Benedictions in which the prayer times are summed up in the following words: "With the coming of day and night . . . and with the outgoing of evening and morning. . . ." However Dupont-Sommer ignores the expression "while they are," בהיותם, later in the same line, which points to two more times, one each for the day and night, corresponding to the term "their circuit," תקופתם, at the head of the column (line 1). The preposition ב in בהיותם is to be given a temporal, not a local, force, as proposed by van der Ploeg, whose view was accepted by Wernberg-Møller (*The Manual of Discipline*, 1. 145 [see above, n. 32]).

45. In the enumeration of prayer times, the first quotation is from 1QS, the second from 1QH.

TABLE A: PSALM OF THE APPOINTED TIMES

Jubilees 2:9 (retroverted)	1Q 27	1Q *34*^{bis}	1QH xii 3-11	1QS ix 26—x 8

Jubilees 2:9 (retroverted)	1Q 27	1Q 34bis	1QH xii 3-11	1QS ix 26—x 8
			(3) ואהללה שמכה בתוך יריאיכה	(26) [בכול קץ נהי]ה יברך עושיו
			(4) [אודך לדור] ודור	בכול אשר יהיה יס[פר כבודו
			ותפלה להתנפל והתחנן תמיד	בתרומת] שפתים יברכנו
		Col. ii	מקץ לקץ	(1) עם קצים אשר חקק א[ל]
			(5) עם מבוא אור ממ[עונתו]	ברשית ממשלת אור
			בתקופות יום לתכונו	עם תקופתו
			לחוקת מאור גדול בפנות ערב	ובהאספו על מעון חוקו
			(6) ומוצא אור	
			ברשית ממשלת חושך	ברשית (2) אשמורי חושך
			למועד לילה	כי יפתח אוצרו וישתהו על ת[בל]
			בתקופתו לפנות בוקר	ובתקופתו
			(7) ובקץ האספו אל מעונתו מפני אור	עם האספו מפני אור
			למוצא לילה ומבוא יומם (8) תמיד	באופיע (3) מאורות מזבול קודש
				עם האספם למעון כבוד
			בכול מולדי עת יסודי קץ	במבוא מועדים לימי חודש
			ותקופת מועדים בתכונם	יחד תקופתם עם (4) מסרותם זה לזה
			(9) באותותם לכול ממשלתם	בהתחדשם
	וזה לכם האות			
	בהסגר מולדי עולה			
	וגלה הרשע מפני הצדק			
	כגלות חושך מפני (6) אור			
	וכתום עשן ואיננו			
	עוד כן יתם הרשע לעד			
	והצדק יגלה			
	כשמש תכון (7) תבל			

(1) וגורל בליעל[

(2) קדוש [

(3)] ומספרם כבל יחד ל[

(4) כול יחד

ראש משמרת[ו]
נשיא אומיי
(4) כול יחד

(5) תשורות ראש בליעתם עלי[ואת]
קהל[ה]ו (3) וארתן
ראש אחת קם[ם]עורתם

לבל עובדי ומספם
להחתים
קדמים לעמרתים

(8) ובזוא מלחמת גבורי וורו
וטורי אנש לעמרתים
וטורי וכל לעמרי ראש

וטורי לוקי ליעם
וכ מבמבל וא ליב
וחלק עד (7) ובזוא
וראשי עיום ועומדש עמרתים

טורם חתום לוז
(9) וחתום פשמ ולחם
וכו קיום הכותם לעורתים
ובאותי יחהה ובכתים עמורתים

(2)] ראש ראשו אלים [
(3)] תחחה עטי אך רחה הלא רחה לא
עו חרדה אלה הוה הן

תורת הדחתונה פגי, אך חיום חוברו (10)
בעום דוחמ יובל בל דוד האמד

לפדי וורת ובמום
ליליום ובנקומ
לקרוחת ובאנותם

לוהיום ובנומים
לפוד על רוחי אומד
מבטט ראש יי הודה ואה י חן

(1)] מאות לקודה ל[יחה] הוום

So far the Covenanters' tradition is seemingly in keeping with that of mainstream Judaism. But one observes an interesting difference. In the book of Psalms and in the *'Amidah,* the times of prayer are mentioned in the order to be expected in the Jewish lunar calendar, in which the day is reckoned from sunset to sunset, "evening and morning and at noon." However in the Qumran solar calendar, the reckoning starts from sunrise, and the expected prayer order would indeed be: morning prayer, midday prayer, and evening prayer.[46] This contrast is exceedingly apparent in the Thanksgiving Psalm: מבוא אור ("the coming of light") parallels the expression "at the beginning of the dominion of light" in 1QS, while מוצא אור ("the outgoing of light") is equivalent to "at the turn of evening" or "its [the sun's] ingathering to its decreed dwelling." Hence בוא,

46. I have suggested that the Covenanters reckoned the beginning of the day from the morning, thereby setting themselves apart from mainstream Judaism even in the observance of the Sabbath and the festivals. See Talmon, "The Calendar of the Covenanters" (in this vol., pp. 147-85) and cp. Cassuto's method of bringing the two systems into accord (*From Adam to Noah* [Jerusalem: Magnes, 1949] 13-14). J. M. Baumgarten (*JBL* 67 [1958] 355-60) has expressed doubts about my supposition. But it seems that it can now be substantiated from new, unpublished material from Qumran, as stated by J. T. Milik in a note appended to the English translation of his "Dix ans de découvertes dans le Désert de Juda": "There also seems to be no doubt that they reckoned the day as starting with sunrise and not sunset" (*Ten Years of Discovery in the Wilderness of Judaea* [trans. J. Strugnell; London: SCM, 1958] 152, n. 5). The prayer order, "morning, noon, evening," which, as stated, indicates the use of a solar calendar, was probably not innovated by the Qumranians. In this, as in their many other deviations from the religious practice of their contemporaries, they probably conserved a tradition which may perhaps be alluded to in the Jerusalem Talmud (*Ber.* 4.1; 7 a): in the course of a discussion arising out of Psalm 55 about the prayer times customary in Israel, R. Samuel bar Nahmani lists the changes in the day with which the times of prayer coincide, beginning from the morning and not from the evening, as did the psalmist. Nahmani's inverted order of prayer times may be dependent on the Mishna (ibid.), but it should be pointed out that in the parallel expostulation in *t. Ber.* 3.6, the original order of the psalm is maintained. A further point to be stressed is the prominence given to the sun and its light in the actual formulae of the prayers quoted in the Talmud. This calls to mind the very important part played by the sun in the religious thought of the Qumranians. The morning prayer also precedes the evening prayer in Psalm 119, which, as already remarked, greatly influenced the author of the Psalm of Benedictions: "I rise before dawn (נשף) and cry for help; I hope for your words. My eyes are awake before the watches of the night, that I may meditate upon your promise" (119:147-48). For נשף in the sense of "the dim light of dawn," cp. Job 7:4; *b. Ber.* 3 b; and see E. Ben-Yehuda (*Thesaurus Totius Hebraitatis,* s.v. נשף).

which in the Bible and the Mishna always indicates the setting of the sun, at Qumran refers to its rising; while יצא, which in the Bible and the Mishna (as in Akkadian and Ugaritic) describes the rising of the sun, in the Judean Scrolls refers to its setting.

The Qumran author now records the times of the prayers to be said during the night:

> The Evening Prayer—"at the beginning of the watches of darkness"[47] or "at the beginning of the dominion of darkness";
> The Night Prayer—"at its [the moon's] circuit [orbit]";
> A prayer at the end of the night—"at its [the moon's] ingathering before the light" or "at the turn of the morning."

This roster seems to indicate that the Covenanters divided the night, like the day, into three watches. In this they concur with the opinion of R. Nathan which became authoritative in mainstream Judaism, in contrast to the opinion of Rabbi Jehuda Hanasi who divided the night into four watches (*b. Ber.* 3 b).[48]

The same division is implied by the statement in 1QS vi 7-8: "And the רבים shall keep vigil together a third of all the nights of the year, reading the book and interpreting[49] the law [?] and worshipping together." From this it may be inferred that during one of the watches, apparently the second, of every night of the year[50] "the רבים" devoted themselves to study and prayer.[51] On the other

---

47. Followed by [בל]ת על וישיתהו אוצרו יפתח כיא, "When he opens his treasure and installs it over the un[iverse]," accepting van der Ploeg's reconstruction based on the letters עלת ("Le 'Manuel de Discipline' des rouleaux de la Mer Morte," *BOr* 8 [1951] 113-26). The metaphor is possibly derived from Ps 104:20: "You spread [תשת] darkness and it is night."

48. Cp. *t. Ber.* 1.1; *y. Ber.* 1.1; 2 d. In the opinion of Y. Rabinowitz, this detail is an indication of the antiquity of 1QS, since the division of the day into four watches was first introduced by the Romans and is, therefore, mentioned in the Gospels and the Talmud ("Sequence and Dates of the Extra-Biblical Dead Sea Scroll Texts and 'Damascus' Fragments," *VT* 3 [1953] 180). An allusion to the division of the night into three watches can already be found in Judg 7:19. Cp. *Lam. Rab.* 2:19.

49. C. Rabin (*Qumran Studies* [Scripta Judaica; Oxford: Blackwell's, 1957], 2. 44) points out that these same words are also used as *termini technici* in talmudic literature (*m. Soṭa* 9.3; *y. Ned.* 8.3; 40 d).

50. Rabin also inclines to this interpretation (ibid., 43). Comparison with *Qohelet Rabbah* 9 shows that the terminology employed by the Covenanters was similar

hand, whenever ten rank and file Covenanters[52] came together, they were duty bound to appoint "a man who studies the law day and night, by turns."[53] That is to say, one out of every ten members of the יחד was constantly engaged in the study of the Law according to a prearranged rota based on the division of the day and night into six vigils.

III

After listing the times of the daily prayers, the authors of the Thanksgiving Psalm and the Psalm of the Appointed Times proceed to specify the order of benedictions for the appointed times of the year. In both the list is headed by a short general summary.

1QH xii 8-9: "At all renewals [literally "births"] of periods [i.e., "new moons"], foundations of time [reckoning] and circuits of seasons in their [fixed] order and [according to] their signs for all [the days of] their dominion."

1QS x 3-4: "At the coming in of seasons, for days of New Moons [when] at one is their [the luminaries'] circuit, with their mutual pledge [literally "binding"] when they renew themselves."[54]

to that of "the Holy Congregation": "Why was it called the Holy Congregation? Because they divided the day into three parts, one third for [the study of] the Law, one third for prayer and one third for work" (ibid., 38). But this purely external resemblance is insufficient to prove a historical connection between these two groups (Wernberg-Møller, *RevQ* 1 [1948] 144). Cp. further *m. ᵓAbot* 2.14; *y. Ber.* 4.2; 7 d.

51. See *b. Ber.* 3 b. In this connection it may be worthwhile to mention the custom adopted in later Judaism of petitioning for the rebuilding of the Temple in the first watch of the night, "at the beginning of the watches" (Lam 2:19). Cp. *Talmudic Encyclopaedia* (vol. 2, s.v. אשמורה). My colleague, Prof. Z. Werblowsky has drawn my attention to the fact that a midnight prayer is also mentioned in the Canons of Hippolytus (§ 37): Ἀποστολίκη παράλοσις.

52. Here the two categories are clearly distinguished. On this question see A. M. Haberman ("Studies in the Judaean Desert Scrolls," *Sinai* 32 [1953] 101-8 [Heb.]); G. Vermes (*Discovery in the Judean Desert. The Dead Sea Scrolls and Their Meaning* [London: SCM, 1957] 37).

53. Reading חליפות instead of על יפות, as proposed by H. Yalon ("Dead Sea Scrolls II 2, ed., M Burrows," *Kiryat-Sefer* 28 [1952] 65 [Heb.]). See also I. Sonne ("Remarks on 'Manual of Discipline' [1QS], Col. VI, 6-7," *VT* 7 [1957] 405-8).

54. See the table. A period should probably be placed after "when they renew themselves [בהתחדשם]," as proposed by Haberman (*ᶜEdah we ᶜEduth*, 83 [above, n. 26]).

The first part of each of these lines is in chiastic parallelism. Both refer to the New Moons (מולדי עת[55] ימי חודש), which are determined by the phases of the moon; and the festivals (תקופת מועדים, מבוא מועדים) which are dependent on the course of the sun. The words in 1QS are probably a kind of paraphrase of Ps 104:19: "You have made the moon to mark the seasons; the sun knows its time for setting," which the rabbis took as a prooftext in their polemic against the solar calendar prevalent among dissident Jews such as the Qumran Covenanters.[56] The second part of the two lines, where the language of the 1QS is more explicit, asserts the correspondence of the courses of the two great luminaries[57] and the consequent synchronization of the festivals dependent upon them.[58] That this is the meaning of the words can clearly be seen by comparing them with *1 Enoch* 41:5: "And I saw the chambers of the sun and moon, where they proceed and whither they come again, and their glorious[59] circuit, and how one is superior to the other, and their stately orbit, and how they do not leave their orbit and they add nothing to their orbit and take nothing from it, and keep faith with each other in accordance with the oath by which they are bound[60]

55. "Renewal" (מולד) is one of the characteristic terms used to describe the phases of the moon in rabbinic as well as in Qumran literature (cp. the use of the expression מולדי עולה) to indicate the times at which the course of the moon is decisive in calendar reckoning (1Q *27*, p. 103). See also E. Ben-Yehuda (*Thesaurus* [see above, n. 46] s.v. מולד).

56. *Midrash Shoher Tov* [ed. Buber, 230]. See Talmon ("The Calendar of the Covenanters," in this vol., pp. 147-85). It is to be doubted whether the author of 1QS interpreted the biblical verse in the manner proposed by Wernberg-Møller (*The Manual* [see above, n. 32], 141, n. 10): "He makes the moon at fixed times, the sun knows its [i.e., the moon's] entering."

57. Cp. Sir 43:1-9 (ed. Segal, p. 288).

58. So Dupont-Sommer, whose view is rejected by Wernberg-Møller (*The Manual* [see above, n. 32]).

59. This is in keeping with the phraseology of the Qumran Scrolls, for instance "the glorious dwelling," מעון הכבוד (1QS x 3).

60. From *1 Enoch* it is clear that the word מסרותם is to be derived from the root יסר = קשר ("to bind") as was rightly discerned by H. Yalon (*Kiryat-Sefer* 28 [1952] 69-70). These last words of the passage quoted are found only in manuscript *k* of *1 Enoch* and were not printed in R. H. Charles' edition of 1893. However in the later, complete edition of the *Apocrypha and Pseudepigrapha* (1913), Charles did include them with the following marginal note: "So *k* alone, probably a fortunate conjecture." It is now apparent that MS *k* has preserved an ancient reading.

together."[61] But the harmony of the orbits of the two luminaries in no way detracts from the superiority of the sun over the moon,[62] seeing that, in the words of the author of *1 Enoch,* "the one [the sun] is higher than the other"; and according to 1QS x 4, God ordained "the great l[uminary] as the holy of holies and [as] a f[aithful] sign,[63] for the beginning of his eternal grace."

At this point 1QS proceeds to list four additional times of prayer which were omitted by the author of the Thanksgiving Psalm, the third and fourth being separated by a line of devotional character (see Table A):

(a) "At the heads of seasons in every period to be";
(b) "At the beginning of months in their seasons";
(c) "And holy days in their fixed order, for a memorial in their seasons";
(d) "At the heads of years."

Bearing in mind that at the beginning of the Psalm of the Appointed Times the author recorded the times of the daily prayers, we should logically expect him to go on and give a list of the other prayers in order of their frequency: Sabbath, New Moons, Festivals. This is precisely what we find in *Jub.* 2:9: "The Lord set the sun as a great sign over the earth for days and Sabbaths and months and seasons and years."[64] However the author of 1QS seems to have inverted this logical order, placing the festivals before the New Moons, and the Sabbaths after both of them.[65] For it is almost certain that "holy days in their fixed order, for a memorial[66] in their seasons" are the same as "His holy Sabbaths" (CD iii 14),[67] which are to be observed at their proper times.[68] The author of 1QS then

---

61. Cp. Ibn Ezra's remark (*Iggereth HaShabbath* 2): "All those learned in the constellations said that the month begins at the moment when the moon and the sun are conjoined in one part. This is what the ancients called מולד."
62. See Talmon ("The Calendar of the Covenanters," in this vol., pp. 147-85).
63. These restorations are based on parallel passages in the Covenanters' writings (see Table A). Cp. Talmon, ibid., pp. 164, 169.
64. New Moons, festivals, and years, in that order, are also mentioned in *1 Enoch* 82:7.
65. In *Jub.* 1:14 the order is: New Moon, Sabbath, festivals; in 6:34: New Moon, festivals, Sabbath.
66. Cp. Exod 20:8: "*Remember* the Sabbath day to keep it holy."
67. Cp. Isa 58:13; Neh 9:14. See Wernberg-Møller, *Manual of Discipline,* 143-44 (see above, n. 32).
68. On this question see Talmon ("The Calendar of the Covenanters," pp. 147-85).

concludes his list of the annual cycle of seasons with a prayer "at the heads of years."[69] Next follows a list of notable days peculiar to the calendar of Qumran. The phrase [70] ובתקופות מועדיהם בהשלם[71] חוק תקונם יום משפטם זה לזה apparently refers to "the leaders of the months," those four days added to the year, one at the end of every quarter, whereby "the order of the year is accomplished through three hundred and sixty four[72] [days which are] the abodes of the year" (*1 Enoch* 75:2).[73]

Ensuingly the seasons of the year are registered, at which, in addition to all previously recorded occasions, every member of the יחד is to offer praise to God. These are: (the season of) reaping, summer, [the season of] sowing, and (the season of) vegetation. The first two would seem to be mentioned in the same sequence in *1 Enoch* 82:[74] "reaping" = "the harvest of wheat" (v 16); and "summer" = "and the trees ripen their fruits and produce all their fruits ripe and ready," etc. (82:19).[75] These two seasons together constitute the first six months of the year. For some unkown reason the list was not completed in *1 Enoch,* the last two seasons being left unmentioned.[76] On the basis of the resemblance to 1QS x 7, Milik has convincingly proposed to restore the terms קיץ, "summer,"

---

69. Cp. Ezek 40:1.
70. The language is similar to the opening of the previous section (1QS x 3-4).
71. Reading בהשלם as nif'al. So Haberman (*'Edah we'Eduth* [see above, n. 26]); Wernberg-Møller (*The Manual of Discipline,* ad loc.).
72. Cp. *1 Enoch* 82:4-6; 10-20. These are the 364 "abodes" or "places" according to another Ethiopic version, through which the sun passes in its annual course.
73. Also *1 Enoch* 82:6: "And the year is completed in three hundred and sixty four days." Hence in the fragment 1Q *34*^{bis} (p. 152), the expression [   ] מועד שלום should probably be related to שלמות ("completeness") and not to שלום ("peace") as proposed by the editor.
74. This may serve as proof that מועד in this context means "a season," as already interpreted by Dupont-Sommer (*Les écrits esséniens découverts près de la Mer Morte* [Paris: Payot, 1959]) in contrast to the view of Wernberg-Møller, *The Manual of Discipline,* ad loc.).
75. An Aramaic or Hebrew wording of this passage (*1 Enoch* 89:19) seems to have been preserved in the fragment 1Q *24* vii (DJD 99): ת[גמורו כולם [. . .] יום לקץ.
76. C. Rabin would explain their omission by the fact that in Ethiopia the year has only two seasons. The translator thus "emended" the text in accordance with the local Ethiopic tradition. But this interpretation is questionable since the writer allocates only 91 days to each of the two seasons. It is worth mentioning that the Slavonic Enoch counts four seasons in the year (*The Secrets of Enoch* [ed. R. H. Charles; London: Bible Society, 1896] 16).

and דשא, "vegetation," in a fragment of the Prayer for the Day of Atonement, 1Q *34bis* (DJD 1, 152-53; see Table A).[77]

The author of 1QS concludes his register of prayer-times with the sabbatical years and jubilees (x 7-8): "The seasons of the years in their weeks[78] and at the head[79] of their weeks for the time of liberty" (cp. Lev 25:10). This conclusion is practically identical with the final sentence of the passage dealing with the division of the times in *Jub. 2:9:* "For years and sabbaths of years and for jubilees and for all the times of the year."

We are now in a position to reconstruct the contents of the first part of the Covenanters' *Manual of Benedictions* from our examination of the data found in their writings and on the basis of a comparison of the various sources which complement each other in several respects.

The *Manual* opened with a song of praise to the Creator (1QS ix 26; 1QH xii 3-4). This was followed by a list of the times of prayer for every day: for Sabbaths, New Moons and festivals; for the seasons of the year and their four "leaders"; (for sabbatical years and jubilees)—in that order. The different sections of the book may have been marked off from each other by short devotional hymns, such as 1QS x 6: "with an offering of the lips I will bless him." A further song of praise rounded off this part of the book[80] (1QH xii 11ff.: 1Q*34bis* i 4).[81]

IV

The second part of the Manual of Benedictions contained references to the actual contents of the prayers. Though the prayers as such have not yet been

---

77. It resembles the וידוי, the confessional prayer which occupies a central place in the later Jewish liturgy for the Day of Atonement (1Q *34bis* [DJD 1, 152]). The prayer for the Day of Atonement (תפילה ליום כפורים) is preceded by a composition which may be connected with the New Year, in view of the clear reference to the seasons of the annual cycle.

78. Cp. Lev 25:1ff.; Dan 9:24-27.

79. H. Yalon proposed to read: ופרושי שבועיהם instead of ובראשי (*Kiryat-Sefer* 28 [1952] 71).

80. In 1QS the conclusion of the Psalm of the Appointed Times also serves as the beginning of the Psalm of Benedictions (x 8-9). See below.

81. Compare the opening of 1QH xii 3-4, "I will praise forever your name among those that fear you," with the last line of 1Q *34bis*, "forever [be] blessed, my Lord, who has given [us] joy."

discovered,[82] they can be partly reconstructed from allusions in the extant writings of the sect.

The Psalm of Benedictions, which is attached to the Psalm of the Appointed Times, is to be interpreted, in the present writer's opinion, as a kind of paraphrase of some of these prayers in terms that were plain and intelligible to any Covenanter.[83] It appears that one can still discern in the Psalm of Benedictions allusions to the prayers that were said at the three ordained prayer times. An examination of the liturgical fragments of Cave 1 will provide further prayers for some of the appointed seasons of the year.

Like the Psalm of the Appointed Times, the Psalm of Benedictions also began with a devotional hymn (1QS x 8-9), followed by an abbreviated summary of the six times of the day at which prayers are to be offered to God: "With the coming of day[84] and night[85] . . . and with the outgoing[86] of evening[87] and morning[88] . . . and while they prevail." This last expression is used in a double sense, simultaneously indicating both the midday prayer[89] and the prayer said in the middle of the night[90] ("at their orbit").

82. In a short preliminary notice, C. H. Hunzinger announces the discovery in Qumran of fragments of a liturgical work in which the morning and evening prayers were recorded for all the days of the month (Cp. "Travail d'édition, Communication de C. H. Hunzinger," *RB* 63 [1956] 67).

83. C. Rabin (*Qumran Studies* [Judaica; Oxford: Clarendon, 1959], 2. 75) is of the opinion that the order of the prayers given in 1QS "has become schematized and lost its connection with ritual practice." From the analysis of the sources proposed here, it appears that we are concerned with the beginnings of institutionalized Jewish prayer and not with developments that occurred after it had already become stereotyped. Contrast with this the argument of A. Büchler: "The author knew the confession in the liturgy of the Jews in Talmudic times, therefore his book [CD] could not have been composed before them" (Review of S. Schechter, *Documents of Jewish Sectaries* in *JQR* 3 [1912-1913] 429-85).

84. Cp. 1QS x 1: "at the beginning of the dominion of light"; 1QH xii 4-5: "with the coming of light from [its] d[welling]."

85. Cp. 1QS x 1-2: "at the beginning of the watches of darkness"; 1QH xii 6: "at the beginning of the dominion of darkness."

86. Based on Ps 65:19.

87. Cp. 1QS x 2: "at its ingathering before light"; 1QH xii 6-7: "and at the time of its ingathering to its dwelling, at the outgoing of night."

88. Cp. 1QS x 1: "at its [the light's] ingathering to its decreed dwelling"; 1QH xii 5-6: "at the turn of evening and the outgoing of light."

89. Cp. 1QS x 1; 1QH xii 5.

90. Cp. 1QS x 2; 1QH xii 6.

The liturgical poet now proceeds to describe the sequence of blessings to be pronounced from the moment a man rises in the morning till he retires at night, according to the three prayer times allocated to the period of daylight. First comes the prayer at dawn: "When I first put forth my hands and my feet, I will bless his name" (1QS x 13). These words most probably allude to a benediction in praise of the Creator, such as "who forms light and creates darkness," which is one of the essential blessings of the morning prayer in the tradition of Rabbinic Judaism (b. Ber. 11 d).[91]

This is followed by an allusion to the Shema[c] prayer: "At the beginning of [my] going out and [my] coming in, when I sit down or rise"[92] (1QS x 13-14).[93] This wording is simply a paraphrase of Deut 6:7: "And you shall talk of them when you sit in your house, and when you walk by the way, and when you lie down, and when you rise," with a tendentious inversion of the parts of the sentence.[94]

At this point the prayer at night, introduced during the Second Temple Period (m. Ber. 1.3), is mentioned in the list. The words "as I lie on my couch, I will sing aloud to Him" are evoked by association with the expression "when you lie down" in Deut 6:7.[95]

The benediction at dawn and at evening appear to have been private prayers, in accordance with ancient Jewish custom.[96] Not so the benedictions that follow which are headed by the line "I will bless him with an offering of the utterance of my lips from within a congregation of men" (1QS x 14). Here the expression ממערכת אנשים is to be interpreted, in the present writer's opinion, as an allusion to communal prayer.[97] Then blessings are to be pronounced before

---

91. Cp. y. Ber 4.1; 7 a.

92. Probably based on Ps 139:2.

93. This reading may be alluded to in a variant of 1QIsa[a] in Isa 37:28: "Your rising up and your sitting down, your going and your coming I know." (See Wernberg-Møller, The Manual of Discipline, 145.) Cp. 1QSa i 16-17.

94. See Talmon, "The Calendar of the Covenanters," in this vol., 147-85.

95. Josephus defined the time of the evening prayer as follows: ὁπότε πρὸς ὕπνον ὥρα τρέπεσθαι (Ant. 4.8.13 §212). See I. Elbogen (Der jüdische Gottesdienst, 99-100 [see above, n. 12]).

96. m. Ber. 1.2 (Elbogen, ibid., 24-26, 100).

97. So also Wernberg-Møller (The Manual of Benediction). This seems to be borne out by the phrase [. . . רבת מע]לכול [יעש]ן הזה וכחוק, in 1QSa ii 21-22. Cp. as well M. Wallenstein's remarks on רנה במכון, 1QH xi 5 ("The Palaeography of the ZAYIN in the Hymns Scroll with Special Reference to the Interpretation of Related Obscure Passages," VT 9 [1959] 102-3).

tasting food: "Before I raise my hand to satisfy myself with the delights of what the world produces" (1QS x 15),[98] i.e., before partaking in the communal meal, which was a salient feature in the Covenanters' way of life.[99]

Possibly a part of a liturgical composition pertaining to this occasion was preserved in a fragment from the Cairo Genizah, which J. Levi already attributed to the group from which the Damascus Document originated.[100]

כהן
[עת] יורנו מבני
עדת בני צדוק
על חוק טמא וט[הור
משפטיי ישפוט
[י]קדישו וחול
[שם] יסובו דוכני
[ב]שיר יהללו און[תו
יי עוז לעמו יתן [יי יברך את עמו בשלום]

From this point on the poet appears to allude to the blessings of the *ʿAmidah,* which together with the *Shemaʿ* form the core of the morning prayer. The list of blessings is not complete. But there is nothing remarkable in this, since in Rabbinical Judaism too their number grew to eighteen only by gradual accretions in the course of generations,[101] and some of them were not added till after the destruction of the Temple.[102] Again, in 1QS the blessings are not listed in the order prevalent in later Jewish tradition. But this different arrangement

---

98. Cp. ארץ ותנובות שמים [לה][דש]ן בעד[נ]י (1Q *34bis* 3 i 4, DJD 1. 153). This seems to me the correct reconstruction required there. בעדי is probably a scribal error and will not bear the interpretations attached to it by the editor. Cp. also the *pesher* on Psalm 37, 1QpPs *37* i 10 (J. Allegro, "A Newly Discovered Fragment of a Commentary on Psalm XXXVII from Qumran," *PEQ* 86 [1954] 69-75). According to my interpretation, 1QS x 15 has no eschatological significance, as Wernberg-Møller opines (*The Manual of Discipline*).

99. See below.

100. "Catalogue des actes de Jaime Ier, Pedro III et Alfonso III Rois d'Aragon concernant les Juifs (1213-1291)," *REJ* 65 (1913) 69-75 (see below, n. 119).

101. Elbogen, *Der jüdische Gottesdienst,* 27-60, 252-56 (see above, n. 12); L. Finkelstein, *The Development of the Amidah* (Philadelphia: Dropsie, 1925).

102. *b. Ber.* 28 b: "R. Levi said: The benediction relating to the Zadokites was instituted at Jabneh," etc., i. e., at the beginning of the second century.

accords with the words of Rab Assi: "The middle benedictions have no order" (*b. Ber.* 34 a). Altogether, the compressed formulation of the blessings in 1QS is reminiscent of the statement in the Mishna. Rabban Gamaliel says: A man should pray the Eighteen (Benedictions) every day. R. Joshua says: *The substance of the Eighteen*. R. Akiba says: "If his prayer is fluent in his mouth he should pray the Eighteen, but if not, *the substance of the Eighteen*" (*m. Ber.* 3).

In the first and the fifth columns of table B, the key words in the Psalm of Benedictions are juxtaposed with those of the Eighteen Benedictions to which they supposedly refer. Columns two and three contain passages from *b. Ber.* 29 a and *y. Ber.* 4.3; 8 a (= *y. Ta⁽an.* 2.2; 65 c), in which the twelve middle benedictions of the Eighteen[103] appear, not in the form customary today, but in a loose paraphrase. These quotations show that paraphrastic allusion was a method employed by the rabbis,[104] no less than by the Covenanters, as long as the benedictions referred to were not mentioned for the express purpose of actual prayer.[105] Set in the fourth column beside these passages from the Talmud are some verses from Ben Sira's Great Song of Praise (Sir 51:21-35),[106] which has been preserved only in Hebrew and is not extant in Greek and Syriac. This Song of Praise is virtually a summary of the morning prayer and particularly of the bendictions of the ⁽*Amidah*. Here too the list of blessings is incomplete, and the order is different from the customary one.[107] Moreover the blessings are not reproduced in full, but only alluded to, exactly as in the Covenanters' Psalm of Benedictions.

---

103. With the addition of the benediction "For the slanderers (למלשינים)," which is not part of the original number (cp. n. 102). In *y. Ta⁽an.* 2.2; 65 c, the number twelve is preserved by combining the benediction for "the shoot of David" with that for "the rebuilding of Jerusalem."

104. Cp. Elbogen, *Der jüdische Gottesdienst,* pp. 14ff. (see above, n. 12).

105. See *b. Meg.* 17 a—18 b.

106. Ed. M. H. Segal, משלי בן סירא (Jerusalem: Bialik, 1953) 355-57. It is important to note that just as the Psalm of Benedictions is one of the three liturgical poems with which 1QS concludes, the Great Song of Praise is one of the three devotional odes that round off the Proverbs of Ben Sira.

107. The analogy of the Psalm of Benedictions makes it evident that the order of verses in Ben Sira should not be changed (as proposed by Segal) to bring them into accord with the order of normative Jewish prayers. Nor is there any reason for supposing that some verses of the "Praise" have been lost (Rabin, *Qumran Studies,* 76, n. 2).

TABLE B

Shema' and 'Amidah	Ben Sira 51:21-35	y. Ber. 4.3 (8 a)	b. Ber. 29 a	1QS x 8—xi 16	
ברוך אתה יהוה אלהינו ואלהי אבותינו אלהי אברהם				וברוב טובו אכפר כל עוני	14-13 x
אלהי יצחק ואלהי יעקב האל הגדול הגבור והנורא		הברכה		וללא חסד כי אל משפטי	15 xi
אל עליון קונה שמים וארץ			דעתנו ממך להבין	ישועתי לעד ומצעדי	16 x
ומביא גואל לבני בניהם למען שמו באהבה				תמיד ובכול יהיה אריב	17-16 x
מלך עוזר ומושיע ומגן ברוך אתה יהוה מגן אברהם	34	חננו מאתך דעה		ומשפטו בידו יכלכל	18 x
אתה גבור לעולם אדני מחיה מתים אתה רב להושיע	27 33	ורצה בתשובתנו		כי אל סלעי ומעוזי	19-18 x
משיב הרוח ומוריד הגשם	28		והלא	מסתרי שכל ומזמת דעת	23 x
מכלכל חיים בחסד מחיה מתים ברחמים רבים	29		סלח לנו אבינו	מעין צדקתי	8-7 xi

There are, however, two important differences between the Great Song of Praise and the Psalm of Benedictions. First there is no parallel expression in the Psalm and still less in the ʿAmidah to the verse in Ben Sira, "Give thanks to Him who chooses the sons of Zadok as Priests" (51:29). Here is a problem that calls for further investigation, since one would have expected the Covenanters to make much of any reference to the sons of Zadok. Indeed, it is this verse that has led some scholars to conjecture that the Song of Praise perhaps originated with the Covenanters or in similar circles.[108]

The second difference between the Psalm and the Song of Praise is that the former contains no allusion to "the flourishing of the horn of David" or to the "rebuilding of Jerusalem," which Ben Sira mentioned in their customary order.[109] The author of the Psalm presumably omitted these two benedictions deliberately as an expression of his community's opposition to the Jerusalem of their day and their preference for the house of Aaron over the house of David.[110] The loss of these benedictions was made good by substituting for them the blessings contained in the following verse: "He has given them an inheritance in the lot of the holy ones, and with the sons of heaven he has associated their company for a council of unity, fundament (סוד = יסוד) of a holy framework for an eternal planting" (1QS xi 7-8). Instead of beholding the rebuilding of Jerusalem, the יחד is to inherit "the lot of the holy ones," and in place of "the flourishing of the horn of David," they proclaim the house of Aaron, meaning the sons of Zadok, to be the "fundament of a holy framework for an eternal planting."[111] The application to the house of Zadok of expressions which in the Bible are always associated with the house of David (Isa 11:1; Jer 23:5; 33:15; Ps 132:17; et al.) is no mere accident, but rather discloses a deliberate tendentious policy. This omission of the house of David and of Jerusalem from the prayers of the יחד, in contrast to the mentioning of them next to the benediction for the house of

108. Ibid.
109. This benediction is not given in the Palestinian text of the "Eighteen" found in the Cairo Genizah (see Rabin, ibid., 77). Elbogen considers it late (*Der jüdische Gottesdienst*, 39-41, 263 [see above, n. 12]). But the reference to it in Ben Sira seems to indicate its antiquity, though it may not have been a component of the ʿAmidah of all the various trends of Judaism in the Second Temple Period.
110. See the *Rule of the Congregation* which describes the future "session of the men of renown" (1QSa ii 11ff.).
111. Reading מבנית as proposed by Y. Yadin ("A Note on DSD IV 20," *JBL* 75 [1955] 40-43). "A holy framework" (מבנית קודש) is the opposite of "a frame of sin," מבנה חטאה (1QH i 22. Cp. 1QS iv 4-5; CD i 7-8).

Zadok in Ben Sira's Song of Praise may point to a steady worsening of the relations between the יחד and its opponents in the period between the composition of the "Song" and the time when 1QS was committed to writing. Traces of such a process can also be detected in the Covenanter's own writings. In fragments of several manuscripts there are explicit references to a Davidic Messiah[112] in terms borrowed from the Bible, especially from Isaiah 11, e.g., "the Messiah of righteousness, the shoot of David." These texts seem to stem from a period prior to the composition of the Psalm of Benedictions and reflect a more favorable attitude to the house of David than that expressed in the Psalm.[113]

V

The suggested reconstruction of the daily routine of a member of the Qumran יחד, based on the foregoing analysis of the Psalm of the Appointed Times and the Psalm of Benedictions, calls to mind the description given by Josephus of the division of the day in the life of the Essenes. In the following table the two sources are printed side by side. The comparison is intended to highlight the similarities in the life-style of these two groups. At the same time it puts in relief the quite different literary character and setting of the sources compared. Josephus details prayer times as an illustration of the Essenes' customary practice and refers to the prayers offered in the morning and the evening without quoting or paraphrasing their actual texts. In contradistinction, the wording found in the Manual of Discipline (1QS) echoes the psalmodic tenor of the prayer texts which the author paraphrases.

112. J. M. Allegro, "Further Messianic References in Qumran Literature," *JBL* 75 [1956] 174-87.
113. For an opposite view, see Y. Liver's detailed examination of this question in *The House of David* ([Jerusalem: Magnes Press, 1959] 117-40).

1 QS x 13-16	*J.W.* 2.8.5 §128-131[114]
When I begin to put forth my hands and my feet I will bless his name.	Before the sun is up they utter no word on mundane matters, but offer to him[115] certain prayers, which have been handed down from their fore-fathers, as though entreating him to rise.
At the beginning of [my] going out or [my] coming in,[116] when I sit down or rise.	They are then dismissed by their superiors to the various crafts in which they are severally proficient and are strenuously employed until the fifth hour, when they again assemble in one place and, after girding their loins with linen cloths, bathe their bodies in cold water.
	Pure now themselves, they repair to the refectory as to some sacred shrine.
Before I raise my hand to satisfy myself with the delights of what the world produces . . . I will bless him, giving special thanks.[118]	Before meat[117] the priest says a grace, and none may partake of food until after the prayer.

114. H. St. J. Thackeray, trans., *The Jewish War* in *Loeb Classical Library* (Cambridge, MA: Harvard University Press, 1927). Cp. Elbogen, *Der jüdische Gottesdienst,* 246, 251 (see above, n. 12).

115. Thackeray and other scholars understand this pronoun to refer to the sun. But it seems more likely that it should be referred to God. Accordingly, the second part of the sentence should be translated: "as if entreating him [God] to make it [the sun] rise." See J. Strugnell's suggestion to give εἰς αὐτὸν a local sense so that the words indicate "a heterodox direction of prayer" ("Flavius Josephus and the Essenes: Antiquities XVIII.18-22," *JBL* 77 [1958] 112).

116. These words have a legal slant, as may be inferred from a comparison with CD xx 27-28. Cp. Table B.

117. The excavations at Qumran have brought to light the Covenanters' refectorium and beside it a kind of store for eating utensils (R. de Vaux, "Fouilles de Khirbet

From a comparison of the Psalm of Benedictions with the Essene order of prayer, it appears probable that the Covenanters, like the Essenes, used to pronounce a blessing similar to the rabbinical "fatten us with the pleasant things of Thine earth" (*b. Ber.* 29 a), not as a part of the morning prayer, "with the coming of the day," but only in the middle of the second watch, after five hours of work and approximately another hour of ritual bathing and purification.[119] Furthermore this was not a private devotion like the prayer at dawn but was said in congregation, ממערכת אנשים, in the language of 1QS x 14.

From the analogous arrangement of the Psalm of the Appointed Times, it may be inferred that the daily prayers specified in the Psalm of Benedictions were originally followed by prayers for festivals and appointed times, seasons of the years, sabbatical years and jubilees. A fragment of a benediction for the seasons apparently has been preserved amongst the remains of a liturgical work, 1Q *34*[bis] 2 + 1, (cp. Table A). It is noteworthy that the presumed blessing for the seasons is followed there by a Prayer for the Day of Atonement (2 + 1, line 6),[120] which we would have expected to find earlier in the list, among the prayers for the festivals. We can offer but a tentative explanation for this apparently surprising displacement.

A pivotal component of the Jewish liturgy of the Day of Atonement is the confessional prayer, ודוי, the essence of which, according to Mar Zutra, are the words "indeed we have sinned": "If one says, 'Indeed we have sinned,' one need say no more" (*b. Yoma* 87 b).[121] The confessional prayer was derived from the liturgical rites performed by the High Priest on the Day of Atonement, as

Qumrân. Rapport préliminaire sur les 3ᵉ, 4ᵉ et 5ᵉ campagnes," *RB* 63 [1956] 542-43). A description of the communal meal is given in 1QS vi 2-6; 1QSa ii 16-21.

118. The sages gave a similar description of a man's acts at the end of his day's work: "When a man comes from the field in the evening he enters a synagogue; if he is accustomed to read [Scripture] let him read; if he is accustomed to study [the Mishna], let him study. Then he reads the *Shemaᶜ* and says the *Tefillah* [Eighteen Benedictions]; after that he eats his meal and says Grace" (*b. Ber.* 4 b).

119. Possibly this was the time when the prayer from the Cairo Genizah, mentioned previously (see above, n. 100), was said. This conjecture finds confirmation in the expression [שם] יסובו דוכני, where דוכן is to be interpreted as "table," as in *b. Kelim* 7 b: "A table, דוכן, which contains a receptacle for pans is pure" (cp. *Aruch Completum,* ed. A. Kohut, s.v. דוכן).

120. Y. M. Grintz has rightly pointed out that this blessing has no connection with the text preceding it ("Tarbuth we Sifruth," in the Hebrew Daily, *Haaretz* 10 Feb. 1956).

121. See also *t. Yoma* 5 (4).14ff. (ed. Zuckermandel, p. 191); *y. Yoma* 8.9; 45 c; *Pesiq. R.* 35.160.

described in Lev 16:21:[122] "And the priest shall lay both his hands upon the head of the live goat and confess over him all the iniquities of the people of Israel, and all their transgressions and all their sins (*m. Yoma* 2.8).[123] This prayer would also seem to be alluded to in the devotional verses that separate the Psalm of the Appointed Times from the Psalm of Benedictions (1QS x 11): "His judgment I will pronounce according to my perversity—and my transgression is before my eyes." It further forms part of the two extant descriptions of the procedure at the annual initiation of new members into the covenant:

CD xx 27-30	1QS i 22ff.[124]
	and the Levites shall recount (23) the iniquities of the sons of Israel and all their guilty transgressions and their sin in the dominion of (24) Belial.
But all they that hold fast to these rules, to [g]o out [and] (28) come in according to the Law; and listen to the voice of the Teacher and confess before God:	[Then all] those who are passing into the covenant
"Indeed, we (29) have done evil both we and our fathers, by walking contrariwise against the ordinances of the covenant of righteousness (30) and truth; thy judgments are upon us."	shall confess after them, saying, "We have committed iniquity (25) [we have transgressed, we have sin]ned, we have done evil w[e] and our [fath]ers before us in walking[125] (26) [contrariwise against the covenant] of truth and righteousness, [and the God of vengeance has performed] his judgment upon us."

122. Cp. Ps 106:6: "Both we and our fathers have sinned; we have committed iniquity, we have done wickedly."
123. Cp. *Dires de Moïse*, cols. iii-iv and additional fragments (*Qumran Cave I*, pp. 94-96).
124. The text is given here as reconstructed by Haberman, *ʿEdah weʿEduth*, 82-83 (see above, n. 26).
125. Reading: ב[ה]לכתנו. Cp. 1QS iii 9.

The confessional prayer on this solemn occasion was accompanied by a description of the contrasting fates of the wicked and the righteous, ending with God's promise to forgive for the sins of the truly penitent, the members of the covenant:

CD xx 34	1QS ii 25—iii 12
	Everyone who refuses to enter [the covenant of Go]d, walking in the stubbornness of his heart . . . (4) he will not be purified by atonement offerings, and he will not be made clean with the water for impurity; he will not sanctify himself with seas (5) and rivers or be made clean with any water for washing. Unclean, unclean he will be all the days that he rejects the ordinances of (6) God, not binding himself to the יחד of his community. Because in the spirit of the true community of God [are] the ways of a man,
And God shall atone for them, and they shall witness his salvation for they have taken refuge in his holy name.	all his iniquities will be atoned . . . (8) and by an upright and humble spirit his sin will be atoned. . . . (11) Then he will be forgiven by pleasing atonements before God, and this will be for him an eternal covenant of (12) the יחד.

This part of the ceremony ended with words of encouragement to the faithful as set out in the previously mentioned Prayer for the Day of Atonement (1Q 34bis):

(2) [   ] in the lot of the righteous. But for the wicked a lot [   ] (3) [   ] in their bones, a disgrace for all flesh and the righteous (4) [   ] to fatten on the delight (בעדני) of heaven and the produce of (the) earth, so that there should be distinction (מבדיל or להיות הבדל)[126] (5) between (the) righteous and (the) wicked. Thou hast given (the) wicked (for) our ransom and traitors [in our stead] (6) [and you played, עשיתה] havoc with all our tormentors. And we will praise thy name forever (7) [and ever]. Because for this thou didst create us and this is that [is due (יאה)] to you.[127]

This close resemblance, both in content and language, between the Prayer for the Day of Atonement and the prayer uttered at the initiation ceremony of the יחד, plus the fact that the confession was an essential part of that ceremony make it highly probable that the initiation ceremony was actually performed on the Day of Atonement. Moreover the prominent part played in it by the priests and Levites indicates that the Covenanters substituted this ceremony for the service of the Day of Atonement in the Temple at Jerusalem, from which they had disassociated themselves.

The fact that the Covenanters held their ceremony of initiation on the Day of Atonement further helps to explain the actions of "the Wicked Priest," their main antagonist, as described in 1QpHab xi 5-8. The author of the *pesher* vents his bitterness against that priest, presumably the High Priest of the Temple at Jerusalem, "who pursued after the Teacher of Righteousness in the indignation of his wrath to the place of his voluntary exile (אבית גלותו),[128] and at the time of rest on the Day of Atonement, he appeared to them to confound them and to make them stumble on the day of fasting, their Sabbath of rest." I have suggested[129] that "the day of fasting, their Sabbath of rest" is the Day of Atonement of the יחד, which did not coincide with the Day of Atonement of mainstream Judaism, because of their different time-reckoning. The High Priest left Jerusalem on that day (a clear indication that it was not the Day of Atonement observed by him) and went to the Covenanter's retreat on the shores of the Dead Sea to prevent them from observing the day which they regarded as

---

126. In Milik's transcription the letters לה[י]ת can be seen. We have completed the line in accordance with the wording of 1QS ii 6.
127. My restorations.
128. H. Yalon, "The Dead Sea Scrolls ed. M. Burrows. The Isaiah MS and the Habakkuk Commentary," *Kiryat-Sefer* 27 (1951) 175.
129. S. Talmon, "Yom Hakippurim," in this vol., pp. 186-99.

holy, and to stop them from performing the ceremony which was the pivot of their communal life.[130]

This double use of the Prayer for the Day of Atonement may serve as an explanation for its being listed in the concluding part of the Covenanters' Manual of Benedictions, apart from the festival benedictions where it naturally belongs. We may also infer that the same liturgical work included benedictions for occasions which are not part of the regular, rhythmically repeated pattern of human life. Possibly, therefore, the Prayer for the Time of Wa[r] referred to in the 1QM xv 5,[131] was also contained in the same work. If so, the actual name of the compilation, the contents of which have been conjecturally reconstructed here, may have been preserved. The author of the *War Scroll* informs us that "the 'Prayer for the Time of War' . . . with all the words of their thanksgiving" was written in the "[B]ook of the Manual of the Appointed Times" (ס[פר סרך] עתו).[132] It may reasonably be conjectured that this was the title which the Covenanters gave to their Manual of Prayer Times and Benedictions.[133]

VI

The propagation of institutionalized prayer among the Qumran Covenanters cannot fully and adequately be explained as arising solely from the historical circumstances of their dissociation from the Temple of Jerusalem and its sacrificial worship. In addition socioreligious factors presumably played a role in this development. One of these, it would appear, was their "commune ideology"

130. It is usually assumed that the annual initiation ceremony of the יחד coincided with the Festival of Weeks, although this is not stated in any of the Covenanters' writings published so far. Passages from *Jubilees* (6:17; 14:14ff.; 19:7; etc.) adduced in support of this assumption never mention the "New Covenant" of the יחד and cannot be considered decisive evidence (*contra* Milik, *Ten Years of Discovery,* 116ff. [see above, n. 6]). The omission from these accounts of the Covenant of Renewal or any reference to the Sinai episode or the Decalogue which are connected in Jewish tradition with the Festival of Weeks (cp. Milik, ibid.), seems to speak against the dating of that ceremony to this festival.
131. 1QM xv 5 (ed. Yadin, p. 346).
132. Yadin's restoration. See his comments, ad loc.
133. As already conjectured by Yadin (ibid.). He rightly compared the title ס[פר עתו with ספר ההגו (CD x 6; xii 2) or ספר ההגי (1QSa i 7). Cp. his further comments on 1QM vii 5 (*War Scroll,* p. 301).

which seriously weakened the position of the individual as a self-contained unit in the group, stressing instead his role and his function as a component of the community's "corporate personality."

It is obvious that sacrificial worship, with its lack of individual variation and its dependence upon agents and institutions (priests, Levites, sanctuaries, and stereotyped ritual) would have been well suited to the basic concepts and needs of the Covenanters. Indeed it can be shown that they never rejected sacrifice *per se*. In their vision of the "New Jerusalem," the restored sanctuary with all its paraphernalia takes prominent rank, and the priesthood continues to play a central role.[134] In their actual, historical situation, however, participation in sacrificial worship had become a practical impossibility for the above-mentioned reasons. But the Covenanters never wavered in their conviction that the Jerusalem Temple was the only site where sacrifices could legitimately be offered. This tension is reflected in the Qumran literature, which shows an intricate development of the presentation of heaven as a temple in which the angels serve as cultic personnel.[135] The idea in itself has roots in biblical and ancient oriental traditions. The Covenanters' intensive preoccupation with the image of a heavenly temple gives expression to their critique of the contemporary Temple operative in Jerusalem, and at the same time it discloses their unwillingness to replace the traditional sanctuary at Jerusalem with any other terrestial center of worship.[136]

Because the Covenanters dissociated from the Temple in Jerusalem, and the substitution of another cultic site was absolutely unacceptable, sacrifice automatically ceased to fulfill any function in the devotional practices of the יחד.[137] In the light of the cessation of sacrificial worship and the resultant quest

---

134. M. Baillet, "Fragments Araméens de Qumrân 2: Description de la Jérusalem Nouvelle," *RB* 62 (1955) 222-45. J. M. Allegro, "Fragments of a Qumran Scroll of Eschatological Midrashim," *JBL* 77 (1958) 350-54 = *4Q 174 Florilegium* (DJD 4, 1968), 5. 53ff. Cp. Y. Yadin, "A Midrash on 2 Sam vii and Ps. i-ii (4Q Florilegium)," *IEJ* 9 (1959) 95-98.

135. J. Strugnell, VTSup (1960), 8. 318-45 (cp. n. 20 above).

136. Cp. D. Flusser ("Two Notes on the Midrash on 2 Sam vii," *IEJ* 9 [1959] 99-109). See the basic treatment of this motif by V. Aptowitzer ("The Heavenly Temple in the Agada," *Tarbiz* 2 [1930] 137-53, 257-87 [Heb.]).

137. The bones found at Qumran do not witness to sacrifice, *contra* S. M. Steckoll ("The Qumran Sect in Relation to the Temple of Leontopolis," *RQ* 6 [1967] 55-69). Cp. R. de Vaux's rejoinder (in postscript to M. Delcor, "Le temple d'Onias en Égypte," *RB* 75 [1968] 204-5) and his discussion of the issue in *Archaeology and the Dead Sea Scrolls* ([London: Oxford University Press, 1973] 11ff.).

for a new form of divine "service," we can better understand the Covenanters' midrashic amplification of Prov 15:8 in CD xi 20-21: "The sacrifice of the wicked is an abomination, but the prayer of the righteous is an offering of delight," זבח רשעים תועבה ותפילת צדיקים כמנחת רצון (cp. 1QS ix 3ff.; 11QPs[a] xviii 8-10).[138] In order to compensate the loss of the sacrificial cult, and by reason of their group-centered ideology, the Covenanters especially promoted de-individualized, stereotyped forms of prayer which could be adapted without further qualification to communal devotion. Their egalitarian principles, the right of each member to scrutinize the deeds of his fellow, the hierarchical structure of the community, and the resulting system of close supervision of the lower-ranking by their superiors were conducive to the development of worship patterns fixed in time, openly observable, and removed from the sphere of subjective *ad hoc* decisions with their concomitant individualized forms of expression: "the prayer formula is stereotyped and strictly obligatory; the wording is inviolable, sacrosanct; no worshipper may dare to alter the words in the slightest degree, any more than he would think of making a change in the ritual acts of sacrifice, expiation, or consecration." In short, all these factors triggered the emergence of institutionalized prayer in the Qumran commune. [139]

It is quite possible that in these matters also, the Covenanters shared with other Jewish groups specific cultic developments, which spring from biblical prototypes. The first mention of three definite prayer times during the day is found in the book of Daniel. We are told that Daniel went into his house, whose windows looked towards Jerusalem, "there he knelt down three times a day and offered prayers to his God as his custom had always been" (Dan 6:11). His enemies pounced upon this opportunity to denounce him to the king, who had issued an ordinance that only he himself should be the object of adoration. Daniel was thrown into the lions' pit in punishment for his transgression (Dan 6:12-17). Now, scholars hold unanimously that the book of Daniel, or its latter part, is among the latest works in the Hebrew canon and that it was committed to writing at the beginning of the second century B.C.E., i.e., approximately at

---

138. See the discussion of the matter by D. Flusser (The Dead Sea Sect and Pre-Pauline Christianity, *ScrHier* 4 [1958] 229-36); B. Gärtner (*The Temple and the Community in Qumran and the New Testament* [Cambridge: Cambridge University Press, 1965] 19ff., 44-46); and J. M. Baumgarten ("Sacrifice and Worship among the Jewish Sectarians of the Dead Sea [Qumrân] Scrolls," *HThR* 46 [1953] 145).

139. F. Heiler, *Prayer*, 66 (see above, n. 2).

the time of the emergence of the Qumran community. The information contained in the book of Daniel, which is extant at Qumran in several copies, can therefore be adduced as corroborative evidence for the emergence of fixed prayers at the time we first encounter them as an institution at Qumran.

In view of these characteristics, it is rather surprising that the priests apparently were not accorded a special standing in the Qumran prayer service and did not function as "cultic virtuosi" (to use a term coined by Max Weber), as they did in the sacrificial service. Only one exception can be elicited from the Qumran writings in this respect. The priests offered the blessing over the bread and wine at group meals which were also an occasion for study (1QS vi 2-8; cp. CD xiii 2-3). The same applies to the "messianic meal" in the "latter days," אחרית הימים, as laid down in the *Rule of the Congregation* (1QSa ii 17-21).[140] But this single reference does not warrant the inference that such was the priests' prerogative at all public prayers.[141] The contrary seems to have been the case, since in no other reference to prayer are priests ever singled out. I tend to explain this circumstance as revealing an intent not to accord to priests in the prayer service the status of intermediaries which they occupied in the sacrificial service. In prayer the community enters into direct communion with God. It is possibly for this same reason that we do not find any reference to a cantor who leads the congregation in prayer, a custom which later developed in the synagogue service. One is tempted to see in this absence an assertion of egalitarian principles to balance the otherwise preferential status of the priests.

A similar intent can be discerned in the composition of the council of the community (עצת הרבים). It consists of fifteen members, of whom twelve are laymen, probably a conceptual representation of the tradition of twelve tribes and three priests (1QS viii 1ff.).[142] It follows that at any given occasion of difference of opinion, the larger number of laymen on the "council" would outweigh the smaller number of priests, notwithstanding their prestigious status, and this

---

140. This appears to have been a generally recognized Jewish custom since it is also mentioned in rabbinic writings (*b. Giṭ.* 59 b). See also Heinemann (*Prayer in the Talmud,* 10 [see n.1 above]).
141. J. Licht, *The Rule Scroll* (Jerusalem: Bialik, 1965) 139, and notes, ad loc.
142. The figure fifteen is taken by Licht (ibid., 112, 119, and especially 167) to be the minimum number required for the constitution of a self-contained Qumran communal unit and nothing more. Differing from this interpretation, I subscribe to the explanation that the fifteen constitute a "governing council," whereas the minimum number required for a "community" is ten, including one priest (see above).

would safeguard the Covenanters' egalitarian principles against disproportionate self-assertion of the priests.

We have pointed to the many affinities between the Qumran Manual of Benedictions and the basic Jewish prayers which developed in the period of the Tannaim and Amoraim and ultimately became the core of the traditional prayer book. This similarity should not cause any surprise since the Covenanters must be viewed, after all, as an offshoot of postexilic Judaism, whose institutions and beliefs ensuingly found their most salient expression in "normative Judaism" of the late Second Temple Period. We have further placed great emphasis on the early emergence of institutionalized prayer at Qumran, a socioreligious development paralleled in normative Judaism only after the destruction of the Temple. However we must also take notice of some fundamental differences in patterns of worship between the Covenanters and the mainstream community.

There is no reference in the Qumran writings to the reading of the Law as a major feature of the divine service. The liturgical reading from the Law is usually viewed as one of the earliest components of synagogue worship, going back to the times of Ezra and Nehemiah (Nehemiah 9), so much so that scholars are inclined to consider it the basis and the core of the service. Some even perceive in it the very reason for the establishment of the synagogue, which at first was not meant to be a "house of prayer," but rather a locale for reading the Law.[143]

In this context it is important to note that the technical term used to designate the Covenanters' place of worship is בית השתחות (CD xi 21) and not בית כנסת or בית תפלה, which are the appropriate terms in the vocabulary of the "normative" Jewish community. בית השתחות equals the Greek προσκυνήσῃ,[144] rather than συναγωγή, and appears to focus exclusively on the invocation character of the service held at that place. The term בית השתחות is possibly derived from the biblical reference to a "house of prostration" dedicated to the Aramean deity Rimmon (2 Kgs 5:18). Its Aramaic equivalent is extant in the

143. Cp. Heinemann, *Prayer in the Talmud,* 83 (above, n. 1) and references to Safrai and Zeitlin adduced there.

144. Cp. T. Olm, "Proskynese," *RGG* 3 (Tübingen: Mohr, 1961) cols. 640-41; E. Rivkin, "Ben Sira and the Non-Existence of the Synagogue. A Study in Historical Method," *In the Time of Harvest: Essays in Honor of Abba Hillel Silver* (New York: Macmillan, 1963) 320-54, esp. Appendix B; also S. Talmon, "A Further Link Between the Judean Covenanters and the Essenes?" in this vol, pp. 61-67.

Elephantine Payrus no. 44, 3 (ed. Cowley, p. 147) and has its counterpart in the Arabic *masjad*.

Without intending to establish any historical links between the Qumran community and the Samaritans (another group of Jewish dissenters that preceded the Covenanters in the secession from the mother community), attention should be drawn to the fact that in the Samaritan worship also the Law is not read. Their service on the morning of the Sabbath consists exclusively of prayer chants. The appropriate portions of the Law are read in private after the service. Another public reading is performed about midday, as an adjunct, as it were, to the morning prayer. This similarity in the liturgical service between the practices of two unconnected, dissident communities, whose traditions are rooted in postexilic times, vouches for the antiquity of the Qumran pattern of liturgical worship.

At Qumran a form of divine service emerged which lacks the distinct features of the Jewish synagogue ritual. It appears that the Covenanters instituted a worship pattern which revolved on prayer to the very exclusion of any other element. This fact puts into even sharper relief the transition from sacrifice to prayer which seems to have emerged at Qumran without any intermediating factors.

We may add one further consideration. Historically, sacrifice in Israel was predominantly group-oriented. Though individual sacrificial offerings have their place in biblical ritual law, the main aspects tie sacrifice definitely to a group, pertaining either to family, clan, or the nation. In some cases, as with the agricultural festivals, we may observe that the prescribed rites and customs oscillate between observance within the family circle and observance by representation on a nationwide basis. Thus the Passover sacrifice initially was conceived as a function of a family unit (בית אב), with every member of the household participating. Side by side with this pattern, rather than superseding it, there emerged the custom of celebrating the Passover at the central sanctuary with the representatives of the family units participating on a nationwide scale.[145] After the cessation of service at a central sanctuary in the wake of the destruction of the Second Temple, the family-bound pattern of observance regained its initial exclusiveness and retains it to this very day.

---

145. This is an important feature of Josiah's reform. See S. Talmon, "Divergences in Calendar-Reckoning in Ephraim and Judah" (*KCC*, 131-35).

Neither the family-oriented nor the nation-centered pattern of worship could gain a hold over the Judean Covenanters, who undervalued family organization to the point of idealizing the exclusive, male commune[146] and conceived of themselves as elite, standing in conscious opposition to the body of the nation. The new form of worship which they adopted, that of institutionalized prayer, gave expression to the egalitarian principles of the group and at the same time furthered group-cohesion based on the principle of election rather than on ascription.

Our analysis suggests that, despite the significant common ground, no definite historical interdependence can be established between the emergence of institutionalized prayer at Qumran and in mainstream Judaism. Jewish prayer developed within the framework of preexisting, ascriptive social entities, the family and the nation, and cannot be linked with elective groupings that have no roots in the natural structure of society. In contrast to this, one could posit a historical connection between the institutionalized prayer of the Covenanters and the institutionalized prayer of early Christians, which developed initially in the monastic movement. In this instance a similarity in the sociological composition of the two groups may have effected a borrowing of devotional practices. This hypothesis, however, calls for further investigation.

---

146. In this respect the Covenanters differ significantly from the Jewish exiles in Babylon who attached prime importance to traditional family bonds and to clan consciousness, as the many family rosters in Ezra-Nehemiah evince.

EXTRA-CANONICAL HEBREW PSALMS
FROM QUMRAN — PSALM 151

I

The *Psalms Scroll* recovered from Cave 11 was published by J. A. Sanders in 1962, merely four years after its discovery.[1] Like most Qumran documents it is written in square Hebrew characters, executed with careful penmanship. Sanders dates the scroll on paleographical grounds to the Hasmonean Period. When unrolled it was found to contain 33 canonical psalms preserved in full or in part. Four fragments (A-D) discovered in the same cave contain portions of four additional psalms. They were most probably already detached in antiquity from that very same manuscript. A fifth fragment (E) was published by Y. Yadin, who tends to date the manuscript about a century later than Sanders.[2] This fragment contains the latter part of Psalm 118, Psalms 114, and 117 in their entirety, and the opening lines of Psalm 105. The ensuing text of this psalm is still preserved at the very beginning of the scroll itself. This fact proves beyond doubt that Fragment E also became detached from 11QPs[a].

All psalms preserved in the manuscript are from the fourth and the fifth book of the Hebrew Psalter in the masoretic subdivision, the first being Psalm 93. The internal sequence of the individual psalms in 11QPs[a] differs from their order in the MT and the ancient VSS. Fragments A-E contain Psalms 101-103; 109; 118; 104; 105:1-12; whereas the main manuscript contains Psalms 105:25-45; 146; 148; 121-23; 119; 135-36; 118; 145; 139; 137-38; 93; 141; 133; 144; 142-43; 149-50; 140; 134.

1. J. A. Sanders, "The Scroll of Psalms (11QPs[a]) from Cave 11: A Preliminary Report," *BASOR* 165 (1962) 11-15; idem, "Ps 151 in 11QPs[a]," *ZAW* 75 (1963) 73-86; idem, "Two Non-Canonical Psalms in 11QPs[a]," *ZAW* 76 (1964) 57-74; idem, *The Psalms Scroll of Qumran Cave 11 (11QPs[a])* (DJD; Oxford: Clarendon, 1965), vol. 4.
2. Y. Yadin, "Another Fragment of the Psalms Scroll from Qumran Cave 11 (11QPs[a])," *Textus* 5 (1966) 1-10.

Interspersed between the canonical psalms are eight additional compositions, none of which was transmitted in either the MT or in any of the ancient VSS of the biblical book of Psalms. The closing line of one, the only one extant (xxvii,1), is in fact the final stanza of "The Last [or possibly "additional"] Words of David" (2 Sam 23:1-7). Therefore it can be considered certain that this psalm-like biblical composition had also been included originally in 11QPs^a.

The scroll holds, furthermore, a variational text of Sir 51:13-30 (xxi,11-17; xxii,1). There are also three Hebrew pieces of a psalmodic nature (xviii; xix), a Syriac version of which is found in a homiletical treatise by the tenth century Nestorian patriarch Elias of Anbar.[3] One of these is known as Psalm 151 from the Syro-Hexaplar, the LXX, and the Vulgate. In addition, it contains three hitherto altogether unknown extra-canonical Hebrew psalms (xix; xxii; xxvi).

To all these we should add a prose composition which gives the sum total of songs and psalms composed by King David. It closes the manuscript (xxvii), bringing up the total of added materials to nine.

The discussion of this important find bears on various aspects of biblical research. Sander's identification of the scroll as the earliest manuscript of the canonical book of Psalms quite obviously invites an evaluation of its meaning for the textual history and the composition of this book and possibly for the history of the biblical text altogether. But it appears to be rather doubtrful that 11QPs^a is indeed an ancient copy of the canonical book of Psalms, as both Sanders and Yadin assume. The numerous extra-canonical additions which have no equal in other Qumran works,[4] or for that matter in fragments of Psalms scrolls found on Masada[5] and at Nahal Hever,[6] give rise to the supposition that what we probably have here is an ancient compilation of liturgical poems which

3. W. Wright, "Some Apocryphal Psalms in Syriac," *PSBA* 9 (1887) 257-66; M. Noth, "Die fünf syrisch überlieferten apokryphen Psalmen," *ZAW* 48 (1930) 1-23.

4. See the synoptic list of psalm-scrolls from the Judean Desert compiled by J. A. Sanders, "Pre-Masoretic Psalter Texts," *CBQ* 27 (1965) 114-23. It should be noted that one of the extra-canonical pieces of 11QPs^a was also found inscribed on the back of a fragment which issued from the same cave and is not part of a copy of the biblical book of Psalms. See Sanders, *ZAW* 76 (1964) 76.

5. For a preliminary account of the biblical fragments from Masada, see Y. Yadin, "The Excavations of Masada—The Documents and Inscriptions," *IEJ* 15 (1965) 103 ff.

6. See Y. Yadin, "Expedition D," *IEJ* 11 (1961) 35-52, esp. p. 40; cp. J. A. Sanders, *JBL* 86 (1967) 439.

served the members of the Qumran community as a kind of breviary.[7] Such compilations may have been in general use among Jews at the end of the Second Temple Period. There are, however, reasons for assuming that the preservation of this unique exemplar among the writings of the Covenanters does not result merely from happenstance. It would rather appear that it evidences their particular concept of worship in which a definite prayer service replaced the customary sacrificial worship to which most Jews still adhered.[8]

Defining 11QPs[a] as a breviary rather than as a copy of the canonical book of Psalms would more easily explain the inclusion of that prose summary (xxvii) which credits King David with the authorship of 4050[9] compositions:

> 3,600 psalms; and songs to sing before the altar over the whole-burnt, תמיד, offering every day, for all the days of the year, 364[10]; and for the קרבן of the Sabbaths, 52 songs; and for the קרבן of the New Moons and for all the Solemn Assemblies and for the Day of Atonement, 30 songs.[11] And all the songs that he spoke were 446, and songs to be entoned on הפקועים, 4. And the total was 4,050.

We may reasonably assume that the four special songs for the פגועים correspond to the "four leaders" of the four quarters of the year into which the Qumran calendar was subdivided. The term פגועים appears to derive from the biblical term

7. See below.
8. S. Talmon, "The Emergence of Institutionalized Prayer in Israel in the Light of the Qumran Literature," in this volume, pp. 200-243.
9. The figure given implies that David's poetic output exceeded that of Solomon, whom tradition accredits with having authored 4,005 poems and proverbs (1 Kgs 4:32). But we should be reminded that the above biblical passage was transmitted with some textual variation, the LXX (1 Kgs 5:12) reading 5000 (πεντακισχίλιαι) for the MT 4005. Therefore it could be surmised that it was extant at Qumran with the Hebrew reading 4050. If this indeed was the case, the author of 11QPs[a] 151 would have acquired the sum total of David's compositions from a biblical prooftext.
10. These figures furnish us with definite proof that the Qumranians adhered to a solar-lunar calendar of 364 days. See "The Calendar of the Covenanters of the Judean Desert" (in this volume, pp. 147-85).
11. See Sir 47:13-14. In both instances this specific praise of David probably derives from 1 Chr 23:30-31.

פגע, which connotes "supplication," "prayer," or "entreaty" (cp. especially Jer 7:16; 27:18; and Gen 23:8; Isa 47:3; 53:12; Jer 36:25; Ruth 1:16).[12]

This detailed enumeration of prayers, properly arranged in their chronological sequence throughout the year, would be out of place in a copy of the canonical book of Psalms. But it is eminently appropriate in a compilation which may have been part of what can be considered a prototype of the daily prayer book which was established later and of the *maḥzor,* the collection of customary prayers for the festivals.[13]

Sanders has equipped his edition of the *Psalms Scroll* with a critical apparatus and valuable exegetical comments. But as is wont to be the case, some of his readings and comments are open to discussion. The recovered Hebrew original of Psalm 151, especially, has attracted the attention of scholars, since against it can be checked the previously accessible translations into Greek, Syriac, and Latin. It is to the examination of this psalm that we shall now turn, bringing under consideration the following three issues:

(a) The Hebrew text and the structure of Psalm 151;

(b) The literary characteristics of the song in comparison with biblical psalmody;

(c) The bearing of the psalm on aspects of the history of the biblical text, with special reference to a distinctive feature of the MT, the inner-sentence caesura, *pisqah beʾemṣaʿ pasuq* (henceforth *p.b.p.*).

II

The entire scroll and the psalm obviously were penned by an accomplished scribe in an easily legible hand. Like other Qumran copyists, this scribe also wrote the tetragrammaton in paleo-Hebrew characters (lines 3 and 8). There are only two scribal errors which, however, he corrected later: in line 1 he inserted supralinearly a forgotten נ in the word מנ. In the last line but one, he inserted supralinearly a previously omitted word, ומשל. It appears that in line 5 he

---

12. The specification "four פגועים" precludes the identification of the שיר על הפגועים of 11QPsᵃ with the שיר פגועים mentioned in rabbinic literature (*y. Šabb.* 6.2 8b; *y. ʿErub.* 10.1 26c; *b. Šebu.* 16b; *Midr. Ps.* on Ps 91) which pertains to invocations against demons and evil spirits. Therefore Sanders' translation of the term "music over the stricken" (*The Psalms Scroll,* 92) is unacceptable.

13. See "The Emergence of Institutionalized Prayer," in this volume, pp. 200-243.

erased a connective ו before the word אלוה. For some unexplainable reason he left space for two letters between the words היפים and בשערם in line 8. Into the empty space he introduced a heavy dot, the first from the right in a series of eight which may have served him as guiding marks for achieving the straight guidelines he impressed with a stylus into the leather. They may also have been intended as markers for the division of the sheet into columns. The second of these dots is placed on the י of the tetragrammaton and the third on the ו of the word וישלח. The remaining five appear on the margin which is otherwise left blank. This part of the sheet served as the end piece of the scroll, as was the custom. A similar dot may be seen on line 1 of the preceding column (xxvii). The last line of our poem contains only one word, בריתו, which is a clear indication that this is indeed the ending of the psalm.

The forms of the two letters ו and י are practically indistinguishable, similar to what can also be observed in other Qumran manuscripts, e.g., in the large Isaiah Scroll (1QIsaᵃ). The upper part of these two letters are almost identical in shape, and the down-strokes are not fixed in length. It is at times impossible to decide whether in this or the other instance a ו should be read or a י. Therefore the exact reading of several words remains open to discussion, especially when the pron. suff. of the first or the third sing. are involved.

The orthography of the psalm, like that of the entire MS, is not uniform. As is also the case in the MT, plene spelling, e.g., in ומושל (lines 2 and 9), appears next to defective spelling, as in הגבהים (line 7). Occasionally the introduction of *matres lectionis* goes beyond what one encounters in the MT. But this is well in line with the extreme plene spelling often found in Qumran manuscripts: אלוה (line 5), הכול (lines 5, 6), and למושחני (line 6). Also the indication of a long vowel by two *matres lectionis,* common in Qumran MSS, occurs in Psalm 151: לוא (lines 3, 4) and צואן (lines 4, 9). On the other hand we also find cases of *scriptio defectiva,* even with the omission of a radical א: לצונו (line 2), יפי התור instead of התואר (line 7).[14]

The language of the poem is not of one cloth. Into the core text are interwoven paraphrases of biblical imagery, culled predominantly from passages which revolve on David's election as king over Israel and his feats of heroism (especially 1 Samuel 16-18 and 2 Samuel 7). Overlying this substratum we find

14. E. Tov now proposes to identify scrolls written originally at Qumran by their specific plene spelling and thus to differentiate them from "imported" manuscripts ("The Orthography and Language of the Hebrew Scrolls Found at Qumran and the Origin of These Scrolls," *Textus* 13 [1986] 31-58).

expressions drawn from Rabbinic Hebrew which prove that the poem achieved its final form in the post-biblical era. The psalm speaks of David's youth in an autobiographical style, highlighting a characteristic trait of his which Ben Sira extols: "In his entire career [or "in whatever he did"], he gave praise to God most high" (Sir 47:8). It is composed of two main parts which reflect two scenes: in the first three lines David speaks of his youth when he, the youngest son, was put in charge of his father's flock. At that time he fashioned a musical instrument for himself, as shepherds are wont to do, so as to praise God and sing his glory. In the closing lines the poet tells of his election as king over Israel: Samuel the prophet elevated him to that rank, as God had commanded him to do, and anointed him with holy oil (lines 5-11). These autobiographical statements are connected by a short interlude phrased in the typical style of biblical psalmody (lines 4-5).

The text is made up of full, continuous lines like the *Thanksgiving Scroll* (1QH). It does not display the specific technique employed in MSS of the MT, which is intended fully to display the poetic structure of longer poems such as the Song of Moses (Deuteronomy 32) or Deborah's Song (Judges 5). Lacking such structural guidelines and also punctuation marks, the correct internal division of sentences and collocations cannot be fully ascertained, and much is left to the ingenuity of the reader and interpreter.

The editor of 11QPs[a] subdivided the text of our psalm into seven verses each composed of two lines, comprising two stichs. The first three verses are arranged according to the descending meter 3:2. They are followed by a verse in even meter (3:3), which seemingly closes the first strophe. Similarly the two verses which start off the second strophe (5 and 6) are in a descending 3:2 meter, whereas verse 7, which concludes that strophe and the entire poem, is in an even 3:3 meter.

Of the 14 lines which make up the poem, ten display a synonymous parallelism. The remaining four are arranged in the manner of complementary parallelism. The superscription "Hallelujah of David the Son of Jesse" is not included in this structural schema.[15]

15. The Arabic numerals to the right of the text indicate the number of the line in the MS. The break between lines is shown by an oblique stroke / in the body of the text. The Hebrew letters on the right pertain to the suggested division of verses. The Arabic numerals on the left indicate the meter of the lines.

	הללויה לדויד בן ישי	1	
3/2	וצעיר מבני אבי	א קטן הייתי מן אחי	
3/2	ומושל בגדיותיו	וישימני/ רועה לצונו	2
3/2	ואצבעותי כנור/	ב ידי עשו עוגב	
3/2	אמרתי אני בנפשי	ואשימה ליי כבוד	3
3/2	והגבעות לוא יגידו	ג ההרים לוא יעידו/ לו	4
3/2	והצאן את מעשי/	עלו העצים את דברי	
3/3	ומי יספר את מעשי אדון	ד כי מי יגיד ומי ידבר	5
3/3	הכול הוא שמע והוא האזין	הכול ראה אלה/	6
3/2	את שמואל/ לגדלני	ה שלח נביאו למושחני	7
3/2	יפי התור ויפי המראה	יצאו אחי לקראתו	
3/2	היפים בשערם	ו הגבהים בקומתם/	8
3/2	אלוהים בם	לוא בחר יי	
3/3	וימשחני בשמן הקודש	ז וישלח ויקחני/ מאחר הצואן	9
3/3	ומושל בבני/ בריתו	וישימני נגיד לעמו	10

The arrangement of the poem suggested by Sanders was met with criticism by scholars who applied themselves to its analysis and interpretation. Some deem Sanders' proposal to be founded on uncertain assumptions and suggest to rearrange the poem in accord with the rhythmical pattern displayed in the *Thanksgiving Scroll* (1QH). Others maintain that the arrangement is too mechanical and that it imposes on the poem an unsuited metrical structure. Most stringent are the critical comments voiced by B. Uffenheimer[16] and I. Rabinowitz.[17] In their view, Sanders' arrangement unhinges the logical cohesion on two counts:

(a) the collocation אמרתי אני בנפשי in line 3 introduces the ensuing phrase ההרים לוא יעידו לו, which starts off the next verse and cannot be construed as a complement of the preceding colon ואשימה לה' כבוד, which actually concludes the line, ידי עשו עוגב ואצבעותי כנור (v 2).

(b) *Metri gratia*, Sanders splits the phrase אדון הכול (line 5) by positioning אדון in the first colon of v 4 and הכול in the second in order to maintain the presumed 3:3 structure of that verse. But this structure falls apart if the construct

16. "A Zealot Scroll from Qumran," *Molad* 187-88 (1964) 70 ff. (Heb.).
17. "The Alleged Orphism of 11QPs^a 28, 3-12," *ZAW* 76 (1964) 193-200.

אדון הכול is kept intact on the ground of linguistic considerations[18] and is put at the end of stich 4a (in Sanders' arrangement), as proposed by R. Weiss,[19] or at the beginning of 4b, as Rabinowitz suggests (see below).

Because of our unsatisfactory knowledge of the metrical rules which govern early Hebrew psalmody, Rabinowitz proposes an arrangement of the text based on *parallelismus membrorum*, which is the most basic and best-established pattern in biblical as well as in Qumran psalmody. He further takes into account logical sequence and continuity of thought. These two criteria also underlie the arrangement of 11QPs[a], suggested here, which however differs from that preferred by Rabinowitz. The psalm is seen to contain verses constituted of four, three, or two cola, whichever is required by considerations of context and content, and no attempt is made to subject it to a consistent metrical balance:

	הללויה לדויד בן-ישי	א	1
רצעיר מבני אבי	קטן הייתי מן אחי	ב	
ומושל בגדיותיו	וישימני/ רועה לצונו		2
ואצבעותי כנור/ ואשימה לה׳ כבוד	ידי עשו עוגב	ג	3
ההרים לוא יעידו/ לו והגבעות	אמרתי אני בנפשי	ד	4
והצאן את מעשה/	לוא יגידו עלי העצים את דברו		5
ומי יספר את מעשו	כי מי יגיד ומי ידבר	ה	
אלוה/ הכול הוא שמע והוא האזין	אדון הכול ראה	ו	6
את שמואל/לגדלני	שלח נביאו למושחני		7
יפי התור ויפי המראה	יצאו אחי לקראתו	ז	
לוא בחר ה׳ אלהים בם	הגבהים בקומתם/ היפים בשערם		8
וימשחני בשמן הקודש	וישלח ויקחני/ מאחר הצואן	ח	9
ומושל בבני/ בריתו	וישימני נגיד לעמו		10

The division of the psalm into two strophes, pace Sanders, does not take into account the marked difference in style between its constituent parts. As said, we must distinguish between the two components of the "narrative envelope"

18. A. Hurwitz, "The Post-biblical Epithet אדון הכול in Psalm 151 from Qumran," *Tarbiz* 34 (1965) 1-4 (Heb.); idem, "Observations on the Language of the Third Apocryphal Psalm," *RQ* 18 (1965) 228.
19. R. Weiss, "Psalm 151," *Massa* 21 (1964) 1-2 (Heb.).

and the central passage which is couched in hymnic phraseology and hymnic style. This center piece also exhibits a sentence structure which differs from that of the opening and closing stanzas.

In the opening stanza v 2 displays a structure of two lines, each consisting of two members in synonymous parallelism, whereas v 3 comprises only one line with three stichs in complementary parallelism.

Similarly the center piece consists of two verses: the first (v 4) is structured of two lines, each with two stichs, with only the second line displaying a clear parallelism; the second verse (v 5) is again shorter. It consists of only one line, which can be subdivided into two parallel stichs and concludes that component of the poem.

The third stanza is composed of three verses (6-8), each consisting of two lines. Of these, five are made up of two stichs in synonymous parallelism, whereas in the sixth (7b) no such definite structural device can be discerned.

In view of this analysis, the poem can be divided into three stanzas which are headed by a superscription:

v 1	Superscription: a Hallelujah of David
vv 2-3	Stanza 1: opening part of envelope
vv 4-5	Stanza 2: hymnic center piece
vv 6-8	Stanza 3: closing part of envelope

The closing phrase of the first stanza, ואשימה לה׳ כבוד, is a prayer formula which requires no explanation. It connects directly with the opening collocation of the third stanza, אדון הכול ראה, as in a cause-and-effect relation. The appropriate place for the hymnic link, from אמרתי אני בנפשי to ומי יספר את מעשיו (vv 4-5), is actually between vv 2 and 3. Realizing that there is no power of speech in the material world, in flora and fauna, to glorify God אדון הכול, David took this task upon himself. The rhetorical question "For who can proclaim . . . his works?" כי מי יגיד . . . את מעשהו, leads to a description of how the young lad's spirit was stirred to make a musical instrument so as to give praise to God (v 3; cp. Sir 47:11-13). God observed his deeds and granted him ample reward (vv 6-10).

However, in the psalm in its present form, the hymnic interlude is construed as an explanation after the fact of the statement "My hands made an instrument and my fingers a lyre" (v 3a-b), and as an amplification of the prayer formula "I rendered glory to God" (v 3c). It is possible that the poet conceived of this structure from the very outset. But in view of the fact that the ancient translations have not preserved a rendition of the hymnic interlude, with the exception of the phrase (כי מי יגיד (לאדוני) (v 5c), we may assume that it did not form part of the original text, but rather was inserted at a later stage into the psalm. This assumption is supported by the vocabulary of the hymnic interlude which differs from that of the main stanzas (1 and 3) and does not share with them in the scheme of recurring words interconnected by antithetical parallelism:

אחי (vv 2, 6, 7); וישימני (vv 2, 6-8, cp. אשימה in v 3);

(v 7); גבוהים בקומתם—(v 2) קטן ‖ צעיר

(v 8); ויקחני מאחר הצואן—(v 2) וישימני רועה לצונו

(v 2); וישימני רועה לצונו ‖ ומושל בגדיותיו

(v 8). וישימני נגיד לעמו ‖ ומושל בבני בריתו

The *parallelismus membrorum* structure was better preserved in the envelope than in the hymnic interlude. Synonymous parallelism is found in the two members of v 2, in v 3, and in the second line of vv 6, and 8. Verse 7 exhibits a chiastic arrangement: 7c parallels 7b, and 7d complements 7a. Similarly, the second member in line one of v 8 complements the first. The hymnic interlude exhibits a partial parallelism in the second line of v 4 and a rather loose complementary parallelism in the first line of the verse.

III

Exegetical Remarks

(1) For the synonymous terms צעיר מ(ן) ‖ (ן) קטן מ(ן), cp. "I am the youngest, הצעיר, in my father's house" (Judg 6:15) "David was the youngest, הקטן" (1 Sam 17:14) and "there is yet the youngest, הקטן" (1 Sam 16:11). These terms do not refer solely to David's young age, but also to his inferior status in his father's house, as can be gathered from the collocation "the smallest, הקטן, shall become a multitude, and the little, הצעיר, a mighty nation" (Isa 60:22; cp. also Ps 119:141). It should be pointed out that while the designation קטן is recurrently applied to David in the basic biblical narratives (1 Sam 16:11; 17:14), the author of 11QPsᵃ 151 may have borrowed the epithet צעיר from Mic 5:1, correctly

identifying David as its object. Also there the term stands in juxtaposition to מושל, "ruler," as in the present passage: ואתה בית-לחם אפרתה צעיר להיות באלפי. יהודה ממך לי יצא להיות מושל בישראל ומוצאתיו מקדם מימי עולם (Mic 5:1).

(2) שים על/ל, with the connotation of (נגיד, 1:10, cp.) וישימני רועה לצונו "appointing to office," occurs in the David narrative in the passage which speaks of his appointment as commander of Saul's army (1 Sam 18:5, 13) and in the reprise of that collocation in the Achish episode (1 Sam 28:2). The interchange of שים על and שים ל is also found in the traditions of Saul's appointment as king over Israel (1 Sam 8:5; 10:19).

ידי ‖ אצבעותי. Whenever these two vocables are used synonymously in the Bible, they invariably turn up in the A ‖ B pattern (Isa 2:8; 17:8; Cant 5:5). This sequence is also maintained when the synonym כף is employed for יד, as in Isa 59:3. It is probably under the impact of this traditional coupling and of the quoted Isaiah passage that the scribe of 1QIsaᵃ inserted the phrase אצבעותיכם באעון in Isa 1:15 next to the MT, ידיכם דמים מלאו, so as to restore the expected synonymous parallelistic structure.

The wording of the Qumran poem seems to paraphrase Ps 144:1, which is also attributed to David, המלמד ידי לקרב ‖ אצבעותי למלחמה. But the Qumran author already introduces into the account of David's annunciation by Samuel that reference to his heroism which became apparent in his later career (see below). Tradition presents Psalm 144 as David's song of thanksgiving after his victory over Goliath. In the LXX (143) it bears the superscription, Τῷ Δαυιδ πρὸς τὸν Γολιαδ, and the targum inserts a reference to Goliath into the text of v 11, דפצי ית דויד עבדיה מחרבא בישא דגלית.

עוגב ‖ כנור. The biblical narrative has it that David was summoned before Saul because he played the כנור (1 Sam 16:16, 23), which was a shepherds' instrument. There is no indication in our sources that this was also the case with the עוגב. But once again the Qumran author appears to follow a standard biblical practice of collocating these two terms or using them interchangeably (Gen 4:21; Job 30:31; and similarly Ps 150:4-5; Job 21:12).

(3) ואשימה לה׳ כבוד. This formula marks a hymn of praise in honor of God (cp. Isa 42:12 and Josh 7:19). Closely akin to it are the collocations זכר כבוד (Ps 66:2), נתן כבוד (1 Sam 6:5; Jer 13:16; Mal 2:2), יהב כבוד (Ps 29:1-2; 96:7-8; 1 Chr 16:28-29), זמר כבוד (Ps 68:2), ספר כבוד (Ps 96:3).

(4) ההרים לוא יעידו לו והגבעות יעידו. יעידו appears to be a denominative verb derived from עדות, which denotes a song of praise in which the singer extols God's works in nature and in history (Ps 60:1; 80:1; and cp. Ps 119:46, 99).

Since the connotation "witness" is unsuitable in the context, there is no room for a comparison of the collocation with Mic 6:1-2. The sentence structure of the verse may be compared with that of Ps 10:7, אלה פיהו מלא ומרמה ותוך; 11:5, טמנו גאים פח לי וחבלים; 140:6, ה' צדיק יבחן ורשע.

(5) נגד. לוא יגידו ... את דברו ... את מעשהו, another psalmodic term, is coterminous with עוד, as, e.g., in Isa 43:9. נגד occurs in the book of Psalms with האל מעשה serving as its direct object (Ps 19:2; cp. 111:6). Analogous expressions are עלילות (92:3); חסד (50:6; 97:6); צדק (50:6; 97:6); הגיד תהלה (Ps 50:6; 97:6); (9:12); and נפלאות (71:17).

For the series of natural phenomena (that cannot praise God), ... ההרים והגבעות ... עלי העצים ... והצואן, cp. the contradictory invocation, הללו את ה' ... ההרים והגבעות עץ פרי וכל ארזים החיה וכל בהמה ... (Ps 148:9-10); further, ישמחו השמים ותגל הארץ ירעם הים ... יעלז שדי ... אז ירננו כל עצי היער (Ps 96:11; 1 Chr 16:31-33).

The author of the extra-canonical psalm employs hyperbolic language to stress the point that the material universe cannot praise the Creator. The rhetorical question "for who shall declare God's greatness?" suggests its own answer. The task falls to the poet, "For who can do so, if not I?" It may well be that he indirectly hints at the poetic biblical statement that the praise sung by the heavenly bodies is without words, and their voice cannot be heard (Ps 19:1-4).

עֲלֵי הֵעָצִים. A construct form of עלים (cp Neh 8:15), viz., "the leaves of the trees." This appears to be the correct reading (and interpretation) of the phrase[20] and not עָלוֹ, as proposed by Sanders or עָלַי, as Rabinowitz suggests. The use of the pi'el of עלה to connote "praise" (Uffenheimer) is late. This meaning had not yet developed in early Rabbinic Hebrew (see y. Sanh. 10.29b).

דברו ... מעשו. It cannot be determined whether these nouns are employed here in the sing. or in the pl. with the defective spelling דברו, מעשו, which is found in 1QIsaᵃ.[21] Cp. Ps 147:17, מגיד דברו, qere, דבריו; Job 5:18, וידו, qere, וידיו.

כי מי יגיד. According to Rabinowitz this is a summons formula. The speaker sees himself called upon to praise the Creator. The verse structure is

---

20. P. Skehan, "The Apocryphal Psalm 151," *CBQ* 25 (1963) 408.
21. For this defective spelling, see E. Y. Kutscher (*The Language and Linguistic Background of the Isaiah Scroll (1QIsaᵃ)* [Leiden: Brill, 1974] 100, 114); I. N. Epstein (*Introduction to the Text of the Mishnah* [Jerusalem: Magnes, 1948] 1240).

similar to that of Ps 106:2, מי ימלל גברות ה' ישמיע כל תהלתו. In the same vein the author of the *Hôdāyôt* (1QH xi 25) alludes to the inadequacy of all creatures to praise God appropriately, ומי בכל מעשיכה יוכל לספר [נפלאותי] כה.

יגיד . . . ידבר . . . יספר. The author presumably borrowed this concatenation of verbs from Ps 40:6 (cp. also Ps 145:4-6, 11-12). We encounter a similar string of verbs in another extra-canonical psalm, . . . להודיע כבוד ה' . . . ולספר . . . להודיע . . . להשכיל (11QPsᵃ xiix 3-5).

The collocation ספר מעשי (האל) occurs in the book of Psalms (107:22; 118:7) and frequently in the Covenanters' literature (CD xiii 8), especially in the *Hôdāyôt* (i 43; iii 23; v 4-5; xi 25; xiii 10-11). Now it is also found in the extra-canonical psalm 11QPsᵃ xviii 3-4, ולספר רוב מעשיו.[22] All these phrases of praise refer to God, both in the Bible and in our poem. They cannot be construed to mean that the sheep and the trees would extol David's deeds and his achievements[23] or that he expresses disbelief that they could indeed do so.[24] The rejection of this interpretation disposes of the unsupported conjectures that they manifest an influence of the Orpheus legend on the psalm.[25]

(6) אדון הכול ראה. This colon probably introduces the second part of the envelope (third stanza). This becomes practically certain if the ensuing colon was opened by a connective *waw* which was erased, so that now two dots before the word אלוה are the only indications of its original presence.

The expression אדון הכול is not biblical but is quite common in post-Biblical Hebrew. To the instructive examples adduced by Hurvitz,[26] one could add the paraphrase on the opening words of the prayer עלינו לשבח, in a piece from the Chariot literature published by G. Scholem, עלי לשבח לאדון הכל.[27] Of special import in the present context is the epithet אדון כל המעשים (*b.Ḥag.* 3b; Sifre Deb. 60, ed. Finkelstein, 304), which is alluded to in our psalm in two separate phrases, מעשו and אדון הכול.

22. See Sanders (*ZAW* 76 [1964] 57-74), above n 1.
23. Uffenheimer, *Molad* 187-88 (1964) 70 ff.
24. Rabinowitz, *ZAW* 76 (1964) 193-200.
25. Sanders, *ZAW* 75 (1963) 82.
26. *Tarbiz* 34 (1965) 1-4.
27. *Jewish Gnosticism, Merkabah Mysticism and Talmudic Tradition* (New York: Ktav, 1960) 105; R. Loewe, "The Divine Garment and Shiʿur Qomah," *HTR* 58 (1965) 153-60. It is appropriate to mention in this context that texts connected with the mystical Merkabah literature have been discovered at Qumran. See J. Strugnell ("The Angelic Literature at Qumran," *VTSup* 7 [1959] 335-45).

הכול הוא שמע אדון הכול. הכול is the direct object of שמע, or else the governed noun of a construct in relationship with אלוה. A similar construction is found in the previous expression אדון הכול.

(7) שלח נביאו ... The closing passage of the psalm reflects the tradition of David's being anointed by Samuel (1 Sam 16:1-13).

לגדלני. In antithesis to קטן הייתי. The verb גדל is not used in the tradition about David's annunciation. It is introduced for the first time in the conclusion of the report of his conquest of Jerusalem which raises the curtain on his effective rule over all Israel (2 Sam 5:9-10; 1 Chr 11:9; cp. the reference to Solomon's rule in 1 Kgs 10:23).

יצאו אחי לקראתו. A verbal sentence, the subject of which is specified in the ensuing colon, יפי התור ויפי המראה. The syntactical structure may be compared with Prov 7:10.

יפי התור. A defective spelling of התואר, which was considered a physical attribute of royalty (cp. Judg 8:18) and is a common biblical synonym of מראה (cp. Gen 29:17; 39:6; Esth 2:7). This descriptive detail of David's brothers is not mentioned in the biblical account of his anointing. For התור cp. 1QIsa[b] 52:13.

ויפי המראה הגבהים בקומתם. A paraphrase of 1 Sam 16:7, אל תבט אל מראהו ואל גבה קומתו.

(8) היפים בשערם. Commentators expressed surprise at the fact that "beauty of hair" is singled out as a special feature of the appearance of Jesse's sons. This detail is not contained in the biblical tradition. Also the report on the luxuriant growth of Absalom's hair does not speak of its "beauty" (2 Sam 14:26). A closer parallel would be the description of the youth in Cant 5:11 ראשו כתם פז קוצותיו תלתלים שחרות כעורב. We should recall that the author of the Genesis Apocryphon (2-3) praises Sarah's fine hair: וכמא [ ] [קיק לה שיער ראישה (30:2-3). It is possible that our poet mentioned this matter here by way of a contrastive comment to David's being אדמוני (1 Sam 16:12; 17:42), which he may have taken to be an undesirable feature (cp. Gen 25:25). But this is unlikely.

I presume that the psalmist speaks not of hair, שֵׂיעָר, but rather of the physical stature, שִׂיעוּר קומתם, of Jesse's older sons, i.e., their unusual height. This was obviously deemed a desirable feature of royalty, as may be gathered from the description of Saul who was chosen to become the first ruler over Israel (1 Sam 10:23-24). The poet broke up the construct (or possibly the hendiadys) שיעור קומה for the sake of parallelism: הגבהים בקומתם || היפים בשערם.

The defective spelling of a noun in the qittul formation, derived from a root with a medial ʿayin, is not without precedence in Biblical Hebrew. Other such instances are, e.g., נְחֻמִים, (Isa 57:18; Zech 1:13), next to the plene spelling נְחוּמִי (Hos 11:10); נְאָפִים (Jer 13:27), next to נאופים (Ezek 23:43).[28] However in the majority of instances, the long vowels ē and ā are indicated in scrolls which seem to have originated at Qumran[29] by a *yod* which serves as *mater lectionis*.

The collocation שיעור קומה is not extant in early Rabbinic Hebrew. Its earliest use may be found in the Hekhalot literature, the roots of which G. Scholem traces to the first century C.E., where it indeed carries the meaning of "greatness," especially in reference to God. The reading proposed here from the Qumran text would make it the first occurrence of that phrase.

לוא בחר ה׳ אלהים בם. Cp. David's provocative words to his wife Michal, Saul's daughter, אשר בחר בי מאביך ומכל ביתו (2 Sam 6:21).

וימשחני בשמן הקודש (9). The phrase clearly echoes the biblical text ויקח שמואל את קרן השמן וימשח אותו (1 Sam 16:13). But the amplification by the use of הקודש (cp. Exod 30:25; 37:29; Num 35:2; in reference to the high priest), appears to disclose the influence of a conception of David's image which developed in biblical psalmody: מצאתי דוד עבדי בשמן קדשי משחתיו (Ps 89:21; cp. Sir 47:2).

וישלח ויקחני מאחר הצואן ... וישימני נגיד לעמו. This motif is frequently found in the biblical traditions about David (2 Sam 5:2 = 1 Chr 11:2; 2 Sam 7:8; Ps 78:70-72).

IV

We distinguished in the Qumran psalm two strata which differ in style and language: an autobiographical narrative framework which envelops a hymnic interlude. Both these strata display characteristics of biblical psalmody, and in both we find linguistic traits which evidence their postbiblical provenance: the phrases אלוה הכול, אדון הכול (line 5) in the hymnic interlude, and בני בריתו[30] in the second part of the envelope (line 10), which occur in postbiblical Hebrew but are not found in biblical literature. The same distinction applies to the collocations הגבהים בקומתם היפים בשערם, construed with a preposition (line 9),

---

28. On the issue of *scriptio defectiva*, see Kutscher (*The Language and Linguistic Background*) and Epstein (*Introduction*), above, n. 21.

29. See Tov, *Textus* 13 (1986) 31-58 (above, n. 14).

30. References are given by Uffenheimer (*Molad* 187-88 [1964] 73).

in contrast to the biblical constructs גבה קומה and יפה תואר without a preposition.

Also the loose application of *parallelismus membrorum* in the hymnic interlude may be taken to indicate a postbiblical composition, since the same feature can be observed in the *Hôdāyôt* (1QH).

The style of the narrative envelope approximates more closely to that of biblical psalmody. But also one observes here some formal innovations which evidence a neo-classic rather than a pristine biblical style. We do not find in the Bible an autobiographical psalm like 11QPsᵃ 151, woven of references and allusions to events described in biblical historiography. By their very nature, historical records are not conducive to a presentation in the genre of prayer and psalm.

In the book of Psalms we do have specimens of the specific "historio-graphical psalm" type. But these compositions are invariably comprised of an invocation-like recital of God's mighty deeds in the past which the poet enumerates in detail to invoke divine compassion for Israel in the present also (see, e.g., Pss 47; 78; 89:48-52; 106; 108:13-14). Furthermore, the "voice" of a biblical psalm, the "I," whether representing an individual or the community, will generally adopt a rather general phraseology which avoids realistic data and details when it comes to describing the events which occasion the prayer, thus making it difficult to place such a psalm in a specific historical situation. Such imprecise phraseology will ease the way for an originally individual psalm to be adapted to the experiences and the needs of the community and finally to become an expression of communal sentiments. An exception is Psalm 137, in which the exile-community recalls the hardship it had undergone in the captivity: "By the rivers of Babylon we sat and wept" (cp. also Psalm 126).

Generally speaking the specifically historical setting of a composition in the book of Psalms, its reference to an event in the life of a personality of national renown, especially in the life of David, will be manifested in a superscription rather than in the intrinsic text of the poem. These superscriptions will not be formulated in the autobiographical mode, i.e., in the 1 pers. sing. or pl., but rather in the 3 pers., by way of description. Therefore such titles indeed are not autobiographical, but rather explanatory. As a result the superscription is often entirely unrelated to the text of the psalm to which it is attached: it does not correspond to its actual content, nor does the wording of the psalm echo the wording and the essence of the superscription. It will suffice to illustrate this well-known fact by adducing just a few examples. The very general complaint of

259

the poet about the many enemies who rise up against him and his plea to be saved from them (Ps 3:2-8) have no direct relation to David's suffering in his flight before the rebellious Absalom of which the superscription speaks (Ps 3:1). The same may be said of a similarly construed lament and entreaty, replete with general terminology (Ps 7:2-18), which again bears a title meant to present that psalm as reflecting a specific, dangerous situation in David's career, an otherwise unrecorded event concerning one "Kush the Benjaminite" (but see 2 Sam 18:21ff.).

The interrelation between the title and the body of the psalm is particularly evident in cases in which the superscription purports to relate to specific events reported in detail in the biblical historiographies, preponderantly in reference to David's contention with Saul. An instance of this kind is the title of Psalm 18 which superficially connects the ensuing text with David's deliverance "from the hand of all his enemies and the hand of Saul" (cp. 2 Sam 22:1). Another example is the superscription of Psalm 34 which ostensibly ascribes the composition of this song to David when he was fleeing before Saul to the city of Gath. There he came from bad to worse. Threatened by the Philistines, he had to extricate himself from the danger by "acting like a lunatic" (cp. Ps 34:1 with 1 Sam 21:13). Again, the line "When Doeg the Edomite came and told Saul, 'David has come to Ahimelek's house'" (Ps 52:2) connects the ensuing poem superficially with an incident in David's life at Saul's court (1 Sam 22:9). Similarly the plea for divine help in Ps 54:3-9 is riveted by an almost verbatim quote in the superscription of another such event, when the Ziphites reported to Saul that David was hiding with them (1 Sam 23:19). Less specific is the occasion on which David composed a *maskil* when "being in the cave" (Ps 142:1). But in spite of its vagueness, it is nevertheless clear that the notation is intended to tie this composition with one of the 'cave tales' in the David-Saul tradition (1 Sam 22:1; 24:3-8). In not one of these instances does the body of the psalm display any specificity which would link it with the event to which the superscription refers, not even when quoting the actual wording of the original tale in the book of Samuel.

Only rarely will there be found a collocation in the body of a psalm which evidences a connection with an event reported in biblical historiography that occasioned its composition. In such instances the reference will be in the 1 pers. sing., formulated as a citation of words spoken by the *dramatis persona* involved and set in a descriptive framework in the narrator's objective voice. An example is Ps 132:1-5, which paraphrases the report of David's intention to build a house for God (2 Sam 7:1-4). Psalm 89, based on Nathan's prophecy in 2 Sam 7:4-17, alludes to that very same situation. In the basic account, the prophet's oration contains the divine reply to David's quest, which is detailed there. The superscription of Psalm 132 alludes to that same situation, and the body of the psalm presents a paraphrastic version of the original dialogue between David and Nathan.

This short review of the pertinent literature induces the conclusion that the extra-canonical psalm of David under scrutiny here exhibits palpable features of stylistic innnovation. It is marked by an autobiographical mode, unprecedented in biblical psalmody: historical events are retold in detail and accurately described. They are portrayed realistically in their uniqueness; no attempt is made to fashion them into prototypes on which could be modelled the portrayal of other similar events. Thus 11QPs^a 151 may be seen to represent a new stage in the development of ancient Hebrew psalmody.

It should be stressed that this novel autobiographical poetry does not display any characteristics which would identify its style as being specifically Qumranian, just as there is nothing particularly Qumranian in the content of the poem.[31] We can discern in it, rather, a conflux of several elements which are extant separately in various genres of biblical literature. The lyrical mode of psalmody is blended with the autobiographical prose account found in the books of Daniel, Ezra, and Nehemiah, to form a new, poetic medium. The autobiographical prose account appears to be a feature of Hebrew literary creativity which evolved in biblical historiography of the post-exilic age. We do not find examples of the autobiographical style in the literature of the First Temple Period (with the possible exception of Deuteronomy) such as we encounter, e.g., in Ezra's report on his return from the Babylonian exile, "I assembled them at the river. . . . I reviewed the people . . . I found no Levite there. So I sent Eliezer, Ariel . . . and Meshullam . . . and I gave them a message. . . . Then I proclaimed a fast," etc. (Ezra 8:15 ff.). Again, "When I heard this, I rent my robe and mantle, and tore my hair and my beard, and I sat dumbfounded. . . . [Then] . . . I rose . . . I knelt down . . . and I said . . . " (Ezra 9:3). Similarly Nehemiah's memoirs are recorded altogether in the first voice, as is well-known: "[When] I was in Susa . . . one of my brothers arrived. . . . They told me. . . . When I heard this . . . I sat down and wept; I mourned for some

---

31. Even the few instances of an alleged Qumranian vocabulary enumerated by Carmignac (*Rev Q* 15 [1963] 376 ff.) cannot be typified thus. On the contrary they are part and parcel of the standard biblical vocabulary.

days," etc. (Neh 1:1 ff.). The same style permeates the entire book. Further reference could be made to numerous comparable passages in the book of Daniel.[32]

This style became a familiar feature in writings of the post-biblical era. An author will ascribe his composition to a post-diluvian hero or to a patriarch of Israel who describes in it, as it were, his own life experiences, holding them up to posterity as lessons to be learned. This is the make-up of the late biblical book of Daniel,[33] *1, 2,.3 Enoch,* the *Testaments of the Twelve Patriarchs, The Apocalypse of Baruch, The Words of Job,* 4 Ezra, Tobit, and likewise of the *Genesis Apocryphon.*

This same autobiographical pattern is also exhibited in a newly discovered composition, of which fragments stemming from two copies were found at Qumran in Caves 2 and 4. Baillet published the 2Q fragment, filling in some lacunae with the aid of the 4Q fragment.[34] The text runs as follows:

ולא שניתי כי שברו י]הוה אלוהינ]ו ל[פי]חרב
ועשיתי ק]לעי המזור עם קשתות ולא
כי . . . . מ] לחמה לתפש ערי מבצרים ולחריד
ו]עתה   [לל   [לל

The editor defined the work from which the fragments stem as an apocryphal composition which portrays David's battle with Goliath.[35] But this is hardly correct. It would appear, rather, that it is Moses who speaks in that apocryphal work, describing his war against Og, King of Bashan, and his country. Og

32. From Qumran comes an interesting parallel to Nebuchadnezzar's autobiographical statement in Dan 4:11ff. It was published by J. T. Milik (" 'Prière de Nabonid' et autre écrits d'un cycle de Daniel," *RB* 63 [1956] 407-415). See further C. Gevaryahu ("The Prayer of Nabonidus from the Judaean Desert Scrolls," in *Studies in the Dead Sea Scrolls,* [ed. J. Liver; Jerusalem: Kiryat-Sefer, 1957] 12-23 [Heb.]); D. N. Freedman ("The Prayer of Nabonidus," *BASOR* 145 [1957] 12-23); R. Meyer (*Das Gebet des Nabonid* [Berlin: Akademie Verlag, 1962]); W. Dommershausen (*Nabonid im Buche Daniel* [Mainz: Natthias-Grünewald-Verlag, 1964]).
33. See S. Talmon, "Daniel," *The Literary Guide to the Bible* (ed. R. Alter and F. Kermode; London: Collins, 1987) 345-46.
34. The readings from the 4Q fragment are given in italics.
35. M. Baillet, J. T. Milik et R. de Vaux, O. P., *Les 'Petites Grottes' de Qumran* (DJD; Oxford: Clarendon, 1962), 3. 81-82.

actually is mentioned by name in the text of the 4Q fragment which precedes the passage adduced here. The latter part of the fragment contains a paraphrase of the biblical description of Israel's war against Og of Bashan (Deut 3:1ff., esp. vv 4-5; cp. Num 21:33):

ונלכד את כל עריו בעת ההיא לא היתה קריה אשר לא לקחנו מאתם ששים עיר כל חבל ארגב ממלכת עוג בבשן. כל אלה ערים בצרת חומה גבהה דלתים ובריח.

It would seem that the wording of the Qumran work shows evidences of the influence of some biblical passages outside the Pentateuch which pertain to Israel's wars against Moab. Some such texts are: והכיתם כל עיר מבצר (2 Kgs 3:19); ומבצר משגב חומותיך השח (Isa 25:12); ויסבו הקלעים ויכוה (2 Kgs 3:25); מי יבילני עיר מבצר מי נחני עד אדום (Jer 48:41); והמצודות נתפשה נלכדה הקריות (Ps 108:1; cp. Ps 108:10). But in any case the first part of the Qumran fragment appears to speak of a battle in which Moses defeated Og. Now such a battle is indeed not mentioned in the biblical sources. However it is referred to in an ʾal tiqrê midrash on Ps 3:8: "שני רשעים שברת . . . Rabbi Simeon ben Laqish said, 'Do not read שברת, but rather שרבבת.[36] Moses was ten cubits tall, he took an axe ten cubits long, smote Og in the ankle and killed him' " (b. Ber. 54b).[37] This midrash was in fact incorporated into Tg. Jonathan in the biblical passage which relates to Og (Num 21:25): "Moses went and took a ten cubits long axe, jumped up ten cubits and smote [Og's] ankle, so he fell and died at the edge of the Israelites' camp. It is written that [Moses] smote him, his sons and all his people, so that none survived; and he threw him to the ground."

Israel's victory over Og, the king of Bashan, and the conquest of his country, according to the midrash (Yalkut Makiri on Ps 136:14; cp. 136:17), were important enough to induce David to compose songs about this event (Ps 135:10-12; 136:17). It could well be that the psalmodic tradition reflected in that midrash also continued to develop in the post-biblical era. One cannot form an opinion on the literary character of the apocryphal composition attributed to Moses on the basis of the small fragment published by Baillet. But the editor opines that it exhibits hymnic characteristics: "un certain caractère hymnique

36. This reading may perhaps explain the unusual phrase in the Qumran fragment: כי שברו . . . לפי חרב.

37. Cp. Midrash Aggadah, end of חוקת (ed. S. Buber, 252-53); Midrash ha-Gadol on Numbers, חוקת (ed. S. Fish, 155).

n'est pas exclu."[38] If it could be established that the fragment(s) indeed stem from an autobiographical psalm, this would provide additional evidence for the emergence of a literary genre in the early Second Temple Period which combined traits of the late biblical autobiographical narrative with characteristics of biblical psalmody. To a degree, a fusion of these elements may be seen in Ben Sira's Psalm (Sir 51:13 ff.; cp. 11QPs^a xxi 11 ff.). But the most complete and perfect specimen of this new genre known today is certainly 11QPs^a 151.

V

There is nothing intrinsically Qumranian in the content or form of most extra-canonical compositions in 11QPs^a or in their interpolation among canonical psalms. Therefore the new scroll is bound to illuminate the process by which biblical literature was interlaced with extra-biblical compilations to meet the cultic needs, not only of dissenting groups, but also of mainstream Judaism in the time of the Second Temple. Viewed thus, the extra-canonical compositions in 11QPs^a, predominantly Psalm 151, and the opening lines of another psalm which follow it, may supply the basis for a fresh approach to a tributary problem in the transmission of the Bible text which has not yet been resolved, namely the question of the *p.b.p.* The history of the research into this issue has been surveyed in an illuminating and amply documented essay by P. Sandler, which makes it unnecessary for us to present it here in detail.[39]

In the discussion of the matter at hand, scholars are divided into two camps. On the one hand we have the monists who posit one key explanation only for all instances of the *p.b.p.* On the other hand are the pluralists, in whose opinion the phenomenon is not of one cloth and is assumed to fulfill diverse functions in the transmission of the MT. Another division of opinion concerns the very nature of the *p.b.p.* Some students would define it as a masoretic note which is meant to draw attention to textual matters pure and proper. It is taken to reveal the Masoretes' doubts about passages which, assumedly, in their opinion had suffered textual corruption, or in which words and even whole text units had been

---

38. Baillet, Milik, and de Vaux, *Les 'Petites Grottes' de Qumran*, 81-82. See n. 35.
39. P. Sandler, "לחקר הפיסקא באמצע הפסוק," *D. Neiger Memorial Volume* (Publications of the Israel Society for Biblical Research; Jerusalem: Kiryat-Sefer, 1959), 7. 222-49.

faultily omitted. Some of these missing components have at times been preserved for us in one of the VSS, above all in the LXX.

In contrast to this, other scholars insist on the integrity of the MT and reject completely the very suggestion that the *p.b.p.* was meant to indicate textual flaws, *a fortiori* omissions of complete textual units in the MT which were still known to its early tradents. M. H. Segal, for example, claims that the *p.b.p.* exclusively pertains to the external form of the text, "indicating the end of one section and the beginning of another" and representing a text division which deviates from the system that underlies the main masoretic tradition. Thus the *p.b.p.* gives witness to a dispute between various schools of Masoretes, with regard to the exact delineation of sections.[40]

Segal's argument is invalidated by the fact that to all appearences the *p.b.p.* does not pertain to a system of sections but rather to the verse division. This is clearly indicated by instances in which the word before the *p.b.p.* carries a double accent—the mid-sentence caesura *'etnaḥ* and the sentence divider *silluq*, as, e.g., in Gen 35:22, וַיִּשְׁמַע יִשְׂרָאֵל . . . וַיֵּלֶךְ רְאוּבֵן; Exod 20:14, לֹא תִנְאָף; Deut 5:18, וְלֹא תִנְאָף. This doubling points to a fusion of two traditions, comparable to the practice of grafting the vowels of the qere upon the consonants of the kethib. In the same manner one can explain the *p.b.p.* which appears in the middle of some other verses without a preceding double accent, as fulfilling the function of the *sof pasuq,* and as substituting for it, for example, in 1 Sam 4:1; 2 Sam 7:4; 10:17; 16:13; 24:10, 23, *et sim.* This contention is strengthened by five instances in the Aleppo Codex (A), in which we can still discern traces of the colon, the symbol by which the scribe customarily marks the end of a verse, in the space left blank to indicate a *p.b.p.* (2 Sam 21:6; 24:10; 11:23; 1 Chr 17:7). In contrast to this no consistent relationship between the *p.b.p.* and the *parashah* system can be established. The *p.b.p.* does not necessarily appear near the end of a *parashah,* indicating, as it were, a section-division which deviated from the norm. True, in many MSS the *p.b.p.* is marked by the letters ס and פ. But this practice derived from the custom of so designating the end of a *parashah,* which itself is a late convention and is not found in superior MSS such as A. However, once the custom of placing the letters ס or פ between sections became prevalent, copyists, by force of habit, at times also placed, or rather misplaced, these *sigla* in the blank spaces indicating a *p.b.p.,* although originally they did not belong there.

---

40. M. H. Segal, "הפיסקא באמצע פסוק," *Tarbiz* 29 (1960) 203-206.

In attempting a clarification of the issue at hand, we are faced with the great difficulty that neither the location of the individual *p.b.p.*, nor their sum total in the MT are in any way fixed in MSS or in the Masorah. Only a few examples have received general recognition.[41] The Masorah Parva on Gen 4:18 enumerates 28 cases of *p.b.p.*, while at Gen 32:22 it expressly corrects this statement to set their number at 31. M. H. Segal lists 30 instances which are certain: 3 in the Pentateuch (Gen 35:22; Num 27:1; Deut 2:8); 1 each in Joshua (8:24), Judges (2:1), 1 Kings (13:20), and Ezekiel (3:17); and 23 in Samuel. Or includes in his exhaustive list "all cases on which we have any tradition of some value." Combining the instances of a *p.b.p.* recorded in BH[3] with additional information culled from Ginsburg's edition, Or arrives at the sum total of 72 *p.b.p.*, of which not less than 40 are found in the book of Samuel.[42]

Since, as stated, the Masoretes obviously did not consolidate one clearly defined system of *p.b.p.* notations, it is best to base our discussion on one authoritative MS. For this purpose the Aleppo Codex was chosen. An examination of A revealed 42 or 43 cases of *p.b.p.* However, in view of the fragmentary state of this MS, we cannot ascertain whether there were marked in it the six occurrences of a *p.b.p.* which Or enumerates in the Pentateuch and the four in the books of Ezra and Nehemiah. This means that of the 62 cases which Or culled from the biblical books that are yet preserved in A, as opposed to 27 in Segal's list, A attests to 42 (or 43), of which 27 (or 28) are found in the book of Samuel. Eighteen (or 19) occurrences listed by Or—1 in the book of Joshua, 2 in Judges, 11 (or 12) in Samuel, and 4 in Chronicles—are for certain not represented in A.

On one point all students of the issue under review are agreed: the comparatively large percentage of *p.b.p.* in the book of Samuel requires an explanation. This phenomenon accounts for some 15% of the total according to Segal, almost 60% of Or's list, about 64% in A, "despite the fact that the book of Samuel only makes up approximately 1/13 (i.e., less than 8%) of the text of the Bible."[43]) It seems that the plethora of *p.b.p.* in the book of Samuel, as is the case with the relatively large number of *kethib* and *qere* found in it, attests to the instability of the textual tradition of this book. This instability becomes even more apparent in the numerous deviations of the Greek text from the MT,

41. A. Or, "פיסקא באמצע פסוק מהי?," *E. Auerbach Volume* (Publications of the Israel Society for Biblical Research; Jerusalem: Kiryat-Sefer, 1955), 1. 33.
42. Ibid., 37.
43. Ibid., 30.

now corroborated by fragments of the book of Samuel from Qumran, whose text is closer to that of the LXX than to the MT.[44]

Attention must also be given to the puzzling, uneven distribution of the *p.b.p.* over the various categories of biblical literature. Not a single case of *p.b.p.* is found either in the Wisdom literature or in the Psalms. In the list given by Or, only one *p.b.p.* occurs in legal literature, but is not included among the certain instances listed by Segal: לא תתעב אדמי כי אחיך הוא [*p.b.p.*] לא תתעב, מצרי כי גר היית בארצו (Deut 23:8). Accordingly the *p.b.p.* is found exclusively in a narrative context. The majority of *p.b.p.* are concentrated in the historiographical literature, which is narrative by its very nature: 26 instances out of 30 according to Segal, 37 (or 38) out of 42 (or 43) in A, and 60 out of 72 by Or's count.[45]

One must also examine the distribution of the *p.b.p.* by the criterion of chronology. All cases adduced by Segal occur in pre-exilic books, the latest citation being Ezek 3:17. However in Or's fuller list, thirteen instances from post-exilic books are found (Ezra, Nehemiah, Chronicles). In A we find five occurrences in Chronicles. However, on closer examination the authenticity of most of these must be held in doubt, since they either are noted only in isolated MSS, or else are suspect of having been inserted into the text of Chronicles in imitation of the parallel passages in the former prophets.[46] Only three of the four *p.b.p.* in post-exilic books hold their own: Ezra 2:69 = Neh 7:68; Ezra 3:1; Neh 11:4 = 2 Chr 14:7 (?); 2 Chr 34:26. One concludes per force that the *p.b.p.* is a phenomenon which originally pertains to the historiographical books of the Pentateuch: Genesis, Exodus, Numbers, and to the former prophets. The concentration of *p.b.p.* in the book of Samuel, in particular in episodes connected with the life of David, accordingly cannot be satisfactorily explained as a mere matter of chance but rather must be considered integral to the very nature and function of this masoretic notation. Therefore methodological considerations require us to base our discussion of the *p.b.p.* primarily upon the book of

---

44. F. M. Cross, Jr., "A New Qumran Biblical Fragment Related to the Original Hebrew Underlying the Septuagint," *BASOR* 132 (1953) 15-26; idem, "The History of the Biblical Text in the Light of the Discoveries in the Judean Desert," *Qumran and the History of the Biblical Text* (ed. F. M. Cross and S. Talmon; Cambridge, MA: Harvard University Press, 1975) 177-95.

45. Ibid, 39, 40; Sandler, "לחקר הפיסקא באמצע הפסוק," 19.

46. In several cases the *p.b.p.* is noted in Chronicles, even when it is absent from the parallel passages in the former prophets. Cp., e.g., 2 Chr 10:18 = 1 Kgs 12:18; 2 Chr 34:26 = 2 Kgs 22:18.

Samuel and subsequently to apply our findings to other books of the Bible. It should also be clear from the preceding deliberations that the *p.b.p.* indeed is not of one cloth, but that it most probably fulfills more than one function of textual notation. It follows that the conclusions to be profferred do not necessarily apply to each and every occurrence of a *p.b.p.*, but only to a certain definite type, or types.

Several scholars who have dealt with the problem of the *p.b.p.* have explained it as being evidence of a textual deficiency at junctures singled out in this way, indicating the loss of supplementary text units. It is then held that these supplementary elements were omitted from the text, either unintentionally through the fault of scribes, or else were intentionally removed by some early Masoretes who felt "that there are many things in the Scriptures which should not be revealed publicly . . . and who left for us, by way of tradition, a special symbol to indicate the omission, which is the *p.b.p.*"[47] However this surmise is rather doubtful. An explanation nearer the mark is offered by Chatzkes, also based on the premise that the *p.b.p.* hints at the absence of text elements in places so marked, namely that it attests to "many secrets which remained in (extra-Biblical) scrolls, and for which the divinely inspired scribes found no room in the Holy Writ."[48] That is to say the *p.b.p.* does not at all point to matters in the transmission of the text, to textual corruption, or to any omissions which might have occurred. Its basic purpose is entirely extra-textual, as Segal correctly stated. However in our opinion the *p.b.p.* does not indicate a *parashah* division which differs from the one that has taken root in the main stream of the masoretic tradition, but rather alludes to literary expansions of the sections in question for liturgical and homiletical purposes. And indeed the *p.b.p.* very often appears in a context in which the author obviously left many things untold, and the reader or expositor requires further information on facts or on the reactions of the biblical figures concerned.

We may divide the literary expansions which are the raison d'être of the *p.b.p.* into two main categories: (1) intra-biblical and (2) extra-biblical supplements. From the point of view of their literary nature, these supplements may be classified further as: (A) additional factual information derived from parallel accounts and formulated in the style and language of the sources; (B)

---

47. D. Cahana, *מסורת סייג למקרא* (Vienna, 1882) 114.
48. M. A. Chatzkes, "*שמחת התרת ספקות*," *Knesset Hagedolah* 2 (Warsaw, 1890) 114.

poetic paraphrases in the style of the Psalms. Here are some examples of these categories:

(1A) The *p.b.p.* which is marked in the Reuben—Bilhah episode as told in Gen 35:22, [*p.b.p.*] וילך ראובן וישכב את בלהה פילגש אביו וישמע ישראל, according to our theory directs the reader's attention to the additional information recorded in 1 Chr 5:1, to the effect that in punishment of his transgression, the rights of the firstborn were divested from Reuben and transferred to Joseph: ובני ראובן בכור ישראל כי הוא הבכור ובחללו יצועי אביו נתנה בכורתו לבני יוסף בן ישראל ולא להתיחש לבכורה.[49]

(1B) a. More often the *p.b.p.* aims at supplementary expositions which are not of a historiographical nature, but are, rather, poetic paraphrases on historical events, such as are found in the book of Psalms. When revealing his desire to build a house for the God of Israel, David's speech to Nathan ends with the words ויהי בלילה ההוא (2 Sam 7:4), after which the MT records a *p.b.p.* We assume that the *p.b.p.* refers to Psalm 132 which treats of this very event:

זכור ה׳ לדוד את כל ענותו
אשר נשבע לה׳ נדר לאביר יעקב
אם אבא באהל ביתי אם אעלה על ערש יצועי
אם אתן שנת לעיני לעפעפי תנומה
עד אמצא מקום לה׳ משכנות לאביר יעקב

b. We may explain the *p.b.p.* which follows David's words of remorse to Nathan after the Bathsheba incident in a similar manner, ויאמר דוד חטאתי לה׳ (2 Sam 12:13), as calling our attention to Psalm 51, מזמור לדוד בבוא אליו נתן הנביא כאשר בא אל בת-שבע, which contains a confession of sin and a petition for forgiveness.

c. Similarly, the *p.b.p.* in 2 Sam 16:13, וילך דוד ואנשיו בדרך, is probably meant to remind the reader of Psalm 3: מזמור לדוד בברחו מפני אבשלום. This *p.b.p.* is set in the story about Shimei ben Gera, who went out to curse the

---

49. Cp. D. Cahana, מסורת סייג למקרא, 19. M. Hacohen Reichersohn takes the *p.b.p.* in Deut 2:8, ונעבור מאת אחינו ... מאילת ומעציון גבר [*p.b.p.*] ונפן ונעבר, to indicate that the verse had been shortened "perhaps for the sake of brevity, since these matters have already been related in the book of Numbers" ("פסקא באמצע פסוק," *Knesset Hagedolah* 2 [Warsaw, 1847] 67).

fugitive David when he was pursued by Absalom. Such a situation appears to be reflected in the Psalmist's words (3:2), ‫ה׳ מה רבו צרי רבים קמים עלי‬.

(2B)   a. And now to Psalm 151. A detailed exegesis shows that by subject matter and language this psalm is intimately related to the story of David's election by Samuel as told in 1 Samuel 16. Actually Psalm 151 can be defined as a paraphrastic expansion of 1 Sam 16:7-13 in the style of an autobiographical ode. Now, in that narrative unit in the book of Samuel, we have again a *p.b.p.*:

‫(11) ויאמר שמואל אל ישי שלחה וקחנו כי לא נסב עד באו פה (12) וישלח ויביאהו‬
‫והוא אדמוני עם יפה עינים וטוב ראי [.p.b.p] ויאמר ה׳ קום משחהו כי זה הוא‬

The *p.b.p.* severs the connection between the preparations for David's unction and the portrayal of his person from the description of the very act of his anointment by Samuel, giving David, as it were, a timely opening to praise his Creator, and the reader an opportunity to meditate upon the greatness of God's deeds. The *p.b.p.* seems to serve a purpose here which the midrash ascribes to the division between sections: "What is the object of the section divisions? To give Moses an opportunity for reflection between one *parashah* and another and between one subject matter and another. Now, if one who hears God directly and himself speaks by divine inspiration [Moses] must reflect between one *parashah* and another and between different subject matters, how much more should an ordinary human being do so" (*Sifra Wayiqra* I, a).

This pause for reflection between the section dealing with matters preceding David's election and the one concerning his anointing was seized upon by the author of Psalm 151. We surmise that to this or to a similar composition the *p.b.p.* in 1 Sam 16:13 draws the reader's attention.

   b. Adjoining Psalm 151 in 11QPs[a] we find the opening lines of another piece of poetry (Ps 151[a]):

‫1 תחלת גב[ו]רה ל[דו]יד משמשחו נביא אלהים‬
‫2 אז [שמע]תי פלשתי מחרף מ[ערכות ישראל]‬

The superscription and the beginning of this psalm show it to be a poetic paraphrase of David's battle with Goliath. We tend to assume that the *p.b.p.* which is recorded in 1 Sam 17:37 alludes to this composition or the like of it: ‫ויאמר דוד ה׳ אשר הצלני מיד הארי ומיד הדב הוא יצילני מיד הפלשתי הזה [.p.b.p]‬ ‫ויאמר שאול אל דוד לך וה׳ יהיה עמך‬. This same *p.b.p.* may possibly be associated with two further extra-canonical psalms which for the present have been preserved in the Syriac tradition only.[50] Their common theme is David's rescue from the lion and the bear, and again their composition is attributed to David:

אמיר הוא לה לדוד כד מתכתש הוא עם אריא וזאבא (Psalm 154)

[51](Psalm 155) אמיר לדוד כד מקבל טיבותא לאלהא דפציה מן אריא וזאבא

The juxtaposition of David's anointing by Samuel (1 Sam 16:1-13) with the episode of his battle against Goliath (1 Sam 17: 1-54) in Psalms 151 and 151[a] of 11QPs[a], and the insertion of elements from Psalm 151[a] into the Greek translation of Psalm 151 call for an explanation. In directly conjoining these two episodes, the poet skipped over an event in David's life which in the basic biblical account is interpolated between them and which, rather surprisingly, he failed to use as a basis for a poetic elaboration and expolation. We refer to the story of the first encounter of David, the young musician, with King Saul, whose soul was troubled by evil spirits (1 Sam 16:14-23). This passage is commonly held to be a parallel version of matters related in another and more suitable context. David's presentation to Saul as "cunning in playing, a mighty man of valor, a man of war, prudent in speech, and a comely person" (16:18) clearly clashes with a subsequent story in which we are told that neither Saul nor Abner knew the youth who went to do battle with Goliath (1 Sam 17:55): "And when Saul saw David go forth against the Philistine, he said unto Abner, the captain of the host, 'Abner, whose son is this youth?' And Abner said, 'As thy soul liveth, O King, I cannot tell.' And the King said, 'Inquire whose son the stripling is.' "

The passing over of the episode of David's playing before Saul by the author of Psalm 151, even though this theme almost begs to be developed by him, achieves, however, one important result: it smooths out the difficulties in the

---

50. See above, n. 3.
51. The graphic and/or phonetic similarity induced the poet, or the copyist, to substitute (א)זאב for דוב, which the Bible employs in the basic story (1 Sam 17:34). Cp. Noth, *ZAW* 48 (1930) 22, n. 2. The same interchange occurs in Sir 47:3, again in a context pertaining to David. There the Hebrew ולדובים is rendered ודאבא in the Syriac translation (D. Barthélemy, O. Rickenbacher, *Konkordanz zum Hebräischen Sirach* [Göttingen: Vandenhoeck & Ruprecht, 1973] 80). Further instances of a זאב-דוב substitution are found in midrashic literature, e.g., in *Gen. Rab.* 99 (ed. Theodor-Albeck, 1273); *Gen. Rab.* 77 (1225); *Lev. Rab.* on Lev 13:5 (ed. Margulies, 288); Ber. Rabbati (ed. Albeck, 253).

present arrangement of the Bible text. This same revised order by which David's anointment is followed immediately by the story of his battle against the defamer of Israel's armies appears also to underly Josephus Flavius' report of David's deeds, as given in his *Antiquities of the Jews* (6.165). After Samuel had anointed David, "He also exhorted him to be righteous and obedient to his commandments, for so would the kingship long continue to be his, and his house would become splendid and renowned; he would subdue the Philistine and . . . he would in his lifetime attain glorious fame and bequeath it to his posterity." Only then does Josephus tell us that the divine spirit was taken from Saul and given to David, who was brought before Saul to calm his stormy spirit with his music (*Ant.* 166-69). It seems to follow that in joining Psalm 151, which portrays David's anointment by Samuel, with Psalm 151[a], which extols David's victory over the Philistine, the author or the scribe of 11QPs[a] followed a biblical text tradition which differed from the section arrangement preserved in the MT and in the ancient VSS of the book of Samuel.

In concluding we wish to stress that there can be no doubt that the tradents who introduced the *p.b.p.* into the MT never considered the extraneous expansions to which they point as integral components of the Bible. They intended them to remain outside the authoritative canon as some kind of appendixes to the original version of Scripture. It is this relation of basic text and paraphrase, with the concomitant relation of primary and supplementary, which caused the *p.b.p.* .as a notation alluding to literary expansion to be especially prevalent in the biblical books that originated in and pertain to the First Temple Period, namely the historiographies which head the canon, the Pentateuch, and the Former Prophets.

Psalm 151 from 11QPs[a]
Courtesy of the Department of Archaeology
The Rockefeller Museum, Jerusalem

Fragment of the Song of the Sabbath Offering
which illustrates the ongoing creation of Psalm-like poems at Qumran;
written at Qumran (Sectarian text), found in Masada
Courtesy of The Israel Museum, Jerusalem, The Shrine of the Book
D. Samuel & Jeane H. Gottesman Center for Biblical Manuscripts

WAITING FOR THE MESSIAH — THE CONCEPTUAL UNIVERSE OF THE QUMRAN COVENANTERS

Introduction

The vision of an Anointed king (Hebrew משיח and Greek χριστός) who will rise in a diversely determined or altogether undetermined future was deemed by Martin Buber to constitute "die zuteifst originelle Idee des Judentums,"[1] deeply rooted in the biblical world. The concept emanates from the existential chasm that exists between the actual socioreligious and political human condition and the fervent hope for an immaculate, ideal, future age that the Anointed will ring in.

The messianic age maintains a focal although differently accentuated position in the Jewish and Christian faiths. Therefore *messianism,* its meaning and evaluation, constitutes a credal and intellectual challenge for each generation of Jews and Christians, calling for a separate, internal reassessment at every juncture of history.

The Qumran Discoveries

In our own time an additional factor justifies a reopening of the discussion: the discovery of documents from the turn of the era that contain new information on some configurations of the messianic idea in the critical period that witnessed the parting of the ways for Judaism and Christianity. These documents are the well-known manuscript finds in caves located in the area of Qumran in the Judean Desert, which at first often were and sometimes still are designated by the

---

1. M. Buber, *Drei Reden über das Judentum* (Frankfurt: Ruetten & Loening, 1911) 91.

misnomer "The Dead Sea Scrolls."[2] Some introductory remarks may be helpful in tracing the coordinates of the context in which a deliberation of the Covenanters' messianism must be set.[3]

In the summer of 1947, bedouin shepherds were grazing their flocks in the Judean Desert at a place known by the modern Arabic name of Qumran, situated near the northwestern shore of the Dead Sea, about seven miles south of Jericho. While searching for a strayed goat, they discovered a crevice in the rocks which, upon investigation, turned out to be an opening in the roof of a large cave. Letting themselves down into it, they found on its floor eight large, oblong, earthenware jars, some still covered with bowl-shaped lids. Seven jars were empty, but the eighth contained one large and two small leather scrolls. Once the find became known, free-lance diggers retrieved from the cave four more scrolls and several large fragments.

At first, because of the clandestine character of the discoveries, doubts about their authenticity and antiquity were entertained by some scholars. The suspicions were allayed, however, when the antiquity of the material was independently established by E. L. Sukenik of the Hebrew University, and J. C. Trever and W. H. Brownlee of the Albright School of Oriental Research in Jerusalem. Properly conducted archeological excavations in the Qumran area between 1951 and 1956 verified the dating of most scrolls to the last two centuries B.C.E. and the first century C.E. The results achieved by paleographic analysis were later confirmed by carbon-14 tests. A search of some 200 caves in the area produced written materials from an additional 10, the richest find hailing from Cave 4. Pottery similar to the jars from Cave 1 was found in about 25 other caves.

Not far from the cave discovered by the bedouin, archeologists laid bare the ruins of fairly large communal buildings that had been occupied in several phases between the beginning of the second century B.C.E. and 67 or 68 C.E., when the Roman legions destroyed the settlement on their march from Jericho to Jerusalem. One may surmise that the inhabitants of that settlement, the

2. It is preferable to use the designation Qumran Scrolls, since unrelated written materials roughly contemporaneous with some of the documents found at Qumran were found in other locations in the Judean Desert, especially in Wadi Murabbaʿat. (The Qumran Scrolls will be designated by the system of sigla detailed in D. Barthélemy, O. P., and J. T. Milik [*Qumran Cave 1, Discoveries in the Judaean Desert* [Oxford: Clarendon Press, 1955], 1. 46-48).

3. For a more detailed discussion of pertinent matters, see "Between the Bible and the Mishna" (in this vol., pp. 11-52).

Covenanters (see below), had secreted the scrolls away before their communal center was stormed by the Roman soldiers. But the exact nature of that assemblage of written materials and the reasons for their having been taken to the caves remain under scholarly debate.

The writings preserved in the collection shed light on the history and conceptual world of a community that emanated from mainstream Judaism at the beginning of the second century B.C.E., gradually diverging and ultimately separating from it completely. The group probably came to an end in the first half of the second century C.E. Thus the Qumran community existed altogether for some three centuries.[4]

The scrolls reflect the credal concepts of that group of dissenters who propounded an extreme messianism. They indeed parted company with proto-Pharisaic Judaism but never amalgamated with Christianity. A probe into their socioreligious history should thus provide new, albeit indirect, information on the contemporary messianic concepts of early Rabbinic Judaism and of nascent Christianity, whether by pointing out similarities the Qumran community shared with either, or else by highlighting views that contrasted with one or the other or with both.

The first lot of manuscripts turned out to be fairly representative of the three categories under which most of the Qumran writings can be subsumed:

(1) Copies of books included in the Hebrew Bible. With the exception of the book of Esther (and possibly Ezra), all books are represented, some by only a few fragments, others by several almost complete manuscripts. Quotations of and allusions to biblical texts abound in the specifically Qumranic works (see below).

(2) Copies of books of the Apocrypha and Pseudepigrapha, such as Ben Sira, *Jubilees, Enoch,* the *Testaments of the Patriarchs,* and Tobit. These works had been preserved in the Bible Canon of the Church in translation. Qumran provides irrefutable proof that originally they had been penned in Hebrew.

It should be stressed that the manuscripts in these categories are not necessarily Qumranian in origin or character. They may have been in the possession of prospective members when they joined the community and thus represent what may be considered the common heritage of Jewry in the Second

4. Comprehensive surveys of the Qumran finds are offered by F. M. Cross (*The Ancient Library of Qumran and Biblical Studies* [New York: Doubleday, 1958, 1961]) and G. Vermes (*The Dead Sea Scrolls: Qumran in Perspective* [London: SCM Press, 1982]), et al.

Temple Period. Therefore, for example, the many textual divergencies from the MT found in biblical manuscripts from Qumran must be taken in part to reflect an all-Jewish tradition. Others may have had their origin at Qumran, where scribes would have copied books for the use of their fellow members.

(3) The third category is of an altogether different kind. It contains manuscripts and fragments of literary works that are peculiar to the Covenanters. There are the *pesharim,* viz., actualizing extrapolations of biblical books, especially of prophetic literature and the Psalms. By this method of interpretation, Scripture is shown to foreshadow the history of the Covenanters, which is presented as the fulfillment of preordained processes and divine promises. The picture is rounded out by works (not based on the Hebrew Bible) which provide an insight into the structure of the Qumran community, its particular understanding of Jewish (biblical) monotheism, and the norms of its socioreligious life.

It is to these specific Qumranian writings of the third category that we must turn our attention, so as to extract from them information on the Covenanters' conception of messianism and the ideal future Eon.

Terms and Methods

Three further preliminary remarks regarding terminology and methodology are in order.

(1) For the sake of brevity, I shall refer to the Qumran Covenanters in the ensuing deliberations as יחד. This term is an apocopated form of the designations יחד בני צדוק or יחד בני אל, "The Commune of the Divine Ones" (or possibly, "The Followers of Zadok"), which the authors of the Qumran writings employ when they make reference to their own community.

(2) Proper methodology requires that Qumran messianism be discussed first and foremost against the background of information gleaned from the literature of the יחד, leaving aside at this stage of the investigation any considerations based on comparisons with other groups in Second Temple Judaism. The overly hasty comparative approach leads to a premature identification of this new socioreligious phenomenon with other previously known streams in Judaism of that period of which ancient sources, Hellenistic, Rabbinic, and Christian, supply partial evidence. None of these is as fully documented as is the יחד, thanks to the rich finds that issued from the Qumran caves.

I shall also steer clear of the prevailing identification of the יחד with the Essenes. As a matter of fact, if these two entities of dissenters from mainstream Judaism are lumped together, the resulting amalgam should be called Qumran-יחד, rather than Essenes, since documentation on the former is incomparably more detailed and comprehensive than the latter. Moreover, whereas information about the Essenes comes entirely from retrospective reports written by authors who had never been members of that community (with the possible exception of Josephus, if his claim is taken at face value), our knowledge of the יחד is derived from firsthand sources authored by its own members and is contemporaneous with the events described in them. This gives the latter an edge over the former.[5] I shall have occasion to demonstrate that the specific configuration in which messianism appears at Qumran, unlike what has been ascribed to the Essenes by any ancient informant, is an important reason to be reticent in identifying the one with the other.

(3) I use the term *messianism* with some hesitation. The notation of the uniqueness of the messianic savior that inheres in this concept as commonly employed is not compatible with the Qumranians' fervently expected rise of Two Anointed, one descended from the House of David and one from the House of Aaron. This distinction should be kept in mind when, for the sake of brevity, I shall nevertheless employ the term *messianism* in the ensuing deliberations.

For similar reasons I shall avoid as much as possible the employment of the term *eschatology,* which bears the stamp of "metahistory" or is understood to designate "the end of historical time." I shall speak rather of the Age to Come, which the Qumranians, like Biblical Israel, perceived within the framework of actual history, expecting it to set in at a preordained stage in the progress of history.[6]

5.   I have argued these points in previous publications. See "Types of Messianic Expectation at the Turn of the Era" (*KCC* [Jerusalem: Magnes Press, 1986]) 202-24; "Qumran und das Alte Testament" (*Frankfurter Universitätsreden* 42 [1971] 71-83); "The Calendar of the Covenanters of the Judean Desert" (in this volume, pp. 147-85); "Between the Bible and the Mishna" (in this volume, pp. 11-52).
6.   See S. Talmon (*Eschatology and History in Biblical Judaism, Occasional Papers No. 2* [Jerusalem: Tantur/Ecumenical Institute for Theological Research, 1986]).

Waiting for the Messiah

The Founders of the יחד

The founding members of the יחד can best be described as a group of Jews possessed by an ardent messianic vision. Viewed from the angle of typology, they represent the most decidedly millenarian or chiliastic movement[7] in Second Temple Judaism and possibly in antiquity altogether, Christianity included.[8] By extrapolating biblical texts, they had worked out the exact date of the onset of the ideal Age to Come and held themselves in readiness to welcome its harbingers, the Anointed, who would usher it in. However they did not live to see their hopes materialize and thus were suspended in limbo between the real and the visionary stage of history. They present to us a prime example of stumped millenarianism. The יחד is a godsend for anyone interested in a typology of religious dissent, its internal development, and the communal structures and organization in which it expresses itself. The study of sectarianism, not only in the framework of Judaism but as a general phenomenon, could greatly benefit from an expertly carried out sociological analysis of the יחד.[9]

We should be reminded that once before Israel had experienced an almost-realized messianism.[10] The returnees from the Babylonian Exile, led by Zerubbabel, Ezra, and Nehemiah, had conceived of their return and the restoration of a religiopolitical Judean entity, however restricted, as the realization of Jeremiah's prophecy in which he had foreseen for Judah a period of doom and

7. A concise discussion of this socioreligious phenomenon and references to relevant literature may be found in Yonina Talmon, "Millenarian Movements" (*EJS* 7 [1966] 159-200); "Pursuit of the Millennium: The Relation between Religious and Social Change" (*EJS* 3 [1962] 125-48). By way of contrast one can compare the Samaritans, whose rejection of the Prophets and Writings apparently led to a lack of development of any truly messianic idea at all.
8. The Judaism at Qumran contrasts starkly with the Judaism of the Mishna, for, as Neusner remarks, "the Mishnah presents us with a kind of Judaism possessed of an eschatology—a theory of the end—without Messiah, a teleology beyond time" (J. Neusner, "Mishnah and Messiah," *Judaisms and Their Messiahs at the Turn of the Christian Era* [ed. J. Neusner, W. S. Green, and E. Frerichs; New York: Cambridge Univ. Press, 1987] pp. 265-82).
9. See S. Talmon ("The Emergence of Jewish Sectarianism in the Early Post-Exilic Period," *KCC*, 165-201).
10. See B. Vawter ("Realized Messianism," *De la Tôrah au Messie, Études d'exégèse et d'herméneutique bibliques offertes à H. Cazelles* [ed. M. Carrez, J. Doré, and P. Grelot; Paris: Desclée, 1981] 175-79).

exile that would last for seventy years (Jer 25:11, 12; 29:10; cp. Zech 1:12; 7:5; Dan 9:2; 2 Chr 36:21; see also Ezra 1:1 = 2 Chr 36:22). At the end of this preordained span of time, God would reverse his people's bitter fate and restore Judah to her fortunes. The postexilic biblical books bear witness to the fact that the returning exiles took Jeremiah's prophecy at face value, surprising as this may sound to us. They questioned whether the appointed time indeed had run its course and whether the stage was set for the rebuilding of the Temple, God's time-honored abode, which would signify his residing again in the midst of his redeemed people (Hag 1:2).

Prophets who were active in those days, Zechariah and especially Haggai, gave divinely inspired sustenance to their contemporaries' conviction that the restoration of Judah's glory of old had indeed set in and that the glory of the New Age that they were to experience would even surpass that of the former (Hag 2:1-9; cp. Zech 1:16; 2:8-9, 14 [Heb.]; 8:1-15). Some utterances of these prophets have distinct messianic overtones. Zerubbabel, scion of the House of David, figures in them as the Anointed Who Had Come (Hag 2:20-23; Zech 4:6-10), and traditional Davidic *Hoheitstitel* are assigned to him (e.g., Hag 2:23; Zech 3:8; 6:12). The oracles are patterned after prophetic "latter-day"[11] visions of the First Temple Period and upon descriptions of the exodus from the Egyptian exile and the ensuing *Landnahme*, as can be seen from a comparison of, e.g., Hag 2:5, 21-22 with Exod 15:4, 19; Zech 3:10 with Mic 4:4; Zech 8:20-23 with Isa 2:2-3 = Mic 4:1-2, et al.

In the final reckoning the returnees' flighty expectations did not come to fruition. The world that had been seen to be in upheaval (Hag 2:20-22) came to rest (Zech 1:11). Mundane, real history took over once more. With the fading of Zerubbabel from the scene, the hopes that had fastened upon the Anointed came to naught. The actual restoration did not measure up to the anticipated profound remaking of the historical world.

The founding members of the יחד may have thus judged the period of the return from the Babylonian exile. The allusions to and mentions of it in their literature are so scanty that one is inclined to assume that they intended to obliterate it entirely from their conception of Israel's history and to claim for themselves the distinction of being the first returnees after the destruction. As will yet be elaborated, they conceived of themselves as exiles from Judah who

---

11. Not "last days," as is the prevalent translation. The distinction will be explained below. See Talmon (*Eschatology and History*, 8-16) and the pertinent literature adduced there.

had missed their chance when the edict of Cyrus had made possible the return foreseen by prophets of the First Temple Period. In any case, in their view, the divine promise had not yet been fulfilled and remained open-ended. Now it fell to their lot to close the circle and to assume the preordained task of the restoration generation.

Working Propositions

The ensuing discussion will be based on the following theses:

(1) The Covenanters of Qumran conceived of themselves as the sole true representatives of biblical Israel. While in reality they existed in the Hellenistic and early Roman Period, conceptually they lived in the biblical age, which for them, in distinction from mainstream Judaism, had not yet concluded. Viewed from this angle, they could be designated the last בעלי מקרא. This characteristic misled some scholars to identify them with the medieval Karaites.

(2) More precisely, the יחד members viewed themselves as the exclusive זרע ישראל (CD xii 2-22),[12] the "holy remnant," זרע הקודש (Ezra 9:1-2; cp. Isa 6:13), who in this קץ, or "generation," had been favored by God again "to fill the universe" (CD ii 11-12) forever and ever (1QH xvii 14).

(3) The יחד assumes the role that postexilic biblical historiography (Ezra-Nehemiah, 2 Chr 36:22-23) and prophecy (Haggai, Zechariah, and Malachi) accord to the returnees from the Babylonian exile in the early Persian Period. The substitution possibly was helped along by contracting the entire Persian Period to a bare minimum, thus linking their own generation "directly" to the post-destruction generation.[13]

(4) Any attempt at elucidating Qumran messianism and the Covenanters' concept of the Messianic Age must take this historical construct into account. Their notions in these matters were directly bound up with the views reflected in the postexilic biblical literature.

Like their precursors, the returnees under Zerubbabel, Ezra, and Nehemiah, the Qumran Covenanters sought to underpin their claim to the task and the title

---

12. Since the end of the last century, this work was known in medieval copies that stem from the Cairo Genizah. Fragments of it discovered in Cave 4 prove its Qumranian provenance. The work (CD) is quoted here according to the edition by C. Rabin (*The Zadokite Documents* [Oxford: Clarendon Press, 1954]).
13. See "Between the Bible and the Mishna" (in this vol., pp. 11-52).

of the "saved remnant" by basing it upon a biblical prophecy. They achieved this aim by focusing on a symbolic act, performed at divine instruction by the prophet Ezekiel, in the face of the Babylonian siege of Jerusalem:

> You lie down on your left side and place the iniquity of the house of Israel on it; for the number of days that you lie on it you shall bear their iniquity. I am converting for you the years of their iniquity into a number of days— 390 days. . . . When you finish these, you shall lie down a second time, on your right side, and bear the iniquity of the house of Judah for forty days; I am converting each year of it into a day for you" (Ezek 4:4-6).

Irrespective of the originally intended meaning of this passage, which at times is interpreted to have a *retrospective*,[14] not a *prospective* thrust, the Qumranians, in a pesher-like fashion, read Ezekiel's symbolic act of woe as an oracle of weal, deftly balancing the explicit threat of exile with an implied message of hope. The account they give of the genesis of the יחד opens as follows (CD i 3-8):

> For when they were unfaithful and forsook him, he [God] hid his face from Israel and his sanctuary and delivered them up to the sword. But remembering the covenant of the forefathers, he left a remnant to Israel and did not deliver it up to [utter] destruction [cp. Jer 5:18; 30:11; 46:28; Neh 9:31]. And in the age of wrath [i.e., their own days], 390 years after he had given them into the hand of King Nebuchadnezzar of Babylon, he remembered them [cp. CD vi 2-5] and caused the root he had planted to sprout from Israel and Aaron to take [again] possession of his land and enjoy the fruits of its soil [cp. Zech 3:10; 8:12; Hag 2:18-19].

Exegetes have found it difficult, if not impossible, to make head or tail of the figure 390,[15] whereas the unit signifying 40 days/years obviously reflects the biblical stereotype that accords this number of years to an average generation.

14. Thus, e.g., Rashi *ad* 2 Chr 36:22. See I. Rabinowitz ("A Reconsideration of 'Damascus' and '390 Years' in the 'Damascus' ['Zadokite'] Fragment," *JBL* 72 [1954] 33-35).
15. See M. Greenberg (*Ezekiel 1-20* [AB; Garden City, NY: Doubleday, 1983], vol. 22); W. Zimmerli (*Ezechiel 1-24* [BKAT; Neukirchen-Vluyn: Neukirchener, 1979] ad loc.).

The Covenanters attached realistic values to these figures.[16] It cannot be pure coincidence that by subtracting 390 from 586, when Jerusalem and the Temple were destroyed by the Babylonians, one arrives at the beginning of the second century B.C.E., which scholarly *communis opinio* takes to be the time in which the יחד arose.[17] I am persuaded that what we have here is yet another piece of millenarian arithmetics.[18] Ezekiel's oracle of 390 years took on for the Covenanters the very same key meaning that Jeremiah's prophecy of 70 years had for the Judeans who returned from the exile.[19]

It may be presumed that then and there the founding members of the יחד, "the first men of holiness," אנשי] הקודש [הרא[שונים] (CD iv 6), readied themselves for the great event, the onset of the New Age. In their millenarian calculations, they still had to account for the 40 years that Ezekiel had foreseen as the period of Judah's exile. It would appear that they took care of this matter in several ways.

Telescoping Deut 2:14, which speaks of the Exodus (from Egypt) generation, with Ezek 4:6, the author of CD tells us that "from the day of the 'Teacher of the יחד' [probably to be identified with the Righteous Teacher of whom I shall yet speak] until all the inimical men [men of war] who sided with

16. I have reasoned thus for some time (see publications mentioned in n. 5 above). Recently B. Z. Wacholder arrived independently at the same interpretation of the opening passage of CD. See his *The Dawn of Qumran. The Sectarian Torah and the Teacher of Righteousness. Monographs of the Hebrew Union College* 8. ([Cincinnati: Hebrew Union College, 1983] 177ff.) and the pertinent literature adduced there. Our views differ, however, in the interpretation of the socioreligious factors that triggered the emergence of the Qumran community.

17. This was already argued before the discovery of the Qumran writings. See E. Meyer (*Eine jüdische Schrift aus der Seleukidenzeit. Abhandlungen der preussischen Akademie der Wissenschaften, Phil.-hist. Klass* [Berlin, 1919] 1-65). See also E. Täubler ("Jerusalem 201-199 B.C.E.: On the History of a Messianic Movement," *JQR* 37 [1946/47] 1-30, 125-37, 149-63); H. H. Rowley ("The History of the Qumran Sect," *BJRL* 49 [1966/67] 203-32; B. Z. Wacholder (*The Dawn of Qumran,* 177 ff.).

18. "Millenarian arithmetics" or "messianic numerology" constitutes realistic historical values for those who take them seriously, while outsiders will view them as mere products of religious fantasy.

19. The figure of 390 from Qumran contrasts with the figure 400 used in the book of 4 Ezra for the duration of the age of the Messiah (cp. M. Stone, "The Question of the Messiah in 4 Ezra," *Judaisms and Their Messiahs* [see above, n. 8] pp. 209-24, esp. pp. 210-15). The significance of this difference cannot be discussed in the present context.

the Liar [their prominent opponent] will come to an end, [exactly] 40 years [will pass]" (CD viii 52-54).

The same figure is given for the duration of the final war, during which time the Covenanters, the Sons of Light, will vanquish all their opponents, the Sons of Darkness, i.e., foreign nations (1QM i-ii) and Jews who had not joined the New Covenant.

However, of more importance for our present concern is the opening passage of CD to which I have already referred. Having elucidated the figure of 390 years, the author goes on to report that as the founding members

> perceived their iniquity and recognized that they [still] were guilty men, for twenty years they were like blind men groping for their way. And God observed their deeds, that they sought him with a whole heart, and he raised for them a [or "the"] Teacher of Righteousness [or Righteous Teacher] to guide them in the way of his heart (CD i 8-11).

This passage forms the continuation of the preceding pesher-like interpretation of Ezek 4:4-6. Therefore, the figure "twenty" requires an explanation. Two possibilities offer themselves. Either the Ezekiel text on which the author relied contained in 4:6 the reading "twenty" instead of MT's "forty,"[20] or (preferably) he divided the stereotype lifespan of one generation into two parts, each amounting to twenty years (cp. the figures given for Samson's "judgeship" in Judg 15:20 and 16:31). This leads to the following understanding of the passage, which, however, is not explicated in the Covenanters' writings:

> After the founding members had been "groping for the way" for twenty years, the Righteous Teacher arose to lead them for another twenty years. Assuming that the Teacher had himself been one of the "gropers," his association with the group would thus have spanned the life of one generation, 40 years, parallelling the figure of 40 years given for the time that elapsed from the day of his demise to the end of the Liar's men (CD viii 52-54).

---

20. Such a variant is most likely to occur when numerical values are indicated by letters of the alphabet, מ standing for "forty" and כ for "twenty." These letters are easily misread for each other, especially in the ancient Hebrew script.

Waiting for the Messiah

The Righteous Teacher

Some attention must now be given to the figure of the מורה הצדק,[21] who at
this juncture enters the scene and from here on will occupy a prominent position
in the Qumran writings. In all likelihood he was of priestly descent. What is
important for our present concern is the role accorded to him in the unfolding
messianic drama, or rather in its impeded dénouement. The Teacher was born out
of intense emotional stress, triggered by the profound disappointment that the
unrealized hope for an imminent onset of the millenium had evoked in the initial
nucleus of Covenanters when the precalculated date passed uneventfully. Thus,
emerging in a second stage of the group's history, and not being its initiator,[22]
he cannot be defined as a "founding prophet" (in the typology introduced by Max
Weber), nor has the occasionally proposed identification with Jesus Christ any
basis.[23] Rather, he must be seen as an inspired interpreter whose latent
inspiration revealed itself in his response to his fellows' despair. It fell to him to
find the means for bridging the gap between the unduly protracted *now* and the
disappointingly delayed *then*. This he apparently did by transforming the loose
group-cohesion of the founding members into a structured socioreligious system.
Under his guidance, their utopian millenarism,[24] which originally had anarchistic
overtones, crystallized into a structured order. Before long the basically
antiestablishment millenarians formed a socioreligious establishment of their

21. See G. Jeremias (*Der Lehrer der Gerechtigkeit* [Göttingen: Vandenhoeck &
    Ruprecht, 1963]) and B. E. Thiering (*Redating the Teacher of Righteousness*
    [Sydney: Theological Explorations, 1979]).
22. This hypothesis is advanced by Wacholder (*The Dawn of Qumran*, especially on
    pp. 99-119, 135, 140 ff.).
23. See J. Carmignac (*Christ and the Teacher of Righteousness* [Baltimore/Dublin:
    Helicon Press, 1962]) for a discussion of this issue.
24. It may be said that in the (comparatively speaking) subdued messianic hope
    which obtained in Pharisaic Judaism, the "restorative" orientation prevailed.
    For Christianity, the "utopian" element, seemingly freed from the fetters of
    actual history, became the most prominent trait of its messianism. In the יחד
    concept of the messianic age, one perceives a distinct fusion of those two diver-
    gent trends: utopia and reality have been blended to the almost total obliter-
    ation of any demarcation lines between them. In this, as in many other aspects,
    the יחד concept shows strong affiliations with the Hebrew Bible and biblical
    Israel, possibly more than any other Jewish community of the Second Temple
    Period (see Talmon, "Types of Messianic Expectation, " *KCC*, 202-24).

own which was soon to surpass in rigidity and normative exactitude the system of the mother community from which they had separated.

The vista of the New Age was not lost from sight. But it appears that once Ezekiel's vision had failed to materialize for them, the Covenanters could not anymore, or would not, venture to establish by chiliastic computations the exact date of the onset of the ideal Eon. One wonders why they did not seize upon the apocalyptic 490 (7 x 70) years' vision in the book of Daniel (chaps. 9-10) for achieving this purpose. To go into speculations about what caused this abstinence would lead us too far afield, although some explanation could tentatively be suggested.[25] In any case it stands to reason that in this crucial second period of 20 years, the founding members retreated into the Judean Desert, led by the מורה הצדק. Reenacting the paradigmatic events that had determined and enfolded Israel's history in the biblical period, life in the arid area of Qumran signified for them the period of exile—Egypt and Babylon rolled into one. There, they located typologically the "Damascus," beyond which Israel would be exiled, according to the prophet Amos (5:27): "I shall take you into exile beyond Damascus, says God" (CD vii 13-14; cp. Zech 6:8). There "they shall escape again in the time of the visitation [or "judgment"]," whereas "they that turn away [from God and the covenant] shall be delivered to the sword when the Anointed of Aaron and Israel shall come" (CD vii 20-21a; cp. Zech 11:11).

Like the "locust" that usually invades the land of Israel from the south and nevertheless can represent the "foe from the north" in the visions of the biblical prophet Joel (Joel 2:10; cp. 1:1—2:11), "Damascus" and the "north" in the Qumran writings should probably be understood as cyphers for "exile in the desert of Judah."[26] There, in that "Damascus," they established the New Covenant (CD vi 19; viii 21). By this token the loosely knit group of founding members achieved the character of a structured community that set out to attract and initiate an ever-growing number of novices (1QS i 1—ii 18, et al.).

---

25. Much depends on whether or not the status of the book of Daniel equaled that of the books of the biblical prophets, such as Jeremiah and Ezekiel. Charlesworth does note that 11QMelch mentions both the book of Daniel and the "seven weeks," but this does not seem to figure prominently in the eschatological chronology of Qumran (J. H. Charlesworth, "From Jewish Messianology to Christian Christology, Some Caveats and Perspectives," *Judaisms and Their Messiahs* [ed. J. Neusner] 225-64 [see above, n. 8]).
26. Scholars are divided on the question of whether "Damascus" stands for the name of the well-known city or whether it is used here as a topos.

It seems that when the Covenanters' millennial expectations consolidated into institutionalized heterodoxy, the authorities of the mother community, who until then appear to have viewed their dissenting concepts with equanimity, took steps to prevent a further solidification of the rebellious community. Led by the Wicked Priest, they pursued the Teacher and his followers to Qumran, his House of Exile (1QpHab xi 4-8), where the Covenanters had meant to weather out the now uncharted period of time that intervened between their own days and the hoped-for Age to Come. Then, and from there, they would embark on the march to Jerusalem, regain the Holy City, and make her the kingpin of the reestablished Commonwealth of Israel, thus bringing once again to its climax the historical cycle of biblical days: exile—sojourn in the wilderness—settlement.[27]

Their ignorance of the (next) "appointed day" brought about a decisive modification in the Covenanters' millenarian stance. In the initial phase they had expected the progress of history toward the divinely ordained onset of the New Age to unfold in a smooth process. Just as the Judeans in the Babylonian exile had passively bided their time until the day that would be ripe for the divinely promised return (Jer 29:1-14), the Qumran millenarians at first adopted a quietist posture in their "waiting for the Messiah": since the date of this rise had been divinely ordained, no human interference was required to bring it about.[28] The changed circumstances engendered a reformulation of this attitude. They began to perceive their own sinfulness (CD i 8-9) as a factor that had contributed to or had altogether caused the retardation of the redeeming event. The need for action was further accentuated by the interference of hostile agents, the Wicked Priest and his followers, who obstructed the expected smooth progress of history toward the New Age. These inimical forces had to be overcome before the New Jerusalem could be achieved. An apocalyptic battle in which all evil powers would be

27. See S. Talmon ("The 'Desert Motif' in the Bible and in Qumran Literature," *Biblical Motifs, Origins and Transformations* [ed. A. Altmann, Studies and Texts of the Philip L. Lown Institute of Advanced Judaic Studies; Cambridge, Mass.: Harvard University Press, 1966], 3. 31-63); idem, *"Midbār"* (TWAT [Stuttgart: Kohlhammer, 1983], 4. 660-95).

28. In contrast to this initial quietist attitude, but more in keeping with the militant later stance of the יחד, was the perception of Bar Kokhba, who, as Neusner notes, was probably seen in his own day as a "messianic general" and his war "as coming at the expected end of time, the eschatological climax to the drama begun in 70" (J. Neusner, "Mishnah and Messiah," *Judaisms and Their Messiahs*, 267 [see above, n.8]).

vanquished was now seen as a *conditio sine qua non* for the aspired transition from the dire *here and now* to the illumined *then and there*. This battle, which was to shake the foundations of the universe, is portrayed in the *War Scroll* (1QM).[29] It is conceived in the image of Ezekiel's Gog and Magog vision (Ezekiel 38-39) and the apocalyptic engagements of which the book of Daniel speaks. In view of this presumed development of the Covenanters' messianism, the *War Scroll* probably was produced during a later stage of the existence of the יחד. However this assumption rests solely on the evolution of ideas presented here and cannot be substantiated by other evidence gained either from a scrutiny of Qumran literature or from a paleographical analysis of the scrolls.[30]

The Anointed

The victorious termination of the final war, the recapture of Jerusalem, and the rebuilding of the Temple will pave the way for the assured advent of the Anointed as a matter of course. As mentioned, in Qumran literature this concept emerges in a distinctive bifurcation: two figures are seen to appear on the horizon, an Anointed of Israel, associated with the royal House of David, and an Anointed of the House of Aaron. The doctrine of a priestly Anointed who officiates next to the royal משיח at the head of Israel's body politic is reflected also in some strata of the apocryphal literature.[31] This wider currency proves that it cannot be considered the Covenanters' exclusive legacy, but rather must have been rooted in a common Jewish tradition. However, in the Qumran literature, the doctrine is accorded a much more significant role than in any apocryphal book.

29. See Y. Yadin (*The Scroll of the War of the Sons of Light Against the Sons of Darkness* [trans., B. and C. Rabin; Oxford: Clarendon Press, 1962]).
30. The different outlook and presumed comparative lateness of 1QM may explain the baffling absence of any reference to the (two) Anointed, which is underscored by Yadin (p. 227, n. 15). In contrast, G. Vermes presumes that 1QM and the "messianic rule" (1QSa, see below) "were both written during the same period, i.e. in the final decades of the pre-Christian era or at the beginning of the first century A.D." See his *The Dead Sea Scrolls in English* ([New York: Penguin, 1972] 118).
31. See A. S. van der Woude (*Die messianischen Vorstellungen der Gemeinde von Qumran* [Assen: Van Gorcum, 1957]).

While at times dissent has been voiced on this matter, the opinion prevails that at Qumran the rise of Two Anointed was indeed expected.[32] L. Ginzberg's conclusion, which he reached on the basis of CD alone, has lost nothing of its poignancy: "we have to reject the [then] dominant opinion which seems to find references to only one Messiah in our document [CD], who unites both priesthood and kingdom in his person."[33] I fully concur with this view, which can now be buttressed by quotations culled from writings from the Qumran caves.

The following are some of the relevant texts on which a discussion of the issue must be based:

1QS ix 10-11:

They shall be judged by the first statutes [or "the statutes laid down by the first/founders"][34] by which the יחד members were first ruled, until there shall arise (בוא) the prophet and the Anointed (ומשחי) of Aaron and Israel.[35]

32. See int. al. A. S. van der Woude (*Die messianischen Vorstellungen*); K. G. Kuhn, ("The Two Messiahs of Aaron and Israel," *The Scrolls and the New Testament* [ed. K. Stendahl; New York: Harper, 1957] 54-64); K. Schubert ["Die Messiaslehre in den Texten von Chirbet Qumran," *BZ* 1 [1957] 177-97); R. E. Brown ("The Messianism of Qumran," *CBQ* 19 [1957] 53-82); idem ("The Teacher of Righteousness and the Messiah(s)," *The Scrolls and Christianity* [ed. M. Black; London: SPCK, 1969] 37-44); H. W. Kuhn ("Die beiden Messias in den Qumran-texten und die Messiasvorstellung in der rabbinischen Literatur," *ZAW* 70 [1958] 200-208); J. Liver ("The Doctrine of Two Messiahs in Sectarian Literature of the Second Commonwealth," *HThR* 52 [1959] 149-85); M. Smith ("What Is Implied by the Variety of Messianic Figures?" *JBL* 78 [1959] 66-72); W. S. LaSor ("The Messianic Idea at Qumran," *Studies and Essays in Honor of A. Neumann* [Leiden: E. J. Brill, 1962] 363-64); J. Starcky ("Les quatres étapes du messianisme à Qumran," *RB* 70 [1963] 481-505); K. Weiss ("Messianismus in Qumran und im Neuen Testament," *Qumran-Probleme* [ed. H. Bardtke; Berlin: Akademie-Verlag, 1963] 353-68); R. B. Laurin ("The Problem of Two Messiahs in the Qumran Scrolls," *RQ* 4 [1963/64] 39-52); E. A. Wcela ("The Messiah(s) of Qumran," *CBQ* 26 [1964] 340-49).
33. L. Ginzberg, *An Unknown Jewish Sect* (updated translation from the German by R. Marcus; New York: JTSA, 1976) 248.
34. The translations offered aim at highlighting the sense of the Hebrew texts rather than rendering them literally.
35. According to Charlesworth in an older copy of *The Rule*, announced by J. T. Milik, the *locus classicus* for two messiahs is missing (see J. H. Charlesworth, "Jewish Messianology" 230-33 [see above, n. 25] and literature adduced there, p. 256, n. 15).

CD xii 22-23:

This is the rule of the assembly of the camps who walk in it in the Age of Wickedness (בקץ הרשעה) until there shall arise the Anointed (עד עמוד משיוח) of Aaron and Israel.[36]

CD xiii 20-22:

This is [the rule for] the assembly of the camps during all the Age of Wickedness (בכל קץ הרשעה), and whosoever will not abide by the[se statutes] shall not be [considered] worthy to live in the land when there shall come the Anointed of Aaron and Israel (באחרית הימים).

CD xix 34—xx 1:

None of the backsliders . . . shall be counted among the "council" of the people and in its records they shall not be entered, from the day of the demise of the Teacher of the יחד (מורה היחיד) until there shall arise the Anointed of Aaron and Israel.

CD xiv 18-19:

This is the exact [or "detailed"] account of the statutes in which [they shall walk in the appointed period of evil until there shall arise the Anoin]ted of Aaron and Israel who will atone for their iniquity.

CD xix 9-11:

Those who watch for him [or "observe his commands"] are the humble of the flock; they shall be saved in the Age of the Visitation (בקץ הפקודה) whereas the backsliders shall be delivered up to the sword when there shall come the Anointed of Aaron and Israel (cp. 4Q 174 ii 5: [the Anointed of Is]rael and Aaron).

The duality of the Anointed appears also to be mirrored in the already-mentioned opening passage of the Damascus Documents.

36. As in the following examples, the distributive singular signifies the plural here.

CD i 5-7:

And in the age of [his] wrath (בקץ חרון) . . . he remembered them and caused the root he had planted to sprout [again] from Israel and Aaron.[37]

The Duality of the Messiah

I intend to show that the duality of a Davidic lay משיח and an Aaronide priestly Anointed reflects a dependence on a biblical pattern that evolved in the postexilic period.[38] At the same time it underscores the sociohistorical character of the messianic idea in Hebrew Scriptures and in Qumran literature, thus revealing the significance of this concept for both biblical Israel and the יחד Covenanters. Also in this matter the extreme Bible-directedness of the יחד, to which attention has already been drawn, comes to the fore. The linguistic and stylistic affinities of the Qumran materials with biblical literature, especially the postexilic books, cannot adequately be explained solely by the chronological proximity of these two bodies of writings. They must rather be understood as revealing a striking spiritual consanguinity. The Qumran authors' predilection for depicting their own community, its structure, history, and future hopes, by having recourse to idioms, technical terms, and motifs that are manifestly drawn from biblical writings, discloses the self-identification of the יחד with biblical, especially postexilic, Israel and its conceptual universe. From this source the יחד drew also the religiopolitical concept of Two Anointed, who in the New Age would together govern their community and ultimately the reconstituted polity of the people of Israel.

The roots of this concept can be traced to the world of ideas of the returnees from the Babylonian exile. At that time, the prophet Zechariah had presented to the repatriates a blueprint for the organization of the province of Jahud as a *state in nuce* in the framework of the Persian Empire. It was based on a concept of

37. A reflection of this duality may be seen in the composition of the יחד tribunal which was comprised of "four men of the tribe of Levi and Aaron, and of Israel six" (CD x 4-6).
38. This is very similar to the Mishna's "blueprint for an Israelite government based on the Temple in Jerusalem and headed by a king and a high priest" (J. Neusner, "Mishnah and Messiah," *Judaisms and Their Messiahs*, 266 [see above, n. 8]). Cp. also J. Collins ("Messianism in the Maccabean Period," *Judaisms and Their Messiahs*, 97-110); and H. Kee ("Christology in Mark's Gospel," *Judaisms and Their Messiahs*, 187-208).

societal structure that differed quite distinctly from the organization of the Judean body politic under the monarchy in the First Temple Period. Then, the king had not only been in charge of the mundane affairs of the realm but had also wielded controlling power over the sacred institutions. The proximity of the sanctuary to the palace had enabled the king to exercise close supervision over its affairs (see, e.g., 2 Kgs 12:7-17 = 2 Chr 24:4-14; 2 Kgs 22-23 = 2 Chr 34-35; 2 Chr 17:7-9; 26:16-19; 29-31; 33:15-16). The priesthood was dependent on the king, so much so that the high priests were considered royal officials (2 Sam 8:17 = 1 Chr 18:16; 2 Sam 20:25-26; 1 Kgs 4:2, 4, 5) whom the king could appoint and depose at will (1 Kgs 2:26-27, 35; see also 2 Chr 24:20-22).

In the early Persian Period the situation changed perceptibly. The loss of political sovereignty with the fall of Jerusalem in 586 B.C.E. had undermined the status of royalty. Probably it was weakened further by the Persian authorities' insistence on granting the returnees only a measure of administrative autonomy—restricted, in fact, to the domain of ritual and sacred institutions (Ezra 5:3-5; cp. 1:1-4 and see 4:8-23)—and at the same time enhancing the status of the priests (Ezra 7:11-26).[39] Moreover, Zerubbabel's position within the Judean body politic seems to have been somewhat tenuous. Being descended not from Zedekiah, the last king of Judah, but from his brother Jehoiachin (1 Chr 3:17-19), who had been dethroned and exiled by the Babylonians in 597 B.C.E. (2 Kgs 24:8-17 = 2 Chr 36:9-10), his claim to royal authority presumably met with some resistance (contrast Jer 22:24 with Hag 2:23; and Jer 22:28 with Jer 28:4).[40] The combination of these factors enhanced the standing of the priesthood, whose position was further strengthened by collaboration (Hag 2:10-14;[41] Neh 13:4-8) and marriage alliances with the upper classes in the Palestinian population that had not been exiled (Ezra 9-10; Neh 6:18). As a

---

39. See E. Meyer (*Geschichte des Altertums* IV, part 1 [photographic reprint; Darmstadt: Wissenschaftliche Buchgesellschaft, 1980] 88-89).

40. K. Baltzer, "Das Ende des Staates Juda und die Messias-Frage," *Studien zur Theologie der alttestamentlichen Überlieferungen*, G. von Rad zum 60 Geburtstag (ed. R. Rendtorff and K. Koch; Neukirchen-Vluyn: Neukirchener Verlag, 1961) 38-41.

41. I concur with Rothstein's interpretation of this passage as a simile: the "unclean bread and wine" symbolize the unclean local population. While the priests seem to have favored their admission into the returnees' community, the prophet(s) opposed their integration and prevailed upon Zerubbabel to reject them (Ezra 4:1-3). See J. W. Rothstein (*Juden und Samaritaner* [BWAT; Leipzig: Hinrich, 1908], 3. 5 ff., 29 ff.)

result, the prestige of Joshua the high priest, Zerubbabel's contemporary, rose to an unprecedented height, so much so that he appears to have contested successfully Zerubbabel's supremacy in matters of the body politic.

It is against this background that the prophet Zechariah's intervention must be evaluated. Realizing the changed circumstances, he proposed a plan of "shared responsibilities": the Davidic Anointed and the Aaronide Anointed were to be assigned separate spheres of competence (Zechariah 3). Monarchy and priesthood were to complement each other, their mutual relations guided by "a counsel of peace" (Zech 6:13), a sign and an example for the entire community (Zech 8:9-17) and, beyond that, for the family of nations (Zech 8:20-23; cp. Isa 2:2-4 = Mic 4:1-5 et al.). In distinction from the "monocephalic" structure of the Judean realm in the First Temple Period,[42] that of the new Commonwealth of Israel was to be "bicephalic":[43] in his vision, the prophet perceives Two Anointed, בני יחר שני, symbolized by "two olives [olive trees/branches] pouring oil through two golden pipes" (Zech 4:2-3, 11-12) "standing before the Lord of the whole world" (Zech 4:14; cp. CD xx 1; xii 22; xiv 19 restored).[44]

This duality is given a more realistic expression in a divine word (Zech 6:9-14; cp. CD i 5-7) that accords a crown to Joshua the high priest and a throne to the shoot (out of David's root—Zerubbabel [cp. 4Q *174* 1-2 i 10-13; *161*, frgs.

42. Because of the obvious predominance of the king in the Israelite body politic of the First Temple Period, the later balanced standing of king and priest cannot be traced to those earlier times, as suggested by Baltzer ("Das Ende des Staates Juda," *Studien zur Theologie* [ed. Rendtorff] n. 50). See also S. Talmon ("Kingship and the Ideology of the State [in the Biblical Period]," *KCC,* 9-38).

43. The emerging picture differs considerably from the still-current portrayal of Judah in the restoration period as a religious community whose sole representative was the high priest of Jerusalem.

44. 1QS ix 10-11 refers to "a [or "the"] prophet who shall come [arise] with the Anointed of Aaron and Israel." This vision brings to mind the closing passage of the book of Malachi—in fact, of biblical prophetic literature altogether—where the prophet Elijah is foreseen to precede the advent of the "Day of Yhwh" (Mal 3:23). Similarly, in a series of messianic testimonia from Qumran (4Q *175*), biblical prooftexts that refer to "the [future] prophet" (Deut 5:27-29; 18:18-19), "the [messianic] ruler" (Num 24:15-17), and "the [future priest out of the] tribe of Levi" (Deut 33:8-11) respectively, are adduced in this very sequence. See J. M. Allegro ("Further Messianic References in Qumran Literature," *JBL* 75 [1956] 182-87).

8-10, line 11, restored]), or preferably, a crown and a throne to each[45] as insignia of their complementary functions.[46]

It cannot be ascertained whether that prophetic concept was indeed realized in the returnees' community. The unexplained disappearance of Zerubbabel, the last scion of the Davidic House, upset the intended balance and turned the scales in favor of the priestly anointed. However, it appears that the יחד embraced this plan as the prototype of the political structure and modeled upon it their vision of the future age. Identifying with an idealized period of return from the exile, they discerned in it the *Vorzeit* in whose image they conceived the ideal Eon to Come. The יחד then were to be established as the axis of a world freed from all tension that had still afflicted the prototypical *Vorzeit*. The New Age will be a shining creation, healed from all religious blemishes and societal evils which had marred the historical Israel also in the the days of that other return, the days of Zerubbabel, Ezra, and Nehemiah.

The character of the Age to Come remains largely restorative. It will unfold in the geographical frame of the land of Israel to which the יחד returns victorious. The Qumranians expected a new *Landnahme*, culminating in the rebuilding of the Temple in Jerusalem, portrayed as an infinitely improved, but nevertheless realistic version, not a spiritualized replica of the historical city. The messianic age will be experienced by the Covenanters as a structured ethnic-national entity—as the renewed People of Israel—not as inspired individuals. This notion again reflects the conceptual universe of biblical, especially early postexilic, Israel. However, the יחד infused into the ascriptive designation People of Israel the idea of *elective* association. They are the chosen remnant of biblical Israel (cp. Mal 3:13-21; Ezra 9:2 with Isa 6:11-13), to whom alone out of all Israel God had granted a new lease on life, the right to reconstitute Israel's sovereignty, epitomized in the Twin-Anointed of Israel and Aaron.

45. The passage presents some textual difficulties both in the MT and in the versions. The interpretation offered here is based on conjectural restoration.

46. The text was thus (correctly) understood by midrashic exegetes. See *Gen. Rab.* 49, 8 *ad* Zech 4:7-23 ([eds. J. Theodor and C. Albeck; Jerusalem: Wahrmann, 1965] p. 1212, lines 1-6); *Num. Rab.* 13 *ad* Num 7:84; *Sifra* (Torat Kohanim) צו 18 *ad* Lev 7:35 ([ed. I. H. Weiss; New York: Om, 1946] 40a); *'Abot R. Nat.* 34 ([ed. S. Schechter; New York: Feldheim, 1945] 100 ff. and elsewhere).

The New Age

It needs to be stressed that the Covenanters invested their conception of the messianic age with the same real-historical character which biblical thinkers gave to their visions of the future. The New Eon was seen by the founding members to be only one step away from their own days. They were standing on the threshold of a new epoch in history, infinitely sublime, but basically no different from preceding stages in actually experienced history.[47] The similarity with the biblical world of ideas shows in the circumstance that in contradistinction to the absence of the historiographical genre from the literature of the sages, the Covenanters cultivated "historiography," spinning out a literary genre handed down to them as a legacy from the biblical writers who had perfected it.

The progress of history is seen as a succession of קצים, i.e., blocks of time or circumscribed periods.[48] In keeping with biblical usage, they can also be defined by means of a generation or generations, דור/דורות (1QS iv 13; cp. Deut 32:7; Isa 41:4 et al.). Beginning with the creation of the world, the series leads up to the קץ/דור אחרון and culminates in אחרית הימים (see 1QpHab vii 1-2, 7-8, 10-14 combined with ii 5-7). This later epoch is not directly designated by the *terminus technicus* קץ אחרית הימים, but it is referred to as קץ נחרצה ועשות חדשה, "the decreed epoch of new things" (1QS iv 25; cp. Dan 9:26-27; 11:35-36; Isa 10:23; 28:22; 43:19)[49] and possibly also by inversion as אחרית הקץ (4Q 169 3-4 iii 3; *173* 1, line 5).

A Qumran work entitled by its editor *The Ages of Creation* (4Q 180; cp. 4Q 181), in which the קצים were consecutively enumerated, beginning with the time before the creation of man (cp. CD ii 7; 1QS iii 15-18; 1QH i 8-12), is preserved in only a few fragments. However, on the basis of data assembled from diverse Qumran writings, the outlines of the יחד concept of history can still be

---

47. This contrasts with the Christian vision of the Messiah as characterized by Neusner, who says that this Messiah "was the Messiah of the end time, savior and redeemer of Israel from its historical calamity" (Neusner, "Mishnah and Messiah," *Judaisms and Their Messiahs,* 263 [see above, n. 8]).

48. The term is similarly employed in late strata of biblical literature, synonymously with עת or מועד, "appointed time." See, e.g., Ezek 7:2-6; 21:25 [Heb. 30], 29 [Heb. 34]; 35:5; Dan 8:17; 11:40; 12:4, 8-9, 11-13; 8:19; 11:27, 35; cp. 9:26. Cp. 1QpHab vii 7 ad Hab 2:3 and Sir 43:6-8.

49. In *b. Meg.* 3a the messianic age is designated קץ משיח. Cp. also *Ber. Rab.* 88 ad Gen 49:1 (ed. Theodor and Albeck, p. 1251).

recovered.[50] The history of Israel, as of all mankind (1QS iv 15-17), is traced from creation to אחרית הימים, with the destruction of the Temple serving as the main watershed (CD v 20-21; vii 14, 21). Events preceding it are reported as having occurred in the days of the דורות ראשונים (CD i 16-20), i.e., in the predestruction period, which for its part is subdivided into a number of "generations" or קצים. The postdestruction era is that of the דורות אחרונים (CD i 11-13). It includes the days in which the דור אחרון (CD i 11-12), i.e., the יחד, arose.[51] Because of the Wicked who opposed the Covenanters and persecuted them, it is designated קץ הרשיע, הרשע, הרשעה (CD vi 10, 14; xii 23; xv 7, 10 restored; cp. xx 23 et al.).[52] This terminology reflects a "relative" (*former* and *later*, not *first* and *last*) chronological system. Events are dated *before* or *after* a middle point (in the case under review, the destruction of the Temple) and not in succession from a primary point of departure, such as the creation. One is again reminded of a facet in the biblical concept of time that shows up especially in the postexilic literature. Zechariah refers to the prophets of predestruction days as נביאים ראשונים (Zech 1:4; 7:7, 12).[53] Likewise, Haggai speaks of the newly built temple as הבית האחרון in contrast to הבית הראשון of the First Temple Period (Hag 2:3-9; cp. Ezra 3:12).

In the present context, the postdestruction era is of focal interest, especially the transition from the ק/דור אחרון, within the wider setting of דורות אחרונים, to אחרית הימים when the Anointed will arise. Some texts give the impression that initially the age of אחרית הימים was considered to be part of the קץ אחרון, the positive ending of its negative beginning as קץ רשעה (CD vi 10-11, 14-15; xii 23; xv 7), קץ עולה (1QS iv 18), or קץ מעל (CD xx 23). The basic continuity of these time spans in the Covenanters' view of history shows in passages such as the following:

---

50. See "Between the Bible and the Mishna" (in this vol., pp. 11-52.)
51. The triad דורות ראשונים, דורות אחרונים, דור אחרון parallels the same triad in Eccl 1:11, where, however, the third component is שיהיו לאחרונה.
52. This period is also referred to by the term בהיות אלה, i.e., "when these [or "they"] were [about]" (1QS viii 4, 12; ix 3; cp. iv 14, 18).
53. This fixed terminology appears to have developed only after the return from the exile. Ezekiel, himself a prophet of the ראשונים, refers to prophets who preceded him as those who were active בימים קדמונים ("in earlier days," Ezek 38:17).

The interpretation of this saying [Hab 1:4-5] concerns the unfai[thful men] in אחרית הימים, the vio[lent breakers of the cove]nant, who will not believe when they hear all [that is to happen] to the דור אחרון from the priest . . . (1QpHab ii 5-8).

Its interpretation [Hab 2:8] concerns the last priests [i.e., the priests of the דורות אחרונים who amass riches and [illicit] wealth by plundering [the] peoples. But in אחרית הימים their riches and plunder shall be delivered into the hands of the army of the Kittim (1QpHab ix 4-7).

When the expected smooth shift from the negative phase of the קץ אחרון (דור/דורות אחרון/נים) did not materialize, history was adjusted to the changed circumstances, and אחרית הימים was now conceived as a self-constituted New Age. The profound disappointment that resulted from the unrealized transition shows distinctly in the *Pesher on Habakkuk*. The author relates plaintively that "God told Habakkuk to write down [Hab 2:2] what would happen to the דור אחרון , but he did not inform him on the termination of that קץ." This explains the fact "that the קץ אחרון shall be prolonged more than the prophets have [fore]told [cp. Dan 10:14; 8:19 and Zech 1:11-12], for God's mysteries are astounding." But "the hands of the men of truth who keep the Torah shall not slacken in the service of truth," even though "the קץ אחרון is prolonged. For [ultimately] all the divine[ly appointed] ages [קצי אל] will come in their destined order as he has decreed in his unfathomable wisdom" (1QpHab vii 1-14). If the above argument concerning the proximity of these קצים or דורות to each other can be sustained, it would imply that in the יחד view of history, אחרית הימים, when the Anointed are expected to arise, is but a generation removed from the דור אחרון. Once again this linguistic-conceptual usage echoes a biblical notion. In the farewell speech of Moses, the phrases אחרי מותי and אחרית הימים are equated by being juxtaposed in two cola of one and the same verse: "I know that after my death . . . you will turn away from the path that I have enjoined upon you and באחרית הימים [i.e., in the days to come] misfortune will befall you" (Deut 31:29; cp. 29:21 and Ps 78:5-6).

All in all it can be said that the Covenanters conceived of the Messianic Age, אחרית הימים, as the preordained period in which the Two Anointed will ring in the New Eon, קץ נחרצה ועשות חדשה (1QS iv 25), as one further link in the chain of historical epochs. The Anointed will not come at the End of Time, but rather at the Turn of Times, after a profound crisis in history, marked by tribulations of cosmic dimensions (cp. Hag 2:20-22). Once these are overcome, the world will settle down to experience "a time of salvation for the people of God" that is *eo ipso* "an age of [world] dominion for all members of his fellowship," i.e., for the יחד (1QM i 5; contrast Zech 1:10 ff.).

The Hierarchy of the Community

The portrayal of אחרית הימים in the wider framework in which the (messianic) Banquet of the Two Anointed is set, reflects distinct characteristics, both of the communal structure of the יחד in historical reality, and of the returnees' community as described in Ezra-Nehemiah. A comparison of relevant texts discloses their striking congruence. In all three instances there emerges the picture of a tightly knit socioreligious entity, restricted in numbers and spatially compressed. The compactness and smallness make for a high degree of direct participation of the membership in daily communal life and in deliberations and decisions concerning the entire group, notwithstanding the pronounced hierarchical structure of the Qumran commune in practice and theory.

The *Rule of the Congregation* prescribes the future standing order of members in the assembly:

1QSa i 1-3

באחרית הימים when they will gather [in the יחד and con]duct themselves in accord with the ordinances of the בני צדוק, the priests and the men of their covenant who re[frained from walking in the] way of the people. They are the men of His council who kept His covenant in the קץ [of] iniquity, expia[ting for the lan]d [or "the world"].[54]

This arrangement is foreshadowed in passages that detail the rules by which the Covenanters' life was regulated in actuality (e.g., 1QS v 1 ff.; CD xii 22-23). At the same time it also mirrors the recurring references in p stexilic biblical literature to assemblies in which rules were laid down and statutory acts

54. D. Barthélemy correctly points out the difference in size of the *community* to which 1QS is addressed and the *congregation* of which 1QSa speaks (see *DJD* I, 28 [1955] 108). But these relative differences do not obfuscate the absolute compactness of both of these units, compared with the *community* of the Essenes and the *congregation* of the Hasidim (ibid.).

proclaimed (e.g., Ezra 9:1 ff.; 10:7 ff.; Neh 5:1 ff.; 8:1 ff.; 9:1; cp. also Haggai and Zechariah).

Especially striking is the linguistic similarity between the passage in the *Rule of the Congregation* that speaks of the future public reading of the statutes in front of the entire community, and the reading of the Torah in Nehemiah 8:

1QSa i 4-5

they [the priests] shall convene (יקהילו) all those who come [including] infants and women, and they shall read in th[eir hearing] al[l] precepts of the Covenant and shall explain to them (ולהבינם) all their sta[tut]es lest they stray in [their] er[ror]s.

Neh 8:1-8

All the people gathered as one man on the square before the Water Gate . . . Ezra the priest brought the Torah before the assembly (קהל) [consisting of] men, women, and all those [children] who understand . . . and he read from it in the presence of the men, the women, and those [children] who understand . . . and the Levites explained (מבינים) the Torah to the people . . . so that the people understood what was read.

Into this יחד באחרית הימים assembly the Anointed are inducted:

1 QSa ii 11-17

[This is (or "shall be") the se]ssion of the men of renown [called to the appointed] meeting of the יחד council, when [God] shall lead to them the [Davidic?] Anointed. With them shall come the [priest] [at the head of the] f[ather (house)s of the] Aaronide priests, the men of renown [called] to the [appointed] assembly. And they shall sit [before him each] according to his dignity and [his standing]. And then shall [come the Anoin]ted of Israel and before him shall sit the head[s of] the [thousands of Israel], each according to his dignity, according to their standing in their camps and marching [formation]s. And all the heads of [clans of the congrega]tion together with the wise [of the holy congregation] shall sit before them, each according to his dignity.

The subdivision into priestly and lay leaders that shall obtain in the Age to Come once again mirrors the Covenanters' community structure and formal seating arrangements, as the following excerpts indicate. At the same time, both reflect the identical subdivision of the returnees' community (Ezra 1:5; 2:2-39 = Neh 7:7-42 et al.).

1QS vi 8-9

This is the rule for an assembly of the congregation, each in his [assigned] place: the priests shall sit first and the elders second and the rest of the people each in his [assigned] place.

These factions are similarly represented on the יחד tribunal of judges:

CD x 4-6

This is the rule concerning the judges [or "the court"] of the congregation: [a number of] ten men selected from the congregation for a [definite] time [or "for the occasion"], four from the tribe of Levi and Aaron, and of Israel six knowledgeable (מבוננים) in the book (ההגו/י) and in the tenets of the Covenant.

In the biblical sources (Ezra and Nehemiah) the lay leaders always precede the priests. As against this, the inverted order obtains in the Qumran texts: the priests precede the lay leaders, both in reference to the actual structure of the יחד and in אחרית הימים.

In keeping with this arrangement, and because of the cultic character of that solemn event, in the messianic banquet the (Anointed?) priest takes precedence over the Anointed of Israel in opening the ceremony:

1 QSa ii 17-22

And [when] they shall assemble for the common (יחד) table [to eat] [and to drink the w]ine, and when the common (היחד) table shall be set and [the] wine [poured] for drinking, [no] man [shall extend] his hand to the first [loaf of] bread and the [first cup of] wine before the [Anointed] Priest; for [he shall] bless the first bread and the wine [and extend] his hand first over the bread. Thereafter the Anointed of Israel [shall ex]tend his hand over the bread;[55] [and then] the entire יחד congregation [shall make a bles]sing [over the food], each [man according to] his dignity. In accord with this statute they shall proceed at every m[eal at which] ten me[n are ga]thered.

---

55. Cp. Ezek 44:3.

Again, the rules foreseen to be operative in the messianic future are effective also in the actual יחד community, when no Anointed are yet involved, as explicated in:

1QS vi 3-5

Wherever there are ten men of the יחד council [together], a priest shall be present, and they shall sit before him according to their rank, and thus they shall be asked for their counsel in all matters. And when they lay the table to eat or to drink, the priest shall first stretch out his hand to make a blessing over the first bread and wine.

It has been argued that these texts give the priest and the Anointed of Aaron pride of rank over the lay leader(s) of the Covenanters and the future Anointed of Israel respectively. But this interpretation remains open to doubt. It would appear, rather, that the precedence accorded to the Aaronides proves the point made above: it is intended to achieve a balance in the standing of the Two Anointed in the community, in contrast to the societal setup of predestruction Israel, which patently favored the (anointed) king over the (anointed) priest.

It is probably for this reason that also in the Zechariah passages to which reference has already been made, the high priest Joshua is mentioned before Zerubbabel, the Davidic scion, when the text speaks of the crown with which each of the בני היצהר (Zech 4:14; cp. vv 3, 11-12), the Two Anointed, is to be endowed (Zech 6:12, restored), whereas in respect to the thrones given to them, the Davidic "sprout" precedes the priest (Zech 6:13).

Conclusion

The above survey points up a striking characteristic of the millenarian-messianic idea at Qumran: the expected New Eon will unfold as an age in which terrestrial-historical experience coalesces with celestial-spiritual utopia. Salvation is viewed as transcendent and imminent at the same time. The New Order to be established by the Anointed is not otherworldly but rather the realization of a divine plan on earth, the consummation of history in history. Qumran messianism reflects the political ideas of the postexilic returnees' community. It is the *politeia* of the New Commonwealth of Israel and the New Universe.

INDICES

SOURCES

HEBREW BIBLE

QUMRAN MANUSCRIPTS

Sources

vii 1-2	40n 294	iv 14		295n
vii 1-14	296	iv 15-17		295
vii 7	46 144 294n	iv 16-17		46
vii 7-8	294	iv 18		295n
vii 10-14	294	iv 25		294 296
vii 12	46	v 1ff.		297
viii 8-10	46	v 1-2		53n
ix 4-5	46	v 5		59
ix 4-7	296	v 7		53n
ix 6	47	v 9		59
ix 12	145	v 13-15		192
x 9	145	v 20		59
x 11	145	vi 2-8		240
xi 4-6	42	vi 3-5		300
xi 4-8	167 187 286	vi 7		69
xi 4-9	152 153	vi 7-8		219
xi 5-8	236	vi 8-9		299
xi 7-8	191	vi 10		53n
xi 9	114	vi 11-13		68
xii 1	145	vii 2		53n
xii 4	53n	viii 4		295n
xii 9	146	viii 9-10		153
xii 15	146	viii 12		295n
		viii 13-15		152
1QpPs37	227n	ix		212
		ix 3ff.		239 295n
1QS	69 177 224n	ix 9		45
i 1	53n	ix 10-11		288 292n
i 1—ii 18	285	ix 11		51
i 8-9	151	ix 20		66n
i 11—ii 25	151	ix 21—x 8		213
i 12	53n 56	ix 26		224
i 13	64	ix 26—x 1		214
i 13-15	151	ix 26—x 8		216
i 14	66	ix 26—x 17		174
i 14-15	171	x		212n
i 16-19	64	x 1		165n 225n
i 22	64 234	x 1-2		225n
ii 1	64	x 1-5		214
ii 6	236n	x 2		176n 225n
ii 22	53n 56	x 3		221n
ii 22-23	57n	x 3-4		220 223n
ii 25—iii 12	235	x 4		165 170 222
iii 2	53n	x 4-6		168
iii 4	150	x 6		154 224
iii 5	63	x 7		223
iii 9	234n	x 7-8		224
iii 10-11	151n	x 8		212
iii 11-12	151	x 8-9		224n 225
iii 19	176n	x 10		175
iv 4-5	230n	x 13	174 175 177 226
iv 13	41 294	x 13-14		226

Sources

RABBINIC LITERATURE

AUTHORS

LIST OF ABBREVIATIONS

AB	Anchor Bible
AJS	Association for Jewish Studies
AJSL	*American Journal of Semitic Languages and Literature*
AJSR	*Association for Jewish Studies Review*
ALW	*Archiv für Liturgiewissenschaft*
ASOR	American Schools of Oriental Research
ASTI	*Annual of the Swedish Theological Institute*
BA	*Biblical Archaeologist*
BAC	*Biblioteca de Autores Cristianos*
BASOR	*Bulletin of the American Schools of Oriental Research*
BASORSS	Bulletin of the American Schools of Oriental Research. Supplementary Series
BHK	R. Kittel, *Biblia Hebraica*
Bib	*Biblica*
BIES	*Bulletin of the Israel Exploration Society*
BJRL	*Bulletin of the John Rylands University Library of Manchester*
BOr	*Bibliotheca Orientalis*
BWAT	Beiträge zur Wissenschaft vom Alten Testament
BZ	*Biblische Zeitschrift*
CBQ	*Catholic Biblical Quarterly*
DJD	Discoveries in the Judaean Desert (of Jordan)
DRMT	S. Talmon, "Double Readings in the Massoretic Text," *Textus* 1 (1960) 144-84
EI	*Eretz Israel*
EJS	*European Journal of Sociology*
EJ	*Encyclopaedia Judaica*
ETL	*Ephemerides Theologicae Lovanienses*
HAT	Handbuch zum Alten Testament
HSM	Harvard Semitic Monographs
HThR	*Harvard Theological Review*
HUCA	*Hebrew Union College Annual*
ICC	International Critical Commentary
IDBSup	Interpreter's Dictionary of the Bible, Supplement
IEJ	*Israel Exploration Journal*
IES	Israel Exploration Society

List of Abbreviations

JAOS	*Journal of the American Oriental Society*
JBL	*Journal of Biblical Literature*
JJS	*Journal of Jewish Studies*
JQRMS	Jewish Quarterly Review Monograph Series
JSOT	*Journal for the Study of the Old Testament*
JSS	*Journal of Semitic Studies*
JTS	*Journal of Theological Studies*
JTSA	Jewish Theological Seminary of America
KCC	S. Talmon, *King, Cult and Calendar in Ancient Israel*
LCL	Loeb Classical Library
PAAJR	*Proceedings of the American Academy of Jewish Research*
PAPS	*Proceedings of the American Philosophical Society*
PEQ	*Palestine Exploration Quarterly*
PSBA	*Proceedings of the Society of Biblical Archaeology*
RB	*Revue biblique*
REJ	*Revue des études juives*
RevQ	*Revue de Qumran*
RGG	*Die Religion in Geschichte und Gegenwart*
RHR	*Revue de l'histoire des religions*
RQ	*Römische Quartalschrift für christliche Altertumskunde und Kirchengeschichte*
ScrHier	*Scripta Hierosolymitana*
SPCK	Society for Promoting Christian Knowledge
SROT	S. Talmon, "Synonymous Readings in the Textual Tradition of the Old Testament," *ScrHier* 8 (1961) 335-83
StJud	*Studia Judaica*
StudOr	Studia Orientalia
ThLZ	*Theologische Literaturzeitung*
TSL	S. Talmon, "The Three Scrolls of the Law That Were Found in the Temple Court," *Textus* 3 (1962) 14-27
TWAT	*Theologisches Wörterbuch zum Alten Testament*
VT	*Vetus Testamentum*
VTSup	Vetus Testamentum, Supplements
ZAW	*Zeitschrift für die alttestamentliche Wissenschaft*
ZDMG	*Zeitschrift der deutschen morgenländischen Gesellschaft*
ZKT	*Zeitschrift für katholische Theologie*

ACKNOWLEDGEMENTS

I wish to thank the original editors and publishers of these studies for their kind permission to reprint them in this volume:

The Qumran יחד — A Biblical Noun, *Vetus Testamentum* 3 (1953) 133-40.

A Further Link Between the Judean Covenanters and the Essenes? *Harvard Theological Review* 56 (1963) 313-19.

A Note on 1QS VI 11-13, *Journal of Jewish Studies* 8 (1957) 113-15.

Aspects of the Textual Transmission of the Bible in Light of Qumran Manuscripts, *Textus: Annual of the Hebrew University Bible Project* 4 (1964) 95-132.

Observations on Variant Readings in the Isaiah Scroll (1QIsa[a]), translated from the Hebrew, *Elias Auerbach Festschrift* (Publications of the Israel Society of Bible Research; Jerusalem: Kiryat-Sefer, 1956), 1. 147-56.

1QIsa[a] As a Witness to Ancient Exegesis of the Book of Isaiah, *Annual of the Swedish Theological Institute, Jerusalem,* 1 (1962) 62-72.

Notes on the Habakkuk Scroll, *Vetus Testamentum* 1 (1951) 33-37.

The Calendar of the Covenanters of the Judean Desert, *Aspects of the Dead Sea Scrolls, Scripta Hierosolymitana*, ed. C. Rabin and Y. Yadin (Jerusalem: Magnes, 1958), 4. 162-99.

Yom Hakippurim in the Habakkuk Scroll, *Biblica* 32 (1951) 549-63.

The Emergence of Institutionalized Prayer in Israel in Light of Qumran Literature, *Qumrân, sa piété, sa théologie et son milieu,* ed. M. Delcor (Bibliotheca Ephemeridum Lovaniensium; Leuven: University Press, 1978), 46. 265-84.   combined with:

The Manual of Benedictions of the Judean Desert Covenanters, *Revue de Qumran* 2 (1959-1960) 475-500.

Extra-Canonical Psalms from Qumran — Psalm 151, translated from the Hebrew, *Tarbiz* 35 (1966) 214-34.

Waiting for the Messiah — The Conceptual Universe of the Qumran Covenanters, *Judaisms and Their Messiahs* (ed. J. Neusner, W. S. Green, and E. Frerichs; New York/Cambridge: Cambridge University Press, 1988) 111-37.